A Clinical
Manual of
Gynecology

Appleton Clinical Manuals

Ayres, et al.: Medical Resident's Manual, 4th edition
Ellis and Beckmann: A Clinical Manual of Gynecology
Ellis and Beckmann: A Clinical Manual of Obstetrics
Gomella, et al.: The Clinician's Pocket Reference,
4th edition

Forthcoming titles

A Clinical Manual of Cardiology
A Clinical Manual of Nephrology
A Clinical Manual of Nuclear Medicine
Surgical Resident's Manual, 2nd edition

A Clinical Manual of Gynecology

Jeffrey W. Ellis, M.D.

Assistant Professor of Obstetrics and Gynecology
Department of Obstetrics and Gynecology
Director, Section of Obstetrics and Gynecology
Northwestern Foundation for Research and Education
Northwestern University School of Medicine
Chicago, Illinois

Charles R.B. Beckmann, M.D.

Assistant Professor of Obstetrics and Gynecology
Director, Undergraduate Medical Education
Department of Obstetrics and Gynecology
University of Illinois College of Medicine—Chicago
Chicago, Illinois

 APPLETON-CENTURY-CROFTS/Norwalk, Connecticut

Notice: Our knowledge in the clinical sciences is constantly changing. As new information becomes available, changes in treatment and in the use of drugs become necessary. The author(s) and the publisher of this volume have, as far as it is possible to do so, taken care to make certain that the doses of drugs and schedules of treatment are correct and compatible with the standards generally accepted at the time of publication. The reader is advised to consult carefully the instruction and information material included in the package insert of each drug or therapeutic agent before administration. This advice is especially important when using new or infrequently used drugs.

84   85   86   87   /   10   9   8   7   6   5   4   3   2

Prentice-Hall International, Inc., London
Prentice-Hall of Australia, Pty. Ltd., Sydney
Prentice-Hall Canada Inc.
Prentice-Hall of India Private Limited, New Delhi
Prentice-Hall of Japan, Inc., Tokyo
Prentice-Hall of Southeast Asia (Pte.) Ltd., Singapore
Whitehall Books Ltd., Wellington, New Zealand
Editora Prentice-Hall do Brasil Ltda., Rio de Janeiro

Library of Congress Cataloging in Publication Data
Main entry under title:
A Clinical manual of gynecology.
      Companion vol. to: A Clinical manual of obstetrics.
      Bibliography: p.
      Includes index.
      1.   Gynecology—Handbooks, manuals, etc.
I. Ellis, Jeffrey W.   II.   Beckmann, Charles R. B.
[DNLM: 1. Gynecology—Handbooks.   WP 100 C6415]
RG110.C55   1983   618.1   82-20623
ISBN 0-8385-1135-X

Design: Jean M.Sabato

PRINTED IN THE UNITED STATES OF AMERICA

Contributors

Barbara M. Barzansky, Ph.D., M.H.P.E.
Assistant Professor of Health Professions Education
Center for Education Development
University of Illinois — Chicago
Chicago, Illinois

Charles R.B. Beckmann, M.D.
Assistant Professor of Obstetrics and Gynecology
Director, Undergraduate Medical Education
Department of Obstetrics and Gynecology
University of Illinois College of Medicine — Chicago
Chicago, Illinois

Guy I. Benrubi, M.A., M.D.
Assistant Professor of Obstetrics and Gynecology
Division of Gynecologic Oncology
University Hospital of Jacksonville
Jacksonville, Florida

M. Yusoff Dawood, M.B., Ch. B., M.D.
Professor of Obstetrics and Gynecology
Director, Division of Reproductive Endocrinology
Department of Obstetrics and Gynecology
University of Illinois College of Medicine—Chicago
Chicago, Illinois

Jeffrey W. Ellis, M.D.
Assistant Professor of Obstetrics and Gynecology
Department of Obstetrics and Gynecology
Director, Section of Obstetrics and Gynecology
Northwestern Foundation for Research and Education
Northwestern University School of Medicine
Chicago, Illinois

John C. Jarrett II, M.D.
Fellow in Reproductive Endocrinology
Division of Reproductive Endocrinology
Department of Obstetrics and Gynecology
University of Illinois College of Medicine—Chicago
Chicago, Illinois

Jeffrey King, M.D.
Assistant Professor of Obstetrics and Gynecology
Division of Maternal-Fetal Medicine
Department of Obstetrics and Gynecology
Georgetown University
Washington, D.C.

Sylvia Lessman, B.A., M.S.W., A.C.S.W.
Assistant Professor of Medical Social Work
Department of Medical Social Work
College of Associated Health Professions
University of Illinois — Chicago
Clinical Assistant Professor of Obstetrics and Gynecology
Department of Obstetrics and Gynecology
University of Illinois College of Medicine—Chicago
Chicago, Illinois

Frank W. Ling, M.D.
Assistant Professor of Obstetrics and Gynecology
Division of Gynecology
Department of Obstetrics and Gynecology
The University of Tennessee Center for the Health Sciences
Memphis, Tennessee

Katherine Y. Look, M.D.
Chief Resident, Instructor
Department of Obstetrics and Gynecology
University of Illinois College of Medicine—Chicago
Chicago, Illinois

John Lurain, M.D.
Assistant Professor of Obstetrics and Gynecology
Division of Gynecologic Oncology
Northwestern University School of Medicine
Chicago, Illinois

Edward L. Marut, M.D.
Assistant Professor of Obstetrics and Gynecology
Division of Reproductive Endocrinology
Department of Obstetrics and Gynecology
University of Illinois College of Medicine—Chicago
Chicago, Illinois

John R. Musich, M.D.
Assistant Professor of Obstetrics and Gynecology
Director of General Gynecology
Division of Reproductive Endocrinology and Infertility
University of Illinois College of Medicine—Chicago
Chicago, Illinois

Gretajo Northrop, M.D., Ph.D.
Associate Professor of Medicine
Associate Professor of Obstetrics and Gynecology
Departments of Medicine and Obstetrics and Gynecology
Rush Medical College
Chicago, Illinois

Ronald W. Richards, M.A., Ph.D.
Professor of Health Professions Education
Director, Center for Education Development
University of Illinois College of Medicine—Chicago
Chicago, Illinois

Ira Rosenthal, M.D.
Professor of Pediatrics
Department of Pediatrics
University of Illinois College of Medicine—Chicago
Chicago, Illinois

Roger P. Smith, M.D.
Assistant Clinical Professor of Obstetrics and Gynecology
University of Illinois College of Medicine
Champaign - Urbana, Illinois

William N. Spellacy, M.D.
Professor and Head
Department of Obstetrics and Gynecology
University of Illinois College of Medicine—Chicago
Chicago, Illinois

Jessica L. Thomason, M.D.
Assistant Professor of Obstetrics and Gynecology
Division of Maternal-Fetal Medicine
Department of Obstetrics and Gynecology
University of Illinois College of Medicine—Chicago
Chicago, Illinois

Edra B. Weiss, M.D.
Formerly, Assistant Professor of Pediatrics
Department of Pediatrics
University of Illinois College of Medicine—Chicago
Chicago, Illinois

Linda A. Wheeler, R.N., C.N.M., Ed.D.
Associate Professor and Director of
Nurse-Midwifery Service
Department of Obstetrics and Gynecology
School of Medicine
University of Tennessee Center for the Health Sciences
Memphis, Tennessee

Contents

Preface

The companion books, *A Clinical Manual of Obstetrics* and *A Clinical Manual of Gynecology*, are designed to bridge the gap between the small pocket guidebooks and "core textbooks" and the large reference textbooks, using an outline format for maximum usability and a pocket size to facilitate availability. They will be of use to the many health professionals involved in the care of women, including medical and nursing students, resident physicians in many disciplines (medicine, surgery, emergency medicine, family practice, pediatrics, etc., as well as obstetrics and gynecology), and practicing physicians and nurses. In each chapter we have struck a balance between too much and too little detail — of pathophysiology, differential diagnosis, evaluation, and management — while at the same time including many of the "practical pearls" so useful in daily health care activities but so often left to be "learned by doing." We trust the resulting books are helpful.

We wish to thank our many authors, the excellence of whose contributions provides the basis for these manuals. We also wish to thank our chairmen, John Sciarra at Northwestern University and William Spellacy at the University of Illinois, for their patience and support. Finally, thanks to Marla Ellis for her forbearance during the long hours of editing; Jeannette West for her tireless typing efforts; and Richard Lampert, John Morgan, Elizabeth Stueck, and Richard Warner of Appleton-Century-Crofts for their support and guidance.

Jeffrey W. Ellis
Charles R.B. Beckmann
Chicago, Illinois
December, 1982

Foreword

This new manual renders an important service in providing readily available, concise, and logically organized information for the busy practitioner involved in the health care of women. The changing mode of clinical practice and the increased expectations of patients dictate that we, as physicians, residents, medical and nursing students, and other health care professionals, are aware of advances in diagnostic and therapeutic procedures, and that we are able to present our planned approach in a clear and understandable manner. Having this manual at our fingertips can aid us in this endeavor.

The material in *A Clinical Manual of Gynecology* is organized and presented in outline form, assuring that the information is easily and rapidly accessible. The chapters are carefully referenced to include both classic and contemporary literature. An important strength of this volume is that the several authors are individuals involved in clinical practice in a variety of institutions, thus, the book provides a national perspective in terms of patient management, not a local or regional point of view.

In addition to giving a comprehensive presentation of the traditional aspects of gynecology, this volume covers a number of important new areas of clinical interest and concern in gynecology: general principles of pre- and post-operative care; a thorough consideration of both surgical and non-surgical alternatives for therapy; a complete listing of indications and contraindications for surgical procedures; a reasonable presentation of the ethical and legal issues involved in abortion, as well as the details of the medical procedures; and a complete discussion of the practical aspects of contraception.

A Clinical Manual of Gynecology, with its companion, *A Clinical Manual of Obstetrics*, should prove invaluable as a resource and guide for the practitioner involved in the health care of women.

John J. Sciarra, M.D., Ph.D.
Thomas J. Watkins Professor and Chairman
Department of Obstetrics and Gynecology
Northwestern University Medical School
Chicago, Illinois

A Clinical
Manual of
Gynecology

1

The House Officer as Teacher, Learner, and Health Team Manager*

Barbara M. Barzansky, Ph.D., M.H.P.E.
Charles R.B. Beckmann, M.D.
Ronald Richards, Ph.D.
William Spellacy, M.D.
Katherine Look, M.D.

PRACTICE PRINCIPLES

A house officer's daily activities often reflect three closely interwoven functions: (1) a responsibility for coordinating patient care services in outpatient and inpatient settings; (2) a continuing need to acquire skills, knowledge, and clinical experience; and (3) a responsibility for supervising the learning of students and more junior house staff. While teaching is an important function of the resident physician, very few are given

---

*This chapter appears in both *A Clinical Manual of Obstetrics* and *A Clinical Manual of Gynecology*.

formal training in this area. This chapter will outline some of the instructional techniques that can be used in clinical settings.

A. House staff generally are involved in informal, task-oriented teaching. Most time with students is spent in operating rooms, labor and delivery rooms, clinics, ward work, and rounds.[1]

B. A number of factors have been identified as contributing to effective teaching in clinical settings.[2,3] These will not be discussed in order of priority. All appear to be important in creating an environment where learning can occur.

C. Throughout this discussion, the term "student" will be used to refer to any learners for whom the house officer has responsibility. These may include medical students in an Ob-Gyn clerkship, more advanced medical students in specialty rotations, or junior house staff in Ob-Gyn or other specialties. Usually, junior house officers will teach and supervise medical students, while senior house staff have responsibilities for both medical students and junior house staff.

GENERAL INSTRUCTIONAL SKILLS

It is important that medical students be accepted as rightful members of the health care team,[4] and therefore, the resident should encourage student participation. This will be facilitated by recognizing that students are at the beginning of their education and require chances to ask questions. Students deserve correct explanations. This requires that the resident both know the material and be able to convey the information clearly. Teaching forces the resident to be critical of the knowledge base that he or she has acquired.

A. *Explain the basis of your actions and decisions.*
   1. It is important when explaining complex content to emphasize the main points.
   2. Summarize the explanation and check to see if students have understood what was conveyed.
   3. Give students a chance to make decisions and critique their thought processes and approaches.

B. *Allow time for discussion and questions.*
   1. Listen carefully to student questions. Rephrase the question if you are unsure what was really being asked.
   2. Answer questions clearly. Make sure the student is familiar with the terminology that has been used.
   3. If time and circumstances permit, allow other students a chance to answer a student's question. Intervene if the group is unable to respond or if incorrect information is being presented.
C. *Teach to the level of the student.*
   1. The needs of third- and fourth-year medical students are quite different. Third-year students should be introduced to their expected role on the clinical management team with increasing responsibility as their knowledge and skills develop.
   2. Fourth-year students can be given responsibilities more commensurate with what will be expected of them as interns.

TEACHING PROBLEM-SOLVING

Often the objective of a formal or informal teaching session is to sharpen the learner's ability to solve clinical problems (e.g., differential diagnoses, management plans). To facilitate this, stress approaches rather than solutions. Guide the session so that generalizations are drawn from specific cases. This makes the most efficient use of instructional time and available patient material.

A. *Whenever possible, "ask" rather than "tell."* Appropriate questioning actively involves the student, and this improves learning and retention.
   1. There are two general types of questions. Each has its proper use as a teaching tool.[5]
      a) *Closed questions* ask the student to recall specific facts (e.g., normal values, definitions). They are best used to check whether students have learned basic information. Problem-solving cannot be done without this base of specific facts.

b) *Open questions* require students to integrate information in order to address a problem (e.g., identify
   relevant variables, develop a hypothesis, suggest possible actions, or defend a position). This type of
   question is used to determine if the student can
   approach a clinical problem in the correct way.

2. *Include both closed and open questions* in a teaching
   session. Usually it is best to start with a few closed
   questions to make sure the students have learned the
   relevant facts. Then use open questions to determine
   whether they can apply the facts to the clinical situation.

3. Use of hypothetical, *"what if,"* questions allows the
   teacher to generalize from a specific finding or situation
   to a broader category (e.g., What would you do if her
   blood pressure had been elevated rather than normal?
   What if the placenta were located over the os rather than
   in the fundus?). This gives students a chance to think
   about clinical cases they may not have the opportunity to
   actually observe.

4. *Questioning should be done in a nonthreatening, nonjudgmental manner.* Avoid high-pressure quiz sessions and
   undue penalty for not knowing. Make students realize
   that questioning is a teaching as well as an evaluation
   strategy. They should be encouraged to admit when they
   are unsure of an answer and taught that this attitude is a
   mark of a maturing professional.

PROVIDING CLINICAL SUPERVISION

The success of a student's learning experience on a clinical
rotation may in a large part depend on the house officer's skills
as a clinical supervisor.[6]

A. Often students and junior house staff learn new procedures
   under the supervision of a more senior house officer. There
   is a general method for teaching manual clinical skills that
   maximizes both students' learning and comfort with doing
   the technique.[5]
   1. Ideally, for common procedures write out the basic steps

in the order and manner they are done. Check with attending physicians to determine if there is general agreement about how to do the procedure. Make this guide available to students. If there is no time to write out the procedure, describe it verbally to the student and allow time for questions.

2. *Demonstrate* the procedure in its entirety. *Describe* the steps as they are being performed. *Highlight* any deviations from the commonly accepted manner of performing the technique that are necessary because of specific patient characteristics.

3. Allow the student to *practice* the technique as soon after the demonstration as possible. If it is feasible, try to arrange practice with models or simulators before students begin to work with patients.

4. *Observe* the student performing the procedure and provide feedback. Determine when the student has achieved competence and then permit some independence.

5. Periodically observe the student to ensure that performance is still satisfactory.

B. Providing *feedback* to students is an important function of a house officer. There are ways to provide the information that make the feedback most useful and effective.

1. Refer to specific behaviors or actions that were either incorrect or well done. Do not just comment on performance in a general way. For example, tell the student "you ignored the patient's question about birth control," rather than saying "you did not deal with the patient well."

2. Identify both strengths and weaknesses in the student's performance.

3. Give the feedback as close to the actual time of performance as possible. However, use discretion in giving feedback in the presence of patients or peers, especially if it is critical.

4. Check to make sure that the student understood what was communicated. Ask the student to repeat and/or rephrase the comments.

C. After giving students a chance to work up patients, review

their history and physical write-up with them. Ask for
explanations about their management plan and correct any
misconceptions.[6]

D. It is important to decide how much control or supervision to
exercise over a particular student. Make an assessment of
the level of expertise displayed in particular areas and use
this as a guide.

HOUSE OFFICER AS ORGANIZER

House officers are responsible for organizing a service or clinic
so that it functions as a site where both patient care and student
learning can take place. Certain *management techniques* can help
to make this difficult balance easier to maintain.

A. *Set realistic goals for learners.*[2]
   1. Often there are general, written objectives for student
      educational activities. Be aware of these objectives and
      attempt to design experiences for students that will
      address them. Try to ensure that each student is exposed
      to information about the procedures, disease states, and
      types of patients that are considered important.
   2. Give feedback to a student about how well each objective
      is being met.
   3. If formal objectives do not exist for an educational
      experience, develop an explicit set of informal expecta-
      tions. Share these with faculty for their input. Make sure
      students are aware that these expectations exist and that
      they understand them.
B. *Include students in discussions* with consultants. Teach
   students how to use these resource persons appropriately.
C. *Familiarize students with the functions of other health professionals* (e.g., nurses, social workers, nutritionists, physical
   and vocational therapists, health educators). Include them,
   where appropriate, in discussions with students about patient problems.
D. *Teach efficiency by example.* Make efficient use of both time
   and personnel. Avoid duplication of activities unless it

serves an educational function. For example, a student and house officer separately examining a patient and comparing results is an educational experience, while two students making separate trips to the same place to deliver samples or to obtain supplies is not.

E. The efficient running of a ward or clinic allows more time to teach informally. Use short blocks of free time to discuss general concepts related to a patient who has just been seen or to review core material (e.g., dating a pregnancy, diagnosis and treatment of infertility).

F. When *"scut" work* must be done, make sure the duty does not always fall on the same individual. Encourage students to be helpful but not to the detriment of other aspects of their education. Stress that routine chores can both increase students' skills and help them learn to organize their time, as well as being part of their new "professional" responsibilities as health care team members.

G. The senior house officer should familiarize junior house staff and students with the setting in which they will be working. This responsibility consists of two general elements.

1. As soon as possible, inform newcomers about the physical environment of the service or clinic (e.g., location of labs, equipment, supplies) and the general procedures to be followed in order to get things done (e.g., how to order tests, get results, and obtain consults). Introduce new staff to others who will be working with them.

2. Acquaint students with the preferences of individual attending physicians. Many faculty have definite ways they want their services to operate, and students are often not sophisticated enough to discover these on their own.

DEVELOPMENT OF
A PROFESSIONAL ORIENTATION

Clinical training from medical school through residency has been described as a continuum with the objective of sequentially increasing the learner's knowledge, skills, and responsibilities.[4] Paralleling this maturation is the development of a professional identity, which requires the adoption of certain attitudes and behaviors consistent with the practice of medicine. Attending physicians serve as role models for both house staff and students. House officers are also important as models, since students are in contact with and observe them in many different situations. Therefore, teaching by example is an important strategy to employ while working with other house staff and students.

A. The clinical environment can be a stressful one for students. Create an atmosphere where feelings and emotions can be expressed and shared.

B. Teach students to recognize and display sensitivity to patient needs and concerns while they are providing care.[2] Model the ways to establish rapport with patients and give students advice and feedback about their interaction skills.

C. Encourage students to accept other health professionals as colleagues and to deal with them in a respectful and friendly manner.[2,3]

D. Model those behaviors that students, house staff, and supervisors consider to be characteristic of a good clinician.[3]

   1. Display self-confidence and be ready to assume responsibility, without being arrogant.

   2. Be self-critical and willing to admit lack of knowledge.

E. Maintain rapport with peers and supervisors. Be flexible and responsive. Assist colleagues in getting things done when necessary and encourage students to act similarly.

F. Help students develop a sense of perspective. Convey the feeling that though the task of learning medicine is difficult, it is also rewarding.

ATTITUDE TOWARD TEACHING

Students consider teacher enthusiasm and interest as an important factor in their learning.[2,3] The house officer should be concerned with facilitating learning in all interactions with students, not just those formally designated as teaching sessions.

A. *Remain accessible to students.* Be receptive to questions and give explanations when time permits. If it is not possible to respond to a student immediately, make sure to return to the subject later.
B. *Foster in students an attitude of independence and responsibility for their own learning.* When appropriate, rather than immediately providing answers, have students research their questions and report their findings.
C. *Have students share information.* If one student has seen a specific pathology or normal variant, have him or her report on it to the other students in the group.
D. *Use teaching as an instrument for self-diagnosis.* The process of explaining things to others is often a useful way of determining your own information base.

CONTENT EXPERTISE/KNOWLEDGE

The senior house officer is still in the process of acquiring the knowledge and skills necessary for independent practice. This learning can come from a variety of sources: faculty, peers, the published literature, and direct clinical experience.

A. Share appropriate references with junior house staff and students.
B. Encourage beginning students to concentrate their reading on their own patients' problems. This strategy makes the information more relevant and more likely to be retained.

REFERENCES
1. Stenchever MA, Irby D, O'Toole B: A national survey of undergraduate teaching in obstetrics and gynecology. J Med Educ 54:467–470, 1959
2. Stritter FT, Hain JD, Grimes DA: Clinical teaching reexamined. J Med Educ 50:876–882, 1975
3. Irby D: Clinical teacher effectiveness in medicine. J Med Educ 53:808–815, 1978

4. Tonesk X: The house officer as a teacher: what schools expect and measure. J Med Educ 54:613–616, 1979
5. Foley RP, Smilansky J: Teaching Techniques: A Handbook for Health Professionals. New York, McGraw-Hill, 1980
6. Byrne N, Cohen R: Observational study of clinical clerkship activities. J Med Educ 48:919–927, 1973

2

History and Physical Examination*

Jeffrey W. Ellis, M.D.
Charles R.B. Beckmann, M.D.
Linda A. Wheeler, R.N., C.N.M., Ed.D.
Frank W. Ling, M.D.

MEDICAL HISTORY

Practice Principles

The patient's medical history should be obtained in an orderly sequence. When dealing with the obstetric or gynecologic patient, *pertinent gynecologic information is emphasized,* although care should be taken to obtain information regarding the patient's entire medical history in order to detect and treat other intercurrent medical problems.

Chief Complaint

The patient's chief complaint (CC) may be recorded either as a quote of the patient's response or as a description of the patient's response using medical terminology, although care must be

---

*This chapter appears in both *A Clinical Manual of Obstetrics* and *A Clinical Manual of Gynecology.*

Format of the Gynecologic History
Identifying Data
   Age
   Menarche
   Last Menstrual Period (LMP)
   Previous Menstrual Period (PMP)
   Obstetric Profile   Gravida ____ Para ____ ____ ____ ____

     Number of Pregnancies ⟶

     Number of Term Pregnancies ⟶

     Number of Premature Pregnancies ⟶

     Number of Aborted Pregnancies ⟶

     Number of Living Children ⟶

Birth Control History (past and present methods, sterilization)
Gynecologic Surgery

---

taken to avoid obscuring the patient's true meaning by the use of technical terminology.

History of Present Illness (HPI)
The following information should be obtained according to the patient's presenting symptoms.

A. *Bleeding Symptoms*
   1. Changes in the menstrual period interval; duration of bleeding; relative amount of bleeding (determine by assessing the number of tampons or perineal pads used); passage of clots

    2. Intermenstrual bleeding: amount, duration, relative time within the menstrual cycle
    3. Contact bleeding: after douching, sexual intercourse
    4. Postmenopausal bleeding: amount, duration, time interval from last menstrual period, history of hormonal (estrogen) therapy
    5. Changes in menstrual pattern in relation to exogenous steroids; estrogen, progesterone, birth control pills

B. *Pain Symptoms*
    1. Date of onset
    2. Relation to the menstrual period
    3. Location
    4. Radiation
    5. Character: sharp, dull, constant, intermittent
    6. Degree: whether the pain incapacitates the patient
    7. Factors that decrease or increase pain: position, urination, defecation
    8. Use of analgesics, muscle relaxants, etc. (type, frequency, amount, duration of use)
    9. Associated gastrointestinal and urinary symptoms

C. *Mass Symptoms*
    1. Date of onset
    2. Relation to the menstrual period
    3. Location
    4. Associated symptoms: pain, bleeding, gastrointestinal or urinary disturbance
    5. Growth: stable, slow, rapid (measured by such things as "changes" in clothing size, "bloated" sensation, etc.)

D. *Vaginal Discharge*
    1. Date of onset
    2. Relation to the menstrual period
    3. Color, odor, consistency, quantity
    4. Associated rectal or urethral discharge
    5. Associated symptoms: pain, pruritus
    6. Relation to use of medications: antibiotics, exogenous steroids
    7. History of previous treatment

E. *Ulceration or Persistent Lesion*
   1. Date of onset
   2. Location
   3. Growth: stable, slow, rapid
   4. Associated symptoms: pain, pruritus, bleeding, discharge
   5. Other body sites with a similar lesion
   6. History of previous treatment
F. *Pelvic Relaxation*
   1. Pressure
   2. Prolapse ("falling out")
   3. Urinary symptoms: urgency, frequency, inability to void, incontinence
   4. Lower gastrointestinal symptoms: constipation, tenesmus, incontinence
G. *Infertility*
   1. Duration
   2. Frequency of intercourse
   3. Prior investigation
   4. Medical or surgical disorders of partner (previous children?)
H. *Pelvic ("Tubal") Infection (Pelvic Inflammatory Disease, PID)*
   1. History consistent with PID: fever (with or without chills), abdominopelvic pain, foul discharge; use of parenteral antibiotics with relief within 48 hours
   2. History of positive GC culture or documented exposure

Gynecologic History

The following detailed information is obtained regarding the patient's gynecologic history:
A. Age at menarche
B. Normal interval between menstrual periods
C. Normal durations of menstrual flow
D. Normal amount of menstrual flow (number of perineal pads or tampons)

E. Associated menstrual symptoms: pain, edema, headache
F. Past gynecologic problems treated medically
G. Past gynecologic surgery
H. Contraceptive use: method, side effects, complications

Sexual History
A. Regularity of intercourse
B. Associated symptoms: pain, bleeding
C. Sexual dysfunction

Medical History
A. Chronic diseases: treatment, results
B. Infectious diseases: venereal diseases, exposure to infectious diseases
C. Current medications
D. Past medications
E. Allergies *(include symptoms of allergic reactions)*
F. Use of drugs, alcohol, tobacco
G. Exposure to toxic agents and radiation

Surgical History
A. Dates of procedures
B. Diagnosis
C. Type of surgical procedures
D. Results

Family History
A. Malignancy, chronic illness
B. Hereditary disease
C. Multiple gestation
D. Pertinent obstetric and gynecologic histories of family members

Social History
A. Occupation and financial status
B. Marital status
C. Education

Review of Systems (ROS)

In general, the standard format of the review of systems should be followed. Pertinent "negatives" should be noted in the following systems:

A. Gastrointestinal
   1. Indigestion
   2. Nausea, vomiting, diarrhea
   3. Constipation
   4. Incontinence, tenesmus, rectal bleeding
   5. Abdominal pain
B. Urinary
   1. Urgency, frequency, dysuria, nocturia, incontinence
   2. Hematuria
   3. Inability to void

Format of the Obstetric History (page 12)

THE PELVIC EXAMINATION

Practice Principles

1. A relaxed and comfortable patient is essential for the performance of the pelvic examination.

2. The patient in the lithotomy position with drapes across her knees is blind to the pelvic examination. Eye contact between the patient and the examiner decreases some of the anxiety about the pelvic examination.

3. It is necessary to alleviate the patient's anxiety and enlist her cooperation.

4. Principles to be followed during the pelvic exam include:

● Assure the patient that all procedures will be demonstrated and explained prior to being performed.
● Inform the patient before an area is examined.
● Use slow and deliberate motions to allow the patient to maintain relaxation.

- Inform the patient of any deep palpation or uncomfortable procedures.
- Warm speculum before insertion if possible.

Format of the Pelvic Examination. The following outline should be used when reporting the pelvic examination into the medical record:

- External genitalia
- Vagina
- Cervix
- Corpus
- Adnexa
- Rectovaginal

Physical Findings

The following physical findings should be noted and recorded.

A. *External Genitalia*
   1. Hair distribution
   2. Labia majora/minora: lesions, ulcerations, masses, induration, areas of different color
   3. Clitoris: size, lesions, ulcerations
   4. Urethra: discharge, lesions, ulcerations
   5. Skene's glands/Bartholin's glands: masses, discharge, tenderness
   6. Perineum: lesions, ulcerations, masses, induration
   7. Anus: lesions, ulcerations, fissures, hemorrhoids
B. *Vagina*
   1. Inflammation or atrophy
   2. Lesions, ulceration, excoriation
   3. Masses, induration or nodularity
   4. Discharge (KOH and saline preparation results; vaginal pH)
   5. Septa, status of hymen/introitus
   6. Relaxation of support: rectocele, cystocele, urethrocele, enterocele, uterine prolapse

C. *Cervix*
   1. Size and position; position of transformation zone
   2. Color
   3. Ulcerations, lesions, lacerations (old, new; size, location)
   4. Consistency (firm, hard, soft, nodular)
   5. Pain on motion
   6. Contact bleeding (after pap smear or contact with the speculum)
   7. Discharge
   8. Parous or nulliparous
D. *Corpus*
   1. Position
   2. Size (describe in weeks size as though pregnant)
   3. Contour (smooth, irregular)
   4. Consistency
   5. Mobility
   6. Pain on motion
E. *Adnexa*
   1. Size
   2. Consistency (solid, soft, "thickened")
   3. Contour (smooth, irregular)
   4. Mobility (if not, fixed to what structure)
   5. Position
   6. Pain on motion
F. *Rectovaginal*
   1. Cul de sac: mass, flutulence
   2. Rectovaginal septum: mass, flutulence, nodularity, induration
   3. Parametria: induration, nodularity
   4. Rectum: mass, bleeding
   5. Uterosacral ligaments: nodularity

PROCEDURE GUIDE: PELVIC EXAMINATION

Procedure	**Comments**
1. Place a glove on one hand.	See comments at end of this section regarding one- and two-glove technique.
2. Make patient as comfortable as possible. If the examiner is male, a female assistant should be present. If the examiner is female, many people also advocate the presence of an assistant who is female.	A female assistant protects the examiner from charges of improper sexual advances and provides the patient with a same-sex support person.
3. Drape the woman so that her knees are covered. The head of the table should be elevated enough that you will have eye contact with the patient.	Covering a woman's knees helps her feel you have some concern for her modesty. Some women feel a drape is unnecessary. However, it is usually best to proceed with the assumption that the patient prefers a drape.
4. Arrange the drape so that it is flat on the patient's abdomen yet covers the patients knees.	A sheet placed flat on the abdomen allows for eye contact between patient and examiner.
5. Sit down. Adjust the light.	
6. Tell the patient you are going to touch the back of her leg. Touch the back of your hand to the inside of the patient's thigh.	This action is relatively noninvasive, assures her you are concerned for her comfort, and involves no discomfort. Watch the muscles around her vagina and rectum. If they contract, make extra efforts to go slowly and be gentle.

7. Observe the perineum and external genitalia. "Chattering" or complete silence at this point will often make the patient anxious.

8. Tell the woman you are going to touch her external genitalia, "privates," "outside," etc. Separate the labia majora from the labia minora. Inspect the urethra.

Normal labia minora may be asymmetrical, and either larger or smaller than the labia majora.

9. Tell the woman you are going to put one finger inside. Insert your index finger to the last phalanx (approximately 1 inch). With palm up, "milk" the urethra.

You are looking for purulent discharge. Most often it is gonorrhea.

10. Using the thumb and index finger, palpate the area at 7 and 8 o'clock, as well as at 4 and 5 o'clock for a Bartholin cyst.

You will feel nothing in the absence of a cyst.

11. Show the patient the speculum if she has not seen one before and tell her you are going to insert it. If you wish, moisten it with warm water to make insertion easier. However, the speculum should be moistened/lubricated for prepubertal girls and postmenopausal women.

Lubricants such as KY Jelly should not be used as they will affect the reading of the Pap smear. If the speculum has not been warmed, warn the patient that it will be cold. Warming the speculum, however, greatly increases patient acceptance of the examination and ease of examination.

12. The speculum can be inserted in many ways. Here are three that are commonly used. Hold the speculum in your ungloved hand:

a) Insert the index and middle fingers of your examining hand into the vagina and press down posteriorly. Insert the speculum on top of your fingers and rotate it so that the handle is down. Remove your fingers from the vagina.

b) Place the index and middle fingers of your examining hand just inside the vaginal orifice on either side. Roll them back onto the external genitalia and press posteriorly and laterally to enlarge the vaginal orifice. Insert the speculum.

c) Place the index and middle fingers of your examining hand on either side of the vagina on the outside. Exert pressure downwards and laterally to

Whatever technique is used, ask the patient to relax (have the patient relax the muscle she uses to cut off her urine stream). It is not unusual for a woman to unconsciously tighten her pelvis muscles at this time. Observe for a cystocele or rectocele as you get ready to insert the speculum.

enlarge the vaginal opening.

Insert the speculum. Whichever method is used remember pressure "posteriorly" presses soft tissue against soft tissue, whereas "anteriorly" soft tissue is "caught" between a hard metal speculum and the bony pelvis.

13. Transfer the handle of the speculum to your other hand. Remember that the vagina angles toward the hollow of the sacrum. Open the speculum. The cervix will appear smooth in comparison with the rugaeted vagina. Its position varies.

The most common reason for not "finding" the cervix is failure to insert the speculum far enough before opening the instrument.

Once the cervix is found, insert the speculum far enough so that the cervix rests within the blades. Set the screw with your ungloved hand.

In most instances it will not be necessary to adjust the lower screw located on the handle of the speculum. Adjusting this screw allows for greater visualization, needed for procedures such as IUD insertion.

14. Observe the vagina and cervix. Saline and KOH preparations should be done on any discharge and pH obtained with litmus paper.

15. Perform a Pap smear and obtain a specimen for the

gonorrhea culture (see procedure guide).

16. Tell the patient you are going to turn and remove the speculum. Unscrew the screw but do not remove the speculum. Rotate the speculum 90° so that you can see the anterior and posterior walls of the vagina. Remove the speculum.

17. Place a small amount of lubricant on the index and middle fingers of your gloved hand. Tell the woman that you are going to examine her internally.

If you obtain the lubricant from a multiple-use tube, be sure you do not touch your fingers to the tube's opening. If you touch the opening, the tube must be thrown away as it may be contaminated with secretions on your gloved hand.

18. Tell the woman you are going to touch the back of her leg again. Then gently and slowly insert your middle and index fingers into the vagina. Turn your palm up and feel for the cervix.

The cervix may be found posteriorly, anteriorly, or any where in between. Its position is most often related to the postion of the uterus: a posterior cervix with an anteverted uterus and an anterior cervix with a retroverted uterus. The cervix will feel like the tip of your nose. Note its shape and consistency. Feel for growths.

19. Now feel the body of the uterus. Place your fingers palm up on top of the cervix. Place your abdom-

It is important to start at the umbilicus with your abdominal hand until you become skilled to avoid missing a

inal hand at the umbilicus. Slowly work your abdominal hand down toward the symphysis trying to trap the anteverted uterus between your two hands (Fig. 2–1).

20. If you cannot feel the uterus with this maneuver, place your fingers *under* the cervix and advance them along the posterior part of the cervix as far as they will go. Move your abdominal hand as in step 21, following.

uterus enlarged by fibroids or pregnancy.

This time you are trying to trap a retroverted uterus between your fingers.

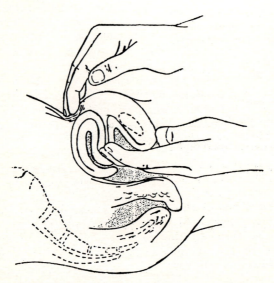

Figure 2–1. Bimanual palpation of the uterus.

21. If you still cannot find the uterus, it is probably in a midposition, i.e., not tilted in either direction. Keep your fingers, palm up, under the cervix and work them toward the patient's head. Place the flat part of the fingers of your abdominal hand above the symphysis. Press toward the examining table trying once again to trap the uterus between your fingers (Fig.2–2).

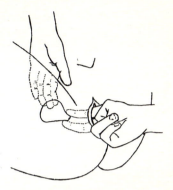

Figure 2–2. Palpation of the uterus in midposition.

22. Once located there are six things about the uterus to be noted; size, shape, position, consistency, mobility, and tenderness.

23. The ovaries and fallopian tubes are located posterior to the broad ligament, which is attached to the uterus. Place your vaginal fingers to the side of the cervix deep in the cul-de-sac (lateral fornix). Move your abdominal hand to the same side just inside the flare of the pelvis. Press down and move your abdominal hand toward the symphysis. Reach up with your vaginal fingers. Bring them together the rest of the

Feeling ovaries is a skill that takes much practice to develop. As a beginner, it is neither necessary nor expected that you will feel ovaries on every patient. Keep the patient's comfort in mind. Even experienced, competent physicians do not *always* feel the ovaries. Inability to feel the adnexa is often just as important as feeling the adnexa. It is a significant negative for the skilled clinician, meaning that no pathology is evident.

way down the abdomen. The ovary should be felt trapped between your fingers. It normally feels about the size of an almond. It should be mobile and free of the side walls. The fallopian tubes will not be palpable unless they are pathologically enlarged (Fig. 2–3).

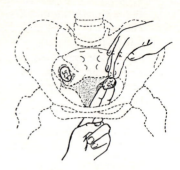

Figure 2–3. Palpation of the adnexae.

24. Tell the patient that the final part of the examination is the exam of the rectum. Repeat rectally the exam of the uterus and ovaries as in step 23. A rectal exam is quite uncomfortable for most people. It should, therefore, be completed as quickly and gently as possible. Tell the patient what you intend to do. Ask her to bear down as if she were going to move her bowels. Besides relaxing the patient, this helps you feel where to insert your finger. Keeping your index finger in the vagina, *slowly* insert your middle finger into the rectum as

The exam is important for three reasons: the information it gives about the rectum, the rectovaginal septum, and confirmation of your vaginal findings. Additionally, you can feel 1 to 2 cm higher into the pelvis than you can feel vaginally. Explaining these facts to a patient helps her to understand why such an uncomfortable procedure is necessary.

the sphincter relaxes. Place your rectovaginal fingers laterally with your abdominal hand on the same side. Move your hands together across the abdomen to the opposite side. Be sure your vaginal finger stays under the cervix.

Feel both uterosacral ligaments. They should be obvious, symmetrical, smooth, and nontender. Feel posteriorly across the uterus. It should feel smooth. The mucosas—or two peritoneal surfaces—should slide across each other. If not, suspect endometriosis. Feel for puckering, shortening, scarring—all suggestive of endometriosis.

25. Offer the woman a tissue to wipe off excess lubricant before she dresses. Ask her to move back on the table and then to sit up.

If she sits up first, she will fall on the floor.

26. Remove your glove(s) and wash your hands.

Remember to turn off the faucet with a paper towel to avoid contaminating your hands with anything (GC, trichomonas) that may be on the faucet.

Hints

1. Many women make extra effort to be clean prior to a pelvic examination by douching. You may want to inquire as to whether or not the patient douches and how often. Ask her not to douche for 48 hours prior to examination, so that you can observe the usual state of her vagina.

2. Clinicians' feelings about a one- or two-glove technique vary, as do their preferences for which hand to use for the examination. The use of two gloves protects the examiner from possible contact with disease organisms such as *Neisseria gonorrhoeae*. However, beginners using this technique often forget to keep one hand clean and, consequently, may contaminate the light and other objects.

3. Once you perform a pelvic exam, you will see that you can feel one side of the pelvis better than the other. The angle of your hand allows the right-handed examiner to examine the patient's right side better and vice versa. To compensate for the difference, some clinicians use their left hand to examine the left side and their right hand to examine the right side.

THE VAGINAL SPECULUM

The vaginal speculum (Fig. 2–4) is an instrument that facilitates visualization of the cervix and vaginal walls. Note the parts of the speculum:

A. Upper blade
B. Lower blade
C. Handle
D. Screw attaching the upper and lower blades
E. Lever separating the upper and lower blades
F. Screw to fix the blades in position

There are two types of specula: the Pederson and the Graves (Fig. 2–5 and 2–6). The Pederson speculum has flat and narrow blades that barely curve on the sides. The standard Pederson works well for most nulliparous women. Occasionally, it is necessary to use the Pederson for a multiparous woman who is sensitive to objects being placed in her vagina.The Graves speculum has blades that are wider, higher, and curved on the sides. Most women who have had a baby can accommodate the standard (medium) Graves speculum. Its wider, curved blades keep the looser vaginal walls of the multiparous woman separated for visualization.

Both specula are available in a pediatric size as well as the standard size (Fig. 2–7). The pediatric specula are usually reserved for young children. The length of the blades does not usually allow the examiner to reach the cervix of girls who are pubertal or older. A Pederson with extra narrow blades is also available (Fig. 2–8).

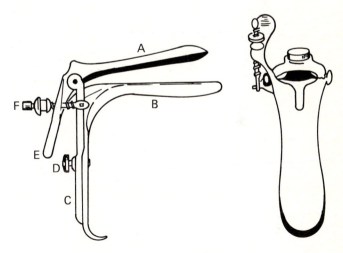

Figure 2–4. Parts of the vaginal speculum.

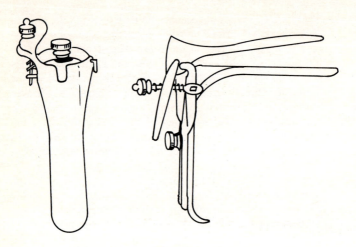

Figure 2–5. Medium Pederson speculum.

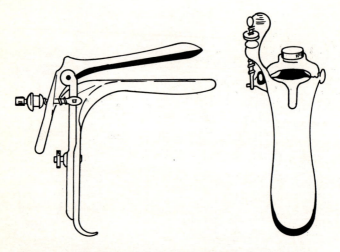

Figure 2–6. Medium Graves speculum.

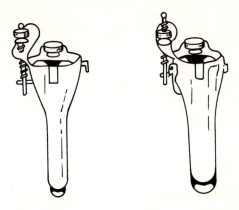

Figure 2–7. Pediatric specula: A. Pederson; B. Graves.

Figure 2–8. Pediatric Pederson speculum with extra-narrow blades.

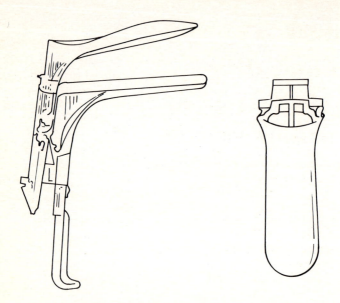

Figure 2–9. Disposable plastic speculum.

The disposable plastic speculum (Fig. 2–9) may be used in some institutions. It makes a loud "click" when the lower blade is disengaged for removal. Women should be alerted to the noise prior to disengaging to avoid startling the patient. Women who perform or plan to begin performing self-examination of the cervix and vagina appreciate being given the plastic speculum to take home. It should be washed after each use. Most women find that, for self-examination, insertion is most easily accomplished with the handle up rather than down.

3

Operative Management*
Jeffrey W. Ellis, M.D.

ROUTINE ADMITTING ORDERS
Admitting orders will vary according to the patient's condition and the planned operative procedure.

Orders should be specified in the following sequence:

1. Vital signs
2. Diet
3. Activity
4. Laboratory studies
5. Radiologic studies
6. Other special studies
7. Medications
8. Special care
9. Respiratory care

1. Vital Signs. In most patients admitted for elective procedures, vital signs (pulse, respirations, blood pressure, temperature) may be taken every 8 hours or every 12 hours (q8h, q12h). More frequent assessment may be required in acutely ill patients (q1h, q2h, q4h).

*This chapter appears in both *A Clinical Manual of Obstetrics* and *A Clinical Manual of Gynecology*.

2. Diet. A regular diet may be given to most patients up to the night before surgery. The patient should receive nothing by mouth (NPO) for at least 8 hours prior to surgery. A clear liquid diet may be required before certain radiographic studies and before some surgical procedures in which bowel surgery is a possibility.

3. Activity. Most patients are allowed unrestricted activity prior to surgery (up ad lib). Special bed positions should be specified if necessary (Trendelenburg position, semi-Fowler's position, etc.).

4. Laboratory Studies. Most hospitals require the following laboratory studies prior to surgery: complete blood count, urinalysis, prothrombin time (PT), partial thromboplastin time (PTT), platelet count, electrolytes, blood urea nitrogen (BUN), creatinine, direct and indirect bilirubin, alkaline phosphatase, SGOT, SGPT. Other studies may be necessary according to significant history and physical examination.

5. Radiologic Studies. Most hospitals require a chest x-ray prior to surgery. Additional diagnostic studies may be required for complete preoperative evaluation: intravenous pyelogram (IVP), lower gastrointestinal series (LGI), voiding cystoure-throgram, and so on.

6. Other Special Studies. An electrocardiogram should be obtained on all patients over the age of 35 years and on all patients with a history of cardiac or pulmonary disease. Additional studies that may be required include: pulmonary function studies (PFT), ultrasound, and computed axial tomography (CAT scan).

7. Medications. Patient comfort medications (analgesics, hyp-notics, laxatives) and therapeutic medications should be specified. Some physicians suggest a "non-PRN" sleeping medi-cation the night before surgery to allow the patient adequate sleep prior to surgery (example: secobarbital, 100 mg at 11 P.M.).

8. Special Care. Specify the following: wound care, catheter care, skin care, and colostomy care.

9. Respiratory Care. Patients who smoke should be vigorously encouraged to cease smoking two to four weeks before elective surgery. Upon admission, all patients should be provided with a voluntary respiratory exiciser (Uniflow, Triflow, etc.) with instructions for the nursing staff to teach the patient the proper use of the instrument and to verify that the patient has acquired facility with the device. This presurgical emphasis fixes in the patient's mind the importance of good respiratory effort in the postoperative period, thus increasing patient compliance in these matters.

PREOPERATIVE ORDERS

Preoperative orders will vary according to the type and site of surgery and the general condition of the patient.

Orders should be specified in the following sequence:

	Example
1. *Diet*	Nothing by mouth after midnight
2. *Patient preparation*	
Abdomen–perineum	Shave abdomen from umbilicus to symphysis
Bowel	Tap water enema until clear two hours before surgery
Vagina	Betadine douche the evening before surgery
Skin	Scrub abdomen with soap and water one hour before surgery
Bladder	Void on call to operating room
3. *Medications*	
Preoperative sedation (to be given IM on call to operating room)	Meperidine (Demerol), 50 mg; hydroxyzine (Vistaril), 25 mg; atropine, 0.4 mg
Antibiotics	If prophylactic antibiotics are

given, the first dose should be administered parenterally within two hours before surgery.

4. *Blood bank* (Every hospital has its own protocol about the availability of blood for surgery.)

Type and crossmatch two units of whole blood.

PREOPERATIVE NOTES

Prior to any operative procedure, the following note should be recorded in the medical record.

	Example
1. *Preoperative diagnosis*	Uterine myomata
2. *Planned procedure*	Vaginal hysterectomy
3. *Surgeons*	Drs. _____
4. *Preoperative laboratory*	Summary of pertinent laboratory studies
5. *Blood bank*	Whole blood, 2 units, available

POSTOPERATIVE NOTES

The postoperative note provides a summary of the surgical procedure.

	Example
1. *Preoperative diagnosis*	Uterine myomata
2. *Postoperative diagnosis*	Same
3. *Procedure*	Vaginal hysterectomy
4. *Surgeon*	Dr. _____
5. *Assistant*	Dr. _____
6. *Anesthesia*	General endotracheal, halothane and thiopental
7. *Anesthesiologist*	Dr. _____
8. *Fluids administered*	2000 mL lactated Ringer's so-

	lution; 2 units of packed red blood cells
9. *Estimated blood loss*	300 ml
10. *Urinary output*	600 ml
11. *Findings* (The careful and detailed description of operative findings and procedures is one of the *most crucial* roles of the operative note, yet it is also the most often neglected aspect of the note.)	Uterus: 12-week size, multinodular; tubes and ovaries: normal
12. *Complications*	None
13. *Tubes and drains*	Foley catheter, nasogastric tube
14. *Condition of patient*	Tolerated procedure well, brought to recovery room awake and extubated

POSTOPERATIVE ORDERS

Minor Procedures. During minor gynecologic procedures, blood loss is usually minimal and the abdominal cavity is not entered. Examples include dilatation and curettage, cone biopsy, Bartholin cystectomy. Postoperatively, the patient should rapidly regain normal preoperative status.

	Example
1. *Vital signs*	Every 15 minutes until stable, then every four hours.
2. *Diet*	Regular diet when fully recovered from anesthesia.
3. *Activity*	Unrestricted activity when fully recovered from anesthesia.
4. *Intravenous fluids*	Dextrose, 5%, in Ringer's lactate at a rate of 125 ml/hour.

	Discontinue when the patient is fully awake and tolerating a diet.
5. *Special observations*	Inform the service of heavy vaginal bleeding or inability to void.
6. *Medications*	Specify analgesics, hypnotics, antibiotics; resume other necessary medications.

Major Procedures. Examples include abdominal hysterectomy, vaginal hysterectomy, salpingectomy. Major procedures usually involve the following:

1. Bowel manipulation with resulting paralytic ileus.
2. Operative blood loss of 100 to 1000 mL or more.
3. Longer anesthesia time with resulting pulmonary atelectasis and accumulation of pulmonary secretions.

Postoperative management is thus aimed at:

1. Careful and frequent monitoring of vital signs.
2. Maintenance of adequate intravascular volume through careful monitoring of intake and output.
3. "Bowel rest" until peristaltic function resumes.
4. Pulmonary therapy.

An example of immediate postoperative orders after an abdominal hysterectomy follows:

	Example
1. *Vital signs*	q 15 minutes until stable, then q1h × 2, then q2h × 2, then q4h.
2. *Diet*	Nothing by mouth (NPO)
3. *Activity*	Complete bed rest for 8 hours, then ambulate with assistance for 10 minutes q4h.

4. *Intravenous fluids*	Dextrose, 5% in Ringer's lactate to run at 125 mL/hour
5. *Tubes and drains*	Foley catheter to closed drainage bag, nasogastric tube to low, intermittent suction.
6. *Intake and output*	Record q2h.
7. *Medications*	Meperidine, 75 mg IM q3h PRN.
8. *Respiratory care* (Whatever respiratory care is selected, it should be ordered "around-the-clock" in the immediate postoperative period, and *not* "while awake.")	Turn, cough, and hyperventilate q2h, ultrasonic nebulizer for 10 minutes q2h.
9. *Laboratory*	CBC at 10:00 P.M. and 7:00 A.M.
10. *Notify service*	Pulse greater than 120; systolic BP less than 90; diastolic BP less than 60; temperature greater than 101F; urine output less than 60 ml in any two-hour interval.

POSTOPERATIVE ROUNDS

During daily postoperative rounds, the following areas should be evaluated and entered into the medical record:

Postoperative Day Number (POD#)

1. *Review of chart*	Vital signs; intake and output; nursing notes.
2. *Patient complaints and observations*	Location and degree of pain; vaginal drainage or bleeding; bowel movement or passage of flatus; nausea or vomiting; difficulty with urination; expectoration.

3. *Physical examination*

Auscultate chest; auscultate abdomen for bowel sounds; palpate abdomen; examine incision; examine lower extremities and IV sites for evidence of phlebitis; evaluate vaginal drainage or bleeding.

4. *Treatment plan*

Re-evaluate diet, activity, frequency of vital signs; intravenous fluids; necessity of tubes and drains; medications; special care. Order new laboratory studies as indicated.

4

Benign Diseases of the Vulva

John R. Musich, M.D.

PRACTICE PRINCIPLES

Vulvar diseases are some of the most common problems seen in the practice of gynecology. Occupying the female external genitalia from the mons pubis to the rectum and bordered by the lateral portions of the labia majora, the vulva can exhibit many variations of normal anatomy while being host to multiple symptomatic and asymptomatic pathologic conditions. Developmental anomalies or abnormalities, such as agenesis, duplication, clitoral hypertrophy, imperforate hymen, urethral epispadias or hypospadias, are possible but infrequently seen. Instead, most vulvar disorders are related to the fact that this region is in large part an organ of skin and, like skin elsewhere, can manifest inflammatory, vascular, dermatologic, dystrophic, cystic, and both benign and malignant neoplastic changes. A complete discussion of the many described vulvar disorders is beyond the scope of this chapter. For detailed reviews the reader is referred to the cited references.[1-3] This chapter considers only those benign entities commonly seen in clinical practice.

ANATOMIC AND
PHYSIOLOGIC CONSIDERATIONS
An understanding of both normal and diseased vulvar conditions can be enhanced by appreciating the following brief considerations of important anatomy and physiology.

A. *Epithelium*
  1. Composed of stratified squamous epithelium with a cornified surface layer, median prickle layer, and basal layer.
  2. Rete pegs, abundant in vulvar epithelium, gradually decrease in prominence as the vulvar epithelium merges with the stratified squamous epithelium of the vagina.
  3. Contains specialized gland structures.
B. *Glands* Four differing gland structures are prominent in vulvar topography.
  1. *Sweat glands*
     a) Small-coiled eccrine glands located in the mons pubis and outer aspects of the labia majora.
     b) Decreased numbers in the inner labia majora.
     c) Absent from the labia minora inward.
  2. *Scent glands*
     a) Large-coiled apocrine glands opening into hair follicles or directly into the skin.
     b) Limited in location to the labia majora.
     c) Respond to hormonal cycle with peak activity at midcycle.
     d) Responsible for the characteristic female vulvoperineal odor in the nondiseased woman. This becomes an important consideration in advising patients who insist on douching as part of their routine perineal hygiene. Normal vaginal secretions are nonodorous, becoming malodorous only when infected, usually with *Trichomonas* or occasionally with *Gardnerella vaginale (Corynebacterium vaginale, Haemophilus vaginalis)*. If bothered by vulvar

malodor, patients must first have vaginal and vulvar infections ruled out and, finding none, be encouraged to practice improved vulvar and perineal hygiene rather than douche vaginally to minimize their normal but self-perceived bothersome perineal "malodor."

3. *Sebaceous glands* and *hair follicles*
   a) Most sebum-producing sebaceous glands are found as part of the prominent pilosebaceous areas of the mons pubis and labia majora.
   b) Sebaceous glands are also present in the labia majora and labia minora.
   c) In hyperandrogenemic conditions, pilosebaceous activity extends to the inner aspects of the thighs and to the perianal area, thereby enlarging the perineal areas susceptible to pilosebaceous disorders.
4. *Mucin-producing glands*
   a) *Bartholin glands* (*major vestibular*), paired and located in the basal portion of the labia majora, are the most prominent of the vulvar mucin-producing glands.
   b) Inflammation of this gland's columnar and squamous epithelial duct is common, resulting in blockage and painful cystic dilation of the underlying gland.
   c) Minor vestibular glands, approximately 12 in number, occupy the inner labia minora surrounding the vaginal introitus and are also possible sites of infection.
C. *Blood supply and lymphatic drainage*[2]
   1. *Arterial supply* mostly from internal pudendal arteries, branches of the internal iliac (hypogastric) arteries.
   2. *Venous drainage* along the internal iliac veins.
   3. *Lymphatic drainage,* crucially important in the spread of vulvar malignancies and of frequent importance in benign conditions, is complex.
      a) The labia minora, labia majora, and posterior perineum drain to the superficial femoral nodes ipsilaterally.
      b) The prepuce and periclitoral areas drain to the

superficial femoral nodes both ipsilaterally and possibly contralaterally.

c) The glans clitoris drains directly to the deeper pelvic obturator and iliac nodes and less commonly to the superficial and deep femoral nodes.

d) The Bartholin gland may drain to either superficial and deep femoral nodes or directly to deep pelvic nodes.

D. *Innervation*[2]

1. Motor and sensory innervation of the vulva and perineum is derived chiefly from the pudendal nerve (S2, S3, S4) and its branches.

2. Mons pubis and anterior portions of the labia majora receive additional innervation from the ilio-inguinal nerve(L1).

3. The posterior portions of the labia majora receive additional innervation from branches of the posterior femoral cutaneous nerve (Sl, S2, S3).

4. *The rich sensory innervation of the vulva accounts for the discomfort associated with many of the vulvar conditions.* In addition, disease states may alter nerve plexus density and sensitivity and exaggerate symptomatology.

E. *Endocrinology*

1. While much is known about the endocrine influences on the embryologic development and differentiation of the external genitalia, little is known about hormonal influences on the adult vulva.

2. *Androgen-excess* conditions, such as adrenal hyperplasia or polycystic ovarian disease, can increase pilosebaceous activity.

3. *Follicular phase activity* will increase apocrine scent gland activity, with subsequent gland activity decrease during menstruation.

4. *Estrogen* considerations are most important in the menopausal patient. Whereas vaginal atrophy is very responsive to exogenous estrogen therapy, *the vulva, lacking the glycogen-rich epithelium that characterizes the*

vaginal mucosa, is virtually unresponsive to estrogen therapy in atrophic conditions.

F. *Moistness*
1. Variations in vulvar moistness will both predispose to pathology and also affect the appearance of the vulvar lesion.
2. Dryness typifies the lateral and central portions of the labia majora.
3. Semi-moist conditions characterize the medial labia majora and labia minora.
4. Moist epithelial surfaces are to be expected in the vestibular areas of the vulva and inner aspects of the labia minora.

COMMON OR IMPORTANT VULVAR INFECTIOUS DISEASES

Two of the most important infectious diseases involving the vulva are herpes and syphilis, which are discussed in other chapters. In this chapter, other vulvar diseases commonly seen or frequently considered in vulvar differential diagnoses are presented.

A. *Candida*
1. *Clinical considerations*
   a) Vulvovaginal infections caused by the fungus *Candida albicans* are frequently referred to as *"yeast"* or *"monilial"* infections.
   b) *One of the most common vulvar disorders seen in everyday practice and represents the most common mucocutaneous surface infected by this organism.*
   c) *C. albicans* is a normal inhabitant of the vaginal flora, and in primary vulvar infections the vagina is usually the source of the vulvar spread.
   d) Pregnancy, diabetes mellitus, oral contraceptive use, antibiotic therapy, *Trichomonas* vaginitis, and cutaneous injury to the vagina or vulva are the most common

inciting circumstances associated with symptomatic vulvar candidiasis.

2. *Symptoms and presentation*
   a) Nearly always causes *vulvar pruritus — indeed, a complaint of vulvovaginal itching should always be considered candidiasis until proven otherwise.*
   b) Characterized by a *yellow-white curdlike vaginal discharge* often forming plaquelike lesions on the ectocervix and vaginal walls.
   c) Causes *labial inflammation* with edematous, tender, weeping areas induced by *intense scratching* and subsequent cracking or fissure formation of the affected vulvar skin.
   d) Frequently spreads to the lateral labia majora, perianal mucosa, and genitocrural areas of the inner thighs.
   e) If in chronic phase, it may present as a dry, slightly scaling lesion with a slightly elevated, reddened margin or, if moist, with a diffuse grayish surface glaze.

3. *Diagnosis*
   a) Usually made solely by observing its classic appearance in a patient with compatible complaints.
   b) Further proof can be obtained by observing budding and pseudomycelia formation on either a Pap smear or on a potassium hydroxide (KOH)-treated microscopic wet preparation of the discharge.
   c) Culture methods are available but rarely indicated.

4. *Treatment*
   a) Primary treatment is usually with one of the following specific antifungal peparations:
      (1) Nystatin (Mycostatin) — daily application for one week.
      (2) Miconazole (Monistat) — daily application for one week.
      (3) Clotrimazole (Gyne-Lotrimin, Mycelex-G) — two tablets daily vaginally.
   b) In certain cases of particularly bothersome vulvar

inflammation, nystatin plus triamcinolone (Mycolog) will be beneficial.

   c) Topical gentian violet or providone-iodine (Betadine) can also be used for primary or concomitant therapy.

   d) Worthwhile adjunctive measures may include cleansing vaginal douche, wearing cotton undergarments rather than heat and moisture-retaining synthetic fabrics, and the use of condoms by the sex partner to prevent reinfection by an asymptomatic male carrier, particularly during the course of antibiotic therapy.

B. *Chancroid*

  1. *Clinical considerations*

    a) *Ulcerating disease* of the external genitalia caused by *Haemophilus ducreyi,* a small gram-negative bacillus.

    b) *Sexually transmitted* and more frequently seen in men than in women (10:1).

    c) Usually involves the urethra, posterior fourchette, and the vestibular mucosa bounded by the labia minora.

    d) After a *3 to 5 day incubation period,* the small single or multiple pustules erode to form shallow, soft, strikingly painful, malodorous ulcers which may become confluent and have virtually no induration.

    e) Ipsilateral inguinal lymphadenopathy occurs in 40 to 50 percent of patients.

  2. *Diagnosis*

    a) The lesion has *no characteristic histologic features,* although stained smears (gram, Giemsa, Wright) obtained from the undersurface of the ragged edges of the ulcers exhibiting chains of gram-negative rods may be helpful.

    b) Conclusive laboratory techniques for confirmation of chancroid are lacking.

    c) Antigen skin testing and complement-fixation studies are of questionable worth in a clinical setting.

    d) Most diagnostic confusion involves distinguishing chancroid ("soft painful chancre") from primary syphilis ("hard painless chancre"), herpes genitalis, granuloma inguinale, and lymphogranuloma venereum.

3. *Treatment*

a) *Sulfa* has long been the standard treatment of chancroid, although streptomycin or trimethoprim-sulfamethoxazole is preferred for treatment failures and may have a role as primary therapy.

b) Erythromycin and cephalosporins are usually reserved for patients with sulfa allergies or in pregnancy.

c) *Treatment modalities* include the following: [4,5]

(1) *Sulfisoxazole (Gantrisin)* — 4 gm/day for 14 days.

(2) Tetracycline — 2 gm/day for 14 days.

(3) Trimethoprim-sulfamethoxazole (Bactrim, Septra) — 2 tablets/day for 14 days (each tablet contains 160 mg trimethoprim and 800 mg sulfamethoxazole).

(4) Streptomycin — 1 gmIM/day for 6 days.

(5) Erythromycin — 2 gm/day for 14 days.

(6) Cephalothin (Keflin) — 1 gm IV qid for 5 days.

C. *Granuloma inguinale* (granuloma venereum, sclerosing granuloma)

1. *Clinical considerations*

a) *Ulcerating disease* of the vulva caused by *Calymmatobacterium (Donovania) granulomatis,* a gram-negative encapsulated bacillus.

b) After an *incubation period of 5 to 6 weeks,* its clinical presentation differs from chancroid mainly in the extent of its vulvar involvement. Initially a reddened papule in the vestibular area, the lesion erodes and extends as a painless, irregular, ragged-edged ulcer with an erythematous, granular base.

c) Local extension of the disease commonly involves the perineum, perirectal skin, genitocrural creases, and inguinal folds.

d) Extension to the vagina and cervix is possible.

e) Oral lesions consequent to oral-genital contact are also possible.
f) Lymphatic spread is uncommon but likely present whenever secondary bacterial infection of the primary lesion occurs.
2. *Diagnosis*
a) Aided by the finding of Donovan bodies in stains or biopsies from the lesion's margins. The Donovan body, a large mononuclear macrophage containing numerous clusters of the encapsulated *C. granulomatis* organism, is best seen in Giemsa or silver stains and is confirmatory of granuloma inguinale when present.
b) As with most genital ulcers, the *differential diagnosis* includes chancroid, lymphogranuloma venereum, syphilis, and herpes. In addition, *a vulvar carcinoma must be ruled out as granuloma inguinale and carcinoma may coexist.*
3. *Treatment*
a) Treatment of choice is *tetracycline* — 2 gm/day for 14 days.
b) Other possible regimens include:
(1) Sulfonamides — 2 gm/day for 14 days.
(2) Streptomycin — 1 gm/day for 7 days.
(3) Ampicillin — 2 gm/day for 14 days.
(4) Chloramphenicol — 2 gm/day for 14 days.
(5) Erythromycin — 2 gm/day for 14 days.
D. *Lymphogranuloma venereum (LGV) (lymphopathia venereum)*
1. *Clinical considerations*
a) LGV is caused by *Chlamydia (Bedsonia) trachomatis*, an organism sharing properties of both bacteria and viruses and very difficult to culture.
b) After an *incubation period of a few days to several weeks,* LGV starts as a small vesicle or papule on the mucocutaneous surfaces of the vulva. The *initial lesion*

may ulcerate but heals rapidly. In a few weeks, the patient will have a symptomatic inguinal lymphadenitis that is usually unilateral but may be bilateral. The enlarged, considerably tender inflammatory *nodal mass (bubo)* is covered by erythematous inguinal skin which may become fixed to the underlying nodes.

   c) In severe cases, a spread to surrounding inguinal and vulvar structures may occur, fluctuance may develop, and destructive ulceration, drainage, scarring, and fistula formation may result in chronic vulvar disease.

2. *Diagnosis*

   a) Dependent on obtaining the *history* of a healed, precursor vulvar lesion followed by the symptomatic appearance of inguinal adenitis.

   b) Biopsy of the nodal lesions can be done, but the histologic appearance is not specific for LGV.

   c) The time-honored Frei test is no longer available.

   d) *Complement fixation* is reliable and obtainable through most laboratories.

   e) The *differential diagnosis* includes chronic vulvar infections, disease, lymphoma, carcinoma with nodal metastases, granuloma inguinale, and, when the perirectal areas are involved, ulcerative colitis must be considered.

3. *Treatment*

   a) Preferences are *sulfa or tetracycline regimens* as described for chancroid and granuloma inguinale (page 48).

   b) Surgical drainage or aspiration of the bubo is frequently necessary to prevent further spread or sinus trace development.

E. *Condyloma acuminata (genital warts, venereal warts)*

  1. *Clinical considerations*

   a) Caused by the *papillomavirus* of the DNA-containing papovavirus group.

    b) As with all other *sexually transmitted* diseases, condyloma acuminata is seen with increasing frequency today.

    c) Presents as a small, pink, soft papillomatous or "warty" lesion, predominantly in the periclitoral, vestibular, posterior perineal, and perianal area.

    d) Lateral spread to the labia majora is uncommon; spread to the vagina, cervix, and urethra is common.

    e) Confluence of many individual warts is frequently seen, giving the impression of a single, fleshy, proliferative lesion.

    f) Secondary infection, bleeding, and discharge are common.

    g) In its early stages, the lesion's growth is rarely appreciated, with the patient usually presenting with a complaint of "feeling a lump" in her vulvar area.

    h) Pregnancy, sexual promiscuity, oral contraceptive usage, and persistent vaginitis may predispose to or stimulate their growth.

2. *Diagnosis*

    a) Condyloma acuminata is one of the most frequently seen vulvar disorders, and for this reason its diagnosis is readily made by its *classic appearance* alone.

    b) Biopsy and histologic verification can be done but are unnecessary unless there is no response to therapy.

    c) Malignant changes are rarely seen, but in patients with atypical wartlike masses or in those refractory to treatment, biopsy is mandatory.

3. *Treatment*

    a) Preferred treatment is *topical podophyllin* (10 to 25 percent) in a benzoin base applied carefully to the lesion with instructions to wash it off 4 to 6 hours later. Several applications may be necessary, and care must be taken to avoid irritating normal mucosal surfaces with the podophyllin resin.

    b) Podophyllin is contraindicated in pregnancy.

      c) Cryotherapy, electrocautery, laser therapy, or surgical excision may be necessary.

      d) Immunotherapy and chemotherapy have been used in research environments.

F. *Bartholin duct cyst*

  1. *Clinical considerations*

      a) The Bartholin gland is an embryologic derivative of the urogenital sinus that in the adult woman is located within the lower pole of the labium majus. The gland is composed of mucin-producing and secreting acini which open to the posterolateral vestibule just external to the hymenal ring through a transitional and squamous epithelium-lined duct.

      b) *Cystic dilation of the gland's duct due to obstruction is probably the most common finding in patients complaining of vulvar masses.* Although obstetric or accidental trauma, congenital atresia, ductal epithelial hyperplasia, or inspissated mucus may cause the occlusion, most symptomatic Bartholin duct cysts are clinically associated with infection and abscess formation.

      c) Contrary to prior thinking, the presence of a ductal abscess should not necessarily imply gonorrheal etiology. Organisms such as *Staphylococcus aureus, Streptococcus faecalis, Escherichia coli*, and *Pseudomonas* may also be etiologically involved.

  2. *Diagnosis*

      a) *Usually readily made by its appearance.* A normal Bartholin gland and duct are nonpalpable, and any cystic swelling in the base of the labia majora almost certainly represents a cyst or abscess.

      b) May range in diameter from 1 to 10 cm, may be asymptomatic, or may be painfully tender, particularly if due to infection.

      c) The *differential diagnosis* may include lipomas, fibromas, hydroceles, accessory breast tissue, or hernias, but unlike duct cysts, these entities usually involve the upper portions of the labia majora and rarely extend into the area of the posterior fourchette.

    d) In women over the age of 40, the rare Bartholin gland carcinoma should be considered.

3. *Treatment*

    a) *Dependent upon the suspected cause and symptoms.* Many small ductal cysts are asymptomatic, do not interfere with intercourse or cause discomfort with walking, sitting, or activity, and may wax or wane in size spontaneously. Most cysts, however, are painful edematous abscesses that require prompt evaluation and treatment.

    b) If left alone, most ductal abscesses will eventually "point" and spontaneously *rupture* resulting in immediate perineal relief. This process may be hastened with frequent sitz baths.

    c) If necessary, *outpatient drainage* can be achieved by simply incising the abscessed duct through the overlying, anesthetized mucocutaneous vestibule. This will provide prompt relief but may not prevent recurrence.

    d) Definitive therapy includes *marsupialization* of the duct during a time when the cyst is readily palpable but before spontaneous rupture occurs. Recurrence after a properly done marsupialization is unlikely.

    e) The other definitive procedure is *glandular excision*. Total excision is infrequently indicated in a young woman, but in an older patient where carcinoma is a possibility, total excision may be necessary for histologic diagnosis.

G. *Pediculosis*

1. Pediculosis pubis, the pubic infestation by the insect *Phthirus pubis* (commonly referred to as "*crabs*"), *may be spread* by *sexual intercourse or by contact with other infested body areas or inanimate objects* (bedding, bedclothes, towels).

2. The affected area always *itches,* and *diagnosis can usually be made by observing the insect near the pubic hair roots.*

3. Because eggs and/or larvae are usually present on the hair shafts, treatment must be aggressive and occasionally repeated. The recommended treatment is *Kwell shampoo* (lindane 1 percent) of the affected area, with repeat shampoo as needed.

VULVAR DYSTROPHIES

A. *Introduction*

   White lesions of the vulva have been the subject of numerous confusing reports in the medical literature. Much of the confusion has resulted from the inconsistent and variable terminology used to describe the many possible lesions that fall into this area of vulvar disease. In this section a simplified classification of the vulvar dystrophies, along with general management guidelines, is presented.

B. *General histopathology*

   Vulvar dystrophies of all types share a common histopathology, that of changes in the vulvar epithelium and underlying connective tissue that are probably secondary to the influences of chronic inflammation and irritation. In deviating from normal epithelium, vulvar skin will become dystrophic in one of two general ways — it becomes atrophic (thinned-out), or it becomes hypertrophic or hyperplastic (thickened). In either case, the wetness of the vulva will cause the superficial and usually increased keratin layer of the epithelium to become *whitish or grayish in color*. The thicker the keratin layer, the whiter the lesion becomes. Along with the response of the keratin to moisture, underlying connective tissue changes, such as relatively decreased vascularity, variable hyalinization, and loss of normal pigmentation, contribute to the pale white appearance of these lesions. These lesions also share a common symptomatic presentation, that of *pruritus and burning*. Malignant differentiation is uncommon (less than 5 percent) but must be considered in all cases. *Basic and mandatory to the approach to all vulvar lesions, dystrophies and otherwise, that do not exhibit an obvious diagnostic appearance is the necessity for biopsy. Only in this way will guesswork be eliminated, malignancies not overlooked, and appropriate management afforded the patient.*

C. *Classification of vulvar dystrophies*
1. *Hyperplastic dystrophies*
   a) *Clinical considerations*
      (1) All *hyperplastic vulvar diseases,* commonly referred to as *leukoplakia,* have a thickened epithelium that is characterized microscopically by hyperkeratosis (thickening of the keratin layer) and hypertrophy of the rete pegs (acanthosis).
      (2) Occurs most frequently in postmenopausal women, although reproductive age occurrences are possible.
      (3) The posterior fourchette, labia majora, lateral labia minora, and clitoral areas are the most likely areas of involvement.
   b) *Diagnosis*
      (1) *Because of pruritus and consequent scratching, the appearance of the lesion may be distorted, making biopsy essential to rule out atypical or malignant changes.*
      (2) Biopsies may be taken by scalpel or punch technique under local anesthesia.
      (3) Multiple biopsies may be necessary, usually under *toluidine blue staining* direction. After applying a 1 percent toluidine blue (aqueous) solution to the affected area and allowing it to dry, the vulva is rinsed with dilute acetic acid, usually 1 percent. Normal epithelium will be left stain-free, while the nuclei of abnormal superficial keratinized epithelium will take up the stain and indicate appropriate areas for biopsy.
   c) *Treatment*
      (1) Primary treatment for the hyperplastic dys-

trophies consists of *topical corticosteroids* with the
adjunctive use of tranquilizers (Librium, Valium)
or antihistaminics (Benadryl, Vistaril, Atarax)
occasionally indicated.

(2) Topical creams are preferred over ointments
because of their lesser likelihood to trap heat and
moisture.

(3) Suggested steroid preparations:
    (a) Hydrocortisone 1 percent.
    (b) Fluocinonide (Lidex) 0.05 percent.
    (c) Fluocinolone acetonide (Synalar) 0.01 per-
    cent.
    (d) Triamcinolone acetonide (Aristocort,
    Kenalog) 0.1 percent.
    (e) Betamethasone valerate (Valisone) 0.1 per-
    cent.

(4) Twice-daily applications of the chosen preparation should give results within 2 to 3 weeks,
although very thick lesions may require long-term
therapy.

(5) Caution must be exercised, however, as chronic
application and overtreatment with steroids may
result in atrophic changes and symptomatic worsening of the original problem.

2. *Atrophic dystrophies*
  a) *Clinical considerations*
    (1) Atrophic lesions of the vulva are the *most com-
    mon of the white dystrophies*.
    (2) Referred to by a *variety of names*: kraurosis
    vulvae, senile atrophy, atrophic vulvitis, atrophic
    leukoplakia, lichen planus atrophicus, and the
    popular lichen sclerosis et atrophicus (LS and A).
    (3) Today the preferred term used to indicate an
    atrophic dystrophy is *lichen sclerosis*.
    (4) Similar in most clinical respects to the hyper-
    plastic lesions, lichen sclerosis differs in one very
    important aspect. Unlike the hyperplastic dys-
    trophies, lesions with underlying atrophy may

destroy the normal vulvar anatomy, causing dissolution of the labia minora, scarring together of the clitoris and periclitoral structures, and introital contracture.

(5) General appearance is characterized by desiccation and thinning-out of the affected areas.

(6) Histologically, hyperkeratosis is frequently present, but the diagnostic features are the relative loss of rete pegs and the homogeneous hyalinization of the subepidermal layers.

b) *Treatment*

(1) Primary therapy consists of *topical testosterone* three times daily for 4 to 6 weeks, after which the frequency of application may be decreased or stopped entirely.

(2) Unlike hyperplastic lesions, atrophic lesions frequently recur and necessitate a program of intermittent but continuing therapy.

(3) Testosterone propionate 2 percent in a petroleum jelly base is standard therapy.

3. *Mixed dystrophies*

a) *Clinical considerations*

(1) Mixed hypertrophic-atrophic lesions are *uncommon* but *demand continuing attention because of a greater tendency to atypia* and *malignant changes* than either of the pure dystrophies.

(2) Because of their variable degrees of atrophic or hypertrophic involvement and tendency to atypia, *mixed dystrophies require multiple-site biopsies* to better define the pathology.

b) *Treatment* options depend on the extent of the predominant lesion:

(1) Corticosteriod therapy followed by testosterone therapy.

(2) Testosterone therapy followed by corticosteroid therapy.

(3) Corticosteroid and testosterone application on alternate days.

PAGET'S DISEASE

A. *Clinical considerations*
   1. Extramammary Paget's disease is *an uncommon vulvar lesion* seen almost exclusively in postmenopausal Caucasian women.
   2. *Clinical presentation* similar to most other vulvar lesions — pruritus, burning, and soreness.
   3. *Delay in diagnosis is common* because of patient delay in bringing the symptoms to the attention of a physician and also because the lesion is easily mistaken for severe vulvar dystrophies, moniliasis, or dermatitis.
B. *Diagnosis and histopathologic importance*
   1. Categorization of Paget's disease of the vulva into "benign" or "malignant" is somewhat unsettled, although it is *usually thought of as an in situ malignant lesion.*
   2. *Histologic confirmation* depends on identifying characteristic *Paget's cells* infiltrating the epidermis — clusters of large, polygonal cells with pale-staining cytoplasm and large hyperchromatic nuclei.
   3. Paget's cells may be found along hair follicles, sebaceous glands, or sweat glands.
   4. Invasion per se, however, through the epithelial basement membrane is rare, hence the hesitation in calling it a true malignancy.
   5. *The concern with Paget's disease is that it frequently heralds the presence of another primary carcinoma of the genitorectal area* — in the vulva, cervix, vagina, apocrine gland, rectum, urethra — *or the possibility of an associated adenocarcinoma of the breast.*
C. *Treatment*
   1. The preferred treatment is total vulvectomy and a diligent search through all portions of the surgical specimen to rule out a coexisting carcinoma.
   2. Superficial cryotherapy, hot cautery, topical therapies, laser treatment, or limited excision all run the risk not

only of incompletely removing the areas involved with Paget's disease but also of missing underlying malignancies.

CLASSIFICATION OF VULVAR DISEASES

The following is a useful comprehensive classification of benign and malignant vulvar diseases:[6]

A. Developmental
1. Agenesis
2. Duplication
3. Hypertrophy of clitoris
4. Synechiae vulvae
5. Imperforate hymen
6. Urethral epispadias
7. Urethral hypospadias
8. Urethral diverticulum
9. Accessory mammary tissue
B. Inflammations
1. Bacterial and spirochetal infections
a) Pyogenic skin and mucosal lesion caused by staphylococcus or streptococcus (folliculitis, furuncle, carbuncle, phlegmon, impetigo, erysipelas, pyoderma gangrenosum, abscess)
b) Gonorrhea (*Neisseria gonorrhoeae*)
c) Chancroid
d) Granuloma inguinale
e) Lymphogranuloma venereum
f) Suppurative hidradenitis
g) Pyogenic granuloma
h) Tuberculosis (primary and secondary)
i) Syphilis and condyloma lata
j) Actinomycosis
2. Viral
a) Herpes genitalis
b) Molluscum contagiosum
c) Condyloma acuminata

    3. Fungal
       a) Candidiasis
       b) Torulopsis
       c) Cryptococcosis
       d) Blastomycosis
    4. Protozoan and helminthic
       a) Trichomoniasis
       b) Amebiasis
       c) Schistosomiasis
       d) Enterobiasis
    5. Other noxious causes
       a) Pilonidal sinus and granuloma (clitoral area)
       b) Simple acute vulvar ulcer (stress)
       c) Salivary vulvitis
       d) Aphthosis (Bechet's syndrome)
       e) Foreign body granuloma
C. Vascular disturbances
    1. Massive edema
    2. Varices and thrombi
    3. Vasculitis
    4. Hematoma
D. Dermatologic lesions
    1. Lichen planus
    2. Lichen simplex
    3. Psoriasis
    4. Seborrheic dermatitis
    5. Dermatitis herpetiformis
    6. Pemphigus
    7. Pemphigoid
E. Cysts
    1. Bartholin's retention cyst (major vulvovaginal gland)
    2. Vestibular retention cyst (minor vestibular glands)
    3. Epidermoid cysts
       a) Sebaceous or pilosebaceous
       b) Epidermal inclusion
    4. Mesonephric cyst (Gartner's cyst, wolffian duct cyst)
    5. Cyst of Skene's gland (periurethral gland cyst)

      6. Cyst of canal of Nuck (cyst of process vaginalis)
      7. Endometriotic cyst
      8. Hydrocystoma (sweat gland cyst)
F. Vulvar dystrophies
      1. Hypertrophic
      2. Atrophic
      3. Mixed
G. Nonneoplastic progressive tissue changes
      1. Hypertrophy — labia, clitoris
      2. Hyperplasia — squamous epithelium, sebaceous glands
      3. Squamous cell dysplasia (atypical hyperplasia)
      4. Urethral caruncle
H. Benign neoplasms and related tumors
      1. Squamous cell papilloma
      2. Condyloma acuminata
      3. Hidradenoma
      4. Pigmented nevi
      5. Supportive tissue tumors — fibroma, leiomyoma, lipoma
      6. Neurogenous tumors — neurofibroma, neuroma, granular cell neurofibroma, granular cell cytoblastoma
      7. Hemangiomas
      8. Endometrioma
I. Malignant neoplasms
      1. Squamous cell carcinoma
        a) Noninvasive (in situ)
          (1) Bowen's type
          (2) Differentiated (simplex) type
        b) Invasive
          (1) Cornifying
          (2) Noncornifying
          (3) Well-differentiated papillary
          (4) Pleomorphic giant cell
          (5) Spindle cell
      2. Paget's disease — invasive and in situ
      3. Basal cell carcinoma
      4. Adenoid cystic carcinoma of vestibular and vulvovaginal glands

5. Adenocarcinoma
   a) Vestibular and vulvovaginal glands
   b) Endometroid
   c) Ectopic breast carcinoma
6. Malignant melanoma
7. Supportive and vascular tissue sarcomas
   a) Leiomyosarcoma
   b) Malignant fibrous histiocytoma
   c) Fibrosarcoma
   d) Hemangiosarcoma
8. Lymphoreticular neoplasms and leukemic infiltrates

REFERENCES
1. Friedrich EG: Vulvar Disease. Philadelphia, Saunders, 1976
2. Ridley CM: The Vulva. London, Saunders, 1975
3. Tovell HMM, Young AW (eds): Evaluation and management of diseases of the vulva. Clin Obstet Gynecol 21:951, 1978
4. Fitzpatrick JE, Tyler H, Gramstad D: Treatment of chancroid: comparison of sulfamethoxazole-trimethoprim with recommended therapies. JAMA 246:1804, 1981
5. Breen JL, Smith CI: Sexually transmitted diseases. II. Bacterial infections. Female Patient 6:14, 1981
6. Abell M, Gosling JRG: Personal communication

5

Benign Diseases of the Vagina and Cervix

Jessica L. Thomason, M.D.

PRACTICE PRINCIPLES

Benign disorders of the vagina and cervix comprise a significant portion of routine gynecologic practice. A knowledge of the anatomy, physiology, and pathophysiology of these areas is essential for their appropriate care.

VAGINA

Development

A. Dependent upon fusion of müllerian (or paramesonephric) ducts and urogenital sinus.
B. *Mesonephric ducts* appear about fourth week after fertilization.
   1. *In male,* becomes epididymis, vas deferens, ejaculatory ducts.
   2. *In female,* regression.
C. *Parmesonephric ducts* appear about sixth week after fertilization.
   1. *In male,* regression.
   2. *In female,* fusion and becomes oviduct, uterus.

D. *Müllerian tubercle*
   1. Formed from paramesonephric ducts, the urogenital sinus, and the mesonephric duct.
   2. Mass of tissue that separates the urogenital sinus and paired paramesonephric ducts.
E. *Uterovaginal canal forms* from medial breakdown of paired paramesonephric ducts.
F. *Solid vaginal plate* begins eleventh week postfertilization and eventually canalizes with stratified squamous epithelium.

Congenital Anomalies

A. *Atresia/agenesis*
   1. Total or partial absence
      a) Often secondary sexual characteristics are normal.
      b) Often associated with uterine anomalies.
      c) Frequently associated with renal anomalies.
      d) May be associated with other system anomalies, e.g., bony, cardiac lesions.
      e) Rokitansky's syndrome — congenital absence of vagina and uterus. The diagnosis is often made at delayed puberty in investigating cause of primary amenorrhea.
   2. Distal versus proximal absence
      a) Must rule out hydrometrocolpos in neonates.
      b) Look for other vesicovaginal/rectovaginal fistula.
   3. Imperforate hymen
      a) Rule out by probing vaginal area since external genitalia may appear totally normal.
      b) Sterility results soon after menses begin unless surgically corrected.
   4. May be associated with intersex conditions.
   5. May be associated with chromosomal syndromes and nonchromosomal disorders.
B. *Duplication*
   1. May be partial or complete.
   2. Often associated with uterine/cervical anomalies.

    3. Double vagina—very rare condition, whereas "septate" vagina is more common.

C. *Canalization failure*
    1. Transverse septa
       a) May occur at any site in the vagina.
       b) Rule out uterine/cervical anomalies and ureterovaginal fistulae.
    2. Hydrometrocolpos, congenital
       a) Always associated with vaginal septum and usually vaginal atresia/agenesis.
       b) Can be genetically transmitted.

D. *Fistulae*
Often associated with imperforate anus.

Benign Cystic Lesions

Differential diagnosis of these lesions is shown in Table 5–1.

A. *Mesonephric duct cysts*
    1. Also known as Gartner's duct cysts.
    2. Are vestigial remnants of the mesonephric ducts (wolffian system).

TABLE 5–1. DIFFERENTIAL DIAGNOSIS OF BENIGN CYSTIC VAGINAL LESIONS

Mesonephric cysts (Gartner's duct cysts)
Paramesonephric duct cysts
Mucoid cysts
Skene's gland cysts
Endometriosis
Adenosis
Urethral diverticulum

   3. Until recently nearly all vaginal cysts were diagnosed as this type.
   4. Clinical appearance
      a) Located laterally along the route of the old meso-nephric ducts, frequently anterolaterally.
      b) Usually ≤ 2 cm, single, unilateral, filled with clear fluid.
      c) Usually *asymptomatic*.
   5. Histologic appearance—lined by nonciliated, columnar, or cuboidal epithelium.
   6. Treatment—none usually necessary. If symptomatic, surgical removal.
B. *Paramesonephric duct cysts*
   1. Cannot be distinguished clinically from Gartner's duct cysts.
   2. Clinical appearance
      a) Located at any area of the vaginal wall.
      b) Usually ≤ 2 cm, single, unilateral, filled with clear fluid.
      c) Usually asymptomatic.
   3. Histologic appearance—lined by any epithelial type derived from müllerian origin, e.g., endocervical, colum-nar, ciliated, and so on.
   4. Treatment—none usually necessary. If symptomatic, surgical removal.
C. *Mucoid cysts*
   1. Usually of urogenital sinus origin.
   2. Clinical appearance
      a) Located near vulvar vestibule, hymen.
      b) Usually ≤ 3 cm, single, asymptomatic.
   3. Histologic appearance—lined by single layer of tall columnar epithelial cells but may be mucinous, ciliated, pseudostratified.
   4. Treatment—none usually necessary. If asymptomatic, surgical removal.
D. *Skene's gland cysts*
   1. Arise from Skene's ducts, usually near the introitus.

    2. Occur secondary to trauma and or infection of the ducts.

    3. May cause urinary retention or obstruction or dyspareunia.

    4. Clinical appearance

       a) May bulge through introitus.

       b) Usually < 2 cm.

       c) May be tender secondary to inflammation.

       d) Occasionally a purulent exudate from the urethra may be seen when pressure is applied to the cyst.

    5. Treatment—surgical excision. Avoid operation during inflammatory episode.

E. *Endometriosis*

    1. Relatively rare disease in this location.

    2. Commonly symptomatic secondary to menstrual cycle hormonal changes with subsequent bleeding.

    3. Clinical appearance

       a) Most frequent location—cul-de-sac.

       b) Usually small, round, reddish or dark blue lesions.

    4. Treatment—excision of lesions or destruction by cryosurgery or cautery; laser therapy.

F. *Adenosis*

    1. Definition—the occurrence of columnar or glandular epithelium in contact with squamous vaginal epithelium.

    2. Origin

       a) Congenital in 3 to 5 percent of women.

       b) Iatrogenic—DES (diethylstilbestrol) induced.

    3. May be associated with other genital tract abnormalities, e.g., incompetent cervical os.

    4. Clinical symptoms

       a) Usually none.

       b) Vaginal bleeding, postcoital spotting.

       c) Occasionally an excessive mucoid discharge.

    5. Clinical appearance

       a) Often multiple lesions can be seen or palpated.

       b) Frequent involvement of anterior upper third of the vaginal wall.

    c) Patchy, granular, often friable lesions having a reddish appearance.

    d) Rarely may appear as polypoid, papillary, or ulcerated area.

    e) On colposcopy, typical grapelike appearance of columnar epithelium.

    f) Affected areas do not stain with iodine.

  6. Treatment — controversial

    a) Consensus of multiple authorities — do nothing.

    b) Patients need examination every six months.

    c) Treatment modalities that have been used include laser therapy, cryosurgery, thermal cautery, acidification of the epithelium, local excision.

  7. Concern for DES-exposed offspring is of increased incidence of adenocarcinoma of the vagina.

G. *Urethral diverticulum*

  1. May be congenital or acquired traumatically.

  2. Clinical symptoms — asymptomatic or symptomatic, e.g., sudden loss of urine, frequent cystitis, repeated dysuria, dyspareunia.

  3. Clinical appearance

    a) Most involve distal two thirds of urethra.

    b) Size — variable.

    c) With palpation, urine loss through urethra seen with decrease in size of cyst.

  4. Histologic appearance — cyst lining may be cuboidal, transitional, columnar, or stratified squamous.

  5. Treatment — surgical excision.

Benign Noncystic Vaginal Lesions

Differential diagnosis of these lesions is given in Table 5–2.

A. *Condyloma acuminata*

  1. Most common solid tumor of the vagina.

  2. Common name: venereal warts.

  3. Sexually transmitted; incubation period — controversial.

  4. Infecting agent — papillomavirus.

TABLE 5–2. DIFFERENTIAL DIAGNOSIS OF BENIGN NONCYSTIC VAGINAL LESIONS

Condyloma acuminata
Vaginal ulcers
Leiomyoma/fibroma
Vaginal polyps

5. Rarely seen prior to puberty or postmenopausally.
6. Often associated with other venereal diseases, e.g., trichomonas.
7. Clinical symptoms
   a) Usually asymptomatic but may be symptomatic, with increased vaginal discharge and pruritis.
   b) Often marked growth with proliferation of lesions during pregnancy.
8. Clinical appearance vaginally is varied
   a) Most easily recognized are the small warty growths that extend from the vaginal wall.
   b) Smaller lesions may coalesce to form more confluent cauliflower-like masses with broad bases.
   c) Most difficult to recognize is the diffuse condylomatous vaginitis in which the entire vaginal canal is involved with the disease, giving the vaginal surface an overall rough appearance.
9. Diagnosis — by biopsy; histologic appearance is characteristic.
10. Treatment
    a) Treat any underlying vaginitis, e.g., yeast, trichomonas.
    b) Many authors do not treat vaginal lesions.
    c) There is *no* treatment available if diffuse disease involving the entire vagina is present.

d) Conventional therapy
   (1) Podophyllin therapy
       (a) Podophyllin is available in a mixture with petroleum jelly or in solution mixed with tincture of benzoin. The former preparation is preferred by many because of ease of application and tendency to adhere in areas where application is desired.
       (b) In whatever vehicle chosen, podophyllin should be applied directly to the lesions, avoiding contact with unaffected areas adjacent to the lesion. Following application the area should be thoroughly cleansed four to six hours after treatment. Treatment may be repeated weekly until all lesions have disappeared.
       (c) Lesions not responsive after a reasonable treatment interval: consider operative removal by any of the methods listed below.
   (2) Cryotherapy
   (3) Thermal cautery
   (4) Laser therapy — excellent form of therapy for vaginal lesions, especially since it may be colposcopically directed.
   (5) Immunologic therapy — due to possible oncogenic potentials of this therapy, only use is at specialized centers.
   (6) Levamisole — antihelminthic drug; experimental use only.
11. During pregnancy
    a) Laryngeal papilloma in infants reported.
    b) If growth of lesions is prolific, outlet obstruction may occur, requiring cesarean section. Also lesions during pregnancy may have increased vascularity. In order to avoid profuse bleeding if lesions are near episiotomy site, cesarean section may be chosen.

    c) Podophyllin—contraindicated: abortion, premature labor, and fetal death reported.

B. *Vaginal ulcers*
   1. Infectious—rule out syphilis, herpes, granuloma inguinale.
   2. High incidence of associated malignancy—rule out by biopsy and Pap smear.
   3. Traumatic
   4. Tampon usage
     a) Seen secondary to prolonged tampon usage.
     b) Mucosal injury progresses from "drying" to "layering" or "peeling up" of the mucosa to frank "ulcerations."
     c) May be related to toxic shock syndrome secondary to specific phase types of *Staphylococcus aureus* invasion of mucosal ulcerations
       (1) Treatment—IV fluids and antistaphylococcal agents, e.g., nafcillin.
       (2) Avoid tampon usage with future menses.

C. *Leiomyoma/fibroma*
   1. Very rare lesions.
   2. Usually small; palpation—firm tissue.
   3. Treatment—surgical excision; some lesions tend to recur.

D. *Vaginal polyps*
   1. Very rare lesion.
   2. Various sizes, firm to palpation.
   3. Treatment—surgical excision.

CERVIX

Development

A. Anatomy
   1. Anatomic and histologic internal os—the "isthmus."
   2. Endocervical canal.

3. External os.
4. Vaginal portion of the cervix — the "portio vaginalis."
B. *Embryology*
   1. At 10 weeks postfertilization, a constriction between the corpus and cervix is visible.
   2. Cervix develops as thickening of surrounding mesenchyme of the uterovaginal canal area.

Benign Lesions of the Cervix

A. *Congenital abnormalities*
   1. Mesonephric duct remnants
      a) Found in approximately 1 percent of cervices.
      b) Located laterally in cervix.
      c) Consists of small tubules or cysts.
   2. Very rarely, heterotropic elements are reported, e.g., cartilage.
   3. Duplication often associated with other genital tract anomalies.
   4. Hypoplasia — "infantile," congenital and DES-induced.
   5. DES-induced
      a) Cervical hood or cockscomb.
      b) "Strawberry" cervix — columns of columnar epithelium.
B. *Nabothian cysts*
   1. Extremely frequent in normal women.
   2. May occur singly or multiply.
   3. Asymptomatic
   4. Clinical appearance
      a) Usually small, < 5 mm, although may enlarge.
      b) Translucent or bluish cysts.
   5. Histologic appearance
      a) Mucus-filled cysts.
      b) Represent ducts of endocervical glands which are pinched off and covered by squamous epithelium.

      6. Treatment—none necessary unless symptomatic or infected, in which case excision may be indicated.

C. *Polyps*
1. Usually derived from endocervical epithelium.
2. Frequently small, < 10 mm, although larger ones occur.
3. Often friable.
4. Usually asymptomatic but may be symptomatic, e.g., postcoital spotting.
5. Clinical appearance
    a) Whitish or reddish elongated or round structures extruding from cervical os.
    b) Often the base of the polyp is visible.
6. Treatment
    a) If base can be isolated, twisting of the polyp from its stalk with cauterization of the base.
    b) If diagnosis of lesion is questionable or lesion is large, surgical excision under anesthesia.

D. *Lacerations*
1. May be stellate but position frequently at 3 and 9 o'clock on the cervix.
2. Usually secondary to delivery injuries.
3. Can involve internal os.
4. Can be etiologic factor in habitual abortions.
5. Clinically usually asymptomatic but may be nidus for associated chronic infections.
6. Treatment
    a) None usually necessary.
    b) Surgical repair if patient has recurrent abortions or recurrent infections.

E. *Ectropion/eversion*
1. A *normal* event.
2. A dynamic, progressively ongoing process whereby endocervical tissue or mucosa extends into the portio vaginalis and slowly is covered by squamous epithelium to become part of the ectocervix.
3. Frequently *incorrectly* diagnosed as a pathologic process and a cause of chronic cervicitis/vaginitis.

4. "Transition zone"
   a) Area of ectocervix in which the columnar epithelium is being transformed into squamous epithelium.
   b) Histologically, phases of metaplasia are seen.
5. Clinical appearance
   a) Irregular in location.
   b) "Bumpy" — like reddened tissue (grapelike tissue of the endocervical epithelium) in close approximation to the shining whitish red, smooth tissue of the ectocervix (squamous epithelium).
6. Clinically — usually asymptomatic.
7. Treatment — *none* necessary.

F. *Condyloma acuminata*
   See Section A, page 68, for discussion.

G. *Adenosis*
   See Section F, page 67, for discussion of etiology, appearance, and treatment.

H. *Endometriosis*
   1. Usually asymptomatic unless lesion is friable.
   2. Clinically, reddish/bluish nodule found in any area on the cervix.
   3. Treatment — surgical removal by biopsy or cautery.

I. *Rare tumors*
   1. Papillomas
      a) Very uncommon tumor (<0.25 percent of all cervical benign tumors).
      b) May occur singly or multiply.
      c) Clinically, often indistinguishable from condyloma acuminata.
      d) Treatment — surgical excision if symptomatic or suspected of malignancy.
   2. Leiomyoma
      a) Can displace cervical portio unilaterally.
      b) Treatment — surgical excision if symptomatic or suspected of malignancy.
   3. Hemangioma
      a) Clinically, reddish/bluish rounded structure.

    b) Treatment — surgical excision if symptomatic or suspected of malignancy.

COMBINED COMMON INFECTIOUS DISEASE OF THE VAGINA AND CERVIX

Normal Discharge Characteristics

A. Normally dependent on age, sexual activity, hormonal status, pH, drug usage, medical diseases.
B. Normal pH of vagina, acidic: 3.5 to 4.5.
C. *Discharge odor*
    1. Secondary to volatile fatty acids in vaginal fluid.
    2. Normally changes during menstrual cycle.
    3. Odor change is obliterated in oral contraceptive users.
D. *Normal bacteriologic flora*
    1. Gram-positive cocci — present in abundance
       a) Aerobes, e.g., *Streptococcus*
       b) Anaerobes, e.g., *Peptostreptococcus*
    2. Gram-positive bacilli — present in abundance
       a) Aerobes, e.g., *Lactobacillus* or Döderlein's bacillus
       b) Anaerobes, e.g., *Propionibacterium*
    3. Gram-negative cocci
       a) Aerobes, e.g., nonpathogenic *Neisseria*
       b) Anaerobes, e.g., *Veillonella*
    4. Gram-negative bacilli
       a) Aerobes, e.g., *Acinetobacter*
       b) Anaerobes, e.g., *Bacteroides*
E. Normal appearance: floccular, whitish/creamy colored.

Common Vaginitis in Reproductive Age

A. General
    1. *Cannot* diagnose by physical appearance of discharge.
    2. Instruments necessary to diagnose 98 percent of causes of vaginitis
       a) Microscope and slides
       b) pH paper (Nitrazine paper)

   c) KOH solution (10 percent)
   d) Normal saline solution
B. *Candida vaginitis,* yeast vaginitis
   1. Infecting agent — a fungus of the *Candida* genus, many species.
   2. Clinical symptoms — hallmark is pruritis; vulvar swelling, occasionally dysuria if excoriations or microulcerations have resulted from pruritis.
   3. Physical signs
      a) Vulvar edema, erythema
      b) Vagina — thick, pastelike discharge that may be difficult to remove from the vaginal walls; color usually whitish.
   4. Microscopic examination of secretions
      a) Use 10 percent KOH to destroy WBC, epithelial cells, and other bacteria.
      b) Hyphae, pseudohyphae, spores, or buds seen.
   5. Diagnosis is made by hallmark of pruritis, positive physical signs, and microscopic examination.
   6. Treatment
      a) Topical antifungal agents — applied by patient
         (1) Nystatin suppositories and cream.
         (2) Micronazole cream.
         (3) Clotrimazole cream and suppositories.
         (4) Whichever agent is chosen, it is important that the patient be instructed to apply cream onto the vulvar surfaces as well as intravaginally. Application to the vulva decreases the patient's discomfort and facilitates eradication of the infection.
      b) Physician application of gentian violet.
      c) Treatment of sexual partner not necessary.
   7. Recurrent infections
      a) Look for underlying predisposing conditions, e.g., diabetes, chronic steroid medication, antibiotics.
      b) Have patient avoid predisposing conditions, e.g., tight jeans, panty hose.
      c) Treatment
         (1) Prolonged clotrimazole therapy for three weeks.

(2) Periodic treatment with vaginal suppositories at the time of menses.

(3) Oral nystatin can reduce GI tract yeast and decrease the risk of repeated self-contamination.

C. *Trichomonas vaginitis*

1. Infecting agent — protozoan, *Trichomonas vaginalis,* many species.

2. Clinical symptoms — from totally asymptomatic to very irritating symptoms with foul odor; postcoital spotting may occur.

3. Physical signs

   a) None may be present — microscopic examination required.

   b) Usual discharge is thin, grayish (previously incorrectly described as green, frothy).

   c) May have foul odor.

4. Microscopic examination of secretions

   a) pH of vaginal secretions > 5.0.

   b) Use body temperature normal saline in preparation of wet smear.

   c) Tetraflagellate protozoan *in motion* is diagnostic.

   d) Marked leukocytic response seen.

   e) Difficult to distinguish between WBCs when protozoan is *not* motile on slide.

5. Diagnosis made by pH of vagina and microscopic examination or positive growth on appropriate culture media. May be diagnosed by cytology report.

6. Treatment with metronidazole (Flagyl) necessary whether patient is symptomatic or asymptomatic

   a) Two dosage regimens are currently equally efficacious:

      (1) One-time dose of 2 gm.

      (2) 250 mg PO tid for 7 days.

   b) Side effects from both dosage regimens are the same and include nausea and occasionally emesis. Alcohol intake should be avoided due to the Antabuse-like effect of Flagyl.

   c) Treatment of the sexual partner is indicated. Patient

and partner should be cautioned to obtain simultaneous therapy prior to the resumption of sexual activity.

D. *Gardnerella vaginitis*

1. Infecting agent — *Gardnerella vaginale* (previously known as *Haemophilus vaginalis* or *Corynebacterium vaginale),* a gram-negative bacillus.

2. Clinical symptoms — increased vaginal discharge with foul odor, *rarely* vaginal itching.

3. Physical signs — homogeneous, grayish discharge, often frothy.

4. Microscopic examination of secretions

   a) pH of vagina — 5 to 6.

   b) "Whiff test" — fishy odor after adding a drop of 10 percent KOH to a glass slide upon which is a suspension of the secretion.

   c) "Clue cells" — epithelial cells dotted with the bacteria.

5. Diagnosis is made by patient's complaint of foul-smelling discharge, wet preparation examination revealing "clue cells," and positive "whiff" test.

6. Treatment

   a) Controversy presently exists concerning the optimum therapy for *Gardnerella* infections. Currently used regimens include:

      (1) Metronidazole (Flagyl) described previously.

      (2) Ampicillin, 500 mg every 6 hours orally for ten days.

   b) Treatment of sexual partner is indicated.

Vaginitis in Nonreproductive Age Groups

A. *Prepubertal age*

1. Any significant vaginal discharge in a prepubertal female warrants thorough examination. Depending upon the age and sensitivity of the patient, examination under anesthesia may be necessary for thorough evaluation. If the

discharge is bloody, such examination is mandatory to rule out lower genital tract malignancy or significant traumatic injury.

2. Causes of prepubertal vaginitis
   a) Traumatic
      (1) Foreign objects introduced into the vagina are the most common cause.
      (2) Both self-induced trauma and that done by another individual must be considered. In the latter circumstance, the possibility of child abuse should be thoroughly evaluated.
   b) Poor hygiene, e.g., pinworm infection (*Enterobius vermicularis*).
   c) Secondary to close physical contact with an adult. This may be nonsexually acquired, such as *trichomonas*, or sexually acquired, such as gonorrhea. If there is any question about the nature of this contact, evaluation for possible child abuse or incest is mandatory.

B. *Postmenopausal age*
  1. Asymptomatic *Trichomonas* infections. See Section C, page 77, diagnosis and treatment.
  2. Atrophic vaginitis
   a) Infecting agent — normal vaginal flora.
   b) Symptoms — dyspareunia, postcoital spotting, mild pruritis.
   c) Physical signs
      (1) Often atrophic vulva.
      (2) Vagina — pale, easily friable vaginal walls without moist rugal pattern.
   d) Microscopic examination of secretions — absence of other vaginal pathogens, multiple WBCs and RBCs.
   e) Diagnosis made by physical symptoms of patient, physical signs, and absence of other pathogens on wet preparation examination of the secretions.
   f) Treatment — local vaginal creams containing estrogen on a continual chronic basis.
      (1) Since such preparations provide a significant sys-

temic dose of estrogen, an evaluation similar to that for postmenopausal estrogen replacement is indicated.

g) Remember that pruritis, irritation, and/or discharge may be the presenting symptoms of malignancy.

BIBLIOGRAPHY

Fleury FJ: Adult vaginitis. Clin Obstet Gynecol 24:407, 1981

Gardner HL, Kaufman RL: Benign Diseases of the Vulva and Vagina. Boston, GK Hall, 1981

Hafez E, Evans T (eds): The Human Vagina. Amsterdam, Vol. 2. North-Holland, 1978

6

Benign Disease of the Corpus

Jeffrey W. Ellis, M.D.

PRACTICE PRINCIPLES

The uterine leiomyoma is the most common benign tumor of the female genital tract, affecting an estimated 20 percent of women over the age of 35. Though they may be asymptomatic, patients commonly present with a variety of symptoms including pain, abnormal bleeding, and pressure effects. Management may be either medical or surgical depending on the nature and degree of symptoms. Other benign tumors are rare.

LEIOMYOMA

A. *Pathology*
   1. *Microscopic.* Bundles of smooth muscle produce a whorl-like pattern. Individual cells are uniform in size and shape. Mitoses are infrequent. Fibrous tissue may be admixed in various amounts, though smooth muscle cells usually predominate.
   2. *Gross.* Myomata may range in size from microscopic to a weight of 100 pounds. There is no definite capsule to the nodule, although a thin areolar tissue pseudocapsule allows them to be readily enucleated from the surrounding myometrium. They have a whitish color. Cross-

section reveals a characteristic whorl-like pattern similar to a cross-section of an onion.

B. *Location* The affected uterus usually contains multiple nodules, although there may be a single nodule. Myomata may be found in multiple positions within the uterus. Since they arise within the myometrium, all myomata are initially interstitial. As they continue to grow, they may extend toward either the mucosal or serosal surface of the uterus and cause distortion of that surface.

1. *Cervical.* Eight percent of myomata are located in the cervix. As they enlarge anteriorly, they may impinge on the bladder and cause urinary retention. Labor may be obstructed by a large growth.

2. *Submucous.* As continued growth occurs, the endometrial cavity becomes distorted. As with subserosal myomata, pedunculation may occur, and the tumor may present as a mass dilating and protruding through the cervix. Impingement upon myometrial vessels may cause passive congestion leading to increased menstrual flow. Necrosis and ulceration may lead to irregular bleeding. Submucous tumors may interfere with implantation and placental growth, leading to infertility and spontaneous abortion.

3. *Intramural (interstitial).* When small, interstitial myomata will cause little or no distortion of the uterus. Eventually, with further growth, they will attain a submucous or subserosal position.

4. *Subserous.* As continued outward growth occurs, pedunculation may result. Lateral growth between the folds of the broad ligament produces an *intraligamentary myoma.* Large subserous growths are usually responsible for pressure effects that cause compression of contiguous pelvic organs: bladder, rectum, ureters, veins. Subserous and pedunculated myomata may be difficult to distinguish from solid adnexal masses.

5. *Parasitic.* Pedunculated myomata may become adherent

to bowel and omentum and obtain a blood supply from these structures. Eventually, their connection with the uterus may be lost, and the myomata will remain adherent to bowel or omentum.

6. *Intravenous leiomyomatosis.* Though uncommon, intravascular projections of leiomyomata have been seen in veins of the parametria and broad ligament.

C. *Degenerative Changes* Myomata are subject to a variety of degenerative changes generally related to local tissue anoxia and subsequent necrosis.

1. *Circulatory impairment* within myomata may lead to *hyaline degeneration, cystic degeneration, fatty degeneration,* and *calcification.*

2. *Infection* may occur when bacteria invade submucous myomata. Less commonly, interstitial and subserous myomata are affected.

3. *Sarcomatous degeneration*

4. *Carneous (red) degeneration*

D. *Hormone dependence* Growth of myomata is associated with estrogen production. Myomata may continue growth during the reproductive years, then stop growth or even regress at the menopause. Postmenopausal growth may be associated with exogenous estrogen or with estrogen producing ovarian tumors. Growth of myomata in young women has been associated with oral contraceptive use.

E. *Signs and symptoms and associated pathology* Many patients with myomata are asymptomatic. However, the following signs and symptoms may occur.

1. *Bleeding*
   a) Excessive and/or prolonged menstruation, *menorrhagia,* may develop due to interference with the normal hemostatic mechanisms of the uterus.
   b) Necrosis and ulceration of a submucous myoma may cause *intermenstrual spotting.*
   c) Bleeding may be excessive and cause significant *anemia.*

   2. *Pain* associated with myomata may be acute or chronic
     a) *Acute torsion* of a pedunculated myoma may give rise to acute abdominal pain.
     b) *Acute degeneration* may give rise to acute abdominal pain.
     c) *Passive congestion* may cause dysmenorrhea.
   3. *Pressure effects.* Large myomata may compress adjacent pelvic structures, giving the following signs and symptoms:
     a) *Bladder compression* — urinary frequency.
     b) *Urethral compression* — urinary retention.
     c) *Ureteral compression* — hydroureter, hydronephrosis.
     d) *Rectal compression* — constipation, tenesmus.
     e) *Vascular compression* — lower extremity edema and venous congestion.
   4. *Pelvic mass.* The patient may present with abdominal distortion due to large myomata.
   5. *Infertility and spontaneous abortion.* Multiple or large submucous myomata may interfere with implantation and placental growth.
F. *Diagnosis*
   1. *Pelvic examination* will generally reveal an enlarged, asymmetric uterus. Nodules of varying size may be palpated over the surface. The uterus is often immobile, although individual pedunculated myomata may be freely movable. Pedunculated subserous myomata or interligamentous myomata may present as adnexal masses that are indistinguishable from solid ovarian tumors. The uterus may range in size from normal to one filling the entire abdominal cavity. Submucous myomata may be detected as an irregularity of the endometrial cavity during curettage or sounding.
   2. *Hysteroscopy* or *hysterosalpingography* may be performed to confirm the diagnosis. Pedunculated submucous myomata may be seen during vaginal inspection as they protrude through the cervix.

3. *Ultrasound* will often identify areas of cystic degeneration.

4. *X-ray* of the pelvis may detect areas of calcification.

G. *Therapy of uterine myomata is dependent upon the patient's age, menstrual status, type and degree of pathology, and desire for further childbearing.*

  1. *Asymptomatic myomata.* The majority of patients will be asymptomatic.

    a) The patient should be examined every six months, preferably by the same examiner, to detect any significant changes in size of the nodules. Careful records should be kept noting the size and location of the masses.

    b) Any significant and rapid increase in size of a nodule warrants immediate removal, as it may represent a sarcoma.

    c) *Any solid adnexal mass warrants laparoscopy or laparotomy to distinguish a pedunculated or ligamentous myoma from a solid ovarian tumor.*

    d) There are no absolute criteria as to what size myomatous uterus must be removed. One must be certain that the pelvic mass does not represent adnexal pathology or render evaluation of the adnexa unduly difficult.

    e) It is recommended that patients with asymptomatic myomata undergo a yearly intravenous pyelogram to detect hydroureter or hydronephrosis. Chronic ureteral compression may cause progressive renal damage. Hysterectomy or myomectomy is indicated if hydroureter is detected.

  2. *Bleeding abnormalities*

    a) *Menorrhagia.* Patients with prolonged or excessive menstrual bleeding can be maintained on oral iron therapy and followed conservatively. Severe anemia or bleeding episodes requiring hospital admission and transfusion are best treated by myomectomy or hys-

terectomy. Other causes of bleeding must be ruled out
by Pap smear and endometrial sampling or fractional
curettage.

b) *Intermenstrual bleeding.* Because of the association
between intermenstrual beleeding and cervical or
endometrial malignancy, appropriate evaluation of
the cervix and endometrium must be performed.

3. *Pressure symptoms*
   a) The findings of hydroureter and hydronephrosis are
   indications for decompression of the ureter by myomectomy or hysterectomy.
   b) Subjective criteria must be applied to other cases of
   compression. If urinary frequency, constipation, or
   lower extremity edema cause the patient significant
   distress, myomectomy or hysterectomy is indicated.

4. *Pain*
   a) *Acute onset of pain* in a patient with uterine myomata
   may indicate acute degeneration or torsion. Hospitalization and observation are indicated. Failure to show
   clinical improvement during observation will necessitate laparoscopy or laparotomy.
   b) *Chronic pain* must be subjectively evaluted. Analgesics may significantly decrease pain. If pain causes the
   patient significant distress, myomectomy or hysterectomy is indicated. Since there are many causes of
   chronic pelvic pain, thorough search for other causes
   is mandatory prior to surgical therapy.

5. *Infertility and spontaneous abortion.* Extensive submucous myomata may significantly distort the uterine cavity
   and interfere with implantation and placental growth.
   a) *Hysterosalpingogram* or *hysteroscopy* will aid in identification of submucous myomata. After all other
   possible causes of infertility and spontaneous abortion
   are excluded, myomectomy may be performed.

6. *Myomata in pregnancy.* Myomata generally enlarge during pregnancy due to estrogen stimulation and increased
   blood supply. They will often regress to pre-pregnancy

size after delivery. Normally, no problems occur during pregnancy. In addition to spontaneous abortion, myomata may be associated with:

a) *Dystocia.* Myomata in the cervix or lower uterine segment may significantly distort the pelvis and prevent delivery (soft tissue dystocia). Abnormal presentations are often due to distortion of the pelvic inlet by lower uterine segment myomata.

b) *Carneous degeneration* occurs most often during pregnancy and is related to impaired circulation to the myoma. Pain and tenderness over a myoma are the presenting symptoms. Fever, tachycardia, and abdominal rigidity may occur. If the patient's condition does not improve with conservative, supportive therapy, laparotomy is indicated. A necrotic, hemorrhagic myoma may require removal.

7. *Myomata in the perimenopausal patient.* Myomata will generally cease growth and even regress as endogenous estrogen levels decline. Symptomatic patients can usually be followed conservatively, since symptoms should cease at the menopause.

8. *Myomata in the postmenopausal patient.* Any growth of myomata in the postmenopausal period demands immediate investigation, as this may indicate sarcoma. Myomata may also enlarge if the patient is receiving exogenous estrogen therapy.

H. *Choice of surgery*

1. *Myomectomy.* The removal of individual myoma and repair of the uterine defects is generally reserved for patients who wish to retain childbearing potential. Most authorities feel that the patient should be delivered by cesarean section if multiple deep myomata are removed, since uterine rupture may occur during labor.

2. *Hysterectomy.* Total abdominal hysterectomy is preferred for large growths. Vaginal hysterectomy, with morcellation if necessary, may be performed, especially if a vaginal repair is also indicated.

3. *Radiation therapy*. Ovarian irradiation to induce menopause through ovarian destruction is uncommonly used today but may be used in symptomatic patients who are poor operative risks.

BIBLIOGRAPHY

Leiomyoma
Abitol MA: Submucous fibroids complicating pregnancy, labor and delivery. Obstet Gynecol 10:529, 1957

Everett HS: Effects of uterine myomas on the urinary tract. Clin Obstet Gynecol 1:429, 1958

Ingersoll FM: Myomectomy and fertility. Fertil Steril 14:596, 1963

Jonas HS, Masterson BJ: Giant uterine tumors. Obstet Gynecol 50:25, 1977

Miller NF, Ludovici PP: Origin and development of uterine fibroids. Am J Obstet Gynecol 70:720, 1955

Morton DG: Symptoms and signs of fibromyomas of the uterus. Clin Obstet Gynecol 1:407, 1958

Newman HF: Clinical observations in patients with myoma of the uterus with particular regard to changes in size and indications for surgery. Am J Obstet Gynecol 68:1489, 1954

Novak ER: Benign and malignant changes in uterine myomas. Clin Obstet Gynecol 1:421, 1958

Sehgal N, Haskias AL: The mechanism of uterine bleeding in the presence of fibromyomas Am Surgeon 26:21, 1960

Hysterectomy
Falk HC, Soichet S: The technique of vaginal hysterectomy. Clin Obstet Gynecol 15:703, 1972.

Hassid RI: Indications and contraindications for vaginal hysterectomy. Clin Obstet Gynecol 15:697, 1972

Heaney NS: Vaginal hysterectomy. Its indications and technique. Am J Surg 48:284, 1940

Levinson CJ: Hysterectomy complications. Clin Obstet Gynecol 15:802, 1972

Richardson EH: A simplified technique for abdominal panhysterectomy. Surg Gynecol Obstet 48:248, 1929

Tancer ML: Total abdominal hysterectomy. Clin Obstet Gynecol 15:769, 1972

White C, et al.: Comparison of abdominal and vaginal hysterectomies. J Obstet Gynecol 37:530, 1971

7

Benign Disease of the Fallopian Tube and Uterine Ligaments

Jeffrey W. Ellis, M.D.

PRACTICE PRINCIPLES

Benign neoplasms of the fallopian tube and uterine ligaments are uncommon and are usually discovered incidentally at the time of surgery. They may occasionally present as an adnexal mass, requiring laparoscopy or laparotomy to differentiate them from an ovarian malignancy.

BENIGN NEOPLASMS OF THE FALLOPIAN TUBE

A. *Clinical types*

The following benign neoplasms may occur in either the wall or the lumen of the fallopian tube:

1. Hemangioma
2. Lipoma
3. Teratoma
4. Leiomyoma
5. Fibroma
6. Fibrodenoma
7. Adenomatoid tumor

8. Mucosal polyp
9. Papilloma
B. *Management*
   1. *Teratomas* and *leiomyomata* may occasionally reach a sufficient size to undergo torsion and infarction. Patients will present with low-grade fever, abdominal pain, and a palpable, tender adnexal mass. Treatment usually involves unilateral salpingectomy unless the mass is pedunculated and can be removed without distorting the fallopian tube.
   2. Frequently, the fallopian tube mass will be found incidentally at the time of pelvic surgery. Salpingectomy should be performed to confirm that the mass is benign. Pedunculated masses may be excised, making salpingectomy unnecessary.
   3. Fallopian tube masses may present as asymptomatic solid or persistent cystic adnexal masses. Identification is thus mandatory, requiring either laparoscopy or laparotomy. Unless a positive visual diagnosis can be made, laparotomy and excision of the mass should be performed.

CYSTS OF THE UTERINE LIGAMENTS

A. *Clinical types*
   These are not true neoplasms but rather remnants of the müllerian or wolffian duct systems.
   1. *Parovarian cysts* of wolffian duct origin.
   2. *Paratubal cysts* of wolffian duct origin.
   3. *Hydatid cyst of Morgagni* of müllerian duct origin.
B. *Management*
   1. Pelvic examination may reveal an adnexal mass indistinguishable from an ovarian neoplasm, requiring laparoscopy or laparotomy for positive identification.
   2. Inspection will reveal fluid-filled cysts in the mesosalpinx, mesovarium, or broad ligament.

3. These cysts should not be removed unless they are symptomatic or large enough to be indistinguishable from an adnexal mass. Cysts less than 2 cm in diameter should not be removed, since dissection may interfere with the blood supply to other structures, thus requiring salpingo-oophorectomy or hysterectomy.

4. *Hydatid cysts of Morgagni* are usually pedunculated and are easily removed.

BIBLIOGRAPHY

Novak ER, Woodruff JD: Gynecologic and Obstetric Pathology. Philadelphia, Saunders, 1979

8

Pelvic Relaxation and Urinary Incontinence

Jeffrey W. Ellis, M.D.

PRACTICE PRINCIPLES

Disorders of pelvic support are generally acquired and result from attenuation of muscular and fascial support within the pelvis secondary to childbirth and advanced age. These disorders usually occur in combination since they have a common etiology. Though many women are asymptomatic, a wide variety of symptoms may occur which will involve the urinary system, and lower gastrointestinal system. Genital fistulas are related to injury to specific pelvic structures that may occur as a result of irradiation, operative injury, or obstructed labor. Symptoms will depend on the size and location of the fistula.

UTERINE PROLAPSE

A. *Definition* The uterus descends in the pelvis as a result of weakened support. Three degrees of uterine prolapse are described.
   1. *First degree prolapse.* The uterus has descended to a point where the cervix is visible at the introitus.
   2. *Second degree prolapse.* The cervix protrudes through the introitus.

3. *Third degree prolapse* (total procedentia). The entire uterus protrudes through the introitus.

B. *Symptoms* Most patients with minor degrees of prolapse are asymptomatic. With greater degrees of prolapse, the patient may complain of pelvic pressure and protrusion of the cervix. Exposed tissue may become inflamed and infected. Symptoms of cystocele and rectocele are often present.

C. *Management* In the management of uterine prolapse, the following factors should be considered: age of the patient, general medical condition, desire for further childbearing, degree of prolapse, associated prolapse of other structures.

1. *Conservative management.* Minor degrees of prolapse will generally require no treatment. In the high-risk or elderly patient, conservative management is indicated. Superficial infection or ulceration of exposed tissue should be treated with a regimen of cleansing with antiseptic solution followed by thorough drying. A pessary may then be inserted. A variety of pessaries is available, and the reader is referred to the Bibliography for a discussion of types and indications for use.

2. *Surgical management*
   a) *Vaginal hysterectomy* is the treatment of choice if the patient does not desire further pregnancy. The *advantages* to this procedure as compared to the abdominal hysterectomy are a shorter operating time, absence of incisional pain that may preclude normal ventilation and ambulation, decreased incidence of postoperative ileus, and opportunity to repair associated prolapse of bladder or rectum. *Disadvantages* of this procedure are decreased surgical exposure and difficulty in performing oophorectomy. Vaginal hysterectomy is *contraindicated* in the presence of adnexal disease and when the posterior cul-de-sac has been obliterated by inflammation or neoplasia.
   b) *Abdominal suspension procedures* are generally only of temporary benefit and should be performed only in

patients with significant prolapse who wish further pregnancy.

c) The *LeFort procedure* involves partial closure of the vagina, thus preventing uterine prolapse. This procedure may be performed relatively rapidly under local anesthesia and is indicated only for patients who may be poor operative risks. The major disadvantages of this procedure are that coitus is no longer possible and evaluation of subsequent vaginal bleeding is compromised.

d) The *Manchester-Fothergill procedure* consists of cervical amputation, plication of the cardinal ligaments, and anterior colporrhaphy. It is rarely performed in the United States and is indicated only in cases of extreme cervical elongation and cystocele in the presence of a normally supported uterus.

CYSTOCELE

A. *Definition* Protrusion of the bladder into the vagina.
B. *Symptoms* Many cases of cystocele are asymptomatic. The following symptoms may occur:
  1. Bladder emptying may be incomplete, leading to a large residual volume. Urinary frequency, urgency, and recurrent urinary tract infection often result.
  2. The patient may complain of pelvic fullness, protrusion, and difficulty with coitus.
  3. Urinary stress incontinence is not associated with cystocele.
C. *Management* Most cases of cystocele require no treatment. In the patient who may be debilitated by her symptoms, the following forms of management may be necessary.
  1. *Conservative*. In the elderly or poor operative risk patient, a pessary may be inserted. Results are often poor, and urinary stress incontinence may develop.

2. *Surgical.* Vaginal hysterectomy with anterior colporrhaphy is the treatment of choice.

RECTOCELE

A. *Definition* Protrusion of the rectum into the vagina.
B. *Symptoms* Many cases of rectocele are asymptomatic. The
following symptoms may occur:
   1. The patient may complain of pelvic fullness, protrusion,
   and difficulty with coitus.
   2. Difficulty in emptying the rectum may necessitate that
   the patient manually reduce the rectocele to complete
   evacuation.
C. *Management* Most cases of rectocele require no treatment.
In the symptomatic patient, the following forms of management may be necessary:
   1. *Conservative.* Nonsurgical management is generally unsuccessful. A pessary may be tried, but this is usually
   unsatisfactory. Perineal exercises are not helpful.
   2. *Surgical.* Posterior colporrhaphy is the treatment of
   choice. Vaginal hysterectomy and anterior colporrhaphy
   are generally also necessary to treat associated prolapse
   of other structures.

ENTEROCELE

A. *Definition* The enterocele is a true hernia occurring in the
space between the uterosacral ligaments, posterior to the
cervix. The hernial sac will extend into the rectovaginal
septum and will contain small bowel.
B. *Symptoms* Enterocele is generally found in association with
other forms of genital prolapse. It may also occur after

previous abdominal or vaginal hysterectomy. Symptoms of pelvic heaviness and protrusion are common.

C. *Management*

1. *Conservative*. Pessaries are ineffective in reducing the hernia.

2. *Surgical*. Repair of the enterocele is usually performed in association with other procedures to correct genital prolapse. Correction of the enterocele follows the general principles of hernia repair in any location: complete dissection of the hernia sac, ligation of the sac, excision of the excess peritoneum.

TOTAL VAGINAL PROLAPSE

A. *Definition* Complete protrusion of the vagina through the introitus may occur in association with uterine prolapse or may occur after hysterectomy.

B. *Symptoms* The patient will generally complain of pelvic fullness, protrusion, and difficulty with coitus. The exposed tissue will usually become inflamed and ulcerated.

C. *Management*

1. *Conservative*. A pessary may be used, but this is generally unsuccessful.

2. *Surgical*

a) *Colpocleisis*. Total vaginal closure may be performed in the elderly patient who is not a candidate for more extensive surgery. After the procedure, coitus will not be possible.

b) *Sacrospinous ligament suspension*. A transvaginal approach is used to suspend the vaginal apex from one of the sacrospinous ligaments. Normal vaginal length is preserved.

c) *Combined vaginal-abdominal approach*. Anterior and posterior colporrhaphy is performed, followed by transabdominal fixation of the vaginal apex to the sacrum.

URINARY INCONTINENCE

Urinary incontinence is the involuntary loss of urine. Many varying etiologies have been identified, including disorders of pelvic support. Careful history, physical examination, laboratory assessment, and clinical assessment are mandatory for correct diagnosis and proper management. The majority of patients with urinary incontinence do not require surgery for correction of the problem. Recent advances in the study of urodynamics have provided methods that more precisely define etiologies. An in-depth discussion of urodynamics is beyond the scope of this text. The reader is referred to the Bibliography for details of specific diagnostic tests and surgical procedures.

A. *Urinary continence* Continence is dependent upon normal detrusor function and a normal sphincter mechanism. Continence requires that the pressure in the proximal urethra exceeds the pressure within the bladder. Voluntary contraction of the detrusor will increase bladder pressure, overcoming urethral pressure, thus initiating micturition.

B. *Evaluation of urinary incontinence*
   1. *History.* A thorough medical and surgical history should be obtained. Records of previous gynecologic or urologic procedures should be reviewed. The patient should be specifically questioned regarding the following symptoms:
      a) Urgency
      b) Frequency
      c) Dysuria
      d) Nocturia
      e) Circumstances surrounding loss of urine (laughing, sneezing, coughing, position change).
      f) Time interval between stress and loss of urine (immediate, delayed).
      g) Pain preceding the urge to void.
      h) Additional areas of questioning should include:
         (1) Current medications (e.g., alpha-blockers contained in antihypertensive medications may lead to incontinence).

        (2) The consistency of symptoms (constant, intermit-
           tent).
        (3) Can urination be stopped once initiated?

2. *Physical examination*
    a) A thorough general physical examination is per-
       formed.
    b) The vagina and external genitalia are examined for
       the presence of prolapse.
    c) With a full bladder or after the instillation of 200 ml of
       saline into the bladder, the patient is asked to cough.
       Involuntary loss of urine may be noted.
    d) The support of the proximal urethra and vesical neck
       is assessed using the *Bonney test.* Two fingers are in-
       serted into the vagina, supporting the bladder neck
       and elevating it toward the symphysis. The patient is
       again asked to cough. If no urine is lost during this
       maneuver, it is presumptive evidence that a disorder
       of support is responsible for incontinence. The princi-
       ple of the *Marshall-Marchetti* test is similar, except
       that the bladder neck is elevated using Allis clamps.
    e) A bimanual examination is performed to detect pelvic
       masses that may be compressing the bladder.
    f) Sensory function over the distribution of spinal seg-
       ments S2, S3, and S4 should be evaluated. Anal
       sphincter tone should be evaluated.

3. *Laboratory studies*
    a) Urinalysis and urine culture.
    b) Appropriate studies if diabetes mellitus or renal
       disease is suspected.
    c) Appropriate x-ray studies if lumbar spine disease is
       suspected.

4. *Additional clinical studies.* One or more of the following
   studies will be necessary depending on symptoms and
   physical examination.
    a) *Intravenous pyelogram*
    b) *Cystoscopy.* The urethra and bladder are examined by
       direct visualization. Residual urine volume is deter-
       mined.

    c) *Cystourethrogram*. Contrast medium is instilled into the bladder to detect anatomic abnormalities. A small beaded chain may be inserted into the bladder to aid in identification of the posterior urethrovesicular angle and axis of the urethra (chain cystourethrogram).

    d) *Urethrocystometry*. This is a neurologic examination of the bladder performed by instilling CO_2 into the bladder at the time of cystoscopy. The capacity and tone of the bladder are assessed. Normal findings include:

        (1) Opening urethral pressure of 80 cm H_2O.

        (2) Intravesical pressure of 5 to 10 cm H_2O.

        (3) No increase in intravesical pressure with filling.

        (4) No involuntary detrusor contractions.

        (5) First sensation of bladder filling occurs at 100 cc.

        (6) First sensation of urge to urinate occurs at 250 to 300 cc.

        (7) Maximum urethral pressure noted 1.5 to 2.0 cm from the vesical neck.

C. *True anatomic urinary stress incontinence*

  1. *Definition*. The involuntary loss of urine with an intact bladder and urethra that follows an abrupt increase in intraabdominal pressure.

  2. *Symptoms*. The patient will complain of varying degrees of urine loss after coughing, laughing, sneezing, and so on.

    a) Pain, frequency, and urgency are absent.

    b) Loss of urine occurs simultaneously with the physical stress.

    c) Loss of urine may occur even after the bladder has been recently emptied.

    d) The patient is generally able to stop the stream of urine while normally voiding.

    e) Over time, symptoms are constant and remissions do not occur.

  3. *Etiology*

    a) True anatomic urinary stress incontinence results

from inadequate support of the proximal urethra, vesical neck, and bladder base.

b) Continence requires that the pressure in the proximal urethra exceeds the pressure within the bladder. Sudden increases in intraabdominal pressure are normally transmitted equally to the bladder and proximal urethra, thereby maintaining the normal pressure differential.

c) Relaxation of the support of the proximal urethra will lead to an unequal pressure distribution when intraabdominal pressure increases. As bladder pressure exceeds urethral pressure, incontinence develops. No detrusor contraction will occur.

d) This condition is most common in older, parous women but may also occur in young, nulliparous women.

e) Incontinence does not depend on the degree of general pelvic relaxation but rather on the degree of relaxation of the support of the proximal urethra, vesical neck, and bladder base.

f) A fixed, fibrotic urethra resulting from previous surgery will maintain a low resting pressure. Incontinence will occur since urethral pressure will not rise in response to increased intraabdominal pressure.

4. *Physical examination*

a) Varying degrees of urethrovesical prolapse may be present. In some patients, there is no visible prolapse.

b) Rectocele and uterine prolapse may be present.

c) Leakage of urine will be demonstrated when the patient coughs or strains.

d) Leakage of urine will be stopped using either the Bonney or Marshall-Marchetti test.

e) Anal sphincter tone and cutaneous sensation over the distribution of spinal segments S2, S3, and S4 are normal.

5. *Clinical evaluation*. The following observations during gas urethrocystometry have been described by Robertson.

a) Low opening urethral pressure (40 cm H_2O or less).
b) Residual urine volume less than 50 ml.
c) Normal bladder capacity.
d) Normal voiding urge.
e) Patient is able to inhibit urge to void.
f) No abnormal detrusor contractions.
g) The bladder fills with normal pressure.
h) The bladder neck is lax and closes sluggishly.
i) Funnelling, opening, and descent of the bladder neck occur with bearing down.

6. *Therapy*. Therapy for urinary stress incontinence depends upon the severity of symptoms. Minor degrees of incontinence are common and require only conservative treatment, if any. Incontinence that results in social embarrassment will generally require surgical correction.

   a) *Conservative*. Weight loss and control of chronic cough are helpful in minor cases. A pessary may be used in the older, debilitated patient, but this is generally unsatisfactory. Perineal exercises (Kegel's exercises) designed to strengthen the pubococcygeal muscles may be of some benefit.

   b) *Surgical*. The aim of surgery is to restore the normal position of the urethra and bladder base to thereby allow normal pressure differentials between the bladder and urethra. All authorities emphasize that the patient must be evaluated for all possible etiologies of incontinence before any surgical procedure is attempted. Numerous surgical procedures have been used, all of which are variations of either a suspension, a plication, or a sling. The reader is referred to the Bibliography for detailed discussions of these procedures. The most commonly used procedures are:

      (1) Kelly plication (vaginal urethroplasty). This transvaginal procedure is most commonly performed as the initial procedure for mild to moderate degrees of incontinence. Overall success rates are generally quoted as approximately 60 percent.

      (2) Marshall-Marchetti-Krantz procedure (sup-

rapubic urethropexy). This procedure is generally performed as the initial procedure for severe incontinence or when a previous vaginal plication has failed. Many authorities consider this procedure to be the most successful and durable procedure, quoting success rates of in excess of 90 percent. No surgical procedure has been 100 percent successful in treating true anatomic stress incontinence. Operative failures may be due to either misdiagnosis or failure to obtain appropriate or durable support. A variety of sling procedures have been used to treat repeated surgical failures. It has been repeatedly emphasized that the initial procedure performed for treatment of incontinence has the best chance of being successful.

D. *Detrusor dyssynergia* (unstable bladder)
   1. *Definition.* The loss of the ability to control detrusor contraction.
   2. *Symptoms.* The patient will complain of involuntary loss of urine after coughing, laughing, running, walking, or change in position. Symptoms may be difficult to distinguish from those of true anatomic stress incontinence.
      a) Urgency and frequency are generally present. Pain does not occur.
      b) Loss of urine generally occurs several seconds after stress.
      c) Involuntary voiding actually occurs. Urine may be lost in a steady stream over several seconds.
      d) The patient is unable to stop the stream during normal voiding.
      e) Symptoms usually occur when the bladder is moderately full.
      f) Symptoms may be intermittent, with several weeks of remission followed by exacerbation.
   3. *Etiology*
      a) No organic disease is present.
      b) Urethrovesical support is normal.

      c) Abnormal detrusor contractions are initiated by sudden increases in intraabdominal pressure or by a critical volume of urine.

4. *Physical examination*
   a) Urethrovesical prolapse may or may not be present.
   b) Urine leakage may be demonstrated after coughing.
   c) The Bonney test and Marshall-Marchetti test will not stop the leakage of urine.

5. *Clinical evaluation.* Urethrocystometry will be necessary to distinguish detrusor dyssynergia from true anatomic stress incontinence. The following observations during gas urethrocystometry have been described by Robertson.
   a) Increased opening urethral pressure.
   b) Residual urine volume less than 50 ml.
   c) Decreased bladder capacity.
   d) Urge to void occurs at low volumes.
   e) Abnormal detrusor contractions are noted.
   f) The bladder fills with increased pressure (over 15 cm H_2O).
   g) The bladder neck is normally supported.
   h) Bladder trabeculations may be present.

6. *Therapy*
   a) Surgical therapy has no role in treatment.
   b) Frequent voluntary urination at specific times during the day may decrease symptoms.
   c) Anticholinergics often give significant but not total relief of symptoms (probantheline bromide 15 mg tid with 30 mg at bedtime, flavoxate hydrochloride 100 to 200 mg tid).
   d) Consistently effective treatment for this condition is lacking.

E. *Urgency incontinence*
   1. *Definition.* The loss of urine due to the inability to control the urge to void.
   2. *Symptoms*
      a) Stress does not cause urine loss.

b) Frequency and dysuria are commonly present.

c) Hematuria may occur.

d) Loss of urine occurs in association with painful bladder distention.

e) The patient reports being unable to control the urge to void.

3. *Etiology.* Urgency incontinence is generally caused by intrinsic bladder disease.

   a) Infection

   b) Calculi

   c) Tumor

   d) Sexual trauma

4. *Diagnosis.* Urologic evaluation including urine culture, urinalysis, and cystoscopy will establish the diagnosis. Urethrocystometry will reveal that painful bladder distention will stimulate voiding by either detrusor contraction or increase in intraabdominal pressure.

5. *Therapy.* Treatment will depend on etiology and may include antibiotics, removal of calculi, or removal of tumor.

F. *Additional causes of urinary incontinence*

1. *Neurogenic bladder.* Involuntary loss of urine is due to bladder dysfunction caused by either an upper or lower motor neuron lesion. Symptoms are that of almost continuous leakage with intermittent large volume loss. A hypertonic form is due to an upper motor neuron lesion (e.g., multiple sclerosis). Spontaneous detrusor contractions occur as the bladder reaches maximum capacity. Urethrocystometry reveals high opening urethral pressure, large residual volume, and small capacity. The hypotonic form is due to a lower motor neuron lesion (e.g., ruptured vertebral disc). Urethrocystometry reveals low opening pressure, large residual volume, and large capacity. These patients should be referred for primary neurologic treatment.

2. *Anomalies of drainage.* Ectopic ureter, hypospadias, and urethral diverticulum may lead to urinary incontinence.

Continuous urine loss is generally associated with both ectopic ureter and hypospadias. Cystoscopy and vaginoscopy will establish the diagnosis. Surgery is indicated to control the anomalous drainage. The urethral diverticulum will fill with urine during normal voiding and will empty at a later time in association with straining or change in position. Diagnosis is made by cystoscopy. Treatment involves marsupialization of the diverticulum.

3. *Psychogenic incontinence.* Symptoms of incontinence are generally related to anxiety or emotional stress. Laboratory and clinical evaluations are normal. Incontinence often occurs in association with headache, backache, and vague gastrointestinal symptoms. These patients should be referred for psychiatric evaluation and treatment.

GENITAL FISTULA

Genital fistulas generally result from tissue injury caused by irradiation, surgery, or childbirth. Invasive malignancies of the bladder, rectum, and genital organs may lead to fistula formation.

A. *Vesicovaginal fistula* (V-V fistula)
   1. *Etiology.* Ninety-five percent of vesicovaginal fistulas occur after surgery, most commonly after abdominal hysterectomy. Fistula formation is less common after vaginal hysterectomy, radical hysterectomy, and anterior colporrhaphy. The fistula may be caused by unnoticed perforation of the bladder or by tissue necrosis secondary to hematoma, infection, or devascularization of tissue. A misplaced suture that enters the bladder may also result in fistula. Fistula formation after obstructed labor or operative delivery is uncommon in the United States. V-V fistula may result from radiation treatment of genital malignancy, especially carcinoma of the cervix.
   2. *Symptoms.* A continuous watery discharge is character-

istic. Pain seldom occurs. Symptoms generally occur within 30 days of the time of surgery, with most fistulas occurring within 7 days. Fistulas may occur up to several years after radiation therapy.

3. *Diagnosis*
   a) Initial evaluation is aimed at determining the nature of the fistula, i.e., is it vesicovaginal, ureterovaginal, or urethrovaginal?
   b) Cotton balls or a gauze sponge is inserted into the vagina, and the bladder is filled with methylene blue dye. If a V-V fistula is present, the cotton balls or sponge will contain dye. If these materials are not stained, a ureterovaginal fistula should be suspected.
   c) A ureterovaginal fistula may be confirmed by retrograde injection of the ureters with methylene blue dye, with subsequent examination of vaginal sponges.
   d) Cystoscopy should be performed to determine the size of the fistula and its location with reference to the ureteral orifices and urethral sphincter.
   e) The location of the fistula within the vagina may be confirmed by instilling water and CO_2 into the bladder and noting the location of bubbles in the vagina.
   f) An intravenous pyelogram is performed to detect any ureteral obstruction.

4. *Management.* A detailed discussion of operative technique is beyond the scope of this text. General principles of management are:
   a) Many small V-V fistulas will heal spontaneously with four to six weeks of catheter drainage.
   b) Spontaneous closure is unlikely if it has not occurred within six weeks.
   c) Surgical correction should be deferred for at least two to four months after the formation of the fistula to ensure adequate tissue healing and treatment of infection.
   d) Fistulas that are a result of radiation injury or malignancy create special problems. In some cases, a

large tissue defect may preclude closure. Treatment of radiation-induced fistula should be deferred for at least one year.

e) A transvaginal or transperitoneal approach to repair may be used depending upon the site of the fistula, the mobility of surrounding tissues, tissue distortion caused by previous attempts at closure, and the experience of the operator.

f) General operative principles include total excision of scar tissue surrounding the fistula, multilayered closure, closure without tension, meticulous hemostasis, and suprapubic catheter drainage.

B. *Ureterovaginal fistula* (U-V fistula)

1. *Etiology*. Most U-V fistulas occur after pelvic surgery and result from either direct trauma or devascularization of the ureter.

2. *Symptoms*. A watery vaginal discharge will generally occur 10 to 21 days after the initial surgery. Evidence of pyelitis may occur prior to vaginal drainage.

3. *Diagnosis*

   a. Retrograde catheterization of the ureters and the injection of methylene blue dye will stain a vaginal sponge.

   b) Cystoscopy will reveal absent urine flow from the affected ureter.

   c) Intravenous pyelogram must be performed to determine if ureteral obstruction is present.

4. *Management*

   a) Expectant management is indicated if the intravenous pyelogram reveals normal ureteral continuity and no evidence of ureteral obstruction. Up to 30 percent of U-V fistulas will heal spontaneously.

   b) If expectant management is chosen, serial intravenous pyelograms should be performed to detect ureteral obstruction.

   c) If progressive hydronephrosis is detected, immediate surgical intervention is indicated. Nephrostomy or ureteral repair is performed depending on local conditions within the pelvis.

d) If detected early in the postoperative period, attempts should be made to insert a ureteral catheter. If successful, the ureteral catheter should be left in place for at least 14 days. Healing of the ureter will often occur. A retrograde pyelogram should be performed to demonstrate an intact ureter before the catheter is removed.

e) If expectant management fails, surgical closure is indicated. The exact nature of the surgery can be determined only at the time of laparotomy and will depend upon the site of the fistula. If the fistula is located within 4 to 5 cm of the ureterovesical junction, ureterovesical implantation is performed. The creation of a bladder flap may reduce the tension on the reimplanted ureter. Ureteroureteral anastomosis will be required if the fistula lies near the pelvic brim.

C. *Urethrovaginal fistula* These fistulas are uncommon and generally occur after surgery, usually anterior colporrhaphy or removal of a suburethral diverticulum. Diagnosis is made by cystoscopy. Surgery involves creating flaps of well-vascularized tissue to cover the defect.

D. *Rectovaginal fistula* (R-V fistula)

1. *Etiology.* R-V fistula may occur after obstetric trauma, gynecologic surgery, irradiation, or perirectal infection. Unsuccessful repair of a third or fourth degree laceration often leads to a low R-V fistula. Surgical causes include perineorrhaphy, posterior colpotomy, posterior colporrhaphy, and hemorrhoidectomy. Radiation injury usually leads to R-V fistula high in the vagina. A perirectal abscess may drain into the vagina, leading to fistula formation.

2. *Symptoms.* A small fistula may lead to only intermittent escape of flatus. Larger fistulas may lead to severe fecal loss through the vagina with tissue irritation and extreme odor.

3. *Diagnosis.* Visual examination of the vagina may reveal feces, and the rectal mucosa may be visible. The location of small fistulas may require the use of a fine metal probe or proctoscopy after instillation of dye into the vagina.

4. *Management*
   a) Surgical therapy is generally delayed for four to six months to allow complete healing of the tissue surrounding the fistula.
   b) In cases of a large R-V fistula, a temporary diverting colostomy may be required to decrease fecal soilage and allow healing of surrounding tissue.
   c) An antibiotic bowel preparation is commonly administered prior to surgical repair.
   d) Details regarding the technique of closure may be found in the bibliography.

E. *Enterovaginal fistula*
   1. *Etiology.* This type of fistula occurs most commonly after radiation therapy and rarely as a result of primary inflammatory disease of the bowel.
   2. *Symptoms.* The patient will lose varying amounts of small bowel content through the vagina. Electrolyte, metabolic, and nutritional balance may thus be lost.
   3. *Diagnosis.* An upper gastrointestinal series using dilute barium will reveal entry of contrast media into the vagina. Speculum examination will reveal the site of the fistula.
   4. *Management.* Surgical correction is indicated in most cases. Initial therapy should be aimed at reestablishing adequate nutrition. A long intestinal tube is inserted to drain bowel contents, and the patient is maintained on hyperalimentation. Spontaneous healing of the fistula has been reported to occur in some cases within two to three weeks. If spontaneous healing does not occur, laparotomy is performed after the patient has had correction of electrolyte and nutritional imbalances. Intestinal bypass of the involved segment of bowel is performed. Resection of bowel is usually not performed because of

dense adhesions and inflammation that surround the fistula site.

BIBLIOGRAPHY
Operative Technique
Mattingly RF: Operative Gynecology. Philadelphia, Lippincott, 1977

Nichols DH, Randall CL: Vaginal Surgery. Baltimore, Williams & Wilkins, 1976

Genital Prolapse
Jeffcoate TNA: Posterior colporrhaphy. Am J Obstet Gynecol 77:490, 1959

Kegel AH: Progressive resistance exercise in the functional restoration of the perineal muscles. Am J Obstet Gynecol 56:238, 1948

Krige CF: The repair of genital prolapse combined with vaginal hysterectomy. J Obstet Gynecol Br Commonw 69:570, 1962

Randall CL, Nichols DH: Surgical treatment of vaginal inversion. Obstet Gynecol 38:327, 1971

Shaw W: Vaginal operations for cystocele, prolapse of the uterus, and stress incontinence. Surg Gynecol Obstet 88:11, 1949

Waters EG: Vaginal prolapse. Obstet Gynecol 8:432, 1956

Weed JC, Tyrone C: Enterocele. Am J Obstet Gynecol 60:324, 1950

Urinary Incontinence
Arnold EP, et al.: Urodynamics of female incontinence. Am J Obstet Gynecol 117:805, 1973

Beck RP, et al.: Recurrent urinary stress incontinence treated by the fascia lata sling procedure. Am J Obstet Gynecol 120:613, 1974

Burch JC: Urethrovaginal fixation to Cooper's ligament for correction of stress incontinence, cystocele, and prolapse. Am J Obstet Gynecol 81:281, 1961

Fantl JA, et al.: Dysfunctional detrusor control. Am J Obstet Gynecol 129:299, 1977

Green TH: Development of a plan for the diagnosis and treatment of urinary stress incontinence. Am J Obstet Gynecol 83:632, 1962

Green, TH: Urinary stress incontinence: differential diagnosis, pathophysiology, and management. Am J Obstet Gynecol 122:368, 1975

Henriksen E: The nonsurgical management of urinary incontinence. Obstet Gynecol 20:887, 1962

Hodgkinson CO: Recurrent stress urinary incontinence. Am J Obstet Gynecol 132:844, 1978

Jeffcoate TNA: Urinary incontinence in the female. Am J Obstet Gynecol 94:604, 1966

Marshall VF, Marchetti AA, Krantz KE: The correction of stress incontinence by simple vesicourethral suspension. Surg Gynecol Obstet 88:509, 1949

Pereyra AJ, Lebhere TB: Combined urethrovesical suspension and vaginourethroplasty. Obstet Gynecol 30:537, 1967

Robertson JR: Gynecologic urethroscopy. Am J Obstet Gynecol 115:986, 1973

Robertson JR: Ambulatory gynecologic urology. Clin Obstet Gynecol 17:255, 1974

Robertson JR: Gas cystometrogram with urethral pressure profile. Obstet Gynecol 44:72, 1974

Fistula
Everett HS, Mattingly RF: Urinary tract injuries resulting from pelvic surgery. Am J Obstet Gynecol 71:502, 1956

Gray LA: Urethrovaginal fistulas. Am J Obstet Gynecol 101:28, 1968

Lescher TC, Pratt JH: Vaginal repair of simple recto-vaginal fistula. Surg Gynecol Obstet 124:1317, 1967

O'Conor VJ, et al.: Suprapubic closure of vesicovaginal fistula. J Urol 109:51, 1973

Symmonds RE: Ureteral injuries associated with gynecologic surgery. Clin Obstet Gynecol 19:623, 1976

9

Sexually Transmitted Diseases

Jeffrey C. King, M.D.
Jeffrey W. Ellis, M.D.

PRACTICE PRINCIPLES

Sexually transmitted diseases affect a significant percentage of patients evaluated by the obstetrician/gynecologist. While syphilis and gonorrhea continue to cause widespread morbidity, the spectrum of sexually transmitted diseases must be expanded to include a variety of bacterial, viral, protozoan, fungal, and parasitic diseases. All studies to date have implicated the new sexual freedom as the primary cause of the increased incidence of this category of diseases.

GONORRHEA

Gonorrhea is *the most common communicable disease.* However, little is known of its pathogenic mechanism. Man is the only known host of this species of *Neisseria.*

A. *Organism*
  1. The causative organism is a gram-negative, nonmotile diplococcus, *Neisseria gonorrhoeae.*
  2. This organism is aerobic, relatively fragile, and requires an alkaline medium of pH 7.2 to 7.6

B. *Symptoms*
1. 80 to 90 percent of infected women are asymptomatic.
2. In those women who are symptomatic, clinical presentation depends upon the organ involved and the degree of infection.
3. The average incubation period is three to five days.
4. There are no characteristic early symptoms of gonococcal infection in women. Some patients may present with only mild *dysuria* and/or *leukorrhea.*
5. Lower genital infection may exhibit the following symptoms:
   a) *Bartholin gland*—painful swelling, fever.
   b) *Skene's glands*—dysuria, discharge.
   c) *Urethra*—dysuria.
   d) *Vulva and vagina*—purulent, irritating discharge.
   e) *Cervix*—mucopurulent discharge.
6. Upper genital and extragenital infection may exhibit the following symptoms:
   a) *Fallopian tubes*—abdominal pain, nausea, vomiting, fever, purulent vaginal discharge.
   b) *Skin*—lesions may be confined to the genital area or may be diffuse. Pustules, erythema, and urticaria may develop.
   c) *Extremities*—joint pain and swelling.
   d) *Liver*—upper abdominal pain.
   e) *Rectum*—rectal pain, purulent anal discharge.
C. *Diagnosis*
1. *Physical examination*
   a) *Inspection* of the Skene's glands, urethra, vagina, or cervix may reveal a purulent discharge. The cervix may appear edematous, with eversion of the endocervical mucosa.
   b) *Bimanual examination* may reveal extreme pelvic tenderness, with pain upon movement of the uterus, cervix, or adnexa. Adnexal masses may be palpable if tubo-ovarian abscesses are present. Fluctuance in the cul-de-sac may represent abscess.
   c) *Abdominal examination* may reveal evidence of

peritonitis, with rebound tenderness, guarding, and hypoactive bowel sounds. Palpation of the liver may reveal tenderness if perihepatitis is present.

   d) In the presence of gonococcal arthritis, joints will be swollen and tender to palpation and movement.

2. *Laboratory evaluation*

   a) *Positive cultures* are essential for the diagnosis of gonorrhea in women, as in only 60 percent of patients can it be diagnosed by gram stain alone. A positive *gram stain* will reveal gram-negative, intracellular diplococci.

   b) *Specimens for culture* should be obtained from the urethral orifice, the endocervical canal, and, if appropriate, the pharynx and rectum. Lubricant should not be used on the vaginal speculum since these preparations have bactericidal properties and can inhibit culture growth.

   c) Cultures should be immediately plated on modified Thayer-Martin or Transgrow medium and incubated at 36C for 48 hours. Colonies that appear smooth and grayish white, give a positive oxidase test, and contain gram-negative cocci can be presumptively identified as gonococci.

   d) In cases of acute pelvic inflammatory disease, many authorities have advocated *culdocentesis* and culture of the peritoneal fluid to identify the causative organism(s).

   e) In cases of acute arthritis, culture of the synovial fluid will confirm the presence of the gonococcus.

D. *Treatment*

Penicillin is the drug of choice for gonococcal infections. The organism is fragile and dies within two to nine hours after exposure to appropriate antibiotics. Organisms resistant to penicillin have developed, and this may complicate therapy.

1. *Uncomplicated genitorectal and pharyngeal infections.*

   a) One gram of probenecid orally followed by 4.8 million units of aqueous procaine penicillin intramuscularly.

   b) Patients with penicillin or probenecid allergy may be

treated with tetracycline 1.5 gm orally followed by 0.5 gm four times a day for four days (total dose 9.5 gms).

c) Treatment failures should be treated with spectinomycin 2 gm intramuscularly after ruling out reinfection.

d) Cultures to confirm cure should be obtained one to two weeks after treatment.

2. *Uncomplicated infection during pregnancy*

a) Procaine penicillin and probenecid is the treatment of choice.

b) The use of tetracycline is contraindicated.

c) Penicillin-allergic patients may be treated with erythromycin 1.5 gm orally followed by 0.5 gm four times a day for four days (total dose 9.5 gm).

d) Cefazolin 2 gm intramuscularly preceded by 1 gm of probenecid may be used. However, the physician must be aware of the 20 percent cross-allergenicity between penicillin and cephalosporins.

e) Cultures to confirm cure should be obtained one to two weeks following treatment and again near term.

3. *Acute pelvic inflammatory disease.* The clinical diagnosis of acute pelvic inflammatory disease (PID) is not synonymous with gonorrhea. However, recent studies have shown that 50 percent of PID patients are culture positive for gonorrhea. *N. gonorrhoeae* may be important in the initiation of pelvic infection, but it seems that its primary role is to allow secondary bacterial invasion of the fallopian tubes and parametria by other organisms of the lower genital tract. Thus, *PID is a polymicrobial infection.*

Acute PID may be mild or may lead to severe symptoms. In the following cases, hospital admission is advised:

a) Temperature greater than 100° F.

b) Evidence of abdominal peritonitis.

c) Persistent nausea and vomiting with evidence of dehydration.

d) White blood cell count greater than 20,000.

     e) Concurrent pregnancy—rare.

     f) When the diagnosis is in doubt.

     g) Suspicion of noncompliance with treatment.

        Because of the association between PID and infertility and ectopic pregnancy, some authorities routinely advise hospitalization and intravenous antibiotic therapy in all cases of PID.

4. *Acute PID not requiring hospital admission*

     a) Tetracycline 1.5 gm orally followed by 0.5 gm orally four times a day for *10 days.*

     b) Alternate treatment is aqueous procaine penicillin 4.8 million units IM, preceded by 1 gm probenecid orally. This should be followed by ampicillin 0.5 gm orally four times a day for *10 days.*

5. *Acute PID requiring hospital admission*

     a) *A standard initial treatment* is aqueous crystalline penicillin G, 20 million units per day in divided doses until clinical improvement. This should be followed by ampicillin 0.5 gm four times a day to complete a 10-day course of therapy. Some authorities now recommend broad spectrum intravenous antibiotic therapy (e.g., Clindamycin and gentamicin) as initial treatment.

     b) Penicillin-allergic patients can be treated with tetracycline 0.5 gm I.V. every six hours until clinical improvement, followed by 0.5 gm orally four times a day to complete a 10-day course of therapy.

     c) *In patients not responding to the above regimens,* antibiotics with a broader spectrum will be necessary. Gentamicin for gram-negative organisms and/or clindamycin or chloramphenicol for anaerobic organisms may be administered in standard doses.

     d) *After administration of antibiotics, clinical improvement should occur in 24 to 48 hours. If improvement does not occur or if the clinical condition worsens, the patient should be evaluated for the presence of intraabdominal abscess or another pathology. Further evalua-*

tion may require ultrasonography, diagnostic laparoscopy and/or laparotomy.

e) Persistent vomiting may require continuous nasogastric suction until the resumption of normal intestinal peristalsis.

f) Abdominal pain often requires the use of analgesics.

6. *Ruptured tubo-ovarian abscess.* The rupture of a tubo-ovarian abscess is an acute surgical emergency that in the past has carried significant mortality.

a) *Symptoms*—fever, severe abdominal pain.

b) *Physical examination*—elevated temperature, tachycardia and tachypnea, abdominal rigidity, clinical signs of shock if septicemia is present. Pelvic examination may reveal fluctuation of the cul-de-sac.

c) *Initial treatment* is aimed at stabilizing the patient

(1) Insertion of a central venous pressure line, indwelling urinary catheter, two secure intravenous lines using 16 gauge catheters.

(2) Intravenous fluids are administered at a rate to maintain adequate tissue perfusion. The CVP and urinary output will provide guidelines for fluid administration.

(3) Broad-spectrum antibiotics are administered that will be effective against gram-negative, gram-positive, and anaerobic organisms.

d) *Surgical treatment.* The mainstay of the treatment of the ruptured tubo-ovarian abscess is removal of the infected tissue and adequate drainage.

(1) Total abdominal hysterectomy and bilateral salpingo-oophorectomy is generally performed.

(2) Conservative surgery involving removal of only the involved adnexa should be attempted only if thorough evaluation of the pelvis reveals no other areas of infection. Many patients treated in this conservative fashion require subsequent surgery for chronic pain or recurrent abscess.

(3) Adequate postoperative drainage is mandatory,

and this may be accomplished through either abdominal drains or a drain inserted through the cul-de-sac.

SYPHILIS

A. *Organism*
   1. The causative organism is the spirochete, *Treponema pallidum,* a slender, tightly coiled, helical cell.
   2. Under darkfield microscopy, this organism shows characteristic motility, rotating in a corkscrew fashion with slight forward or backward movement.
B. *Stages* The diagnosis and management of syphilis can best be understood when the various stages are identified. Untreated, acquired infection progresses through three stages: primary, secondary, and tertiary.
   1. *Primary syphilis.* Clinical evidence of primary syphilis occurs after an *incubation period of 10 to 90 days,* with an average of 21 days. *Chancres* will develop at the point of inoculation. They begin as papules and subsequently ulcerate. Examination reveals an ulcer with raised edges and a punched-out appearance. The lesions are generally painless. Regional lymph nodes may be enlarged but are usually nontender. Since the serologic test for syphilis does not become reactive until at least four weeks after infection, the importance of darkfield microscopy for identification of organisms must be emphasized. The classic chancre of primary syphilis is rarely seen today.
   2. *Secondary syphilis.* Six to eight weeks, or as long as six months, after the initial infection, a variety of symptoms develops. The most common clinical manifestation of early secondary syphilis is a generalized symmetrical cutaneous eruption, *condyloma lata,* characterized by macular, papular, pustular, or papulosquamous lesions. While painless and nonpruritic, these lesions may involve both skin and mucous membranes. Since secondary syphilis is a systemic disease, a variety of *constitutional*

symptoms may be present, such as generalized lymph-adenopathy, low-grade fever, malaise, anorexia, and arthralgia. Although darkfield examination may be positive, the diagnosis is confirmed by the demonstration of a positive serologic test. This form of syphilis may disappear with or without treatment and may last for a few weeks or as long as a year.

3. *Latent syphilis.* Untreated patients then enter the latent phase where there is no clinical evidence of disease. Approximately 25 percent of patients may have recurrence of the cutaneous lesions, which are infectious. The latent phase is divided into *early latency* (less than four years from initial infection) and *late latency* (more than four years). Late latency is not infectious. The diagnosis of latent syphilis is made on serologic testing since physical examination is usually negative. The patient may remain in the latent stage for the rest of her life, but 30 percent of patients will develop the tertiary form of the disease.

4. Tertiary syphilis involves osseous structures (gummas, Charcot's joints), the cardiovascular system (aortic aneurysm), or the nervous system (chronic meningitis, dementia).

C. *Diagnosis*

1. *Nontreponemal tests*

   a) The most commonly used test is the *Venereal Disease Research Laboratory (VDRL) slide test.* Since this test is nonspecific, false-positive reactions may be seen in a variety of conditions, such as febrile illnesses, drug addiction, and collagen-vascular disease. This test is easily quantified, and response to therapy can be followed by serial VDRL titers. Stable or rising titers may mean inadequate treatment, reinfection, or a false-positive test.

   b) The *rapid plasma reagin (RPR) card test* is a modification of the VDRL. Several studies suggest that the RPR is more sensitive in primary syphilis than is the VDRL.

2. *Treponemal tests* are used when false-positive results are suspected on nontreponemal tests.
   a) The *Treponema pallidum immobilization (TPI) test* is expensive and offers no advantage over the other treponemal tests.
   b) The most widely accepted treponemal test is the *fluorescent antibody absorption (FTA-ABS) test.* The FTA-ABS will remain positive for life even after adequate therapy.
3. *Darkfield examination.* In the presence of active lesions, the spirochete may be visualized using darkfield microscopy.
   a) The lesion is cleansed to remove purulent material and scab and is gently abraded.
   b) Serous exudate is collected from the base of the lesion.
   c) The serous exudate is then applied to a clean slide and examined under the darkfield microscope.
4. *Interpretation of results*
   a) Nontreponemal tests may be nonreactive in the early stages of primary syphilis, since the immune response may not be measurable for three to six weeks after inoculation. If the initial test is negative, it should be repeated in one week, one month, and three months.
   b) A reactive treponemal test and a reactive non-treponemal test usually indicate the presence of syphilis.
   c) If the initial darkfield examination of a lesion does not show the spirochete, the examination should be repeated daily for three days.
D. *Treatment*
   1. *Penicillin* is the treatment of choice for syphilis as there has been no evidence of resistant strains. Primary, secondary, and early latent disease of less than one year's duration may be treated with *benzathine penicillin G, 2.4 million units IM* at a single visit. Patients who are allergic to penicillin may be treated with either tetracycline or erythromycin 0.5 gm orally four times a day for 15 days.

Follow-up serology should be obtained at 1, 3, 6, and 12 months after treatment. A falling titer should be demonstrated if treatment was adequate and reinfection has not occurred.

2. Latent syphilis of undetermined duration (or more than one year's duration), cardiovascular syphilis, or neurosyphilis should be treated with benzathine penicillin G, 7.2 million units total dose: 2.4 million units IM on a weekly schedule for three weeks. Penicillin-allergic patients are treated with either tetracycline or erythromycin 0.5 gm orally four times a day for 30 days. Follow-up serology should be obtained every three months for two years to demonstrate falling titers.

3. *Treatment of syphilis during pregnancy* is with the same antibiotics as mentioned previously with the exception of tetracycline, which is contraindicated. Monthly serology should be obtained to document a falling titer. *Adequate screening and follow-up of the neonate is essential to prevent the effects of congenital syphilis. The belief that transplacental passage of the treponemal organism was impossible prior to 18 weeks of gestation has been proven false.*

CHLAMYDIA

Chlamydia trachomatis accounts for a wide variety of obstetric and gynecologic diseases. *Lymphogranuloma venereum* has been found to be caused by immunotypes L1, L2, and L3.

A. *Organism*
   1. The causative organism is a small, obligate, intracellular, bacterium-like parasite that develops within inclusion bodies in the cytoplasm of the host cells.
   2. The incubation period is unknown.
B. *Symptoms*
   1. *Chlamydia* has been implicated as the causative agent for cervicitis, urethritis, and even salpingitis in various studies.
   2. Chlamydia conjunctivitis or chlamydial ophthalmia in the

neonate may be acquired by delivery through an infected birth canal.

3. In cases of lymphogranuloma venereum, the first sign of infection is a small papule on the genitalia from 5 to 21 days after contact. While inguinal adenopathy is common in men, women may develop rectal lesions in the form of proctocolitis, rectal strictures, abscesses, and fistula formation.

C. *Diagnosis*
   1. Culture of the organism will confirm the diagnosis. However, laboratories to perform the culture may not be generally accessible.
   2. Diagnosis of lymphogranuloma venereum is classically based on the Frei skin test for delayed hypersensitivity, fourfold rise in complement-fixation titers on paired serum samples, or the microimmunofluorescent antibody test.

D. *Treatment*
   1. Effective treatment of genital infections can be obtained using minocycline, doxycycline, or erythromycin at appropriate doses for seven days.
   2. Ocular infections may be treated with topical ophthalmic preparations of tetracycline or sulfonamides for 21 days.
   3. Lymphogranuloma venereum is treated with tetracycline, 500 mg four times a day for 21 days.

GRANULOMA INGUINALE

This is a chronic, ulcerating disease involving the genitalia, perineum, or thighs. It most frequently occurs in the tropics and is seldom seen in temperate climates.

A. *Organism*
   The causative organism is a gram-negative, pleomorphic, microaerophilic bacillus, *Calymmatobacterium granulomatis*.

B. *Symptoms*
   The initial lesions may be papular, vesicular, or nodular and appear after an incubation period of a few days to three

months following infection. As the lesions arise, an ulcer with a red granular base develops which bleeds easily but is usually painless. Inguinal adenopathy due to secondary infection is commonly present.

C. *Diagnosis*
Giemsa-stained smears of the ulcer should be obtained. The diagnosis is confirmed by identifying *Donovan bodies,* large mononuclear cells with intracytoplasmic vacuoles containing the organism.

D. *Treatment*
Recommended treatment is tetracycline or erythromycin 500 mg four times a day for 14 days.

CHANCROID

This disease is found more often in men than in women. It is relatively uncommon.

A. *Organism*
The causative organism is *Haemophilus ducreyi,* a short, nonmotile, gram-negative bacillus.

B. *Symptoms*
After an incubation period of 12 to 24 hours, a small macule rapidly changes to a pustule, which then ulcerates. The edges of the ulcer become irregular. In contrast to the chancre of syphilis, the ulcers of chancroid are very painful.

C. *Diagnosis*
Demonstration of the *H. ducreyi* on gram stain is diagnostic.

D. *Treatment*
Recommended treatment is sulfonamide at a dosage of 1 gm four times a day for 14 days.

CONDYLOMATA ACUMINATA (Venereal Warts)

A. *Organism*
The causative organism is a DNA virus of the papova group.

B. *Symptoms*
Lesions occur in the urogenital and anorectal areas, which offer a warm, moist environment for viral replication. They are virtually never seen on the trunk or medial aspects of the

thighs. The lesions begin as a minute papillomatous growth, and as they enlarge they assume a cauliflowerlike appearance. Depending on the location and quantity of the lesions, the patient may be asymptomatic or may complain of a variety of symptoms including dyspareunia, vulvar pruritis, pain on defecation, and bleeding.

C. *Diagnosis*

The lesions are generally easily identified by visual examination. If doubt exists as to the nature of the lesion, the area should be biopsied, with treatment pending histologic examination.

D. *Treatment*

1. *Small lesions* in the *nongravid patient* can be treated with a single application of 25 percent *podophyllin* in tincture of benzoin. Care must be taken to prevent injury to adjacent tissue by the podophyllin. The patient should be instructed to thoroughly wash the lesions with soap and water within four hours of application.

2. Condyloma within the vagina or on the cervix should not be treated with podophyllin because of the lack of protective surrounding tissues and also because neurotoxicity may develop from rapid mucosal absorption. These lesions may be treated with surgical excision, electrocautery, or laser. Large lesions should be treated by either surgical excision or electrocautery.

3. *During pregnancy,* podophyllin usage is contraindicated because of potential toxic or teratogenic effects.

4. Recently, successful treatment of persistent or recurrent lesions has been seen with *immunotherapy.* An autogenous vaccine can be made from the lesions.

5. Sexual partners must be carefully examined and treated to prevent recurrence.

HERPESVIRUS HOMINIS

A. *Organism*

The human herpesviruses have been divided into two distinct antigenic subgroups, type I and type II. Originally it was thought that type I infection was limited to the upper body and that type II infection affected the lower genital tract. It has now been determined that type I infections account for up to 15 percent of all genital herpetic infections. Sexual transmission of the virus is well documented, with an incubation period of three to six days.

B. *Symptoms*

The patient will complain of exquisitely painful genital lesions. Dyspareunia and dysuria are often present. Systemic symptoms of fever, malaise, and myalgias are common with primary infections. Pain in the inguinal areas results from inguinal adenitis. Symptoms are generally more intense with the primary infection as compared to recurrences.

C. *Diagnosis*

1. *Physical examination.* Multiple shallow ulcerations may involve the cervix, vagina, and vulva. The lesions usually present as small vesicles that rapidly progress to ulcers, which may become confluent.

2. *Laboratory studies.* Serous material should be obtained from an active ulcer and immediately applied to a slide. Giemsa, Papanicolaou, or Wright stain will reveal multinucleated giant cells with characteristic intranuclear inclusion bodies. In tissue culture, herpesvirus demonstrates a characteristic pattern of cell destruction (cytopathogenic effect) that can be seen in 72 hours.

D. *Treatment*

1. Healing occurs within three weeks when uncomplicated by bacterial superinfection.

2. At present, effective therapy for genital herpes infection is lacking. Symptomatic treatment is generally helpful in reducing pain and may include cleansing with Betadine solution to prevent secondary infection, sitz baths, and dry heat applied with a blow hair dryer.

3. Recently, new topical preparations have been released (e.g., Acyclovir) that may provide some benefit in reducing the duration of the acute phase of the infection. Further clinical studies are necessary to confirm this benefit.

PEDICULOSIS PUBIS

Infestation with crab lice, *Phthirus pubis,* has become relatively common. They generally inhabit pubic hair but may be found in other hair-bearing areas.

A. *Symptoms*
   None to severe pruritis.

B. *Diagnosis*
   Physical examination often reveals severe excoriation. Adult organisms may be seen. Microscopic studies of the affected hair follicles will reveal the 1 to 2 mm crablike form of the adult and the 0.5 mm transparent oval eggs (nits).

C. *Treatment*
   Gamma-benzene hexachloride as a cream or shampoo.

SCABIES

This is a common skin infection caused by the mite, *Sarcoptes scabiei.* Transmission is by close personal contact and is not limited to sexual contact.

A. *Symptoms*
   Intense pruritis is the most common symptom. The usual location of infection is between the fingers, and on the wrists, breasts, abdomen, buttocks, and genitalia.

B. *Diagnosis*
   Physical examination will reveal slightly raised mite burrows and follicular-papular eruptions due to allergic reaction. Diagnosis is made by scraping multiple burrows with a scalpel and examining the unstained scrapings microscopically for the 200 to 450 μ turtle-shaped mites or for eggs. A drop of mineral oil applied to the lesions prior to scraping improves the diagnostic yield.

C. *Treatment*
   Liberal applications of gamma-benzene hexachloride.

OTHER SEXUALLY TRANSMITTED DISEASES

Infections caused by *Trichomonas, Gardnerella vaginalis* (*Haemophilus vaginalis*), and *Candida albicans* may be transmitted by sexual contact. They are discussed in Chapter 5.

BIBLIOGRAPHY

Charles D: Infections in Obstetrics and Gynecology. Philadelphia, Saunders, 1980

Cunningham F, Hauth J, Gilstrap L, et al.: The bacterial pathogenesis of acute pelvic inflammatory disease. Obstet Gynecol 52:161, 1978

Eschenbach D, Holmes K: Acute pelvic inflammatory disease: current concept of pathogenesis, etiology, and management. Clin Obstet Gynecol 18:35, 1975

Evans T: Sexually transmissible diseases. Am J Obstet Gynecol 125:116, 1976

Ledger W: Bacterial infections during pregnancy. In Quilligan E, Kretchmer N (eds): Fetal and Maternal Medicine. New York, Wiley, 1980

Lee R: Sexually transmitted infections. In Burrow G, Ferris T (eds): Medical Complications during Pregnancy. Philadelphia, Saunders, 1975

McMaster A: Sexually transmitted diseases. In Rommey S (ed): Gynecology and Obstetrics. New York, McGraw-Hill, 1981

Monif G: Infectious Diseases. In Obstetrics and Gynecology. Hagerstown, Maryland, Harper, 1974

Sweet R: Diagnosis and treatment of acute salpingitis. J Reprod Med 19:21, 1977

Sweet R: The case for a polymicrobial etiology of acute salpingitis. Contemp Ob/Gyn 15:93, 1980

10

Sexual Assault
Psychosocial Aspects, Evaluation, and Treatment

Sylvia Lessman, M.S.W., A.C.S.W.
Charles R.B. Beckmann, M.D.

PRACTICE PRINCIPLES

A. The sexual assault victim confronts the physician and other members of the health care team with unique issues.
   1. *Nature of the trauma* — the assult itself may interfere with the patient's acceptance of medical treatment.
   2. *Treatment of emotional trauma* is often the primary need of the patient. The patient feels helpless and powerless, since the assault is more than a sexual violation but may also be perceived as a threat to her life.
   3. The physician must consider collection of *evidence and related legal issues*.
   4. It is difficult for *health professionals to cope with their feelings* that are elicited by the victim.

DEFINITIONS[1–5]

A. *All sexual assaults are acts of violence* against the victim's will.[6] Some involve minor violence apart from coitus to the extreme of lust-murder, but *all involve the common element*

131

of nonconsent, usually associated with violence or the threat of violence.[2–4]

B. The American College of Obstetrics and Gynecology has provided the following *definitions* that may be used as guidelines:[5]

1. *Rape is unlawful carnal knowledge of a female, forcibly and against her will.* This can mean coitus with ejaculation of semen on one extreme to the slightest penetration of the female genitalia by the male penis without emission of seminal fluid on the other extreme.

2. *Statutory rape* is coitus with a female below the age of consent. This is usually 16 but differs in the various states.

3. *Sexual molestation* is noncoital sexual contact without consent.

4. *Deviant sexual assualt* is contact between the sexual organs of one person and the anus or mouth of another without consent.

C. In addition, a sexual assault is usually classified as rape when the victim is mentally incapable, intoxicated, drugged, anesthetized, unconscious, or asleep, or tricked into believing the assailant is her husband.[2,3]

PREVALENCE[7]

A. Historically, rape is an underreported crime because many victims choose to remain silent out of fear, shame, guilt, or other reactions or feelings.

B. There has been an increase in reported rapes in the United States. In 1976, there were 56,000 cases of reported rape (approximately one every nine minutes). The rate of reported rape in 1976 per 100,000 in the population was more than double the number of rapes reported in 1966.[8]

C. Estimates are that the actual number of rapes is 3.5 to 10 times greater than the number reported.[6] The FBI estimates that 50 to 90 percent of all rapes go unreported.[8]

D. Single women between 17 and 34 years of age are the most

frequently reported rape victims,[9] most rapes being intraracial.[2]

E. Just as there are many different types of people, so there are many types of rapists. Cohen et al.[10] provides an extensive review of the types of rapists, possible therapy, and their prognosis.[3,11]

SOCIETAL RESPONSE TO SEXUAL ASSAULT VICTIMS.

A. Many of the misconceptions regarding rape tend to shift the blame from the offender to the victim. Stereotypic responses that substantiate this may be "nice girls don't get raped," "many women secretely want to be raped," and "she must have been asking for it."

B. The reluctance of some victims to report rape or to share the trauma with someone else is based on their perception of the response they may get. Many women are fearful of sharing with a spouse or boyfriend that they have been sexually assaulted because they fear rejection.

C. It has been found that regardless of the situation, police, families, and sometimes the victims themselves are reluctant to accept the fact that the violent crime was accidental.[12] There is often the implication that the victim might have been able to prevent her injuries. This may be attributed to our need to feel less helpless and vulnerable to such attacks. If one can find a rational explanation for violent behavior one can feel more in control.

D. A frequent response is to attack the patient's lifestyle as a reason for her accessibility to the sexual assault. There is a tendency to do this with populations who may be at high risk for such an attack. Prostitutes, illegal aliens, alcoholics, or drug abusers may be reluctant to seek medical care and tend to increase the health professionals' anxiety, thereby making medical care more difficult for them to provide and for the patient to obtain.

EMOTIONAL IMPACT OF SEXUAL ASSAULT

A. Three phases of the *emotional reaction of the rape victim* have been identified:[16,9,13–15]

   1. The *acute phase*[13] is seen in the emergency room. It is characterized by:

     a) *Psychologic trauma* masked by individual defenses and an initial reaction of shock. The individual may appear to be subdued, stunned, quiet, numb.

     b) *Cognitive dysfunction*

       (1) The patient may have difficulty in making decisions.

       (2) The patient may have difficulty concentrating, so questions and/or instructions often need to be repeated several times.

       (3) The victim may appear to be preoccupied or distracted. She may experience flashbacks or be reliving the experience, particularly the moment when she felt that she lost control and felt that there was no way out of the situation.

       (4) The victim may use denial as a defense. She may be resistant to talking about the experience and try to engage personnel in very social conversation unrelated to the traumatic experience. The victim may have difficulty in giving a history of the attack or events immediately thereafter.

     c) Frequently, following a sexual assault the victim may engage in routine activity (such as cleaning the house) before going to the emergency room for care. This behavior helps the victim to reaffirm a sense of self and of control. Such a *retreat to routine activities* and the fact that there are often not any physical signs of assault may contribute to a feeling of disbelief on the part of the health professional that a sexual assault really has occurred. If the victim's behavior is understood, the professional's judgmental error may be avoided.

    d) During this phase it is important for the health professionals to help the victim to confront her feelings rather than to support her defenses. Victims frequently have few opportunities to share the flood of anxiety, grief, and anger that may accompany an assault.

    e) In addition, the victim needs help at this time with pragmatic concerns. Issues of pregnancy, VD, how or who to tell about the experience and how they may feel in the days and weeks to come are important issues to discuss.

2. *The second stage*[13] takes place from several days to several weeks immediately following the experience. It is characterized by:

    a) *Somatic symptoms,* such as sleep and/or appetite disturbance and gynecologic complaints. The patient may have continued flashbacks and trouble sleeping accompanied by violent nightmares.

    b) *A sense of fear* that may be expressed as a generalized vulnerability or may be more specific to, for example, the location where the assault occurred, being alone, or the possible return of the assailant.

    c) The patient may be moody, irritable, cry frequently, and have lost her sense of humor.

    d) Symptoms are often very disturbing to the patient because they are disruptive of her normal routines.

    e) The patient may have *difficulty in concentrating.*

    f) There may be *problems with sexual functioning.* This differs among patients but may be related to the age of the patient, previous sexual experience, and her culture values.

       (1) The patient may initially withdraw from a partner, not wanting any intrusion or demands and may find that requests for sexual activity may trigger flashbacks to the sexual assault. This reaction does not mean that the patient does not have a need for physical comfort and closeness, which, on the contrary, *is very important.*

(2) The reaction is heavily influenced by the response
of the patient's sexual partner to the assualt.

g) *In an attempt to integrate the experience, the victim tries
to find some reason for the assault.* She may exaggerate her own responsibility as a way to regain a sense of
control. If the victim is able to find a reason for the
assault, she can begin to feel that she might be able to
prevent such an incident from happening again. The
historical social myths as discussed previously may
contribute to this susceptibility for self-blame.
Another factor that may be operating is that it is often
less disturbing to blame one's self than to accept the
reality that one has no control and may experience
such victimization again.

3. *The third stage*[13] is one that determines the long-term
resolution of the assault:

a) During this stage the individual must reexamine her
life and self. The feelings of vulnerability and concerns about safety will last over a long period of time,
although the intensity of the feelings will diminish.

b) The victim may feel a sense of loss and spontaneity in
response to life. She may be more cautious and may
exhibit a change in lifestyle.

c) Counseling may be needed to help the patient resolve
any issues that may be troubling her. Often the patient
has no awareness of unresolved issues related to the
assault until they are triggered, sometimes later, by
something that is happening in her life (marriage,
pregnancy, a new relationship).

d) In resolving the feelings regarding the assault, the
victim may be strengthened and have a new apprecia-
tion of life.

4. *It is important to remember that rape violates the individual's basic beliefs and assumptions about the environment,
other people, and the self. The usual things that the victim
depends upon fail her, and the result is a sense of loss, i.e.,
loss of sense of safety, loss of control, loss of trust, loss of*

self-esteem, and loss of physical and emotional integrity.

B. Issues in the *treatment of the emotional crisis*

1. In treating the sexual assault victim, there is a *need for a purposeful, well-thought-out approach. Crisis intervention* is the method of treatment. There are three factors that must be dealt with as part of the crisis:[13]

   a) The hazardous, stressful event.

   b) The *perceived* loss or threat to the victim's integrity. This will include the meaning of the event to the victim and whether it is perceived as a crisis by the victim. When the event is perceived as a threat to her integrity, the victim generally displays anxiety. When the event is perceived as a loss, it is often expressed through depression. For many victims, the event is perceived as a threat, and therefore there is a high degree of anxiety, which is the usual immediate response. The depression is related to a loss of trust, security, and control as mentioned previously, and is usually a long-term reaction.

   c) Inability to respond with adequate and appropriate coping mechanisms.

2. *Initial interview in the emergency room.* The emergency room staff can help *limit the trauma the woman experiences* as she arrives.

   a) A supportive individual should remain with the victim at all times. This person should be nonjudgmental in approach and encourage the victim to talk.

   b) If possible, the victim should be interviewed in a quiet area, thus minimizing exposure to interruption and embarrassment. One must remember that the individual has had an assault on her sense of privacy and needs to regain her composure and some sense of control. This is impossible to do in a waiting room or public area of the emergency room.

   c) Because of the cognitive dysfunction and the multiple stimuli in the emergency room, it is important to reinforce directions. Ideally, this information should be prepared in writing for the patient, along with a telephone number where she can call for support or counseling or to ask additional questions.

d) The patient should be encouraged to find someone to take her home, or, if that is not possible, some arrangement should be made so that the patient does not have to go home alone, as feelings of abandonment at this time might intensify her feeling about the event and herself.

e) The modality of treatment for sexual assualt victims is primarily crisis intervention. The helping person, i.e., physician, nurse, should be aware of the usual reactions to sexual assault and must communicate confidence that the victim can cope and actively look for strengths in her coping skills and point them out to her.

3. *The tasks of the initial interview.*
   a) Cognitive understanding of the event.
   b) Management of the victim's affect and feelings and acknowledgment that they are normal in the context of such a traumatic event.
   c) Helping the victim to develop coping mechanisms and encouraging her to seek out and use the various helping systems that are available, i.e., the medical system, legal system, victim's assistance groups.

4. *Minimal goals to be accomplished while the patient is in the emergency room.*
   a) Helping the victim to begin to express her feelings.
   b) Conceptualizing the experience.
   c) Helping to reduce the victim's anxiety by demonstrating to her her own ability to utilize skills and coping strategies. This can be accomplished through the development of a short-term plan that includes issues such as where she plans to stay upon leaving the emergency room, who she plans to tell, what her follow-up care will be.
   d) The victim should be made aware of possible sequelae, i.e., the feelings and reactions that she will

have in the coming days and weeks, as discussed under Emotional Impact of Sexual Assault, Section A, pages 134 to 137.

e) The victim should be given information about how to handle feelings and situations and resources that she can contact for help.

f) Helping the victim to manage her feelings will make her more accessible to medical treatment. This may be a time-consuming and difficult process for the physician who may be required to deal with all aspects of the sexual assault victim on his own.

g) The victim who is asked to submit to medical treatment prior to dealing with those issues (when that is not a necessary task to save her life) often feels that she is being assaulted for the second time. When the victim is able to deal effectively with her feelings, she can participate in the examination having cognitive awareness that this is in her best interest. Throughout the examination the physician needs to help the victim to have a sense of control. This can be accomplished by gaining the victim's permission and keeping her informed of what procedures are being done and why they are being done. It is important to emphasize that the victim must be an active participant in her medical treatment.

MEDICAL STAFF REACTIONS
THAT MAY INTERFERE WITH TREATMENT

A. There are various *blocks to the effective and sensitive response to rape victims*. Some of these are reflected in the cultural biases that prevail within our society. Others may be related to personal or medicolegal issues. Some of the reactions may be as follows:

1. Staff may feel uncomfortable because they feel that they lack the knowledge and experience to deal with the intense feelings that are often exhibited by the patient and generated within themselves and a sense of fear

about doing something wrong with regard to these feelings.

2. Many physicians are concerned about the legal implications of getting involved. This problem should not be allowed to interfere with the care of the patient.

3. Sometimes it is believed that it would be better for the patient not to discuss the incident as a way of helping her to feel better. This is not the case. It is also not true that it is a violation of the victim's privacy to try to discuss the issue with the patient.

4. The rape victim brings to mind in all of us the personal issue of dealing with our own vulnerability.[13] Medical personnel must deal with that on a daily basis, but in this case the patient personifies the sudden arbitrary and catastrophic events that we come into contact with daily in the hospital and are subject to ourselves. This confrontation makes it difficult to provide immediate and sensitive care of the victim, and we must be in touch with how this type of trauma affects each of us.

5. Individuals involved in rape crisis counseling "burn out" very quickly. This is related to the intensity of the feelings that must be dealt with and the issues that are elicited in the helping person. This is a significant factor for physicians who must deal with rape victims on a regular basis and indicates the need for a supportive team that can intervene with the patient so that one individual is not bombarded regularly with this type of stress.

EXAMINATION AND TREATMENT OF THE SEXUAL ASSAULT PATIENT AND COMPLETION OF THE MEDICAL REPORT[1,2,4,9,11]

A. Because of the many responses elicited in patient and physician, examination and treatment of the assault patient are often difficult. The medical record is often incomplete, from both medical and legal aspects, and the follow-up plan fragmentary and ill conceived. To help avoid this, *we provide an Alleged Sexual Assault Report form (Figs. 10–1,10–2,10–3,10–4). Careful completion of it will help the physician to avoid many of the common errors and provide the victim with comprehensive health care.* The form is in four parts, dealing with alleged assault itself (Section G), the patient's medical history (Section H), the physical examination (Section I), and the laboratory evaluation and treatment plan (Section J).

B. *The initial triage of the victim is crucial, as life-threatening conditions must be quickly identified and treated. If no such emergent medical problems exist, an interval of time in a quiet private place with someone assigned to the patient is of great value prior to the actual examination. If at all possible, the same counselor should stay with the patient throughout the process.*[1] *It should be remembered that the medical and legal procedures following an assault may be perceived by the patient as traumatic as the assault itself. Great care must be taken to ameloriate this tendency.*[2]

C. A written consent should be obtained from the patient (or her guardian if she is a minor) for everything that is to be done.[1] This helps reinforce the patient's sense of control as well as being legally sound practice.

D. All staff actively involved in the evaluation should sign the record.[1] Great care must be taken to identify and label all specimens and reports fully and completely (including patient's name, date, examiner's name, and any hospital identifying number).[1] The legal value in apprehending, prosecuting, and possibly convicting the alleged assailant has medical value as well as social implications, as it has been shown that a major determinant in the eventual emotional well-being of the victim depends in part on the successful outcome of such legal action.[2]

E. The use of nontechnical terms, when feasible, often makes the record more useful for all those who need it. This should not be done, however, at the expense of accuracy.[2]

F. *No matter how much time has elapsed between the alleged assault and the patient's arrival for help, a full evaluation and treatment plan are essential.*[2]

G. *Alleged assault information (Fig. 10–1)*
  1. Description of alleged assault
      a) Needs to be as detailed as possible, using the patient's own words where possible. This facilitates careful, complete, and appropriate medical evaluation. That the record is also legible is of great importance.
      b) Avoid judgmental statements.[1,4]
  2. Legal counsel is valuable for the victim and may be gently encouraged. However, it is not appropriate for the physician or other nonlegally trained member of the health care team to offer specific legal advice.[14]
  3. Police notification requirements vary in different areas for adults, but whether or not the patient wishes to make a report and/or discuss the assault with the police is her decision. Separate consents may be needed for this interview and for the release of specimens and evidence to the police. Most areas require reporting an alleged sexual assault on a minor.[1,4]

H. *Medical history (Fig. 10–2)*
  1. A thorough general physical examination is as important medically and legally as is the genital examination. Evidence of bleeding, lacerations, bruises, and so on are of great importance from both aspects.[1,7]
  2. Genital trauma is more common in the old and young than in women of reproductive age, although such injury may be present and severe in some cases.[2]

I. *Physical examination (Fig. 10–3)*
  1. Clothing worn during an attack should be preserved in a paper bag for forensic use (plastic containers promote secretion deterioration.) Stains, blood, possible semen, and so forth should be left undisturbed.[1]
  2. If possible, photographs of lacerations, bruises, and other injuries are very useful, especially for legal purposes. Separate consents are usually required if these are to be taken.[2]

J. *Laboratory evaluation and therapeautic plan (Fig. 10–4)*[2,4,11]
  1. Combing the pubic hair may collect hair transferred from

the alleged assailant to the victim, which may be compared with the sample of pubic hair taken from the patient.[1]

2. All internal examinations should be done with a water-moistened, nonlubricated speculum. Use PAP fixative (not air drying) for all permanent slides.[4]

3. Motile sperm may be found up to 72 hours after coitus, and nonmotile sperm for three to four days.[2,4]

4. All permanent slides should be marked with a diamond stylus so that the identifying information is permanent, rather than with a pencil or ink.[1]

5. Wet mounts should be made with body temperature normal saline solution.[2]

6. Acid phosphatase reflects the presence or absence of ejaculation only.[2] It may be especially useful in the alleged assailant who has had a vasectomy.[2]

7. Blood typing of the patient may be useful in comparison studies with samples from the alleged assailant.[2]

8. Treatment
   a) Warm sitz baths[2] or the use of any of the local postpartum topical episiotomy sprays may offer some relief from local vaginal/perineal irritation.
   b) Postcoital contraceptive medication. At present there is no FDA-approved medication for this purpose. Those listed have found wide acceptance. The patient should understand that there is a 1 to 5 percent possibility of pregnancy, hence some patients may wish to wait four to eight weeks, have a repeat pregnancy test, and elect for an abortion if pregnancy ensues. If diethylstilbestrol (DES) is used, the possible risks to offspring should be explained. Most of these medications have nausea as a side effect, and an antiemetic (such as Compazine) is often helpful.[1,2]

9. Follow-up
   a) Initial follow-up should be arranged within 24 to 48 hours of the first visit, alone or with family as the patient wishes.[1,11]
   b) A six-week follow-up should also be arranged at

ALLEGED SEXUAL ASSUALT REPORT

Page 1 – ALLEGED ASSUALT INFORMATION

Date _____ / _____ / _____ Time _____ am/pm

Patient ID Stamp

Incident data

Date _____ / _____ / _____

Time _____ am/pm

Elapsed time to presentation for care _____

Alleged assailant(s)

Identity, if known _____

Description(s) _____

YES	NO	NOT KNOWN	Item
			Was there penile penetration of the
			vulva
			vagina
			mouth
			anus
			ear
			other

Description (place, events, sequence, actions afterward; use patient's words where possible; describe patient's emotional status, again with quotes if possible):

Did the alleged assailant
use a foreign object in any
   manner sexually
bind or tie the victim
threaten the patient
wear a condom
ejaculate
strike the patient
threaten the victim's family,
   friends, etc.

Does patient have legal counsel? _____

If so, has counsel been notified? _____

Does patient wish counsel notified? _____

Who has patient notified? _____

Does patient wish anyone notified? _____

Has police notification been made? _____

(Date _____/_____/_____, Time _____ am/pm)

Does patient wish police notification? _____

Has patient been sexually assaulted before? _____

If so, when? _____

_____ M.D.
(/   /   )

_____ R.N.
(/   /   )

_____
(/   /   )

Figure 10–I. Alleged sexual assault form. Alleged assault information.

ALLEGED SEXUAL ASSAULT REPORT

Page 2 – MEDICAL HISTORY

Patient ID Stamp

Date ___ / ___ / ___ Time _____ am/pm

Age: _____ years

Race: White ___ Black ___ Hispanic ___ Oriental ___ Other ___

Marital status:

Single ___ Married ___ Separated ___ Widowed ___ Other ___

Menstrual history:

Menarche _____ years old

Menses: regular _____ (interval in days _____)

irregular _____ (how so: _____)

usual flow: duration _____

amount _____

Last normal menstrual period: ___ / ___ / ___

Previous menstrual period: ___ / ___ / ___

Last bleeding of any kind: ___ / ___ / ___

(describe: _____)

Does patient think she is now pregnant? _____

(If so, how many weeks? _____)

Obstetric history:

Pregnancies _____ Abortions _____ Other _____

Item	YES	NO	NOT KNOWN
Since incident, has patient			
washed face			
bathed			
applied make-up			
changed clothes			
douched			
defecated			
urinated			
used any medications:			
been unconscious			
been to any other healthcare facility			

Patient's personal physician:

_____

Does patient wish him notified? _____

146

Contraceptive history:

( ) None. Why? _____

( ) Oral contraceptive

type _____

since _____

compliance _____

cycle position _____

( ) IUD

type _____

since _____

( ) Condoms _____

( ) Foam _____

( ) Condoms and foam _____

( ) Diaphragm

type _____

since _____

with gel _____

in place at time of alleged assault _____

( ) Rhythm _____

( ) Other _____

_____

Allergies: _____

Habits: alcohol use _____

drug use _____

Past history of VD/PID _____

_____

Treatment _____

Was patient sexually active within 24 hours of the alleged

assault? _____

Comments:

_____ M.D.

(/ /)

_____ R.N.

(/ /)

(/ /)

Figure 10–2. Alleged sexual assault form. Medical History.

ALLEGED SEXUAL ASSAULT REPORT | Patient ID Stamp

Page 3 — PHYSICAL EXAMINATION

Date _____ / _____ / _____   Time _____ am/pm

Description of clothing (items, stains, state, whether they were worn at time of assault):

Physical examination: BP _____ / _____   P _____   T _____   R _____

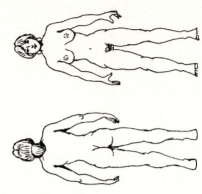

Head:

Throat:

Chest:

Breasts:

Back:

Neck:

Heart:

Abdomen:

Extremities:

Neurologic:

Pelvic examination:

Vulva:

Mons:

Urethra:

BUS:

Vagina:

Clitoris:

Perineum:

Cervix:

Uterus:

Adnexae, right:

left:

Cul-de-sac:

Anus/rectum:

Rectovaginal:

Other comments:

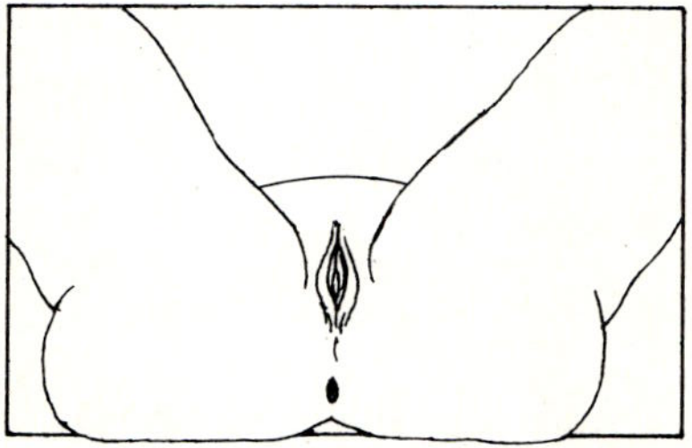

_____ (/ /) M.D.

_____ (/ /) R.N.

_____ (/ /)

Figure 10–3. Alleged sexual assault form. Physical examination.

149

ALLEGED SEXUAL ASSAULT REPORT
Page 4 — LABORATORY EVALUATION &
     THERAPEUTIC PLAN

Date _____ / _____ / _____   Time _____ am/pm

Patient ID Stamp

YES	NO	Specimen
		Foreign material from body (blood, semen;
		location: _____
		Finger nail scrapings (individually marked,
		wrapped)
		Pubic hair combing
		Pubic hair sample
		Other: _____
		Wet preparation of
		vagina (motile sperm: _____)
		cervix (motile sperm: _____)
		PAP (double set, slides scribed with diamond
		stylus with patient name, date, your name)
		vagina
		cervix
		throat
		anus
		other _____

Therapy:

Antibiotic
( ) none; risks explained to and understood by patient
( ) Procaine Penicillin, 4.8 million units IM plus 1 gm Benemid PO
( ) Tetracycline 500 mg PO every 6 hours for 5 days

Postcoital contraceptive medication
( ) none; patient understands risks
( ) none; effective method in use
( ) Diethylstilbestrol, 25 mg PO bid for 5 days
( ) Ethinylestradiol 5 mg PO bid for 5 days

Tetanus toxoid
( ) given
( ) refused, given last _____
( ) Compazine
( ) Tranquilizer; what _____

Laceration repair: _____

150

G.C. culture
- vagina
- cervix
- throat
- anus
- other

Seminal fluid for acid phosphate
- vagina
- cervix
- throat
- anus
- other

Patient's blood type/Rh

Pregnancy test
- urine
- RIA for β-hCG

RPR/VDRL

FTA-ABS

UA

Urine C&S

Radiographs _____

Ultrasound _____

Hepatitis antigen

CBC

Follow-up (describe, give dates and times of appointments, give patient this information in writing)

Medical: _____

Gynecologic: _____

Counseling: _____

Psychiatric: _____

Legal: _____

Pastoral: _____

Other: _____

Patient: _____

Address: _____ Phone: _____

_____ (/ /) M.D.

_____ (/ /) R.N.

_____ (/ /)

Figure 10–4. Alleged sexual assault form. Laboratory evaluation and treatment plan.

which time repeat studies for gonorrhea, syphilis, and pregnancy may be done, as well as any other care that is needed.

c) If the patient is treated in a hospital or clinic that does not have a comprehensive rape crisis program[6,9,16,17] where counseling is available, the patient should be given a list of resources. These may involve professional services and/or self-help organizations.

   (1) Hospital department of social work.
   (2) Family service agencies.
   (3) Community mental health center.
   (4) Local women's health centers or organizations.

d) Many patients will deny the need for counseling but should be given the resources regardless, since the emotional reactions of the second and third phases may cause her to change her mind.

BIBLIOGRAPHY

Brownmiller S: Against Our Will. New York, Simon & Schuster, 1975

Symonds M: The rape victim: psychological patterns of response. Am J Psychoanal 36:27, 1976

REFERENCES

1. McCombie SL: The Rape Crisis Intervention Handbook. New York and London, Plenum, 1980
2. Woodling BA, Evans JR, Bradbury MD: Sexual assualt: rape and molestation clinic. Obstet Gynecol 20:509, 1977
3. Shiff AF: Rape. Med Aspects Human Sexuality 6:76, 1972
4. Evrard J: Rape: the medical, social, and legal implications. Am J Obstet Gynecol 111:197, 1971
5. American College of Obstetrics and Gynecology: Technical Bulletin Number 52, November, 1978 (Replaces Number 14, April, 1972)
6. Abarbanel G: The sexual assault patient. In Green R (ed): Human Sexuality: A Health Practitioner's Text. Baltimore, Williams & Wilkins, 1979, pp 227-241

7. Shiff AF: A statistical evaluation of rape. Forensic Sci 2:339, 1973

8. Uniform Crime Reports for the United States, prepared by the Federal Bureau of Investigation Washington, D.C., 1972 and 1976

9. Vaught C, Woods F: Aftermath of sexual assault: rape. In Woods NF (ed): Human Sexuality in Health and Illness. St. Louis, Mosby, 1979, pp 252-271

10. Cohen M, Garofalo R, Boucher R, Seghorn T: The psychology of rapists. Semin Psychiatry 3:307, 1971

11. Massey J, Gracia C, Emich J: Management of sexually assaulted females. Obstet Gynecol 38:29, 1971

12. Symonds M: Victims of violence: psychological effects and aftereffects. Am J Psychoanal 35:19, 1975

13. Abarbanel G: Emergency care of the sexual assault victim. In-Depth Training for Social Workers. April 19, 1979

14. Fox SS, Scherl D: Crisis intervention with victims of rape. Soc Work 21:27, 1972

15. Sutherland S, Scherl D: Patterns of response among victims of rape. Am J Orthopsychiatry 40:503, 1970

16. Abarbanel G: Helping victims of rape. Soc Work 21:478, 1976

17. Peterson M, Linnane P: Sexual Assault: A Client-centered Training Program. Sexual Assault Treatment Center of Greater Milwaukee-Family Hospital, 1978

11

Malignant Disease of the Vulva

Jeffrey W. Ellis, M.D.

PRACTICE PRINCIPLES

Primary malignancy of the vulva is uncommon but must be considered in a patient in any age group who complains of a persistent vulvar ulcer or long-standing pruritis. Appropriate treatment is often delayed due to both patient neglect of the lesion and delay in diagnosis.

INCIDENCE

Primary malignancies of the vulva account for between 3 and 5 percent of gynecologic malignancies. The majority of cases occur in women over the age of 60. However, 15 percent occur in women under the age of 40.

PATHOLOGY

A. *Squamous cell carcinoma* is the most common lesion and is found in 80 percent of patients. The lesion most commonly occurs on the labia majora.
B. *Melanoma* is found in 10 percent of patients. The lesion most commonly occurs on the labia minora and clitoris.

C. *Adenocarcinoma* is an uncommon lesion that arises in the Bartholin gland.
D. *Paget's disease of the vulva* is an uncommon lesion that may occur in an intraepithelial or invasive form. An underlying apocrine adenocarcinoma has been reported to occur in 10 percent of patients.
E. Rare lesions of the vulva include basal cell carcinoma, verrucous carcinoma, sarcoma, and lymphoma.

SYMPTOMS

Symptoms of vulvar malignancy are generally of a chronic nature as a result of patient neglect of symptoms and delay in diagnosis.

A. Pruritis
B. Ulcer
C. Mass
D. Vulvar pain
E. Inguinal pain or swelling
F. Bleeding

DIAGNOSIS

A. *Gross appearance*
   Primary vulvar malignancies may appear as an ulcer, mass, pigmented lesion, or white lesion.
B. *Evaluation*
   1. *Biopsy. All suspicious lesions must be biopsied* using either a dermal punch or biopsy forceps. These biopsies may be performed in the office using a local anesthetic. Multiple biopsies may be required to establish the diagnosis. *Any area of vulvar "infection" or "inflammation" not responding to medical therapy should also be biopsied.*

2. *Vital staining.* Toluidine blue dye may be applied to the vulva to aid in identifying abnormal epithelium. This technique is useful in determining areas for biopsy in symptomatic patients who have no gross lesions.
   a. *Technique:* 1 percent toluidine blue dye is applied to the vulva using a sponge or cotton-tipped applicator. After two to three minutes, the vulva is washed with 1 percent acetic acid solution. Areas that retain the blue stain should be biopsied.
3. *Colposcopy* performed by physicians experienced in vulvar disease may aid in the direction of biopsies.
4. *Exfoliative cytology* may aid in establishing the diagnosis of vulvar malignancy but should not be relied upon as the sole means of evaluation of a vulvar lesion.
5. *Sexually transmitted diseases* must be considered in the differential diagnosis of any vulvar lesion. Appropriate studies should be undertaken.
6. *Surveillance for other genital malignancies.* Since primary malignancies of the vulva may be associated with malignancy of the vagina and cervix, a thorough examination of the entire lower genital tract is mandatory.

CLINICAL COURSE

A. *Local extension* to adjacent organs may occur with advanced lesions. The vagina, bladder, urethra, and rectum may become involved, often resulting in fistula formation.
B. *Lymphatic spread* initially involves the inguinal and femoral regions. Further spread will involve the deep pelvic nodes. The incidence of nodal metastases increases with the size of the primary lesion.

Size of Primary Lesion	Percent of Cases with Nodal Metastases
Less than 2 cm in diameter	15
Greater than 2 cm in diameter	40
Has spread beyond the vulva	50

CLINICAL STAGING

Staging of malignancies of the vulva considers the following factors: size and extent of local spread of the primary lesion, involvement of regional lymph nodes, and the presence of metastases. Staging of vulvar malignancy depends upon tumor (T), nodal involvement (N), and metastatic involvement (M). The International Federation of Gynecology and Obstetrics (FIGO) system of classification is described.

T	Primary Tumor
T1	Tumor confined to the vulva—2 cm or less in larger diameter
T2	Tumor confined to the vulva—more than 2 cm in diameter
T3	Tumor of any size with adjacent spread to the urethra and/or vagina and/or perineum and/or anus
T4	Tumor of any size infiltrating the bladder mucosa and/or the rectum mucosa, or both, including the upper part of the urethra mucosa and/or fixed to the bone

N	Regional Lymph Nodes
N0	No nodes palpable
N1	Nodes palpable in either groin, not enlarged, mobile (not clinically suspicious of neoplasm)
N2	Nodes palpable in either one or both groins, enlarged, firm, and mobile (clinically suspicious of neoplasm)
N3	Fixed or ulcerated nodes

M	Distant Metastases
M0	No clinical metastases
M1a	Palpable deep pelvic lymph nodes
M1b	Other distant metastases

Clinical Stage Groups

Stage I	T1	N0	M0
	T1	N1	M0
Stage II	T2	N0	M0
	T2	N1	M0
Stage III	T3	N0	M0
	T3	N1	M0
	T3	N2	M0
	T1	N2	M0
	T2	N2	M0
Stage IV	T1	N3	M0
	T2	N3	M0
	T3	N3	M0
	T4	N3	M0
	T4	N0	M0
	T4	N1	M0
	T4	N2	M0

All other conditions containing M1a or M1b

PRINCIPLES OF MANAGEMENT

A. *Pretreatment evaluation*

1. Thorough *inspection* of the vulva, vagina, and cervix is necessary to determine the extent of the primary lesion and to detect multicentric lesions.

2. A *bimanual examination,* under anesthesia if necessary, is performed to assess involvement of the vagina, rectovaginal septum, and vesicovaginal septum.

3. The inguinal and femoral regions should be carefully *palpated* for the presence of suspicious lymph nodes. Several studies have shown that clinically suspicious lymph nodes contain tumor in 75 to 85 percent of patients. Clinically negative lymph nodes may contain tumor in 20 to 30 percent of patients.

4. *Cystoscopy and proctoscopy* are performed to detect invasion of the bladder or rectum in advanced cases.

5. *Chest x-ray, barium enema,* and *intravenous pyelogram* are performed on all patients. Lymphangiogram and CAT scan are performed as indicated by symptoms or suspicious physical examination.

6. Management and prognosis will then depend upon clinical staging.

B. *Squamous cell carcinoma*

1. *General principles.* Squamous cell carcinoma is the most common malignant vulvar lesion. The labia majora are the most common site of inolvement.

2. *Treatment of carcinoma in situ.* This lesion is often multicentric, therefore requiring careful examination of the entire vulva, vagina, and cervix. Therapy will depend upon the location and extent of the lesion(s). The following treatments are currently accepted.

   a) Wide local excision is generally accepted as the treatment of choice for both single and multiple lesions.

   b) Simple vulvectomy is performed if the lesion is large or multicentric.

   c) A "skinning" vulvectomy followed by skin graft may be performed to prevent vulvar distortion in the young, sexually active patient.

   d) The use of topical 5-flourouracil is currently under investigation.

3. *Treatment of invasive lesions — Stage I/Stage II.* Therapy for these lesions consists of radical vulvectomy with en bloc removal of all lymph nodes in the inguinal and femoral groups. Deep pelvic lymph nodes should be treated in the following cases.

   a) Tumor involves the inguinal or femoral lymph nodes.

   b) The lesion involves the vaginal mucosa, urethra, or anus.

   c) The primary lesion is a melanoma or adenocarcinoma. Controversy exists regarding the benefits of pelvic lymphadenectomy. If tumor-bearing lymph nodes are found, postoperative pelvic radiation is generally administered. Many authorities will not perform pelvic lymphadenectomy but will administer pelvic radiation in cases where inguinal and femoral lymph nodes are positive for tumor and in cases of adenocarcinoma and melanoma.

4. *Treatment of invasive lesions — Stage III.* The extent of surgery is individualized according to the degree of spread of the lesion. Lesions that are staged as either T1N2 or T2N2 are treated by radical vulvectomy and inguinal and femoral lymphadenectomy. Lesions involving the anus may require proctotectomy, and lesions involving the urethra may require partial urethrectomy. Preoperative pelvic radiation is often administered.

5. *Treatment of invasive lesions — Stage IV.* Pelvic exenteration may be performed if there is contiguous organ involvement and no evidence of distant metastases. If the lesion is not resectable, chemotherapy or radiation therapy may be initiated. Exenteration should be performed only if total resection of the lesion is anticipated.

C. *Melanoma*

1. *General principles.* The most common sites of melanoma are the labia minora and clitoris. This lesion may spread directly to deep pelvic lymph nodes in the absence of inguinal node involvement.

2. *Treatment.* Surgical treatment of melanoma of the vulva involves radical vulvectomy and inguinal lymphadenectomy. Deep pelvic lymph nodes must be treated. Chemotherapy may be used in cases of disseminated lesions.

D. *Adenocarcinoma*

1. *General principles.* Adenocarcinoma of the vulva is a rare lesion that usually develops in the Bartholin gland. It is mandatory that tissue be sent for pathologic evaluation in all cases of Bartholin cystectomy or marsupialization. Enlargement of the Bartholin gland in the postmenopausal period should be treated by total gland excision, since adenocarcinoma may be present.

2. *Treatment.* Surgical treatment involves radical vulvec-

      tomy with inguinal and femoral lymphadenectomy. Deep
      pelvic nodes must be treated. Chemotherapy may be used
      in the presence of disseminated lesions.

E. *Sarcoma*
   1. *General principles.* Sarcoma of the vulva is a rare lesion
      that may occur in any age group. Leiomyosarcoma is the
      most common lesion. Any solid vulvar lesion should,
      therefore, be treated by prompt total excision.
   2. *Treatment.* Surgical treatment is somewhat controversial,
      with some authorities advocating wide local excision of
      the mass and others advocating radical vulvectomy and
      lymphadenectomy. Chemotherapy or radiation therapy
      may be used for disseminated lesions.

F. *Paget's disease*
   1. *General principles.* Paget's disease of the vulva may exist
      in an intraepithelial and a locally invasive form. It is
      associated with an underlying apocrine gland carcinoma
      in 10 percent of patients.
   2. *Treatment.* Radical vulvectomy, which will remove all
      apocrine gland-containing tissue, is the treatment of
      choice. If subsequent pathologic examination reveals an
      apocrine gland carcinoma, inguinal and femoral lym-
      phadenectomy is performed.

FOLLOW-UP EVALUATION

Following treatment, the patient should be evaluated every three
months for the first two years and then every six months. A chest
x-ray should be obtained every six months. Evaluation should
include Pap smears of the cervix, vagina, and vulva. All
suspicious lesions should be immediately biopsied.

BIBLIOGRAPHY

Chung A, et al.: Malignant melanoma of the vulva, a report of 44 cases.
Obstet Gynecol 45:638, 1975

Davos I, Abell M: Soft tissue sarcomas of vulva. Gynecol Oncol 4:70,
1976

DiSaia P, Creasman W, Rich W: An alternate approach to early cancer of the vulva. Am J Obstet Gynecol 133:825, 1979

Franklin E, Rutledge F: Prognostic factors in epidermoid carcinoma of the vulva. Obstet Gynecol 37:892, 1971

Krupp P, et al.: Prognostic parameters and clinical staging criteria in epidermoid carcinoma of the vulva. Obstet Gynecol 46:84, 1975

Morley G: Infiltrative carcinoma of the vulva: results of surgical treatment. Am J Obstet Gynecol 124:874, 1976

Parker R, et al.: Operative management of early invasive epidermoid carcinoma of the vulva. Am J Obstet Gynecol 123:349, 1975

Shingleton H, et al.: Carcinoma of the vulva: influence of radical operation on cure rate. Obstet Gynecol 35:106, 1970

12

Malignant Disease of the Vagina

Jeffrey W. Ellis, M.D.

PRACTICE PRINCIPLES

Primary malignancy of the vagina is uncommon, with most lesions occurring as an extension of other pelvic malignancies. Early diagnosis is possible, since most patients develop early symptoms of irregular vaginal bleeding and purulent discharge. Exfoliative cytology and colposcopy have proven to be useful screening methods.

INCIDENCE

Primary malignancies of the vagina account for 1 to 2 percent of gynecologic malignancies.

PATHOLOGY

A. *Malignancies of the vagina are commonly secondary,* due to extension of malignant lesions of the ovary, corpus, cervix, vulva, bladder, urethra, and rectum.
B. *Primary vaginal malignancies are uncommon*
   1. *Squamous cell carcinoma* is the most common lesion and is found in 85 to 90 percent of patients.

2. *Less common lesions* are adenocarcinoma, malignant melanoma, and sarcoma (leiomyosarcoma, rhabdomyosarcoma, mixed mesodermal sarcoma, sarcoma botryoides).

SYMPTOMS

A. *In situ lesions* generally have no associated symptoms.
B. *Invasive lesions* are usually associated with bloody or purulent vaginal discharge, most often occurring in a postmenopausal woman. In advanced stages, symptoms may include pelvic pain, urinary symptoms (urgency, frequency, hematuria), and lower extremity edema.

CLINICAL COURSE

A. *Local extension* to adjacent organs will occur with advanced lesions, commonly involving cervix, vulva, rectum, bladder, and/or urethra. Involvement of the rectovaginal septum or vesicovaginal septum may lead to fistula formation.
B. *Lymphatic spread* depends upon the site of the vaginal lesion. Lesions located in the upper one third of the vagina will spread in a pattern similar to cervical malignancies. Lesions located in the lower one third of the vagina will spread in a pattern similar to vulvar malignancies. Lesions located in the middle one third may spread in either pattern.
C. *Hematogenous spread* will occur with vaginal sarcoma.

DIAGNOSIS

A. A vaginal malignancy may appear as a flat, ulcerated, or papillary lesion. Central necrosis may be present. *All suspicious lesions should be biopsied.*
B. A vaginal malignancy should be suspected if evaluation of

the cervix, endometrium, and vulva fail to reveal the source of abnormal exfoliative cytology. Colposcopy and Schiller's test using Lugol's solution will aid in identifying vaginal lesions.

C. Vaginal malignancy should be suspected in the following patients:

1. Patients exposed to nonsteroidal estrogens while in utero (diethylstilbestrol, dienestrol, hexestrol, benzestrol). An increased incidence of clear cell adenocarcinoma has been proven.
2. Patients with known or treated squamous cell carcinoma of the cervix or vulva. Independent squamous cell lesions of the vagina are commonly found in these patients.
3. Patients in any age group who complain of irregular vaginal bleeding or bloody, purulent discharge.

STAGING

A malignant lesion of the vagina should be classified as a *primary* vaginal malignancy only if the lesion is confined to the vagina and adjacent structures, excluding vulva or cervix. If the lesion involves the cervix, it should be classified as a malignancy of the cervix. If the lesion involves the vulva, it should be classified as a malignancy of the vulva. The following system for staging primary carcinoma of the vagina has been recommended by the International Federation of Gynaecology and Obstetrics (FIGO).

Preinvasive Carcinoma

- *Stage 0* — Carcinoma in situ

Invasive Carcinoma

- *Stage I* — Carcinoma limited to the vaginal wall
- *Stage II* — Carcinoma has involved subvaginal tissue but has not extended to pelvic wall
- *Stage III* — Carcinoma has extended on to pelvic wall
- *Stage IV* — Carcinoma has extended beyond true pelvis or has involved mucosa of bladder or rectum

PRINCIPLES OF MANAGEMENT

A. *Squamous Cell Carcinoma*
   1. *General principles.* Squamous cell carcinoma of the vagina is most commonly found in women 55 to 65 years old. The lesion may be located anywhere in the vagina, although the majority are located on the posterior surface of the upper one third of the vagina. Multicentric lesions are common, necessitating thorough examinations of the vagina, cervix, and vulva.
   2. *Management.* Therapy will depend upon the following factors: size, location, and extent of spread of the lesion and age and general medical condition of the patient. Management of each patient is individualized. Vaginal carcinoma may be treated by either primary radiation therapy or surgery.
      a) *Pretreatment evaluation*
         (1) Thorough inspection of the vagina, cervix, and vulva is necessary to determine the extent of the lesion and to detect multicentric lesions.
         (2) A bimanual examination, under anesthesia if necessary, is performed to assess involvement of the parametria, rectovaginal septum, and vesicovaginal septum.
         (3) Cystoscopy and proctoscopy are performed to detect invasion to the bladder and rectum.
         (4) Chest x-ray, barium enema, and intravenous pyelogram are performed on all patients. Lymphangiogram and CAT scan are performed when indicated by symptoms or by physical examination suggesting advanced disease.
      b) *Treatment of carcinoma in situ*
         (1) *Localized lesions* may be treated by wide excision.
         (2) *Multicentric or extensive lesions* may be treated by either vaginectomy or radiation.

    (3) *Topical 5-fluorouracil* is currently under investigation as primary treatment.

  c) *Treatment of invasive lesions*

    (1) *Stage I and Stage II.* Radiation therapy is the primary form of therapy in most patients because of their often advanced age and poor medical status. In patients who are considered suitable for surgery, the procedure will depend upon the site of the lesion and the most probable site of lymphatic spread.

      (a) *Lesions of the upper one third of the vagina:* radical hysterectomy, pelvic lymphadenectomy, vaginectomy.

      (b) Lesions of the mid-third of the vagina: radical hysterectomy, pelvic lymphadenectomy, radical vulvectomy, inguinal lymphadenectomy, vaginectomy.

      (c) *Lesions of the lower one third of the vagina.* radical hysterectomy, vaginectomy, radical vulvectomy, inguinal lymphadenectomy.

    (2) *Stage III and Stage IV.* Advanced lesions are generally treated with radiation. Pelvic exenteration may be performed in suitable patients in whom the tumor has involved the bladder or rectum. Distant metastases and bony involvement are absolute contraindications to exenteration.

  d) *Radiation therapy.* Primary radiation therapy requires individualization of the dosage and site of application. The proximity of the rectum and bladder will limit dosage. Rectovaginal and vesicovaginal fistulas are common complications.

  e) *Chemotherapy.* Chemotherapy has little application in the treatment of primary vaginal malignancy and is used only when all other treatment methods fail.

B. *Adenocarcinoma*

  1. Adenocarcinoma is found in 5 to 10 percent of primary

vaginal malignancies. Though it may occur in any age group, clear cell adenocarcinoma has been associated with young women who have been exposed to non-steroidal estrogens in utero.

2. *General management principles* are the same as those of squamous cell carcinoma. Local and lymphatic spread will occur in the same pattern. Radical surgery or radiation therapy may be used. Primary surgical therapy has the benefit of preserving ovarian function in young women.

C. *Sarcoma*

1. Primary sarcomas of the vagina are rare, accounting for 1 to 2 percent of vaginal malignancies. *Leiomyosarcoma* is the most common cell type. Radical surgery, radiation and chemotherapy have been employed as primary therapy depending upon the site and extent of the lesion.

2. *Sarcoma botryoides* is the most common malignant tumor of the lower genital tract in young girls. Most patients are 2 to 3 years old at the time of diagnosis. Vaginal bleeding and blood-tinged vaginal discharge are the most common symptoms. Grossly, the tumor is polypoid in appearance, arising from multiple points on the vaginal wall and cervix. Primary therapy is total pelvic exenteration and pelvic lymphadenectomy. Prognosis is poor.

D. *Melanoma*

Malignant melanoma of the vagina is rare, accounting for less than 2 percent of vaginal malignancies. General management principles are the same as those of squamous cell carcinoma.

FOLLOW-UP EVALUATIONS

A. Following therapy, the patient should be evaluated every three months for the first two years after therapy and every six months thereafter. A chest x-ray is performed every six months.

B. Suspicion of residual tumor or tumor recurrence will require biopsy and further work-up as indicated.

BIBLIOGRAPHY

Gallup P, Morley G: Carcinoma in situ of the vagina. Obstet Gynecol 46:334, 1975

Herbst A, Green T, Ulfelder H: Primary carcinoma of the vagina. Am J Obstet Gynecol 106:210, 1970

Herbst A, Ulfelder H, Poskanzer D: Adenocarcinoma of the vagina, association of maternal stilbestrol therapy with tumor appearance in young women. N Engl J Med 284:878, 1971

McGowan L: Gynecologic Oncology. New York, Appleton-Century-Crofts, 1978

Perticucci S: Diagnostic, prognostic, and therapeutic considerations in invasive carcinoma of the vagina. Obstet Gynecol 40:843, 1972

Wharton T, Rutledge F, Gallagher H, Fletcher G: Treatment of clear cell adenocarcinoma in young females. Obstet Gynecol 45:365, 1975

13

Malignant Disease of the Cervix

Guy Benrubi, M.D.

PRACTICE PRINCIPLES

Invasive cervical carcinoma, which in 1981 was diagnosed in over 20,000 women and killed over 7,000 women, is a disease for which an excellent screening test exists and for which a definite curable precursor lesion has been identified. Almost every death from this disease in the United States is a failure of public health information and health care delivery. The tools for eradication of this disease are available. Unfortunately, they are often not taken advantage of by the population at risk and are occasionally misused by medical practitioners. There has been a great decrease in the incidence of this disease. It now accounts for 30 percent of all gynecologic malignancies and is no longer the most commonly diagnosed malignancy of the female reproductive tract, having been replaced by endometrial carcinoma. The decreases in incidence and mortality are both due to the use of the Papanicolaou (Pap) cervical cytology smear. Improvements in radiotherapy technology and surgical techniques have not improved the cure rate significantly. Cervical carcinoma can become extinct if every woman at risk in this country is regularly and correctly screened.

EPIDEMIOLOGY

A. Cervical carcinoma can be thought of as a *venereal disease.* Whether a carcinogenic factor is transmitted during intercourse or risk factors for venereal disease and cervical carcinoma are fortuitously similar, the fact remains that *the woman who is most likely to develop a venereally transmitted malady is most likely to develop dysplasia and, if untreated, invasive carcinoma of the cervix.*

B. *Risk factors for cervical carcinoma*
   1. *Low socioeconomic status.*
   2. *Age at first intercourse.* A woman who first experienced sexual intercourse at age 16 has a fivefold greater chance of developing cervical carcinoma than does a woman whose first intercourse was at age 24.
   3. *Sexual activity,* including total number of coital events and total number of sexual partners. Prostitutes are the most likely candidates for developing carcinoma of the cervix. Conversely, nuns almost never do.
   4. *Viral agents.* Infection with herpes simplex type II and condyloma viruses has been implicated in carcinogenesis in the cervix. To date, data are conflicting.
   5. *Carcinogenic males.* Some male sperm may be carcinogenic. The histone:protamine ratio of the sperm may be the etiologic factor. Difficulty has been encountered in determining whether this is an independent variable, however, because carcinogenic sperm seems to be more prevalent in lower socioeconomic males.

C. *The peak incidence for caricnoma in situ is 35 years of age. The peak incidence of invasive carcinoma is 45 to 49 years of age.*

CYTOLOGY AND HISTOLOGY

A. *Squamous metaplasia*
   This is a benign process, which occurs in every woman, by which areas of the cervix that were covered by columnar

epithelium become covered by squamous epithelium. There has been controversy as to the mechanism by which this transformation is accomplished. It is probably done by the shedding of the columnar epithelium and its replacement by squamous cells, which differentiate from reserve or immature cells. This process is greatest during the adolescent and early reproductive years.

B. *Squamocolumnar junction*

This is the line at which the columnar epithelium of the endocervix comes in contact with the squamous epithelium of the exocervix.

1. During childhood the squamocolumnar (S-C) junction is found on the portio of the cervix. As the process of squamous metaplasia exerts its effects and starts replacing the columnar epithelium with squamous epithelium, the S-C junction recedes past the os and up into the endocervical canal.

2. In postmenopausal women, the S-C junction may be found very high up in the endocervical canal.

C. *Transformation zone*

1. The area of the portio and endocervical canal originally covered by columnar epithelium but now covered by squamous cells because of squamous metaplasia is called the transformation zone. It is essentially that part of the cervix between the initial squamocolumnar junction, and the current S-C junction. Its size may vary from patient to patient.

2. *All dysplasia and, therefore, all cervical cancer arise in the transformation zone.* Therefore, adequate follow-up for an abnormal Pap smear can be done only if the entire transformation zone is meticulously evaluated.

3. That early age of initial intercourse is a high risk factor and that dysplasia and carcinoma arise in the area of the cervix that has undergone transformation lead to the supposition that a carcinogen introduced by intercourse somehow interacts with the "reserve" or immature cells which are causing the transformation and leads to dysplasia and carcinoma.

D. *Atypia*

This is a cytologic situation requiring only one cell for diagnosis. An atypical cell is one in which the nucleus has different characteristics from those of the nucleus of a normal cell. In addition, its nucleus:cytoplasm ratio will be greater, as it will have a small amount of cytoplasm compared to a normal cell. A Pap smear is an examination of fixed cells on a slide. An abnormal Pap smear means that there are cells on the slide that appear atypical.

E. *Dysplasia*

A piece of cervical epithelium, when seen under the microscope, has a very orderly appearance. There are no atypical cells. The cells closest to the basement membrane look different from those at the top of the epithelium. There is a precise orientation and maturation of the layers of cells as they progress up the epithelium. *In dysplasia the cells are atypical, and the orientation and maturation of the tissue are lost.*

   1. *In mild dysplasia* the bottom third of the epithelial tissue shows the above changes. *In moderate dysplasia* two thirds of the tissue are involved, and *in severe dysplasia or carcinoma in situ* the full thickness of the epithelium shows dysplastic changes.

   2. Atypical cells shed from a dysplastic epithelium are picked up on Pap smear and result in an abnormal smear. When the pathologist reads a Pap smear as "Class II — moderate dysplasia," what he in fact is saying is, "There are atypical cells on this slide. Based on my past experience, this degree of atypia is seen in cells that are shed from a moderately dysplastic epithelium."

   3. *What must be kept in mind is that a Pap smear is a cytologic screening tool. A patient with a Class III smear may have moderate dysplasia or invasive carcinoma. However, these are hystologic diagnoses, and they cannot be definitely made until the cervix is biopsied.*

F. *Cervical intraepithelial neoplasia (CIN)*

This is new terminology for describing dysplastic changes in the cervical epithelium. It implies that mild dysplasia to invasive carcinoma is a disease continuum which, if untreated, will become invasive cancer. It is divided into three groups:

1. CIN I — corresponds to mild dysplasia.
2. CIN II — corresponds to moderate dysplasia.
3. CIN III — corresponds to severe dysplasia and carcinoma in situ (CIS).

SCREENING METHODS

A. *Dysplasia* is a 100 percent curable disease. The decrease in incidence of cervical carcinoma is due to the availability of an excellent screening method. In order to get maximum benefit for this method, it must be carried out carefully.

B. *Pap Smear Technique*
   1. *A two-slide technique* is probably best. A moist cotton swab is placed in the endocervix and is gently twisted. It is taken out of the vagina and gently rolled over the slide. The slide should be sprayed with fixative within three seconds. Then a spatula can be used to gently scrape the exocervix, and the spatula is scraped over a second slide. The second slide should then be sprayed with fixative within three seconds.
   2. The patient should be told not to douche prior to coming to the physician, and she should not be menstruating.
   3. *There is a 10 to 15 percent false-negative rate with the Pap smear* under the best of circumstances.

C. *Frequency of Pap Smear Screening*
   There is currently considerable controversy as to the proper interval between Pap smears. According to the American Cancer Society: "The Society recommends that all asymptomatic women age 20 and over, and those under 20 who are sexually active, have a Pap test annually for two negative examinations and then at least every three years from age 20 to 40 and annually thereafter."

However, the American Cancer Society qualifies this, saying that women at risk of cervical carcinoma should have more frequent Pap smears. One of the risk factors is defined as more than two sexual partners over a lifetime. It is the opinion of the author that a great many women would fall into the group at risk. Furthermore, as the Pap smear is a relatively inexpensive and nonmorbid procedure, I would recommend that an annual Pap smear be done on all women who are sexually active. Women who are not sexually active do not require annual Pap smears, although they should have an annual pelvic examination.

EVALUATION OF ABNORMAL PAP SMEARS

The best hope of preventing invasive carcinoma in a patient is to promptly and thoroughly evaluate an abnormal Pap smear. An all too frequent mistake is to repeat the Pap smear. As there is a 15 percent chance of obtaining a false-negative smear, repeating an abnormal smear may be disastrously reassuring. The steps to evaluating an abnormal smear follow.

A. *Review the smear* with the cytologist in order to understand precisely what he means by the classification of the observed abnormality. For example, if it is a Class II smear, are there only inflammatory changes, or is there atypia associated with dysplasia present on the slide? Are the atypical cells seen consistent with an adenomatous or a squamous lesion?

B. If the abnormalities are thought to be purely inflammatory, the patient can be treated with an antimicrobial drug and then have the Pap test repeated.

C. *Any smear demonstrating atypia that cannot be accounted for on the basis of inflammation must be evaluated further.*

D. *Colposcopy* is the next step in the evaluation.
   1. *An adequate colposcopy* presupposes that the colposcopist is well trained, the colposcope is functioning, and the whole transformation zone (including squamocolumnar junction) is completely and thoroughly visualized. Col-

poscopically directed biopsies of any abnormal areas are then done.

2. *If the S-C junction is not visualized or if the entire transformation zone cannot be evaluated* for whatever reason, a *cone biopsy* of the cervix under general anesthesia must be done.

3. If the colposcopically directed biopsies show a microinvasive carcinoma of the cervix, a cone biopsy must be done to completely rule out a more invasive cervical carcinoma.

E. If an abnormal Pap is not explained on the basis of the colposcopic findings or by the cone biopsy, a fractional dilatation and curettage should be done. If there are still no positive findings, a laparoscopy should be done. Occasionally, adnexal disease can cause an abnormal Pap test.

MANAGEMENT OF CERVICAL INTRAEPITHELIAL NEOPLASIA (CIN)

The first step in the management of CIN lesions is the thorough evaluation of the abnormal Pap smear, either by complete colposcopy or conization of the cervix.

A. *CIN I—mild dysplasia*
   If the lesion is focal, quite often all that is necessary is excisional biopsy under colposcopic direction. If it is more extensive, cryotherapy may be used provided the colposcopic evaluation has been adequate and the most abnormal looking areas have been biopsied. The laser has been used, but it is currently an investigational tool.

B. *CIN II—moderate dysplasia*
   This can be treated similarly to CIN I.

C. *CIN III—(severe dysplasia or CIS)*
   If the patient has completed her family, CIN III is best treated by hysterectomy, either vaginal or abdominal. If further fertility is desired, a conization is done. Under certain well-controlled situations where there is no question

that colposcopy has been done adequately, where there is confidence in the competence of the colposcopist and in the pathologist who has read the directed biopsy specimens, where the patient has been adequately informed of all the risks, and when there is no dysplasia in endocervical glands (where cyrosurgery may not destroy abnormal cells), a cyrosurgical procedure may be done.

MANAGEMENT OF INVASIVE CERVICAL CARCINOMA

A. *Histology*
   1. Ninety-five percent of cervical carcinomas are squamous. Five percent are adenocarcinoma.
   2. Pathologists now grade squamous tumors according to their *degree of differentiation*, with grade 1 being well differentiated and grade 3 poorly differentiated. Stage for stage, the grade 3 tumors have the worst prognosis, but over all, the *single most important determinant of survival is stage of disease at the time of diagnosis.*

B. *Symptoms*
   1. *Early* cervical cancers may be totally symptom free. Once the tumor has grossly invaded the cervix, the most common symptom is vaginal bleeding, especially after intercourse or vaginal douching.
   2. In more *advanced* vaginal lesions a malodorous discharge may occur. In metastatic lesions, systemic signs, such as weakness, cachexia, and shortness of breath, are all possible.

C. *Clinical presentation*
   Tumors may be *exophytic* and appear to be fungating from the cervix. Other tumors may be *excavating,* and almost the whole cervix may necrose and slough and be replaced by a crater. Still others, especially adenocarcinomas and lesions arising within the endocervical canal, may be *endophytic,* and the whole diameter of the cervix will grow.

D. *Staging*

Stage	Involvement
Stage	**Involvement**
Stage IA	Microinvasive carcinoma
Stage IB	Invasive carcinoma
Stage IB (occult)	Invasive carcinoma recognized histologically but not clinically
Stage IIA	Involvement of the vagina but not the lower third
Stage IIB	Involvement of the parametria but not to the pelvic side wall
Stage IIIA	Involvement of the lower third of the vagina
Stage IIIB	Involvement of one or both parametria to pelvic side wall or obstruction of one or both ureters on intravenous urogram
Stage IVA	Involvement of mucosa of bladder or rectum
Stage IVB	Distant metastases

The definition of microinvasive disease (stage IA) is controversial and varies from center to center. A common definition is invasion limited to 3 mm below the basement membrane with no invasion into vascular or lymphatic spaces.

E. *Therapy*

1. For years the standard therapy for cervical carcinoma was radiation therapy. With the increasing availability of trained pelvic surgeons and with the improved anesthesia, antibiotics, and ancillary care facilities in modern centers, surgery is now playing a major role in the treatment of the early lesion. The decision on which modality should be used is individualized, and it depends on the patient's age, presentation of the tumor, medical status and personal preference. When all other factors

are equal, the decision is often based on which department has the best trained personnel.

2. In broad terms, *therapy* available is as follows:

Stage	Therapy
Stage IA	Simple hysterectomy
Stage IB or IIA	Radical hysterectomy and node dissection or radiation therapy
Stage IIB	Radiation therapy
Stage IIIA	Radiation therapy
Stage IIIB	Radiation therapy
Stage IVA	(a so-called central IV lesion) Primary pelvic exenteration
Stage IVB	Individualized — with palliative radiation or palliative surgery or chemotherapy

3. *Radical hysterectomy and node dissection*

   a) The rationale for a radical hysterectomy is to remove the uterus and adequate vaginal cuff and the parametria *en bloc*. What makes the dissection delicate is the fact that the ureters run through the parametria. Therefore, they must be dissected out of their paracervical tunnel prior to removal of the specimen. A pelvic lymphadenectomy and a common iliac and para-aortic node dissection are routinely added to the radical hysterectomy. The para-aortic and common iliac node dissection is done first. The nodes are sent for frozen section. If there is tumor present, the procedure is stopped, and radiation therapy is given.

   b) *The complications of radical hysterectomy* appear early. Intraoperatively the main problem that can arise is excessive bleeding. Postoperatively the main complication is fistula formation. As the ureter is dissected out of its tunnel, it becomes denuded and part of its vascular supply is disrupted. A ureterovaginal fistula may often result. Depending on the operator and how radical his procedure is, the ureterovaginal fistula rate varies from 1 to 5 percent of all cases. A vesicovaginal fistula is also possible. The bladder becomes denervated after a radical hysterectomy, and it must be drained until it can resume normal function. In some cases this may take several months. In the author's experience, a suprapubic drain works best postoperatively.

4. *Radiation therapy*
   a) Effective in cervical carcinoma because, although squamous carcinoma is a relatively radioresistant tumor, the cervix and uterus can tolerate extremely high doses of radiation.
   b) There are many different *systems of radiation delivery*. Broadly, they combine external beam radiation with brachytherapy or intracavitary cesium implants. One of the systems used bases its dosimetry on an imaginary point in the pelvis called point A. It is defined as a point located 2 cm from the midline of the cervical canal and 2 cm. superior to the lateral vaginal fornix. There is also a point B, defined 3 cm lateral to point A. This system aims to deliver about 7,000 to 8,000 rads to point A and 5,000 to 6,000 rads to point B. This can be done with 4,000 to 5,000 rads whole pelvic radiation (i.e., every point in the pelvis receives a minimum of 4,000 to 5,000 rads) followed by a cesium implant which will deliver a further 2,000 to 3,000 rads to point A. Under such a system, the tumor dose on the cervix may approach 20,000 rads.
   c) The *complications of radiation therapy* are divided into immediate and delayed problems.
      (1) *Immediate complications* are nausea and, more commonly, diarrhea. They can be controlled by diphenoxylate (Lomotil), plus prochlorperazine (Compazine) and delay of subsequent radiation treatments.
      (2) *Long-term complications* appear from 6 to 18 months after termination of radiation. They include rectal ulcers, chronic hemorrhagic proctitis,

rectovaginal fistulas, sigmoid obstruction, small bowel (enteroentero) fistulas, hemorrhagic cystitis, and many others. Fortunately, when dealing with small tumors, the doses or radiation can be kept low, and the resulting complication rate is low. However, frequently, complications can be severe, requiring such surgical intervention as colostomy or bowel resection.

5. In the case of endophytic lesion, leading to a barrel-shaped cervix, radiation alone is not sufficient. It must be followed by a simple hysterectomy.

SURVIVAL RATES

With some reported variation between institutions, radiation therapy and surgery have identical *five-year survival rates*.

Stage	Survival Rates
Stage IA	95 to 100 percent
Stages IB and IIA	80 percent with either radiation or surgery. If the positive pelvic nodes are discovered on surgery, cure rate drops to 40 percent.
Stage IIB	50 percent
Stage IIIA or IIIB	35 percent
Stage IV	10 percent

Rarely does a patient survive if the para-aortic nodes are found to contain tumor at the start of a radical hysterectomy and node dissection, whether or not they are treated with radiation therapy.

MANAGEMENT OF RECURRENCE

A. *Distant recurrence*

In such a situation the clinician can only hope for *palliation*. Rarely is a patient with squamous cell carcinoma metastases saved. If metastatic lesions (e.g., lung, bone) cause discomfort, radiation can be directed to specific areas to attempt to reduce tumor size and thereby decrease discomfort. Chemotherapy may be used. The most active agent now available is *cis*-platinum. There has been some limited success in terms of tumor response to the use of combinations of bleomycin, methotrexate, vincristine, and mitomycin-C. Chemotherapy for this disease is less than satisfactory.

B. *Local recurrences*

Local recurrences are the most common ones encountered. Their treatment depends on the initial treatment of the lesion. If the patient was treated first with surgery, the recurrence can be treated with *radiation*. If radiation was the original treatment, reradiation is not possible as the abdominal and pelvic organs have already reached their limiting doses. In carefully selected patients, a *pelvic exenteration* can be done. This operation involves removal of the bladder, rectum, uterus, and vagina. A colostomy, ileal conduit, and, in some cases, vaginal reconstruction are done. It is an extremely morbid procedure. Prior to its initiation a careful work-up has to be done. The patient must be emotionally and physically able to withstand the operation. A metastatic work-up including liver scan, bone scan, IV urogram, barium enema, CT scan, scalene node biopsy, and skinny needle aspiration of suspicious retroperitoneal nodes must be done. If there is histologic evidence that any pelvic or para-aortic nodes have tumor, the exenteration should not be done, as these patients almost always die. If the pelvic side walls are involved with tumor, surgery cannot be done. Thus, on starting an exenteration, peritoneal surfaces in the abdomen are checked first. If there is tumor on any peritoneal surface, the operation is temporarily stopped. A node dissection is then done, and all nodes are sent for frozen section. If any are positive, the operation is stopped. Finally, if the pelvic side walls are involved with tumor, the operation is terminated. In properly selected patients, five-year survival postexenteration is 35 to 40 percent.

CONCLUSION

When all is said and done, however, the real salvation in this disease is the aggressive and thorough screening of all women at risk.

BIBLIOGRAPHY

Anderson B: Management of early cervical neoplasia. Clin Obstet Gynecol 20:815, 1977

Averette HE: Indication for radical hysterectomy. Med Opinion Rev 7:73, 1971

Barber HRK: Relative prognostic significance of preoperative and operative findings in pelvic exenteration. Surg Clin North Am 49(2):431, 1969

Beral V: Cancer of the cervix: a sexually transmitted infection? Lancet 1:1037, 1974

Boronow RC, et al.: Defining cervical microinvasive carcinoma. Contemp Obstet Gynecol 5:121, 1975

Cramer DW: The role of cervical cytology in the declining morbidity and mortality of cervical cancer. Cancer 34:2018, 1974

Creasman WT, Parker RT: Management of early cervical neoplasia. Obstet Gynecol 18:233, 1975

Creasman WT, Rutledge F, Fletcher GH: Carcinoma of the cervix associated with pregnancy. Obstet Gynecol 36:495, 1970

DiSaia PS: Surgical aspects of cervical carcinoma. Cancer 48:548, 1981

Fletcher GH, Rutledge FN: Extended field technique in the management of the cancers of the uterine cervix. Am J Roentgenol 114:116, 1972

Herbst AL: Clear cell adenocarcinoma and the current status of DES-exposed females. Cancer 48:484, 1981

Kaufman RH, Rawls WE: Herpes genitalis and its relationship to cervical cancer. Cancer J Clinicians 24:258, 1974

Liu W, Meigs JW: Radical hysterectomy and pelvic lymphadenectomy. Am J Obstet Gynecol 69:1, 1955

Lucas WE, Benirschke K, Lebhenz TB: Verrucous carcinoma of the female genital tract. Am J Obstet Gynecol 119:435, 1974

Mikuta JJ, et al.: The "problem" radical hysterectomy. Am J Obstet Gynecol 128:119, 1977

Miyamoto T, et al.: Effectiveness of a sequential combination of bleomycin and mitomycin-C on an advanced cervical cancer. Cancer 41:403, 1978

Perez CA, et al.: Irradiation alone or in combination with surgery in stages I-B and II-A carcinoma of the uterine cervix: a nonrandomized comparison. Cancer 43(3):1062, 1979

Stehman FB, et al.: Cis-Platinum in advanced gynecologic malignancy, Gynecol Oncol 7:349, 1979

Sedlis A, et al.: Microinvasive carcinoma of the uterine cervix: A clinical-pathologic study. Am J Obstet Gynecol 133:64, 1979

Stofl A, Mattingly RF: Colposcopic diagnosis of cervical neoplasia. Obstet Gynecol 41:168, 1973

14

Malignant Disease of The Corpus

Guy Benrubi, M.D.

PRACTICE PRINCIPLES

Endometrial carcinoma is the most common gynecologic malignancy. If diagnosed promptly, it is the most readily curable, with therapeutic modalities that are well tolerated by the patient. An understanding of the risk factors, premalignant conditions, staging, and available treatments is a prerequisite to proper management of the patient with this disease.

Sarcoma of the uterus is fortunately much less frequently encountered. The optimal therapy for this disease is controversial. The classification, biologic behavior, and epidemiology of the disease will be discussed in order to provide a rationale for selection of proper treatment.

ENDOMETRIAL CARCINOMA

A. *Incidence*
　　1. It is *the most common genital malignancy.* In 1981 there were an estimated 38,000 new cases and 3,100 deaths from this disease.

2. Incidence rates rose throughout the early 1970s, although they now appear to be stabilizing.

3. There was a 50 percent increase (one and one-half fold) in the incidence of endometrial carcinoma during the 1970s, despite a 30 percent hysterectomy rate in women under age 70.

4. The lifetime risk for developing this disease is 2.2 percent among whites and 1.1 percent in blacks.

5. There are currently 40 million women in the United States over age 50. This number should double in the next 15 to 20 years as the baby boom generation reaches maturity. It is obvious that the gynecologist will see more and more of this disease.

6. The median age for endometrial carcinoma is 60 years. Those women between 50 and 60 years of age are at greatest risk.

B. *Risk factors*

Obesity, nulliparity, hypertension, late menopause, diabetes, infertility, polycystic ovaries, and postmenopausal estrogen use have all been implicated as risk factors. It is difficult to differentiate between independent risk factors and concomitant ones. The conclusion that can be reached after careful review is that just as cervical carcinoma can be thought of as a venereal disease, endometrial carcinoma can be seen as an endocrinopathy.

1. *Obesity.* There is unanimous agreement among most investigators that obesity is the most important risk factor for development of endometrial carcinoma. The increased risk is three times normal for those women 20 to 50 pounds overweight and nine times normal for those women greater than 50 pounds overweight. The presumed mechanism is conversion of androstenedione to estrone by fat cells, with deleterious effect of the estrone on the endometrium. Another view is that obesity is just a reflection of a general hormonal imbalance that may have endometrial carcinoma as one of its manifestations.

2. *Hypertension.* The association between high blood pressure and endometrial carcinoma has been widely studied. From one third to three quarters of these patients have been noted to be hypertensive. Whether this is a concomitant factor, secondary to obesity, has been a difficult question to answer. A recently completed multicentric review of the literature concluded that when controlled for obesity, hypertension as a risk factor persisted to some extent.

3. *Diabetes mellitus.* The association between diabetes and endometrial carcinoma has not been confirmed. There are some studies that show up to 20 percent incidence of diabetes mellitus in patients with endometrial carcinoma versus 3 percent in controls, but its role as an independent risk factor is yet to be clearly defined.

4. *Nulliparity and infertility.* It has been epidemiologically very difficult to decide whether pregnancy bestows protection against this disease or whether the increased incidence of the disease among nulliparous women is not an additional manifestation of the previously mentioned general hormonal imbalance — an imbalance which makes these women obese, hypertensive, diabetic, and infertile. One study has shown that married nulliparous women have a higher risk of developing this disease than do unmarried women or married, parous women. This implies that infertility, rather than parity, may be the factor that is important. However, a recent study showed that the use of oral contraceptives for one year bestowed a protective effect, possibly indicating that the hormonal changes during pregnancy may be all important in preventing this disease.

5. *Early menarche and late menopause.* Women whose menarche occurred before age 12 were shown to have a 1.6-fold increase in risk for developing the disease over women who had menarche after age 12. Those women who had menopause after age 52 had 2.4 times the risk of

developing endometrial carcinoma compared to those women who experienced menopause at age 49 or younger. Other studies, however, have not confirmed these findings.

6. *Polycystic ovary syndrome.* Women with this disorder have been found to develop endometrial carcinoma at a much earlier age than the rest of the population. They account for most of the cases diagnosed before age 40. In some series, 25 to 40 percent of the women with polycystic ovaries were noted to have developed this disease. It remains to be seen whether long-term use of oral contraceptives is protective in this group of women.

7. *Postmenopausal estrogens.* Since the middle of the 1970s, there have been several retrospective studies showing that postmenopausal estrogen increases the risk of development of endometrial cancer from fourfold to ninefold The proportional increase in risk is greater for women without other risk factors than it is for women with those risk factors. However, estrogen use imparts an additive risk to those women who are obese or nulliparous. In view of the well-documented deleterious effect of estrogen, *the use of postmenopausal estrogen should follow the guidelines discussed in Chapter 22.*

8. The three risk factors other than postmenopausal estrogen use that are most clearly implicated are obesity, nulliparity, and late menopause. They are additive, so that a woman who is nulliparous, is over 50 pounds overweight, and experienced menopause after age 52 is five times more likely to develop endometrial cancer than a woman who is parous, of normal weight, and who had menopause before age 49.

C. *Precursor lesions*

Agreement is fairly unanimous that cervical dysplasia is a precursor lesion of cervical carcinoma. Though agreement is slowly being reached, there is still great controversy as to what constitutes a precancerous lesion in endometrial cancer. Many investigators agree that there is a *spectrum of disease* leading from benign to precancerous endometrial changes. They agree that the changes are due to excessive endogenous unopposed estrogen effect. The lesions are classified into *cystic hyperplasia, adenomatous (glandular) hyperplasia, atypical adenomatous hyperplasia, and carcinoma in situ.* Some consider cystic hyperplasia also an atrophic change and, therefore, not really part of this spectrum. Others never use the designation "carcinoma in situ." There is further controversy over whether adenomatous hyperplasia without atypia does or does not progress to endometrial carcinoma. Various studies have found various progression rates. These range from 5 to 40 percent progression to invasion, with obviously the most atypical lesion being the most likely to invade. The management of percursor lesions is equally controversial. What must be kept in mind, however, is the age of the patient and the histologic appearance of the lesion. The more atypical the lesion and the older the patient, the more the treatment should be surgical.

1. *Reproductive age.* If the patient desires further fertility, she can be treated by estrogen-progestin combinations in order to ensure regular endometrial shedding. These patients are anovulatory. When pregnancy is desired, it can be induced by Clomid or Pergonal. In late reproductive age or in more atypical lesions, hysterectomy is indicated.

2. *Perimenopausal women.* A dilatation and curettage should be done in order to assess the severity of the lesion. If there is moderate or severe hyperplasia, hysterectomy and bilateral salpingo-oophorectomy should be recommended. If there is mild hyperplasia, progestins can be used. One gram of Depo-Provera can be used biweekly. The endometrium should be sampled, preferably by a suction curettage (e.g., Vabra aspirator) or dilatation and curettage, after three months and again at

six months. Therapy should be continued for at least six months. Up to 20 percent of these lesions will progress despite hormonal therapy. Up to 60 percent will remit.

3. *Postmenopausal women.* The recommended treatment has been hysterectomy and bilateral salpingo-oophorectomy for any postmenopausal woman with adenomatous hyperplasia.

4. *In all women with hyperplasia,* careful evaluation of the ovaries should be done to rule out coexisting hormone-producing ovarian neoplasia.

D. *Sampling of the endometrium*

As in all cancers, the earlier the diagnosis, the more efficacious the treatment. In cervical carcinoma, an excellent screening method in the form of the Pap smear exists. No similarly easy and accurate method exists for endometrial carcinoma screening.

1. *Routine screening.* There is much controversy over the frequency and method of endometrial screening. Pap smear is inadequate for showing endometrial pathology. Four-quadrant endometrial biopsy with the Novak or Kevorkian curette is probably 90 percent effective in diagnosing precursor lesions, but it is too painful a method for screening purposes. Aspiration techniques are generally well tolerated. These yield a histologic, not a cytologic, sample and in some series have been shown to be as effective as a dilatation and curettage in identifying the presence of hyperplasia and/or carcinoma. The frequency of routine endometrial sampling has to be tailored to each patient. Those women who demonstrate many risk factors for development of endometrial carcinoma should be sampled preferably yearly. Low-risk women probably do not have to be sampled unless there is postmenopausal bleeding or an abnormal pelvic examination.

2. *Endometrial sampling in postmenopausal bleeding.* Whether the most common cause of postmenopausal

bleeding is atrophy of the endometrium or endometrial hyperplasia and carcinoma is a controversial point. Nevertheless there is agreement that *in the presence of postmenopausal bleeding, the endometrium should be sampled. If office biopsy does not show carcinoma, a fractional dilatation and curettage must be done in order to completely rule out that possibility.*

E. *Histology*

  1. Most endometrial carcinomas are *adenocarcinomas.* They are graded according to their appearance, with good correlation between grade and prognosis. *Grade 1* or well-differentiated adenocarcinomas have a glandular pattern with atypical cells. *Grade 2* or moderately differentiated tumors show a glandular pattern with some partly solid areas. *Grade 3* tumors are undifferentiated, the glandular pattern is absent, and sheets of cells are present.

  2. About 5 percent of patients with adenocarcinoma have the clear cell variety. These tend to be at more advanced stages at the time of diagnosis.

  3. In about 15 percent of patients there is benign squamous metaplasia associated with an adenocarcinoma (*adenoacanthoma*). These tumors tend to behave somewhat less aggressively, as the glandular elements are usually well differentiated.

  4. In about 12 percent of patients the tumor has both glandular and squamous elements which are malignant (*adenosquamous carcinoma).* These tend to occur in an older age group and are aggressive tumors, as the cellular elements are poorly differentiated.

  5. Another variant is the *papillary adenocarcinoma,* which has a histologic appearance similar to a serous cystadenocarcinoma. These tend to be more aggressive than the glandular tumors.

F. *Diagnosis*

  1. *The most common symptom of early endometrial car-*

cinoma is vaginal bleeding. Because early endometrial carcinoma is symptomatic, this disease is most often diagnosed in stage I and, therefore, is curable in the vast majority of cases.

2. *The most important aspect of early diagnosis is the thorough and prompt evaluation of all postmenopausal bleeding,* as described above.
3. Patients who exhibit multiple risk factors should be carefully watched in the postmenopausal years.

G. *Staging*

The International Federation of Gynaecology and Obstetrics (FIGO) classification of endometrial carcinoma follows.

Stage	Description
Stage I	The carcinoma is confined to the corpus
	Stage IA: The length of the uterine cavity is 8 cm or less.
	Stage IB: The length of the uterine cavity is more than 8 cm
	Stage I cases should be subgrouped with regard to the histologic type of adenocarcinoma as follows:
	G1: Highly differentiated adenomatous carcinoma
	G2: Differentiated adenomatous carcinoma with partly solid areas
	G3: Predominantly solid or entirely undifferentiated carcinoma
Stage II	The carcinoma involves the corpus and cervix
Stage III	The carcinoma extends outside the corpus but not outside the true pelvis (it may involve the vaginal wall or the parametrium but not the bladder or the rectum)
Stage IV	The carcinoma involves the bladder or rectum or extends outside the pelvis

H. *Treatment*
   1. *General Comments*

      What constitutes proper management of endometrial carcinoma is a question without a definitive answer. Certain principles are agreed to by most investigators.
      a) Radiation therapy alone does not cure the disease.
      b) The mainstay of therapy in stage I is total abdominal hysterectomy and bilateral salpingo-oophorectomy.
      c) Grade is a crucial prognostic factor.
      d) Size of uterus is not very significant.
      e) Depth of myometrial invasion and metastasis to pelvic and para-aortic lymph nodes are the chief determinants of recurrence.

   2. *Stage I.* The questions in the treatment of *stage I* lesions are whether to add radiation therapy to surgery, if added, whether to do it before or after surgery, whether to give whole pelvis or vaginal radiation. At the same time, the role of routine lymphadenectomy is in the process of being defined. A possible scheme of treatment for *stage I* lesion follows.
      a) *Grade 1 tumors.* The chance of lymph node metastasis is only 2 to 3 percent. Therefore, a total abdominal hysterectomy and bilateral salpingo-oophorectomy and peritoneal washing should be done. If there is no myometrial invasion or if there is only minimal (less than 50 percent) invasion, no further therapy is needed. If there is greater than 50 percent myometrial penetration, 5,000 rads whole pelvic radiation is given, and 3,000 rads surface dose by vaginal ovoids is added.
      b) *Grade 2 tumors.* The chance of lymph nodes metastasis is 10 to 15 percent. In these cases, a total abdominal hysterectomy and bilateral salpingo-oophorectomy, selective para-aortic and pelvic lymph node dissection are done. If lymph nodes are negative and there is no myometrial invasion, no further therapy is given. If there is minimal invasion with

negative nodes, vaginal radiation alone is given. If there is deep myometrial invasion or mestastasis to pelvic nodes, whole pelvic radiation, followed by vaginal radiation, is administered. If para-aortic nodes are positive, progestational or chemotherapeutic agents are added, depending on the estrogen/progesterone receptor assay of the main tumor. If a receptor assay is unavailable, progestational agents are started.

   c) *Grade 3 lesions.* A total abdominal hysterectomy and bilateral salpingo-oophorectomy, para-aortic and pelvic lymphadenectomy are done. The incidence of lymph node metastasis is 25 to 30 percent. Radiation therapy is added for the same indications as in grade 2 lesions.

   d) *Adenosquamous carcinomas* are treated as are grade 2 and 3 lesions. Those patients who have positive peritoneal cell washings are at risk for peritoneal recurrence and should be treated with either progestational agents or chemotherapy.

3. *Stage II.* For *stage II* disease, the treatment is similar to that for stage IB carcinoma of the cervix. If the patient is medically able, a radical hysterectomy can be done. If not, 4,000 to 5,000 rads whole pelvic radiation is given, followed by an intracavity radium application of approximately 2,000 to 3,000 rads to point A, followed in six weeks by an extrafascial hysterectomy.

4. *Stages III and IV.* For *stages III and IV,* therapy must be individualized. In recurrent carcinomas, the decision must be made whether to use progestational agents or chemotherapy. Progestational agents alone cause a remission in approximately one third of recurrences. There is now some evidence that the combination of progestational agents with chemotherapy may be self-defeating. The tumors that respond to progestins are those that have progesterone receptors. There is some evidence that tumors with estrogen receptors may respond poorly to chemotherapeutic drugs. Furthermore, those tumors that have estrogen receptors may respond best to Tomoxifen.

The distribution of receptors in endometrial carcinoma has been shown in at least two studies to be:

Estrogen positive	70 percent
Estrogen positive/progesterone positive	50 percent
Estrogen negative/progesterone negative	30 percent
Estrogen positive/progesterone negative	20 percent
Estrogen negative/progesterone positive	0

If these figures turn out to be valid and if the capability of receptor assay becomes widespread, endometrial carcinoma recurrence can be treated as shown.

Type	Distribution	Therapy
E−/P−	30 percent	Chemotherapy (Adriamycin and/or Cytoxan and/or *cis*-platinum)
E+/P+	40–50 percent	Progestin (Depo-Provera—1 gm IM weekly, or Megace 160 mg po daily)
E+/P−	20–30 percent	Tomoxifen

I. *Survival*
   1. *Five-year survival rates* for endometrial carcinoma are quoted as:

Stage	Survival Rate
Stage I	70–75 percent
Stage II	50 percent
Stage III	25–30 percent
Stage IV	5–10 percent

   2. *Prognostic factors* for survival in this disease are:
      a) Grade of tumor
      b) Myometrial invasion

    c) Lymph node metastasis

    d) Peritoneal cytology

3. The last three factors above are functions of histologic grade, i.e., the more undifferentiated the tumor, the more likely it is to have myometrial invasion and/or lymph node metastasis and/or peritoneal cytology positive for malignant cells.

4. In stage I disease, the patient with a grade 1 tumor with no nodal metastasis and no myometrial invasion has a 95 percent chance of being alive and disease free at five years from time of diagnosis. A patient with stage I, grade 3 disease with deep myometrial invasion and pelvic node metastasis probably has only a 20 to 30 percent chance of five-year survival. If para-aortic nodes are positive, the prognosis is even worse.

5. Between the above two extremes are all the various possible combinations that can exist with stage I disease, such as stage I, grade 1, with deep myometrial invasion and negative nodes, or stage I, grade 2, with superficial invasion and positive nodes. The important point is that five-year survival is in inverse proportion to the number of serious risk factors present.

THE UTERINE SARCOMAS

Uterine sarcomas are uncommon tumors that account for approximately 3 to 4 percent of all uterine malignancies. They are, however, very malignant in their behavior. There is little agreement among oncologists as to the behavior, spread patterns, and optimal management of this disease.

A. *Classification of uterine sarcomas*

The nomenclature for sarcomas has been ambiguous in the past, perhaps adding to the confusion as to their optimal management. The Kempson modification of Ober's classification is now the accepted nomenclature (Table 14–1).

TABLE 14–1. UTERINE SARCOMAS

Pure sarcomas

  Pure homologous

    Leiomyosarcoma

    Stromal sarcoma

    Angiosarcoma

    Fibrosarcoma

  Pure heterologous

    Rhabdomyosarcoma

    Chondrosarcoma

    Osteogenic sarcoma

    Liposarcoma

Mixed sarcomas

  Mixed homologous

  Mixed heterologous

  Mixed combined

Malignant mixed müllerian tumors (MMT)

  MMT homologous type

  MMT heterologous type

Sarcoma unclassified

Malignant lymphoma

"Pure" refers to a sarcoma made up of one cell type. "Heterolgous" refers to a sarcoma that has cells not normally found in a uterus, i.e., bone, cartilage. These probably arise from totipotential mesenchymal cells. Mixed müllerian tumors have both sarcomatous and carcinomatous elements. They arise either from totipotential müllerian cells or totipotential mesenchymal cells.

The three most common varieties of sarcomas encountered at most referral centers are *leiomyosarcomas, endometrial stromal sarcomas, and mixed müllerian tumors.* The remaining sarcomas are very rare. Their clinical behavior is not sufficiently different from the more common tumors to warrant more detailed discussion.

1. *Leiomyosarcomas.* Leiomyosarcomas are malignant smooth muscle tumors that can arise in preexisting leiomyomas or in normal myometrium.

    a) Incidence. They account for approximately *1 to 1.5 percent of all malignancies of the uterus* and, in most series, for about 20 to 30 percent of all uterine sarcomas. Their incidence is between 0.5 and 1 per 100,000 women over age 20. In most studies, the average age of patients with this disease is lower than that of patients with other sarcomas. The overall average age is 45, though a wide span from the second to the eighth decade is seen. The incidence of sarcomatous change in diagnosed leiomyomata is below 0.25 percent. The overall incidence is probably significantly less if clinically undiagnosed fibroids are taken into account.

    b) *Symptoms and diagnosis. The most common presenting symptom is vaginal bleeding,* occurring in about 80 percent of patients. Pain is a less frequent symptom, occurring in 20 percent of patients. There is no good evidence that there is a racial predilection for this disease. There may be some association with obesity and hypertension, but this is less clearly established than with endometrial carcinoma. History of prior irradiation has not been shown to be related to subsequent development of this disease. The most frequent method of diagnosis is incidental finding at hysterectomy.

2. *Endometrial stromal sarcomas*

    a) Incidence. Endometrial sarcomas are rare lesions and in most series account for approximately 10 percent of all uterine sarcomas. They are presumed to arise from the endometrial stromal cell. They comprise a continuous spectrum of lesions from relatively benign to very malignant. The terms *stromatosis* and *stromal nodule* are used to describe the more benign conditions. *Endolymphatic stromal myosis* is an intermediate entity and is malignant but behaves more indolently. The term *stromal sarcoma* is used to describe the most malignant varieties.

b) Symptoms and diagnosis. The average age at time of diagnosis is 50 to 55, but tumors have been seen in teenagers. The most common presenting symptom, as in all sarcomas, is vaginal bleeding, with pelvic pain being a less common symptom. As in leiomyosarcomas, diagnosis is most frequently made during the pathologic review of the hysterectomy specimen.

3. *Mixed müllerian tumors*

a) Incidence. Mixed müllerian tumors are now the most frequently seen sarcomas. They account for *60 to 80 percent of all sarcomas and for 2 to 4 percent of all uterine malignancies*. They have been referred to by a plethora of names, such as mesenchymal tumors, mixed mesodermal tumors, carcinosarcoma, dysontogenic tumors, and many more. It is currently believed that they arise from a totipotential mesenchymal cell located just beneath the surface epithelium.

b) Symptoms and diagnosis. The average age at the time of diagnosis is 65, and these tumors tend to occur in the post menopausal age. Vaginal bleeding is again the most frequent complaint. As these tumors tend to spread more rapidly than do leiomyosarcomas, frequently the diagnosis of malignancy can be made prior to the pathologic inspection of a hysterectomy specimen. The tumor is frequently present within the endometrial cavity, and dilatation and curettage can be a useful tool for diagnosis. Obesity, hypertension, and disorders of ovulation show some association with this tumor but, again, less than is the case with endometrial carcinomas. Previous radiation therapy for benign or malignant conditions has been implicated as, but not definitely shown to be, a factor in the development of this lesion.

B. *Treatment*

The most important determinant in the treatment of uterine sarcomas is the stage at the time of diagnosis. *Staging* is the same as that used for endometrial carcinomas. Histologic type is not an important variable in choosing treatment, and all of the above-mentioned sarcomas are treated in the same way. However, at the time of diagnosis the vast majority of leiomyosarcomas will be stage I (probably 80 percent), while mixed müllerian tumors will show a 40 to 60 percent incidence of tumor outside the uterine corpus.

1. Surgery. *The mainstay of adequate control of this disease is surgery, specifically total abdominal hysterectomy and bilateral salpingo-oophorectomy.* Radiation as a sole mode of therapy has been shown consistently to be inadequate. There are few surgical histologic studies reviewing the incidence of pelvic nodes and peri-aortic node involvement in the different stages of this disease. It is difficult to be dogmatic as to the desirability of node sampling in those cases where diagnosis has been made prior to surgery in stage I disease. A possible incidence of nodal metastasis in these cases may be 20 to 25 percent.

2. Radiation. In the treatment of disease limited to the uterus (stages I and II), there is a disagreement as to the role of radiation. No good prospective studies have been published. There are some ongoing studies that show clearly that adjuvant radiation therapy does decrease pelvic recurrence but does not significantly alter five-year survival rates.

3. Chemotherapy. The role of adjuvant chemotherapy is still not defined at this time for stage I disease.

C. *Prognosis*

Stage I patients have a five-year survival of approximately 50 percent in most series. Those that do recur do so within the first 24 to 30 months. The most frequent site of failure is a combination of pelvis, upper abdomen, and lung (45 percent). Next most common is failure in the lung and upper abdomen with no pelvic recurrence (40 percent). Isolated pelvic failure is much less frequent (10 percent). For stage III and IV disease, results are uniformly poor. Few authors describe any treatment successes in these patients. The average time of treatment failure is six months to a year. Palliative radiation and chemotherapy may be used.

BIBLIOGRAPHY

Bonte J, et al.: Hormonoprophylaxis and hormonotherapy in the treatment of endometrial adenocarcinoma by means of dioxyprogesterone acetate. Gynecol Oncol 6:60, 1978

Cohen DJ, Deppe G: Endometrial carcinoma and oral contraceptive agents. Obstet Gynecol 49:390, 1977

Cohen C, Gusberg SB: Screening for endometrial cancer. Clin Obstet Gynecol 18:27, 1975

Creasman WT, Weed JC Jr: Screening techniques in endometrial cancer. Cancer 38:436, 1976

Davies JL, et al.: A review of the risk factors for endometrial carcinoma. Obstet Gynecol Surv 36:107, 1981

Fehr PE, Prem KA: Malignancy of the uterine corpus following irradiation therapy for squamous cell carcinoma of the cervix. Am J Obstet Gynecol 119:685, 1974

Gallup D, Cordray D: Leiomyosarcoma of the uterus. Obstet Gynecol Surv 34:300, 1979

Gray LA, Christopherson WH, Hoover RN: Estrogens and endometrial carcinoma. Obstet Gynecol 49:385, 1977

Gusberg SB: Precursors of corpus carcinoma, estrogens and adenomatous hyperplasia. Am J Obstet Gynecol 54:905, 1947

Ingram JM Jr, Novak E: Endometrial carcinoma associated with feminizing ovarian tumors. Am J Obstet Gynecol 61:774, 1951

Jones HW: Treatment of adenocarcinoma of the endometrium. Obstet Gynecol Surv 30:147, 1975

Lutz MH, et al.: Endometrial carcinoma; a new prognostic significance. Gynecol Oncol 6:83, 1978

Lyon FA, Frisch MJ: Endometrial abnormalities occurring in young women on long-term sequential oral contraception. Obstet Gynecol 47:639, 1976

MacDonald PC, Siiteri PK: The relationship between extraglandular production of estrone and the occurrence of endometrial neoplasia. Gynecol Oncol 2:259, 1974

Malkasian GD, et al.: Progestrogen treatment of recurrent endometrial carcinoma. Am J Obstet Gynecol 110:15, 1971

Rutledge FN: The role of radical hysterectomy in adenocarcinoma of the endometrium. Gynecol Oncol 2:331, 1974

Salazar OM, et al.: Uterine sarcomas; analysis of failures with special emphasis on the use of adjuvant radiation therapy. Cancer 42:1152, 1978

Salazar OM, et al.: Uterine sarcomas; natural history, treatment, and prognosis. Cancer 42:1161, 1978

Silverberg SQ, Makowski EL: Endometrial carcinoma in young women taking oral contraceptives. Obstet Gynecol 46:503, 1975

Underwood PB, et al.: Carcinoma of the endometrium; radiation followed immediately by operation. Am J Obstet Gynecol 128:86, 1977

Walker AM, Jick H: Declining rates of endometrial cancer. Obstet Gynecol 56:733, 1980

Wharom MD, Phillips TL, Bagshaw MA: The role of radiation therapy in clinical stage I carcinoma of the endometrium. Am J Roentgenol 1:1081, 1976

Ziel HK, Finkle WD: Increased risk of endometrial carcinoma among users of conjugated estrogens. N Engl J Med 293:1167, 1975

15

Malignant Disease of the Fallopian Tube

Jeffrey W. Ellis, M.D.

PRACTICE PRINCIPLES

Primary malignant neoplasms of the fallopian tube are the least common malignancies of the female genital tract. Patients usually do not become symptomatic until extensive spread has occurred. There are no suitable screening methods to detect the malignancy, and the diagnosis is rarely made preoperatively.

INCIDENCE

Malignancies of the fallopian tube account for 0.2 to 0.5 percent of pelvic malignancies.

PATHOLOGY

Malignancies of the fallopian tube commonly are extensions of malignancy of either the ovary or the endometrium. The following *primary* malignancies may occur:

A. *Adenocarcinoma* is the most common lesion, with 20 percent of the tumors bilateral.

B. Less common lesions are *choriocarcinoma, malignant teratoma, mixed mesodermal tumors, lymphoma, and sarcoma.*

SYMPTOMS

The majority of tubal malignancies occur in women between the ages of 45 and 60 years. There is often a history of nulliparity and past pelvic inflammatory disease. Extensive spread often occurs before symptoms become severe enough for the patient to seek medical attention.

A. *Postmenopausal or irregular vaginal bleeding* occurs when there is discharge of bloody secretions and tumor debris from the involved fallopian tube.
B. *Watery vaginal discharge* occurs when there is release of secretions and tumor debris from the tumor mass. Colicky, unilateral abdominal pain, relieved after the vaginal discharge of a profuse, clear, yellow fluid (*hydrotubae profluens*) is a sign often considered pathognomonic.
C. *Abdominal pain* is usually vague and intermittent. Sudden, severe, unilateral pain may be due to acute distention of the involved tube.

DIAGNOSIS

There are no specific diagnostic tests for malignancy of the fallopian tube. It should be suspected during evaluation of the following:

A. *Solid adrenal mass*
B. *Abnormal Papanicolaou smear* when evaluation of the cervix, endometrium, vagina, and vulva fails to reveal the origin of the abnormal cytology.
C. *Irregular vaginal bleeding* when evaluation by inspection and curettage fails to reveal the origin of the bleeding.

CLINICAL STAGING

No specific staging system has been adopted. Many clinicians will use the International Federation of Gynaecology and Obstetrics (FIGO) staging system for ovarian malignancy.

MANAGEMENT

A. *Adenocarcinoma*
   1. *En bloc removal* of uterus, tubes, and ovaries and omentectomy for all stages.
   2. If extensive spread has occurred or if the tumor mass is large, as much of the tumor should be removed as is possible.
   3. Since the tumor will spread as does an ovarian malignancy, a thorough *staging laparotomy* should be performed.
   4. *Postoperatively* the patient should receive radiation therapy according to the protocol for ovarian malignancy. If extensive tumor remains, the patient should receive chemotherapy that is known to be effective for epithelial ovarian tumors.
   5. Overall survival is 20 to 30 percent with all stages. Survival is 50 to 60 percent if the tumor is confined to the tube.
B. *Sarcoma, malignant teratoma*
   1. En bloc removal of uterus, tubes, ovaries.
   2. Irradiation and/or chemotherapy.
C. *Choriocarcinoma*
   1. Salpingectomy
   2. Chemotherapy protocol as used with gestational trophoblastic disease (page 244).

BIBLIOGRAPHY

Boutselis J, Thompson J: Clinical aspects of primary carcinoma of the fallopian tube. Am J Obstet Gynecol 111:98, 1971

Glen J: Adenocarcinoma of the fallopian tube. Am J Obstet Gynecol 120:200, 1974

McGowan L: Gynecologic Oncology. New York, Appleton-Century-Crofts, 1978

Turunen A: Diagnosis and treatment of primary tubal carcinoma. Int J Gynecol Obstet 7:294, 1969

16

Ovarian Neoplasia
Guy Benrubi, M.D.

PRACTICE PRINCIPLES

Ovarian neoplasia can be a perplexing disease. It is often not diagnosed until far advanced because of the lack of symptoms, the difficulties involved in the physical examination of the adnexae, and the lack of biochemical or histologic/cytologic screening tests. The best hope for cure in ovarian neoplasia is early diagnosis, and the proper and prompt evaluation of the adnexal mass, once discovered, is imperative. Adequate management requires an understanding of the pathologic classification of these tumors, a knowledge of the biologic behavior of the different ovarian tumors, and a comprehension of the roles (and limitations) of the various modes of therapy, including cytoreductive surgery, radiation and chemotherapy.

EVALUATION OF THE ADNEXAL MASS

A. In the *premenarchal female*
   1. Any adnexal mass requires surgical exploration.
   2. The most likely cause would be a germ cell tumor. The possibility of malignancy, particularly dysgerminoma, is high, although the most common tumor is mature cystic teratoma (dermoid cyst).

B. During the *reproductive years*
   1. An adnexal mass may have several possible etiologies.
      a) Ovarian — such as functional cysts, neoplastic cysts, solid tumors, endometriosis.
      b) Tubal — such as abscess, hydrosalpinx, ectopic pregnancy.
      c) Uterine — such as fibroids.
      d) Bowel — such as inflammation, carcinoma, distention, adhesions.
   2. *The most common cause of adnexal mass in this age group is a functional ovarian cyst.* If the patient is having ovulatory cycles, the cyst should not persist through a normal period. If the patient is placed on oral contraceptives, the mass should resolve after 28 days. These cysts usually arise from a nonovulatory follicle or a corpus luteum and may be as large as 8 to 10 cm.
C. The normal *postmenopausal ovary* is 1.5 by 0.75 by 0.5 cm and, therefore, should not be palpable on pelvic examination.
   1. *Any adnexal mass or palpable ovary in the postmenopausal female requires exploratory surgical evaluation.*
   2. There is a 10 to 20 percent chance of finding malignancy, although the most common finding would be benign ovarian or uterine neoplasia.
D. *Proper evaluation of the adnexal mass*
   1. Complete *history,* including information on prior diagnosis of endometriosis, accurate menstrual history, symptoms of pregnancy, bowel or bladder complaints, previous pelvic surgery, prior episodes of pelvic inflammatory disease, and fertility.
   2. *Physical examination,* including estimation of size of mass, whether cystic or solid, whether fixed or mobile, tender or not, evidence of pregnancy, other abdominal signs, and the presence of such systemic signs as fever. Examination as a minimum requires meticulous abdominal, pelvic, and rectovaginal palpation.

3. If the adnexal mass is:
   a) Cystic
   b) Eight centimeters or less in diameter.
   c) Shows no evidence of inflammation or endometriosis.
   d) Not associated with an elevated beta-hCG or alpha-fetoprotein. It may be a *functional cyst,* and:
   e) The patient may be placed on oral contraceptives for one month. If the cyst resolves, no further evaluation is necessary. If it persists, laparotomy is indicated.

4. *If a functional cyst is ruled out, the patient must be explored. Prior to laparotomy:*
   a) An *intravenous urogram* is of value. It will rule out a pelvic kidney and will identify any abnormalities of the ureteral path, including prior obstruction. Pelvic calcifications, such as those occurring in a dermoid cyst, will also be identified.
   b) A *barium enema* should be done if bowel symptoms are present.
   c) *Ultrasonography* of the pelvis would be of value if an experienced consultant is available. However, in most cases it adds little to the evaluation.
   d) If the adnexal mass is immobile and fixed by what is suspected to be either a neoplastic, inflammatory, or endometriotic process, a *bowel preparation* should be taken prior to laparotomy. Then, if there is bowel injury during a difficult resection, the bowel may be primarily repaired without sequela. Furthermore, if a neoplastic lesion is encountered and a bowel resection is required for optimal debulking, it can be carried out. A successful bowel preparation involves both a mechanical and an antibacterial regimen. A typical preparatory regimen follows.

Day 1   Low residue diet, one-half bottle of magnesium citrate in the morning, tap water enema in the evening, neomycin 500 mg/erythromycin 500 mg po q6h.

Day 2   Same as Day 1 except clear liquid diet.

Day 3   Same as Day 2 except enemas till clear on
the night before surgery.

Day 4   *Day of surgery*—enemas on call to the
operating room. (Be sure to check electrolyte levels at the end of this preparation.)

CLASSIFICATION OF OVARIAN NEOPLASMS

A. *Epithelial tumors*

1. Epithelial tumors are *the most common ovarian neo-plasms,* representing 60 to 70 percent of all ovarian tumors. They can be found in all age groups but are most frequently seen in the late reproductive years. They are thought to arise from the celomic epithelium covering the ovary.

2. *Serous cystadenoma*

   a) Accounting for 25 percent of all benign ovarian neoplasms, they are usually seen between the ages of 30 and 40. Up to 20 percent of the time they occur bilaterally.

   b) Histologically, they occur in simple and papillary varieties, frequently exhibiting small calcified areas called "psammoma bodies."

   c) One of the two most common ovarian neoplasms that occur in pregnancy.

3. *Serous cystadenocarcinoma*

   a) The most common malignant ovarian tumor, account-ing for 40 percent of all ovarian malignancies and presenting bilaterally 50 percent of the time.

   b) They exist in different histologic grades from well to poorly differentiated, as well as a borderline malig-nant variety which reveals microscopically numerous papillary projections covered with two or three cell layers but distinguished by the lack of stromal in-vasion.

    c) Serous cystadenocarcinomas tend to be in a more advanced stage at the time of diagnosis than do endometroid or mucinous carcinomas. However, stage for stage and grade for grade, the behavior of all three tumors is similar.

4. *Mucinous cystadenoma*
   a) Representing 15 percent of all ovarian neoplasms, they are bilateral in 10 percent of patients. They can attain tremendous sizes, with tumors weighing 100 to 200 pounds not infrequently encountered.
   b) There is some controversy as to whether these tumors are truly epithelial in origin or whether they represent a teratoma which has developed along a single cell line.
   c) If these tumors, which are filled with gelatinous material, rupture, implantation of the benign tumor cells may occur over the peritoneal surfaces, leading to a condition known as "pseudomyxoma peritonei." This condition may necessitate repeated laparotomies for the removal of gelatinous material.

5. *Mucinous cystadenocarcinoma*
   a) They account for 10 percent of all malignant ovarian tumors, presenting bilaterally 20 percent of the time.
   b) As in the other epithelial malignancies, they range from well to poorly differentiated and may be the borderline malignant variety.

6. *Endometroid carcinoma*
   a) They represent 20 percent of all ovarian malignancies and may arise bilaterally in up to 50 percent of patients.
   b) Histologically, these tumors are similar to endometrial carcinoma of the uterus. As in other epithelial tumors, they may be well, moderately, or poorly differentiated and are also seen in a borderline malignant variety.
   c) *In 20 percent of patients they are associated with carcinoma of the endometrium.* Therefore, the uterine cavity must be carefully evaluated.

d) *Up to 30 percent of these tumors are associated with pelvic endometriosis.*

7. *Clear cell carcinoma*

   a) Once erroneously referred to as "mesonephromas," these tumors are now thought to arise from the celomic epithelium covering the ovary. They are made up of cells with clear cytoplasm and round hyperchromatic nuclei. Careful histologic analysis will, on occasion, reveal areas of serous, mucinous, or endometroid cells.

8. *Brenner tumor*

   a) They represent 0.5 percent of all ovarian tumors and arise bilaterally in 10 percent of patients. Their peak incidence is between 40 and 50 years of age. Most of these tumors are benign, but a malignant variety exists.

   b) Histologically, nests of epithelial cells with "coffeebean" nuclei are seen surrounded by strands of fibrous connective tissue.

9. *Undifferentiated carcinoma*

   a) In 10 percent of the malignant tumors of the ovary, no differentiation can be made histologically into either serous, mucinous, or endometroid type.

   b) These carcinomas are highly malignant and are usually in an advanced stage at the time of initial diagnosis.

B. *Sex chord stromal tumors*

1. Accounting for 5 to 10 percent of all ovarian tumors, these neoplasms are derived from specialized stromal cells of the ovary called "nurse cells," which surround the germ cells in the embryonic gonad. *They may be associated with excessive hormonal release, but most of these tumors are nonfunctioning. At the same time, any ovarian neoplasm may exhibit excessive hormonal release.*

2. *Granulosa tumor*

   a) Accounting for 1 to 2 percent of all ovarian tumors, they are unilateral in 90 percent of patients.

b) They present in various histologic patterns, but the constant characteristic is the presence of granulosa cells. Call-Exner bodies, which are small cavities containing esoinophilic fluid surrounded by granulosa cells, are often seen in the microfollicular histologic pattern of this tumor.

c) These tumors usually occur late in the reproductive years and postmenopausally, but they are also seen in prepubertal children. They can cause anovulatory *precocious puberty* in children. Those tumors that produce estrogen cause a *hyperplasia of the endometrium, which may be cystic or adenomatous. Up to a 20 percent incidence of endometrial carcinoma has been reported in these patients.*

d) These tumors have low malignant potential, and if they do recur they do so several years after initial diagnosis. Though most functioning granulosa tumors are estrogenic, a small percentage may actually be androgen secreting.

3. *Thecoma*
   a) These tumors may occur alone or in conjunction with granulosa cell tumors or with fibromas.
   b) They are almost always benign and unilateral.
   c) They occur more often in older women than do ganulosa tumors, and they are frequently estrogenic.

4. *Sertoli-Leydig cell tumors*
   a) These tumors represent less than 0.5 percent of all ovarian neoplasms, occur most frequently in young women (but can be seen at any age), and are unilateral in 95 percent of patients. Most are not malignant.
   b) Often referred to as arrhenoblastomas or androblastomas.
   c) These tumors have varying histologic appearances. Some are composed of only Sertoli cells arranged in tubules, other exhibit both Sertoli and Leydig cells, and still others are made up of pure Leydig cells

containing Reinke crystals (hilus cell tumors) composed of remnant embryologic hilar Leydig cells. Some are very undifferentiated and may resemble sarcomas or carcinomas.

d) Although they are commonly associated with masculinization and androgen production, many of these tumors are endocrinologically inert and some may even be estrogen secreting.

5. *Gynandroblastoma*

a) An interesting rare tumor composed of well-differentiated sex chord stromal cells, both male and female. As the cellular elements are well differentiated, the vast majority of these tumors behave benignly. When they do recur, it is frequently after several years.

b) These tumors may secrete estrogens or androgens.

C. *Germ cell tumors*

1. Comprising 15 to 20 percent of all ovarian neoplasms, these tumors arise from the primitive totipotential germ cell of the embryonic gonad. Thus, within this group are found tumors ranging from dysgerminomas, which are composed of totally undifferentiated germ cells, to embryonal carcinomas, which exhibit minimally differentiated cells, to mature cystic teratomas (dermoid cysts), which are composed of completely differentiated elements of all three germ cell layers. *Most germ cell tumors occur in children and young adults, but some varieties are seen throughout life.*

2. *Dysgerminoma*

a) Accounting for 1 to 2 percent of all ovarian neoplasms and about 5 percent of all malignant ovarian tumors, they are unilateral 85 percent of the time.

b) Made up of undifferentiated germ cells, identical to those seen in seminomas in males. Microscopically, they are composed of islands of tumor cells surrounded by connective tissue infiltrated with lymphocytes.

c) They are the most common malignant ovarian tumors associated with pregnancy and one of the most common ovarian malignancies in the first three decades of life.

d) Clinically, they are unique because they are extremely radiosensitive.

3. *Embryonal carcinoma*

a) A malignancy of children and young adults, it is an extremely rare ovarian tumor and is often seen in combination with other germ cell tumors.

b) It is composed of minimally differentiated germ cells and is identical to the tumor seen in the testes in males.

c) It has an aggressive behavior and a poor prognosis.

4. *Endodermal sinus tumor*

a) Bilateral in 50 percent of patients, it is an extremely malignant ovarian neoplasm seen primarily in the first 30 years of life.

b) Also known as *yolk sac tumor, mesoblastoma,* or *Teilum tumor,* this malignant neoplasm can be thought of as an embryonal carcinoma which has differentiated toward yolk sac structures. Histologically, some of these tumors exhibit the Schiller-Duval body (endodermal sinus), which is a narrow band of connective tissue with a capillary in the middle lined by cuboidal cells.

c) It *secretes alpha-fetoprotein (AFP),* which can be used for diagnosis or for assessment of efficacy of treatment or evidence of recurrence.

5. *Choriocarcinoma*

a) A very malignant rare tumor of children and young adults, it usually presents unilaterally.

b) This is the nongestational, germ cell variety and can be seen as an embryonal carcinoma that has differentiated toward trophoblastic structures. It is composed of cytotrophoblast and syncytiotrophoblast, and *it secretes human chorionic gonadotropin (hCG),* which can be used clinically in the same manner that AFP is used in the endodermal sinus tumor.

   c) Because hCG can stimulate the prepubertal ovary, *it may be a cause of precocious puberty.*

6. *Teratomas*

   a) These are the most differentiated germ cell tumors. Ninety-five percent of these are composed of the benign nature cystic forms also known as "dermoid cysts." The rest are immature forms.

   b) *Immature teratoma*

      (1) These are tumors of early life and are almost never seen after the reproductive years.

      (2) They are made up of germ cells that have differentiated into immature elements derived from all three layers (endoderm, mesoderm, ectoderm). If mature elements are seen, the tumor may be hard to distinguish from a mature teratoma with malignant transformation.

      (3) These tumors have a poor prognosis, though better than endodermal sinus tumors.

   c) *Solid mature teratoma*

A rare tumor, also known as "adult teratoma," it occurs unilaterally and primarily in the first two decades of life. It should be classified as "adult" teratoma only if all elements are mature, in which case this tumor is benign.

   d) *Mature cystic teratoma*

      (1) These are the most common germ cell neoplasms, accounting for 10 percent of all ovarian neoplasms and 25 percent of all childhood tumors. Most commonly referred to as *dermoid cysts* or *benign cystic teratomas,* they occur most frequently during the early reproductive years (although they can be seen throughout life) and are bilateral 15 percent of the time.

      (2) Mature elements from all three germ cell layers

can be seen, though ectodermal elements, such as hair, sebaceous glands, and other dermal appendages, predominate. Macroscopically, these are cystic tumors filled with sebaceous material.

(3) In 2 percent of patients, these tumors undergo malignant transformation. The malignant elements are usually squamous, and the condition is usually seen in postmenopausal patients.

e) *Monodermal teratoma*

(1) These tumors may be thought of as cystic teratomas where one germ cell line predominates over the others.

(2) The two most frequently mentioned are carcinoid and struma ovarii. *Ovarian carcinoids* are syndrome-producing ovarian neoplasms in one third of cases, without the requirement of liver metastasis. They are seen in slightly older age groups than are dermoid cysts. *Struma ovarii* appears microscopically exactly like mature thyroid tissue, in some cases causing a true thyrotoxicosis.

(3) Some of these tumors may be malignant and metastasize.

(4) Mucinous cystadenoma is though by some to be a monodermal teratoma.

7. *Gonadoblastoma*

a) An uncommon tumor, it is usually seen in patients with gonadal dysgenesis, the majority of these patients being phenotypic females. Gonadoblastomas usually occur in the first three decades of life.

b) They are composed of undifferentiated germ cells and sex chord stromal derivatives, such as granulosa cells or Sertoli cells.

c) They are associated with dysgerminomas in 50 percent of patients.

D. *Mesenchymal tumors*

1. These are tumors that arise from supportive and vascular

structures in the ovary, and they are similar to tumors that may arise from these structures in any organ system of the body.

   2. Examples include fibromas, leiomyomas, lipomas, lymphomas, and sarcomas.

E. *Mixed müllerian tumors*

   1. Also referred to as *mixed epithelial-mesenchymal tumors.* It is now felt that these tumors arise from the multipotential germinal epithelium lining the ovary. Thus, they can be classified as epithelial tumors.

   2. There are two varieties, both very malignant. The *carcinosarcomas* consist of adenocarcinomas with a stroma composed of sarcomatous spindle cells. *Mixed mesodermal tumors (MMT)* have a sarcomatous component that consists of malignant cartilage, striated muscle, or bone, in addition to spindle cells.

F. *Metastatic neoplasms*

   1. About 10 percent of ovarian tumors are metastatic in origin.

   2. The most common primary site is the *endometrium.* Difficulties may arise in deciding whether there is a concomitant endometroid carcinoma of the ovary and/or endometrial carcinoma of the uterus or a metastasis to the ovary from the uterus. The other two most common primary sites are the *gastrointestinal tract* and the *breast.* The *Krukenberg tumor* is one consisting of epithelial cells filled with mucin, giving a signet-ring appearance. Ninety percent of these tumors arise in the stomach. Less commonly, they arise in the colon, gallbladder, or breast.

EVALUATION OF OVARIAN NEOPLASIA

A. *Epidemiology*

   1. Sixty to seventy percent of ovarian neoplasms are epithelial.

   2. They occur at any age but most frequently in patients

over 40. Most epithelial varieties occur between ages 50 and 59.

3. Ovarian cancer accounts for 20 percent of gynecologic malignancies but 50 percent of gynecologic cancer deaths. There are approximately 17,000 new cases diagnosed per year, with approximately 11,000 yearly deaths.

4. At birth the risk of eventually having ovarian cancer is 1.5 percent.

5. Whites have a higher incidence of ovarian neoplasia than have blacks.

B. *Risk factors*

1. Denmark has the highest incidence of ovarian neoplasia in the world, six times greater than Japan, which has the lowest. The United States incidence is somewhere in the middle. Interestingly, third-generation Japanese in the United States have rates identical to the total United States population.

2. Breast cancer patients are at an excess risk for ovarian carcinoma, and vice versa.

3. There have been families studied where familial predisposition to ovarian neoplasia has been demonstrated.

C. *Diagnosis and evaluation*

1. *Benign epithelial neoplasia is usually symptomless* unless the tumor is large enough to cause pressure on the bladder or rectum or cause abdominal pain due to torsion.

2. *Malignant epithelial tumors, unfortunately, may likewise be symptomless* until far advanced. The following symptoms are common:

   a) Bloating
   b) Loss of appetite
   c) Inability to ingest usual volumes of food.
   d) Nausea and emesis
   e) Generalized distention from ascites (clothes tighter, too small).
   f) Abdominal pain
   g) Vaginal bleeding or menstrual irregularity.

    h) The classic description of the patient with advanced disease is a cachectic, middle-aged female with ascites and symptoms of intermittent small bowel obstruction. She if often hungry but can tolerate only minimal quantities of food.

  3. *Other varieties of ovarian neoplasia* may manifest symptoms as discussed, depending on their growth potential and hormonal productions.

  4. *Laboratory studies* should include:

    a) Complete blood count, electrolyte evaluation, liver function tests (including lactic dehydrogenase, which is elevated in ovarian neoplasia), clotting studies, intravenous urogram, chest x-ray, barium enema, beta-hCG, AFP, CEA.

    b) Liver and bone scans are used by some centers as baseline studies.

    c) Ultrasonography and computerized axial tomography have a use commensurate with the expertise of the consulting radiologist.

  5. *Ultimate diagnosis of ovarian neoplasia is histologic and made at laparotomy.*

D. *Staging of ovarian malignancies*

  1. *In ovarian carcinoma, staging is surgical and not clinical.*

  2. The International Federation of Gynaecology and Obsterics (FIGO) classification for staging of ovarian carcinoma follows.

Stage I	Growth limited to the ovaries.
	Stage IA: Growth limited to the ovary, no ascites.
	1. No tumor on the external surface, capsule intact.
	2. Tumor present on the external surface, or capsule(s) ruptured, or both.

Stage I (Cont.) **Stage IB:** Growth limited to both ovaries, no ascites.

      1. No tumor on the external surface, capsule intact.

      2. Tumor present on the external surface, or capsule(s) ruptured, or both.

Stage IC: Tumor either stage IA or IB but with ascites present or with positive peritoneal washings.

Stage II Growth involving one or both ovaries with pelvic extension.

Stage IIA: Extension and/or metastases to the uterus and/or tubes.

Stage IIB: Extension to other pelvic tissues.

Stage IIC: Tumor either stage IIA or stage IIB, but with ascites present or with positive peritoneal washings.

Stage III Growth involving one or both ovaries, with intraperitoneal metastases outside the pelvis, or positive retroperitoneal nodes, or both. Tumor limited to the true pelvis with histologically proven malignant extension to the small bowel or omentum.

Stage IV Growth involving one or both ovaries with distant metastases. If pleural effusion is present, there must be positive cytology to allot a

Stage IV (Cont.)

        case to stage IV. Parenchymal liver
        metastasis equals stage IV.

Special category

        Unexplored cases that are thought to
        be ovarian carcinoma.

3. *Intraoperative technique for staging.*
   Ovarian carcinoma, especially epithelial varieties,
   *spreads over peritoneal surfaces. An adequate staging
   laparotomy is easy if there is widespread disease* throughout the peritoneum. *If,* on the other hand, *the tumor is
   limited to the ovary or pelvis, a careful sequence of steps at
   laparotomy must be followed.*
   a) Cell washings must be obtained, on entering the
      abdomen, from the pelvis, both paracolic gutters,
      both subdiaphragmatic areas.
   b) All peritoneal surfaces must be inspected and pal-
      pated.
   c) The bowel should be run, and mesenteric surfaces
      examined, with any enlarged mesenteric nodes sam-
      pled.
   d) If no disease is seen outside the pelvis, random
      biopsies should be taken from the peritoneum, from
      both paracolic gutters, from both diaphragms, and
      from the bladder serosa.
   e) The surface of the liver and spleen should be pal-
      pated.
   f) Using a sterile sigmoidoscope or laparoscope, the
      diaphragms should be visualized.
   g) Omentectomy should be carried out.
   h) If the above steps are completed and still no tumor is
      identified outside the pelvis, paraaortic, common
      iliac, and external iliac retroperitoneal nodes should
      be sampled. About 15 percent of these would be
      positive in stage I disease.

THERAPY FOR OVARIAN
EPITHELIAL NEOPLASIA

A. For benign epithelial ovarian neoplasia, the mainstay of therapy is surgery. For malignant epithelial tumors, it is surgery and chemotherapy. The role of radiation therapy is still being defined.

B. *Therapy for benign epithelial ovarian neoplasia.*
   1. Pelvic cell washings should be obtained on entering the abdomen.
   2. Salpingo-oophorectomy is the next step.
   3. If conservation of the contralateral ovary is desired, a careful frozen section of the removed ovary should be done to rule out malignancy.
   4. Wedge biopsy of the remaining ovary should be done.

C. *Therapy of epithelial ovarian neoplasms demonstrating borderline malignancy.*
   1. Obtain cell washings on entering the abdomen.
   2. If fertility is not an issue, total abdominal hysterectomy and bilateral salpingo-oophorectomy should be done.
   3. If the uninvolved ovary is left behind, it must be wedge biopsied.
   4. Because of the possibility that what appears to be a borderline malignancy on frozen section may be frankly invasive on review of permanent sections, an aggressive staging as described should be done, including multiple peritoneal biopsies and washings.
   5. As the prognosis for these lesions is 95 percent or higher for ultimate cure, most centers do not now add chemotherapy as part of the initial treatment.

D. *Therapy of malignant epithelial ovarian tumors.*
   1. Treatment varies from center to center, although some general principles of treatment apply.
      a) *Surgery is the primary mode of therapy.*
      b) *All such tumors,* except for the most confined, well-differentiated ones, *must have adjuvant therapy. Most*

centers rely on chemotherapy. Some use pelvic or whole abdominal irradiation.

c) In advanced stages, *the best hope of long-term survival and for possible cure is in direct proportion to the completeness of the tumor excision at the initial laparotomy. Meticulous cytoreductive surgery,* or debulking, is crucial. (That is why bowel preparation prior to surgery is necessary.)

d) In stage III and IV disease, combination chemotherapy is more effective than use of a single agent.

e) The following is a *schema of treatment of epithelial cancers of the ovary. It must be remembered, however, that treatment in this disease must be highly individualized.*

Stage	Treatment
Stage IA1, grade 1	TAH,BSO; staging laparotomy
Stage IA1, grade 2,3 Stage IA2, all grades Stage IB Stage IC	TAH, BSO; staging laparotomy; alkylating agent for 12–18 months
Stage IIA	TAH,BSO; staging laparotomy; alkylating agent for 12–18 months
Stage IIB	TAH,BSO; staging laparotomy; debulking of all disease in pelvis, then depending on amount of residual disease, either combination or single-agent chemotherapy ± radiation
Stage III Stage IV	TAH,BSO; maximal cytoreductive surgery; combination chemotherapy

f) Agents commonly used in chemotherapy have included melphalan (Alkeran) when a single agent is used and cyclophosphamide (Cytoxan) plus doxorubicin (adriamycin) when a combination is desired. The addition of *cis*-diaminodichloroplatinum (*cis*-platinum) to the latter combination has been found to be very effective.

E. *Second-look laparotomy.*

1. If after a specified number of treatments with chemotherapy, the patient is free of clinical disease, a decision must be made whether or not to discontinue therapy. The patient undergoes a *repeat metastatic work-up,* including intravenous urogram, barium enema, liver scan, bone scan, cystoscopy, and proctoscopy.

2. *If the repeat metastatic work-up is negative, a second-look exploratory laparotomy is done.*

   a) If no tumor is seen, the maneuvers described for initial staging at laparotomy are repeated. If all biopsies and all washings are negative, chemotherapy can be stopped. If positive results are found, therapy is continued, revised as indicated.

   b) If tumor is seen, the therapeutic plan is revised as indicated by the new data.

   c) Laparoscopy can be used prior to laparotomy, and if tumor is seen, celiotomy can be avoided. However, negative laparoscopy is not sufficient evidence for absence of disease. Laparotomy must still be done prior to discontinuing chemotherapy. In some situations, even if tumor is known to be present, laparoscopy and laparotomy can be used to assess the efficacy of the drugs being given and progress being made.

F. *Survival statistics for epithelial ovarian cancers.*

1. Five-year survival statistics for epithelial ovarian cancers as well as mean survival time in months are difficult to determine accurately for these reasons.

   a) Possible understaging of what appear to be early lesions but which, in reality, are stage III tumors. For example, a grade 3 carcinoma limited to one ovary may have metastasized to the para-aortic nodes, but a retroperitoneal node dissection was not done at the initial laparotomy.

  b) Nonuniformity in the thoroughness of cytoreductive surgery at initial laparotomy.

  c) The use of new drugs and new drug combinations which have not been in use long enough to judge their potency.

2. Survival statistics

  a) For *stage I disease* the five-year survival is quoted as being 70 percent. However, in those series of patients where aggressive staging was done, survival was 90 percent in stage IA and IB. In stage IC the usual figure is 40 percent.

  b) In *stages II and III* five-year survival depends on whether or not the tumor was completely excised.

    (1) In *stage II patients with completely excised tumor* there is a 35 to 50 percent five-year survival. *If the tumor is not completely excised,* survival drops to 15 percent.

    (2) In *stage III patients where the tumor is completely excised,* 30 to 40 percent will survive for five years. *If the tumor is partially excised,* five-year survival is 5 percent.

    (3) One other subgroup of stage III is those patients who are optimally debulked. In these patients tumor is still present, but no individual tumor nodule is greater than 1.5 cm in any dimension. In several centers a 50 percent two-year survival has been obtained in these patients.

  c) *Stage IV patients* have a 5 percent five-year survival.

3. If mean survival time in months is examined, patients on a single agent who are in stage III and minimally debulked have a survival time of one year. Maximally debulked patients in the same category have a mean survival time as high as three years. Although the data are not complete, anecdotal evidence suggests that combination regimens double the mean survival time.

MANAGEMENT OF SEX CHORD STROMAL TUMORS

A. These tumors are managed in the same basic manner as are epithelial tumors. Salient differences in the management of each tumor are discussed.

B. *Granulosa cell tumors*
   1. Many of these tumors are estrogenic which may cause endometrial stimulation and/or postmenopausal bleeding. Careful evaluation of the endometrium must be done.
   2. These tumors are of low malignant potential, and recurrence may occur several years after initial therapy. When recurrence does occur, it is most often residual pelvic structures. Therefore, optimal therapy includes total abdominal hysterectomy and bilateral salpingo-oophorectomy.
   3. Disseminated or recurrent granulosa tumors respond to doxorubicin (adriamycin).
   4. Five-year survival is 70 to 90 percent.

C. *Sertoli-Leydig cell tumors*
   1. May present with increasing masculinization, including acne, hirsutism, voice change, cliteromegaly, and amenorrhea.
   2. Some may present with hyperestrogenic effects.
   3. Optimal therapy is total abdominal hysterectomy and bilateral salpingo-oophorectomy, although conservation of the contralateral ovary and the uterus is safe if the tumor is limited.
   4. These tumors have a low malignant potential.
   5. Five-year survival is 70 to 90 percent.

MANAGEMENT OF GERM CELL TUMORS OF THE OVARY

A. These tumors comprise 15 to 20 percent of all ovarian neoplasms and are most frequently seen in young women. The discussion of diagnosis, staging, therapy, and prognosis for epithelial tumors is broadly applicable to these tumors, with some specific differences dictated by the unique natures of each germ cell tumor.

B. Diagnosis
 1. *Benign cystic teratomas* can sometimes be diagnosed on pelvic x-ray because they frequently contained radiodense material, such as teeth.
 2. Benign cystic teratomas may present with acute abdominal pain because of torsion.
 3. Malignant germ cell neoplasms tend to enlarge rapidly.
 4. Certain *tumor markers* are associated with these tumors
    a) *Endodermal sinus tumor—alphafetoprotein (AFP).*
    b) *Choriocarcinoma—human chorionic gonadotropin (hCG).*
    c) *Embryonal carcinoma—* both *AFP and hCG.*
    These tumor markers can be used both in making the diagnosis and in determining persistence or recurrence of the disease. *Any patient with suspected germ cell neoplasm should have hCG and AFP assays done.*
 5. With hCG-secreting tumors in prepubertal children, anovulatory precocious puberty may result.

C. *Therapy*
 1. *Benign cystic teratoma.* Cystectomy is the only procedure necessary. As 15 percent of these tumors are bilateral, careful palpation and, probably, wedge biopsy of the contralateral ovary should be done.
 2. *Dysgerminoma.* Pure dysgerminomas are exquisitely sensitive to radiation therapy. A problem is deciding between using a conventional therapeutic modality and a more experimental one that would conserve the patient's fertility. Each case must be individualized, with parental and patient input playing a major role. Recurrences of this tumor are also radiosensitive, and 75 percent show an excellent response.
 3. *Endodermal sinus tumors, embryonal carcinomas,* and *choriocarcinoma* are best treated with *surgery, followed by combination chemotherapy.* Regimens used include

cis-platinum-bleomycin-vinblastin, vincristine-actinomy-
cin D-cyclophosphamide (VAC), methotrexate-actino-
mycin D-chlorambucil (MAC), and actinomycin D-5
fluorouracil-cyclophosphamide (ActFUCy).

4. *Immature teratomas.* As these are almost always unilateral, oophorectomy followed by VAC has shown some
success.

5. *Many germ cell tumors may contain more than one
element. Therapy should be tailored toward successful
treatment of the element with the worst prognosis.*

D. *Survival*

1. *Dysgerminoma.* Five-year survival is 70 to 90 percent.

2. *Endodermal sinus tumor.* Very poor, with minimal five-
year survival.

3. *Embryonal carcinoma.* Survival of 50 percent for stage I,
30 to 40 percent overall.

4. *Choriocarcinoma.* Very poor prognosis.

5. *Immature teratoma.* When in stage I, five-year survival
ranges from 30 to 80 percent depending on histologic
grade. Prognosis is much worse if tumor is present
outside the ovaries.

CHEMOTHERAPEUTIC AGENTS

A. Chemotherapy for ovarian cancer is a rapidly changing field.
New drugs and combinations are constantly being evaluated
in multicenter studies. Below is a classification and brief
description of those agents most often used in gynecologic
oncology.

B. *Alkylating agents*

1. These are noncyclo-dependent cytotoxic agents that work
by crosslinking strands of DNA.

2. *Melphalan (Alleran)*

a) The standard by which efficacy of other chemotherapeutic drugs or combinations is measured in the
treatment of ovarian epithelial cancers.

      b) Usually given orally, though may be given intravenously.

      c) Usually given intermittently over a four-to five-day period, once every four to six weeks.

  3. *Cyclophosphamide (Cytoxan)*

      a) It inhibits DNA synthesis and, therefore, is the only alkylator which is cycloactive.

      a) May be given as intermittent intravenous therapy or daily oral dose.

      c) It is a potent immunosuppressant.

      d) It is platelet sparing.

      e) It causes alopecia.

  4. *Chlorambucil* (Leukeran)

      a) Given orally

      b) Is relatively nontoxic

      c) May cause macroglobulinemia

C. *Antimetabolites*

  1. These are cycloactive and work by inhibiting DNA and RNA synthesis. Their action is usually in the S phase of the cell cycle. Purine and pyrimidine metabolism are primarily affected.

  2. *Methotrexate (amethopterin, MTX)*

      a) It inhibits dehydrofolate reductase, thus preventing biosynthesis of thymidylic acid, which is required for DNA and RNA synthesis.

      b) Its effects can be countered by bypassing the enzymatic inhibition by giving citrovorum factor.

      c) It can be given orally, intramuscularly, or intravenously.

      d) It is toxic to bone marrow and causes stomatitis, nausea, and vomiting.

      e) Ninety percent is excreted unchanged in the urine.

  3. *5-Fluorouracil (5-FU)*

      a) It inhibits thymidylate synthesis needed for DNA synthesis.

      b) It competes with uracil at RNA sites.

      c) It may be given intravenously, orally, or as a topical cream.

    d) It causes diarrhea, alopecia, stomatitis, and bone marrow toxicity.

    e) It is metabolized primarily by the liver.

D. *Antibiotics*

  1. These drugs are derived mainly from *Streptomyces* species. They exert most of their effect on DNA synthesis.

  2. *Actinomycin-D (dactinomycin, Cosmegen)*

    a) Inhibits DNA-dependent RNA synthesis.

    b) Excreted unchanged in bile. Therefore, it can be given even with impaired renal function, but patient must have good hepatic function.

    c) Given intravenously only. Can be very irritating to tissue if it extravasates.

    d) It has a synergistic effect with radiation on skin.

  3. *Bleomycin (Blenoxane)*

    a) Acts by causing breaks in DNA strands.

    b) Has no bone marrow toxicity.

    c) It is broken down by enzymes in all tissues of the body except skin and lungs. It is toxic, therefore, to skin and lungs and may cause fevers.

    d) If total dose administered is greater than 400 units, a high risk of pulmonary fibrosis is encountered.

  4. *Doxorubin (adriamycin)*

    a) Reacts by forming complexes with DNA that break down helix.

    b) Given intravenously.

    c) May cause necrosis and sloughing of skin if it extravasates into subcutaneous tissue.

    d) If the total lifetime dose exceeds 550 mg/sq m, the patient may develop cardiomyopathy and heart failure unresponsive to cardiotonic drugs.

    e) It is also toxic to hair, bone marrow, and gastrointestinal tract.

E. *Vinca alkaloids*

  1. These are plant alkaloids that work by arresting cell division in the metaphase of mitosis. They also affect biosynthesis of RNA.

2. *Vinblastine*
   a) Given intravenously, it can cause severe local irritation if it extravasates.
   b) Metabolized in liver
   c) Causes bone marrow depression, alopecia, peripheral neuropathy.

3. *Vincristine*
   a) Given intravenously, it may cause local irritation.
   b) Metabolized by the liver.
   c) Causes minimal marrow toxicity.
   d) May cause marked peripheral neurotoxicity, severe constipation, and alopecia.

4. *Cis-Diaminodichloroplatinum*
   a) Works by creating cross-linkages with DNA.
   b) Must be given only after aggressive hydration. Urinary output must be monitored carefully posttreatment.
   c) Renal, neural, and vestibulocochlear toxicity.

F. The present treatment for malignant neoplasms of the ovary leaves much to be desired. There are two areas where advances need desperately to be made. The first is the combination of immunotherapy and chemotherapy. The use of *Corynebacterium parvum,*and bacillus Calmette-Guérin (BCG) has had some success, but this has been far from universal. The second is the identification of a specific tumor marker for epithelial ovarian carcinomas similar to AFP or HCG. This could be used as both a screening test for ovarian cancers and as a method of follow-up after initial therapy. A Nobel prize awaits its discoverer.

BIBLIOGRAPHY
Barber HRK, Graber EA: Gynecological tumors in childhood and adolescence. Obstet Gynecol Surv 28:357, 1973

Creasman WT: The adnexal mass; its diagnosis and management. Contemp Ob/Gyn 9:45, 1977

Creasman WT, Fetter BF, Hammond CB, Parker RT: Germ cell malignancies of the ovary. Obstet Gynecol 53:226, 1979

Creasman WT, Gall SA, Blessing JA, et al.: Chemoimmunotherapy in the management of primary stage III ovarian cancer; a Gynecologic Oncology Group study. Cancer Treat Rep 63:319, 1979

Dembo AJ, et al.: The Princess Margaret Hospital study of ovarian cancer; stages I, II and asymptomatic III presentations. Cancer Treat Rep 63:249, 1979

Evans AJ III, et al.: Clinicopathologic review of 118 granulosa and 82 theca cell tumors. Obstet Gynecol 55(2):213, 1980

Freel JH, et al.: Dysgerminoma of the ovary. Cancer 43:798, 1979

Griffiths CT, Parker LM, Fuller AF: Role of cytoreductive surgical treatment in the management of advanced ovarian cancer. Cancer Treat Rep 63:235, 1979

Knapp RC, Friedman EA: Aortic lymph node metastases in early ovarian cancer. Am J Obstet Gynecol 119:1013, 1974

Kurman RJ, Norris HJ: Malignant germ cell tumors of the ovary. Hum Pathol 8:551, 1977

McGowan L, et al.: The woman at risk for developing ovarian cancer. Gynecol Oncol 7:315, 1979

Meigs JV, Cass JW: Fibroma of the ovary with ascites with a report of 7 cases. Am J Obstet Gynecol 33:249, 1937

Moore JG, et al.: Ovarian tumors in infancy, childhood and adolescence. Am J. Obstet. Gynecol 99:913, 1967

Omura GA, et al.: Randomized trial of melphalon versus melphalan plus hexamethylmelamine versus adriamycin plus cyclophosphamide in advanced ovarian adenocarcinoma. Proc Am Assoc Cancer Res 20:358, 1979

Piver MS: Incidence of subclinical metastasis in stage I and II ovarian carcinoma. Obstet Gynecol 52:100, 1978

Scully RE: Ovarian tumors; a review. Am J Pathol 87:686, 1977

Smith JP, Delgado G, Rutledge F: Second-look operation in ovarian carcinoma. Cancer 38:1438, 1976

Sotrel G, et al.: Acute leukemia in advanced ovarian carcinoma after treatment with alkylating agents. Obstet Gynecol 47:675, 1976

Spanos W: Preoperative hormonal therapy of cystic adnexal masses. Am J Obstet Gynecol 116:551, 1973

White KC: Ovarian tumors in pregnancy. Am J Obstet Gynecol 116:544, 1973

Young RC, et al.: Advanced ovarian adenocarcinoma; a prospective clinical trial of melphalan (L-PAM) versus combination chemotherapy. N Engl J Med 299:1261, 1978

17

Gestational Trophoblastic Disease

John Lurain, M.D.

PRACTICE PRINCIPLES

Growth disturbances of the human trophoblast manifest a wide range of clinical behavior, but three distinct clinical-pathologic forms are recognized: (1) hydatidiform mole; (2) invasive mole; and (3) choriocarcinoma. Approximately 15 to 20 percent of patients with hydatidiform mole will require treatment for invasive mole (10 to 17 percent) or choriocarcinoma (3 percent). Choriocarcinoma can also occur in association with term pregnancy, abortion, or ectopic pregnancy, accounting for 50 percent of cases. The overall cure rate in the treatment of gestational trophoblastic disease now exceeds 90 percent. This high success rate is the result of (1) effective use of sensitive assays for the tumor marker human chorionic gonadotropin (hCG); (2) the inherent sensitivity of trophoblastic tumors to chemotherapy; (3) the referral of patients to specialized treatment centers; (4) the identification of high-risk factors which enhance individualization of therapy; and (5) the aggressive use of combination chemotherapy, irradiation, and occasionally surgical intervention in the care of high-risk patients.

INCIDENCE

The incidence of hydatidiform mole in the United States is approximately 1 in 1,500 pregnancies. It is much more common in areas of the Orient, where the incidence is 1 in 125 pregnancies. Choriocarcinoma is reported to occur in 1 in 40,000 pregnancies.

PATHOLOGY

A. *Hydatidiform mole* is characterized by vesicular swelling of placental villi and usually the absence of an intact fetus. Microscopically, there is proliferation of the trophoblast (cytotrophoblast and syncytiotrophoblast), with varying degrees of hyperplasia and dysplasia. The chorionic villi are fluid filled and distended, and there is a scantiness of blood vessels.

B. *Invasive mole,* a benign tumor arising from a hydatidiform mole, invades the myometrium by direct extension or by venous channels and may metastasize to distant sites, most commonly to the lung and vagina. The tumor is characterized by swollen villi and accompanying trophoblast, with hyperplasia and usually dysplasia located in sites outside the cavity of the uterus.

C. *Choriocarcinoma,* a malignant disease, is characterized by abnormal trophoblastic hyperplasia and anaplasia, absence of chorionic villi, hemorrhage and necrosis, direct invasion of the myometrium, and vascular spread to the myometrium and distant sites, the most common being the lungs, vagina, brain, liver, spleen, and kidney.

SIGNS AND SYMPTOMS

A. *Hydatidiform mole*

The single outstanding clinical feature of hydatidiform mole is *uterine bleeding,* usually occurring during the sixth to sixteenth week of gestation in over 95 percent of patients.

About 50 percent of patients will have rapid *uterine enlargement* to a size greater than expected for gestational dates. Toxemia of pregnancy in the first or second trimester and hyperemesis occur in about one fourth of patients. Clinical hyperthyroidism and trophoblastic emboli with symptoms and signs of congestive heart failure and pulmonary edema occur in a small number of patients. Bilateral theca lutein cyst enlargement of the ovaries occurs in about 15 percent of patients. Fetal heart tones are usually absent. The hCG levels are usually, but not always, higher than in normal gestation; an LH/hCG level in excess of 100,000 IU/liter should arouse suspicion.

B. *Invasive mole*

After evacuation of a hydatidiform mole, symptoms and signs suggestive of invasive mole are continued uterine bleeding, a plateaued or rising hCG titer, appearance of a metastatic lesion in the lung or vagina, an enlarged irregular uterus, or bleeding from a metastatic lesion or uterine perforation.

C. *Choriocarcinoma*

Symptoms are abnormal uterine bleeding following any pregnancy event and/or bleeding from metastatic lesions.

DIAGNOSIS

A. *Hydatidiform mole* is confirmed by:
1. Spontaneous expulsion of typical molar tissue,
2. X-ray that fails to visualize a fetal skeleton after 16 weeks gestation,
3. Amniography or ultrasonography which demonstrates the so-called snow storm pattern diagnostic of hydatidiform mole. Ultrasound has virtually replaced all other means of preoperative diagnosis of hydatidiform mole.

B. *Invasive mole* is positively diagnosed by histologic identification of molar villi with hyperplastic and often anaplastic trophoblast in the myometrium or in metastatic sites. In most cases this would require removal of the uterus or metastatic lesions to obtain suitable tissue for study. Because of the excellent success with chemotherapy, those surgical procedures are seldom performed simply to establish the diagnosis. Most often the diagnosis is made clinically following hydatidiform mole evacuation, based on a rising or persistently elevated hCG titer, persistent bilateral ovarian enlargement, occasionally angiography, and/or detection of metastases to the lung or vagina. While these criteria do not distinguish between invasive mole and choriocarcinoma, they do indicate the presence of trophoblastic disease. Thus, if a pathologic diagnosis of choriocarcinoma is not made, the clinical diagnosis of invasive mole is used under these circumstances.

C. *Choriocarcinoma* is most often diagnosed by the finding of an elevated hCG titer and the detection of metastatic lesions by radiologic studies and scans of various organs. Pathologic diagnosis can sometimes be made by curettage, biopsy of metastatic lesions, or occasionally examination of hysterectomy specimens or placenta. Biopsy of a vaginal lesion is infrequently performed because of the massive and uncontrollable bleeding that may occur.

STAGING

A. *Nonmetastatic*
   1. Hydatidiform mole
   2. Invasive mole
   3. Choriocarcinoma
B. *Metastatic*
   1. *Low risk (good prognosis)*
      a) Pretreatment LH/hCG titer less than 100,000 IU/liter or β-subunit hCG titer less than 40,000 IU/liter.
      b) Duration of disease less than four months.
      c) Metastases limited to lungs or pelvis.
      d) No previous chemotherapy.

2. *High risk (poor prognosis)*
   a) Pretreatment LH/hCG titer greater than 100,000 IU/liter or β-subunit hCG titer greater than 40,000 IU/liter.
   b) Duration of disease longer than four months.
   c) Metastases to brain and/or liver.
   d) Previous failed chemotherapy.
   e) Disease following term pregnancy.

PRINCIPLES OF MANAGEMENT

A. *Hydatidiform mole*
   1. *Preoperative evaluation.* History and physical examination, CBC and platelet count, coagulation profile, serum chemistries, VDRL, thyroid panel, blood type and cross-match, hCG titer, urinalysis, chest x-ray, (PA and lateral), pelvic ultrasound, EKG.
   2. *Surgical evacuation*
      a. Suction curettage followed by sharp curettage is the preferred method of evacuation. Intravenous pitocin should be infused after starting evacuation and continued for 24 hours.
      b. Hysterectomy is an alternative to suction curettage if childbearing is complete.
   3. Follow-up hCG titers should be obtained every one to two weeks until negative, then in one month, followed by every three months for one year.
   4. Postoperative physical examination and chest x-ray should be performed in one month.
   5. Contraception should be maintained for one year.
   6. Plateauing or rising hCG titers or detection of metastases demands metastatic evaluation and treatment.
B. *Invasive mole or choriocarcinoma*
   1. *Pretreatment evaulation.* History and physical examination, CBC and platelet count, coagulation profile, serum chemistries, VDRL, thyroid panel, blood type and Rh,

urinalysis, chest x-ray (PA and lateral), chest tomograms if indicated, pelvic ultrasound, intravenous pyelogram, liver-spleen scan, brain CT scan, EKG, serum hCG level, CSF, hCG level (optional). Following this initial work-up, the patient is categorized as having nonmetastatic or metastatic disease, with further subcategorization of this latter group into low-risk and high-risk groups.

2. *Treatment of nonmetastatic gestational trophoblastic disease*

   a) Hysterectomy is used as initial treatment if there is no desire for further fertility and as secondary treatment if resistance to chemotherapy develops.

   b) Chemotherapy protocols include:
      (1) Methotrexate 15 to 25 mg daily for five days.
      (2) Actinomycin-D 10 to 13 mcg/kg IV for five days.
      (3) Intermediate-dose methotrexate 1 mg/kg IM on days 1, 3, 5, 7 with citrovorum rescue, Folinic acid 0.1 mg/kg IM on days 2, 4, 6, 8. An interval of seven to nine days between repetitive courses is utilized, toxicity permitting. During chemotherapy CBC and platelet counts are obtained every other day. No treatment course is started if the WBC is below 3,000, if the platelet count is below 100,000, or if there are significant elevations of renal or liver function studies. Treatment is continued until three consecutive normal hCG titers have been obtained and two courses have been given after the first normal hCG titer.

   c) If the hCG titer plateaus while on therapy, alternate therapy with either methotrexate or actinomycin-D, depending on which was used initially, should be used.

   d) If there is a significant elevation in hCG titer or development of metastases, the patient should be started on multiagent chemotherapy.

3. *Treatment of low-risk metastatic gestational trophoblastic disease.* Patients in this category can be treated with

single-agent chemotherapy, either methotrexate or actinomycin-D, sequentially or alternately, as noted above. Follow-up is done and treatment continued as for non-metastatic disease. Appearance of new metastases or failure of the hCG titer to drop is indication for changing therapy to multiagent chemotherapy.

4. *Treatment of high-risk metastatic gestational trophoblastic disease*

   a) *Chemotherapy* (multiagent). The standard treatment regimen has been triple therapy (MAC) employing methotrexate 15 mg IV, actinomycin-D 8 to 10 mcg/kg IV, and cyclophosphamide 3 mg/kg (maximum 200 mg) IV, each given daily for 5 days and repeated as soon as toxicity permits after 10 days without treatment. Recently, a modification of Bagshawe's multiagent regimen, which employs six drugs, has been used with good success and low toxicity as either initial therapy or after failure of MAC. Chemotherapy is continued until three consecutive normal hCG titers are reached and from two to four courses have been given after the first normal hCG titer.

   b) *Radiation therapy.* If cerebral or hepatic metastases are detected, radiation therapy (3,000 rads to brain, 2,000 rads to liver) is begun simultaneously with the start of chemotherapy.

   c) Experimental chemotherapy protocols, employing agents such as *cis*-platinum, bleomycin, VP16-213, and vinblastine, or adjuvant surgery may be required for patients with resistant disease.

5. *Follow-up*

   a) HCG titers should be obtained every two weeks for six weeks, every month for six months, every two months for six months, then every six months indefinitely.

   b) Contraception should be maintained for one year after a normal hCG titer is first achieved before pregnancy is permitted.

SUMMARY

With the utilization of active diagnosis, thorough evaluation, and proper treatment, nearly 100 percent of patients with nonmetastatic and low-risk metastatic gestational trophoblastic disease can be cured. Intensive therapy in trophoblastic disease centers has resulted in cure rates of 70 to 80 percent in patients with high-risk metastatic disease.

BIBLIOGRAPHY

Bagshawe KD: Risk and prognostic factors in trophoblastic neoplasia. Cancer 38:1373, 1976

Brewer JI, Halpern B, Torok EE: Gestational trophoblastic disease: selected clinical aspects and chorionic gonadotropin test methods. Curr Probl Cancer Vol. 3, No. 10, 1979

Brewer JI, Torok EE, Kahan BD, et al.: Gestational trophoblastic disease: origin of choriocarcinoma, invasive mole and choriocarcinoma associated with hydatidiform mole, and some immunologic aspects. Adv Cancer Res 27:89, 1978

Curry SL, Hammond CB, Tyrey L, et al.: Hydatidiform mole. Diagnosis, management, and long-term follow-up of 347 patients. Obstet Gynecol 45:41, 1975

Hammond CB, Weed JC, Currie JL: The role of operation in the current therapy of gestational trophoblastic disease. Am J Obstet Gynecol 136:844, 1980

Hammond CB, Borchert LG, Tyrey L, et al.: Treatment of metastic trophoblastic disease: good and poor prognosis. Am J Obstet Gynecol 115:4, 1973

Morrow CP, Kletzky OA, DiSaia PJ, et al.: Clinical and laboratory correlates of molar pregnancy and trophoblastic disease. Am J Obstet Gynecol 128:424, 1977

18

Diagnosis of Pregnancy
Jeffrey W. Ellis, M.D.

PRACTICE PRINCIPLES
The diagnosis of pregnancy can often be made on the basis of history and physical examination. Sensitive laboratory studies may be necessary to confirm an early gestation. The use of potentially teratogenic drugs or radiographic studies in women in the reproductive age range requires testing in any case where pregnancy is suspected. Pregnancy complicated by serious maternal disease, such as diabetes, is best managed when the diagnosis is made early.

SIGNS AND SYMPTOMS OF PREGNANCY

A. *Presumptive signs and symptoms*
   1. Cessation of menstruation
   2. Nausea and vomiting
   3. Breast changes: tenderness, enlargement, increased pigmentation
   4. Cyanosis of the vagina and cervix
   5. Frequent urination
   6. Easy fatigability
   7. Increased pigmentation of the skin
   8. Abdominal striae

*This chapter appears in both *A Clinical Manual of Obstetrics* and *A Clinical Manual of Gynecology*.

B. *Probable signs and symptoms*
   1. Abdominal enlargement
   2. Changes in the size, shape, and consistency of the uterus (enlarged, globular, soft)
   3. Softening of the cervix
   4. Painless uterine contractions
   5. Ballottement of the abdomen revealing a discrete mass (fetus)
   6. Palpation of fetal parts
C. *Positive signs of pregnancy*
   1. Auscultation of fetal heart sounds
   2. Active fetal movements perceived by an examiner
   3. Radiographic or ultrasound demonstration of a fetus

BIOLOGIC TESTS OF PREGNANCY

Biologic tests are no longer used in clinical practice. They are all based on the observation that chorionic gonadotropin in the urine of pregnant women will, when injected subcutaneously into a variety of test animals, induce ovulatory phenomena.

CLINICAL TESTS OF PREGNANCY

High doses of oral or parenteral progesterone will often induce withdrawal bleeding if pregnancy is not the cause of amenorrhea. Progesterone is no longer approved for this use, as it is implicated in teratogenicity.

RADIOLOGIC TESTS OF PREGNANCY

1. *Abdominal x-ray films* should not be used to diagnose pregnancy because of the potential hazards to the fetus.
2. *Ultrasound* can demonstrate a gestational sac 21 ± 3 days after ovulation. Fetal cardiac activity can be detected reliably 5 weeks after ovulation.

ENDOCRINE TESTS OF PREGNANCY

These tests are based on the detection of human chorionic gonadotropin (hCG) in either urine or serum. The β- subunit of hCG confers biologic and immunologic specificity.

A. *Urinary tests.* Detection of hCG is based on various immunologic reactions. The first urine voided in the morning should be used for evaluation since it is usually the most concentrated urine produced during the day. Table 18–1 summarizes currently available urine pregnancy tests. In performing the pregnancy test, instructions for use of the specific product must be followed carefully. Sensitivities of the individual tests must be noted.

TABLE 18–1. QUALITATIVE IMMUNOLOGIC (URINE) TESTS FOR PREGNANCY

Test	Source	Sensitivity* (IU)
SLIDE TESTS		
Latex Aglutination Inhibition†		
Gravindex 90	Ortho Diagnostics	3.5
Pregna β-slide	International Diagnostics	2.0
Pregnate	Fisher Scientific	2.0–4.0
Pregnosis	Roche Diagnostics	1.5–2.5
Prognosticon Dri-dot	Organon Diagnostics	1.0–2.0
Prognosticon Slide Test	Organon Diagnostics	1.0–2.0
UCG Slide Test	Wampole Laboratories	2.0
Direct Latex Agglutination‡		
Dap Test Macro	Wampole Laboratories	2.0

(*Continued*)

TABLE 18–1. QUALITATIVE IMMUNOLOGIC (URINE) TESTS FOR PREGNANCY (Cont.)

Test	Source	Sensitivity* (IU)
TUBE TESTS		
Hemagglutination Inhibition§		
Gravindex 90	Ortho Diagnostics	0.5
Neocept	Organon Diagnostics	0.2
Pregna-β	International Diagnostics	0.4–0.8
Prognosticon Accuspheres	Organon Diagnostics	0.75–0.85
UCG-Lyphotest	Wampole Laboratories	0.5–1.0
UCG-Quik-Tube	Wampole Laboratories	1.0
UCG-Test	Wampole Laboratories	0.5–1.3
Indirect Agglutination Inhibition‖		
Placentex	Roche Diagnostics	1.0
Sensi-Tex	Roche Diagnostics	0.25

*Minimal detectable levels of hCG/ml urine.
†End points: *positive*, no agglutination; *negative*, agglutination.
‡End points: *positive*, agglutination; *negative*, no agglutination.
§End points: *positive*, red blood cells settle to the bottom of the tube and form a ring; *negative*, red blood cells agglutinate but remain in suspension.
‖End points: *positive*, milky white solution; *negative*, flocculation.

1. *False-negative results.* hCG is present in the urine but is not detected.
   a) Dilute urine (low specific gravity)
   b) The amount of hCG in the urine is below the minimum sensitivity level of the test

        c) Damaged reagents

        d) Excessive vibration (tube tests)

    2. *False-positive results*

        a) *hCG is present but the patient is not pregnant*

           (1) Trophoblastic diseases

           (2) hCG-producing ovarian tumors (choriocarcinoma)

           (3) Nontrophoblastic tumors that produce hCG (colon, pancreas, breast, lung, thyroid)

           (4) After injection of hCG to induce ovulation

        b) *Cross reactivity with high levels of LH*

           (1) Perimenopausal and postmenopausal women

           (2) After injection of substances to induce ovulation that contain LH

           (3) Normal preovulatory LH surge

        c) *Substances that interfere with the immunologic reaction*

           (1) Proteinuria

           (2) Nonspecific agglutinins in the urine

           (3) Drugs (chlorpromazine, thioridazine, trifluoperazine)

           (4) Soaps and detergents in the urine specimen containers

           (5) Blood

           (6) Bacteria

B. *Serum tests.* Detection of hCG is based on radioassay techniques. These tests may be used when greater sensitivity is required than may be obtained with urine tests. Numerous tests are currently marketed with differing sensitivities. The physician should be aware of the sensitivities of the test used in his institution. Table 18–2 summarizes several currently available radioassays.

    1. *Radioreceptor assay* (RRA)

        a) *Principle.* A bovine corpus luteum membrane is the receptor site for binding hCG.

        b) *False-negative results*

           (1) The amount of hCG in the serum is below the minimum sensitivity of the test

           (2) Defective materials

**TABLE 18–2. RADIOASSAY (SERUM/PLASMA)
TESTS FOR PREGNANCY**

Test	Source	Sensitivity* (mIU)
Beta-Tec	Wampole Laboratories	3–50
β-hCG Radioimmuno-assay Kit†	Becton Dickinson	30 (serum) 100 (urine)
Biocept-G‡	Wampole Laboratories	200
Chorio-Shure	NML Laboratories	40
Concept-7-BHCG†	Leeco Diagnostics	30 (serum) 100 (urine)
HCG-β Radioimmuno-assay Kit	BIO-RIA	<6
Preg-CG Assay	Cambridge Nuclear	40
Preg-Stat	Sereno Laboratories	25
Roche β-hCG RIA	Roche Diagnostics	6

*Minimum detectable levels of hCG/ml.
†Tests which may detect hCG in urine
‡Radioreceptor Assay

    c) *False-positive results*
        (1) High levels of LH may bind receptor sites
        (2) hCG may be detected from sources other than pregnancy
  2. *Radioimmunoassay* (RIA)
    a) *Principle.* Antibody specifically detects the presence of the β-subunit of hCG
    b) *False-negative results*
        (1) The amount of hCG in the serum is below the minimum sensitivity of the test
        (2) Defective materials

c) *False-positive results*
   (1) At lower levels of sensitivity, LH may be detected
   (2) hCG may be detected from sources other than pregnancy

BIBLIOGRAPHY

Arkin C, Noto T: A false positive immunologic pregnancy test with tubo-ovarian abscess. Am J Clin Pathol 58:314, 1972

Derman R, et al.: Early diagnosis of pregnancy. J Reprod Med 26:149, 1981

Gailani S, et al.: HCG in non-trophoblastic neoplasms. Cancer 38:1684, 1976

Hogan W, Price J: Proteinuria as a cause of false positive results in pregnancy tests, Obstet Gynecol 29:585, 1967

Marshall J, et al.: Plasma and urinary chorionic gonadotropin during early human pregnancy. Obstet Gynecol 32:760, 1968

Ravel R, et al.: Effects of certain psychotrophic drugs on immunologic pregnancy tests. Am J Obstet Gynecol 105:1222, 1969

19

Abortion

Spontaneous and Induced Abortion in the First and Second Trimester*

Charles R.B. Beckmann, M.D.
Jessica L. Thomason, M.D.

PRACTICE PRINCIPLES

The threat of loss or loss of intrauterine pregnancy is one of the most personally traumatic events that may face a couple and one of the most common clinical situations encountered by the gynecologist. The sensitive and careful management of the various presentations of abortion, salvaging the pregnancy where possible and reducing psychologic and medical morbidity in all cases, then becomes a major goal of good gynecologic care.

INTRODUCTION

Elective second-trimester abortion is a difficult topic, with great controversy in both its medical and legal aspects. Because of this, together with the fact that it is not performed as an

---

*This chapter appears in both *A Clinical Manual of Obstetrics* and *A Clinical Manual of Gynecology*.

emergency procedure and should be done in a facility where such procedures are performed regularly, limited attention will be devoted to this topic. The reader is referred to several excellent references for detailed discussion and procedural guides.[15,29,71,76] Techniques for dealing with spontaneous abortion in the second trimester, especially dilatation and evacuation and hysterotomy, are given more attention.

A. *Abortion* is the loss or termination of pregnancy prior to *viability*.
   1. If one uses the concept of viability to imply a reasonable potential for extrauterine life, present developments in neonatology cause difficulties in definition and application, especially in the second trimester.[76]
   2. An *abortus* is generally defined as:[29,76]
      a) Less than 500 gm in weight.
      b) Less than 20 weeks in gestational age, measured from the first day of the last normal menstrual period (LMP).
      c) From these data The Committee on Terminology of the American College of Obstetrics and Gynecology has proposed defining abortion as "expulsion or extraction of all or part of the placenta or membranes, without an identifiable fetus, or with a liveborn infant or a stillborn infant weighing less than 500 gm. In the absence of known weight, an estimated length of gestation of less than 20 completed weeks (139 days) calculated from the first day of the last normal menstrual period may be used."[29]

B. *Classification of abortion*[72, 73, 76]
   1. *Indication or cause*
      a) *Spontaneous.* Abortion that begins without human intervention. A "miscarriage" in lay terms.[76]
      b) *Elective (induced).* Abortion initiated by human intervention at maternal request.
      c) *Therapeutic (induced).*[76] The guidelines of the American College of Obstetrics and Gynecology for

therapeutic abortion define the conditions where abortion may be so classified.

(1) When continuation of the pregnancy may threaten the life of the woman or seriously impair her health. In determining whether or not there is such risk to health, account may be taken of the woman's total environment, actual or reasonably foreseeable.

(2) When pregnancy has resulted from rape or incest. In this case the same medical criteria should be employed in the evaluation of the patient.

(3) When continuation of the pregnancy is likely to result in the birth of a child with grave physical deformities or mental retardation.

d) *Criminal.* Termination initiated by human intervention outside an approved medical facility.

2. *Clinical presentation* (Table 19–1)

a) *Threatened abortion.* Vaginal bleeding, with or without pain, in a pregnancy before the 20th completed week where clinical judgement suggests that the pregnancy may continue.

b) *Inevitable abortion.* A clinical diagnosis in cases of vaginal bleeding and crampy lower abdominal pain, in a pregnancy before the 20th completed week, so severe that no hope for salvaging the pregnancy exists.

c) *Incomplete abortion.* Expulsion of some of the products of conception before the 20th completed week of gestation.[29]

d) *Missed abortion.* The fetus dies in utero before the 20th completed week of gestation but is retained in utero for eight weeks or more.[29]

e) *Septic Abortion.* Any infected abortion.[29]

3. *Gestational age.* Usually from the first day of the last normal menstrual period.

a) *First trimester.* Conception to 12 completed weeks. Often subdivided into early (conception to 6 weeks) and late (7 to 12 weeks).

TABLE 19–1. DIAGNOSIS AND TREATMENT OF THE ABORTIONS

Diagnosis	Threatened Abortion	Inevitable Abortion	Incomplete Abortion	Missed Abortion
SYMPTOMS				
Crampy, bi-lateral LQ pain	+/–	++	+++	+/–
Symptoms of pregnancy	+	+	+/–	Usually
Preceding amenorrhea	+	+	+	+
Vaginal bleeding	Spotting	Heavy	Heavy with clots and/or tissue	+/–
PHYSICAL EXAM				
Cervix open	Usually not	Usually	Yes	+/–
Blood from cervix	Yes (min.)	Yes	Yes	+/–
Tissue/fluid from os	No	No	Yes	+/–
Uterus soft	Yes	Yes	+/–	+/–

Uterus tender	Often	Yes	Yes	Usually not
Abdomen tender	+/−	Usually	Usually	Usually not
LABORATORY TESTS Urinary test—pregnancy	+/−	+/−	+/−	Usually neg., often positive previously
β-hCG by RIA	+	+	+	+/−
Ultrasound exam	Gestational sac if 6 weeks or more with fetal movement	Gestational sac if 6 weeks or more; +/− fetal movement; halo sign +/−	Unnecessary unless ectopic gestation or uterine anomaly suspected	Disorganized cystic or collapsed intrauterine sac; +/− fetus or placenta
TREATMENT	Observation of patient, bed rest, treatment of infection, counseling and support	Evacuation of uterine contents, counseling and support	Evacuation of uterine contents, counseling and support	Evacuation of uterine contents, counseling and support

b) *Second trimester.* Thirteen to 20 completed weeks of gestation.

FIRST-TRIMESTER ABORTION

A. *Prevalence*
1. At least 10 to 15 percent of pregnancies undergo spontaneous abortion. It is difficult to assess this accurately because of variation in definitions of abortion and their application as well as incomplete and inaccurate record keeping. Finally, with the advent of more sensitive pregnancy testing (radioimmunoassay and radioreceptor assay for human chorionic gonadotropin), it is clear that pregnancy and spontaneous loss (often subclinical) occur far more frequently than previously believed. Thus, the true spontaneous abortion rate may be two or three times that previously suggested.[11,29,75,76,78,79]
2. It is also difficult to estimate the number of elective first-trimester terminations done in the United States each year. Estimates vary, but perhaps as many as one-quarter to one-third of all pregnancies are terminated electively.[76] The repeat abortion rate may be as high as 20 percent.

B. *Etiology*
1. In early gestation, in utero demise usually precedes abortions, whereas in late pregnancy this may not be the case. *A specific etiology is often never ascertained.*[76]
2. *Associated phenomena*
   a) Pathologic ("blighted") ovum[75,76]
   b) Visible embryomal anomalies[76]
   c) Placental anomalies, either intrinsic, metabolic, or implantational[76]
   d) Chromosomal anomalies, present in one-third to one-half of spontaneous abortions.[18,75,76,85,90,96]
   e) Increased maternal age[76,85]
   f) Incompatible intrauterine environment, including

uterine anomalies and myomas, although the latter more often causes infertility rather than abortion.[76]

  g) Teratogens and mutagens (chemical and micro-biological)[76]

  h) Maternal disease (acute or chronic)[76]

  i) Laparotomy[76] (especially if performed before 16 to 20 weeks of gestational age)

  j) Trauma. Often implicated, but unless very extensive, probably plays a small part in the etiology of abortion[76]

  k) Intrauterine devices[1,30,52,76,84,95]

  l) Maternal request (elective abortion)

  m) Radiation exposure[85]

  n) Maternal alcohol use[41,51]

  o) Maternal smoking[41]

  p) Luteal dysfunction[64]

C. *Threatened abortion*

  1. Very *common.* Estimated to occur in one of three pregnancies.[76]

  2. *Symptoms*[29,76]

    a) *Vaginal bleeding (usually minimal spotting)*

      (1) A "physiologic" bleeding, analogous to the placental sign described by Hartman in monkeys, may occur in humans 2½ or 4½ weeks after conception.[43]

      (2) Evaluation for other causes of bleeding must be made, such as cervical polyps, severe vaginal infection (especially *Trichomonas*), cancer, trauma, foreign body, etc.

    b) *Crampy lower quadrant pain may or may not be present*

      (1) Multiparas may identify this as like "labor" pains.

      (2) Prognosis is worse when pain accompanies the bleeding.

  3. *Physical examination*[29,76]

    a) *Abdomen.* Usually not tender

    b) *Cervix.* Usually closed, although blood will be iden-

tified coming from the os. No signs of labor (effacement or dilatation, nor loss of tissue or fluid).
- c) *Cervical tenderness,* if present, is usually minimal.
- d) Examine for evidence of *vaginal infection* (G.C.
  culture, saline and KOH preparations and PAP
  smear).
4. *Laboratory evaluation*[76]
   - a) *Pregnancy test*
     - (1) Urinary test. Positive or negative, depending on
       gestational age
     - (2) β-hCG by radioimmunoassay. Positive
   - b) *Ultrasonography*[17,23,80]
     - (1) Gestational sac with smooth contours; absence of
       halo sign; fluid collections unassociated with preg-
       nancy may occasionally be misleading.[51A]
     - (2) If greater than six weeks' gestational age with
       fetal heart action or fetal motion on real-time
       scan.
     - (3) Be alert for evidence of trophoblastic disease,
       which may present in this manner.
   - c) Clean void urine for urinalysis and culture and sen-
     sitivity.
   - d) A continued research goal is to establish accurate
     predictions for the outcome of threatened abortion.
     The combined measurement of serum estradiol and
     use of ultrasound shows promise as such an index,[44] as
     do various ultrasound measures used alone. As yet,
     no method is uniformly accepted.[32]
5. *Treatment*[29,76]
   - a) *Bed rest* or significant restriction in activity
     - (1) Generally accepted as the most common and
       useful therapy.
     - (2) Hospitalization is rarely indicated, but may be if
       rest cannot be assured in the home.
   - b) *Treat any infection vigorously.*
   - c) Progesterone[35,65,76,87]
     - (1) Demonstrated as ineffective
     - (2) May be teratogenic

    d) Sedation
        (1) Not demonstrated as effective
        (2) May *occasionally* be appropriate if there are other
            indications concomitant to the threatened abor-
            tion that are exacerbated.
    e) *Counseling and assurance*[75]
        (1) An *extremely important* part of the therapy. *Take
            the time to talk with the patient and her partner,
            fully explain the situation, and answer all their
            questions.*
        (2) *Be sure they have means of obtaining care and or
            counsel during this time* (e.g., answering service).
    f) There is debate about the effectiveness of any mea-
       sures, the argument being that any patient having real
       threatened abortion will eventually abort.[76] Never-
       theless, therapy as indicated is appropriate.
D. *Inevitable abortion*
    1. *Symptoms*[29,76]
        a) *Excessive vaginal bleeding.* Diagnosis calls for *clinical
           judgement* based on the amount of bleeding in the
           context of the balance of the clinical situation.
        b) *Moderate to severe crampy bilateral lower-quadrant
           pain,* which a multipara may describe as "labor."
           Often associated with a sensation of pressure or
           fullness.
    2. *Physical examination*[29,76]
        a) *Abdomen.* Often tender
        b) *Cervix.* Shows signs of labor (effacement and dilata-
           tion) with excessive bleeding from the os
            (1) No tissue loss
            (2) Membranes intact (There is controversy on this
                point, with some authorities including ruptured
                membranes in this diagnosis.)
            (3) Cervical tenderness to motion
        c) Uterus remains soft, feeling "pregnant" on examina-
           tion, but is usually tender to movement.
    3. *Laboratory evaluation*
        a) *Pregnancy tests.* As in threatened abortion

    b) *Ultrasound examination*[17,23,80]

       (1) Fetal heart activity and/or fetal motion may or may not be present.

       (2) Gestational sac contour may be irregular and its diameter smaller than expected for the gestational age based on dates.

    c) Maternal blood type and Rh

  4. *Treatment*

    a) Once the *clinical judgement* that the pregnancy is beyond salvage has been made, evacuation of the uterine contents by an appropriate method is indicated.

    b) If the patient is Rh-negative, anti-Rh_o immunoglobulin should be given.[3,37,39,59,76,77]

E. *Incomplete abortion*

  1. Loss of the gestation is begun and must be completed with medical assistance as described below. (The concept of the "complete abortion," where all the products of conception are spontaneously expelled, should be discarded. All patients with incomplete abortion need surgical evacuation of the uterus to assure that there are no retained tissues.[28])

  2. *Symptoms*

    a) Severe *vaginal bleeding,* with the *passage of blood and tissue and/or amniotic fluid*

       (1) If tissue is brought with the patient, it should be sent for pathologic evaluation.

    b) *Severe bilateral lower-quadrant pain*

       (1) Often described by a multipara as labor.

       (2) There is often a sensation of fullness or pressure, with a desire to "bear down" as the process progresses.

       (3) Unilateral pain should alert the physician to the possibility of ectopic gestation.

  3. *Physical examination*

    a) *Cervix.* Open and effaced, showing active signs of "labor"[29,76]

       (1) Usually tender on palpation

    (2) Blood coming from the os, often with clots
    (3) Evidence of ruptured membranes is common.
    (4) Products of conception, either in the vaginal canal
        or protruding from the os (Fig. 19–1)
    (5) Conceptus and placenta are often expelled simul-

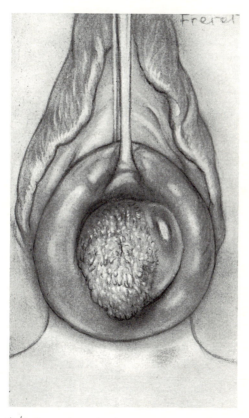

Figure 19–1. Incomplete abortion showing placental fragments extruding from the cervical os. (From Quilligan EJ, Zuspan F: Douglas-Stromme Operative Obstetrics, 4th ed. New York, Appleton, 1982, p 211.)

taneously before the 10th week, separately thereafter.

   (6) Retained tissues, especially placental tissue, may
       impede myometrial contraction, which constricts
       the placental vascular bed and causes hemostasis.
       The resulting hemorrhage may be profound, and
       appropriate precautions for evaluation and treat-
       ment of such an eventuality are indicated. Im-
       mediate removal of large pieces of protruding
       tissue at initial examination (by traction with a
       ring forceps) may reduce the bleeding signifi-
       cantly.
  b) *Uterus.* May be somewhat firmer and smaller than
     expected for the gestational age. This is because of
     loss of part of the products of conception.
  c) *Abdomen.* Usually tender
4. *Laboratory evaluation*
  a) *Pregnancy test.* As in threatened abortion
  b) *Ultrasonography.* Unnecessary unless ectopic gesta-
     tion or uterine anomaly is suspected.[63]
  c) *Blood type and Rh of mother*
  d) *Complete blood count*
  e) Other laboratory tests as clinically indicated, in-
     cluding:
     (1) Sickle cell status of black patients
     (2) Any clinical suspicion of coagulopathy warrants
         appropriate evaluation, including, minimally,
         platelet count, PT/PTT.
5. *Treatment*[29,76]
  a) *Evacuation of uterine contents*[76]
     (1) This may be done on an inpatient or outpatient
         basis, depending on facilities. More advanced
         pregnancies, and those in which there is excessive
         hemorrhage (especially with anemia or hy-
         povolemia) should be hospitalized.
     (2) If the patient is febrile, broad-spectrum antibiosis
         should be begun, before the procedure if possible,

but after appropriate cultures (aerobic and anaerobic) are taken.

(3) All tissues should be sent for pathologic examination, to identify the gestation and to screen for trophoblastic changes.[24]

b) It should be emphasized to the patient and her husband that most spontaneous first-trimester abortions are nonrecurring. *Counseling and appropriate reassurance at the time of pregnancy loss are key aspects of complete therapy.*[71,76]

c) *Dilatation, suction, and curettage*[29,75,76,93]

(1) Gross fetal or placental identification is often difficult due to maceration of the tissues by evacuation procedures or delay from the time of in utero demise.

(2) Both dilatation and curettage and suction and curettage are used in the first trimester, both in induced and spontaneous abortions. In either case, morbidity caused by uterine perforation, cervical laceration, hemorrhage, and incomplete abortion increases after the 12th week of completed gestation.

(3) Suction instead of sharp curettage has been shown to reduce the complication rate, lower operative blood loss, and shorten operative time.[7,71] The need for extensive sharp curettage (with the possibility of denuding the decidua basalis and causing hemorrhage or Asherman's syndrome) is lessened. There is little advantage, however, to a blunt rather than sharp curette, since it is the surgical technique rather than the instrument that causes most problems.

(4) Details of dilatation and suction or curettage may be found in several excellent texts, to which the reader is referred.[29] A brief outline is offered as a general guide.

(5) *Dilatation and suction or curettage.* Following

appropriate preoperative evaluation and preparation, the anesthesia of choice is administered. The
bladder should be empty, with catheterization if
necessary to ensure that the bladder is empty.[66]
Perineal shaving is unnecessary, as no decrease in
infectious or surgical morbidity in shaved patients
has been demonstrated.[29] A careful bimanual
examination under anesthesia is performed. A
weighted vaginal speculum or a Graves bivalve
speculum is placed, the cervix identified, and the
vagina and cervix cleaned with an antiseptic
solution such as povidone-iodine (Betadine). If
the patient is awake, the Graves speculum may be
more comfortable and hence preferable.[93] The
anterior lip of the cervix is then grasped with a
tenaculum, ring forceps, or Allis clamp and
pulled outward gently to lengthen and straighten
the endocervical canal and, to some extent, the
uterine cavity. Care must be taken not to place
the tenaculum too high so as to impinge on the
bladder or to pull too hard so as to pull the
tenaculum through the cervical tissue, lacerating
it. A second tenaculum may be used if significant
traction is anticipated. The uterus is then carefully
measured with a uterine sound, first within the
endocervical canal, and then part way into the
uterine cavity (Fig. 19–2). This helps determine
the need for dilatation, as well as further estimat-
ing the size and direction of the uterine cavity,
which will aid in the subsequent instrumentation.[7,53] Pratt or Hegar dilators are then *slowly*
used as needed to dilate the cervix sufficiently to
allow instrumentation and removal of the products of conception (Fig. 19–3). Laceration of the
cervix may be avoided by the slow and gentle use
of these instruments. *There is no rush* to complete
dilatation.

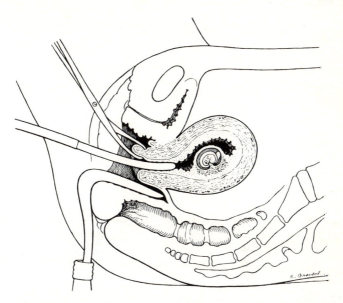

Figure 19–2. Sounding of the uterus with weighted vaginal speculum in place and anterior lip of the cervix grasped with a tenaculum. (From Quilligan EJ, Zuspan F: Douglas-Stromme Operative Obstetrics, 4th ed. New York, Appleton, 1982, p 184.)

If a vacuum suction is to be used, it is inserted, without the suction being engaged. The suction machine has previously been set up and tested to show that it maintains an appropriate amount of suction (usually 50 to 60 mm of Hg). An intravenous infusion of oxytocin is begun "piggyback" into the main intravenous line as the suction procedure is begun (20 to 40 units of oxytocin in one liter of solution is usually sufficient). This oxytocin infusion is maintained during the procedure and for a few hours afterward. Blood loss is significantly reduced and uterine tone increased,

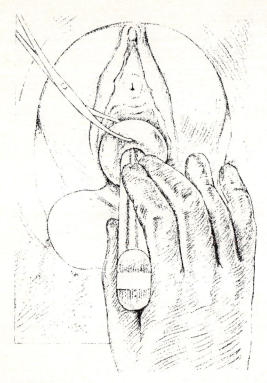

Figure 19–3. Dilatation of the cervix. (From Quilligan EJ, Zuspan F: Douglas-Stromme Operative Obstetrics, 4th ed. New York, Appleton, 1982, p 185.)

the latter decreasing the chances of uterine perforation of the pregnancy-softened uterine wall.[29,56] Suction is then applied, and the suction tip is gently revolved about the inside of the uterine cavity to remove the products of conception (Fig. 19–4). This may need to be done several times to remove all of the tissue. Sufficient repetition is usually indicated by the absence of retrieval of

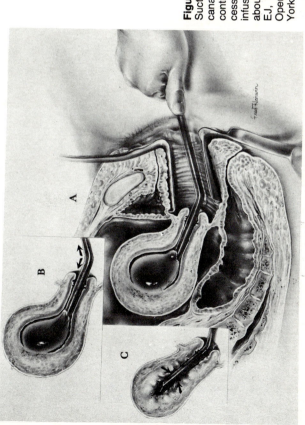

Figure 19–4. Suction curettage. A. Suction tip inserted through cervical canal. B. Suction applied, with uterine contraction due to the suction process as well as intravenous oxytocin infusion. C. Empty uterus contracted about the suction tip. (From Quilligan EJ, Zuspan F: Douglas-Stromme Operative Obstetrics, 4th ed. New York, Appleton, 1982, p 186.)

tissue, a frothy bloody return, and a "rough scratchy" ("gritty") feeling on the tip of the suction catheter against the uterine wall.[93] Sometimes, tissue pieces too large to pass the cannula are encountered (Fig. 19–5). These are easily removed with an ovum or other forceps, whereupon the suction procedure may be completed. Such pieces should be checked for routinely at the end of these procedures. The size of the suction tip chosen will vary with the gestational age, the estimated size of the uterus, and the amount of dilatation accomplished. Tips vary from 7 to 12 mm in diameter.[93]

Sharp curettage may be used to check for

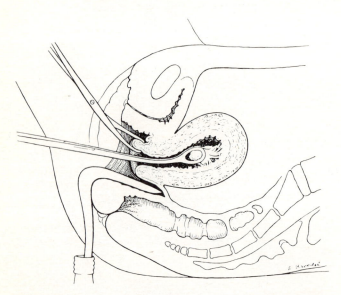

Figure 19–5. Use of ring forceps to remove large adherent products of conception. (From Quilligan EJ, Zuspan F: Douglas-Stromme Operative Obstetrics, 4th ed. New York, Appleton, 1982, p 199.)

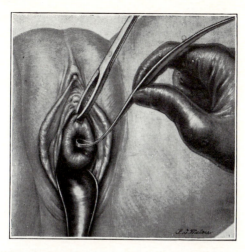

Figure 19–6. Introduction of the curette. Note that in order to avoid excessive pressure application by the curette, the instrument is held between the thumb and forefinger. (From Pritchard J, MacDonald P: Williams Obstetrics, 16th ed. New York, Appleton, 1980, p 606.)

retained products, or as a primary method of removal. In the latter case, blood loss is increased somewhat. In either case, the sharp curette is gently introduced into the uterine cavity and pulled out under mild pressure in smooth, even strokes (Fig. 19–6). Excessive pressure may lead to perforation or denuding of the basalis. To help avoid this, the curette should be held in thumb and forefinger only, so that excessive pressure cannot be exerted. After the products of conception are removed, all implementation is removed, and the sites of the traction or tenaculum insertion on the cervix are checked to ensure that there are no lacerations and that any bleeding is ceasing. *A second careful bimanual examination at the end of the procedure is essential,* to help check for completeness of procedure, trauma (as a developing hematoma), and for adnexal abnormality (as in a combined gestation).

(6) *Dilatation may be difficult,* especially in nulliparous or older patients. This is also more common in elective and some missed abortions compared with the treatment of the inevitable or incomplete abortion. *The use of laminaria tents* may help with this procedure, as well as reducing the incidence of cervical trauma or laceration.[68] Made from the stems of a seaweed (*Laminaria japonica*), laminaria are small sterile "sticks" of material that are carefully placed into the endocervical canal and then beyond so that their tips just pass the internal os but without rupturing the membranes (Fig. 19–7). They come in three sizes, small (3 to 5 mm in diameter) medium (6 to 8 mm), and large (8 to 10 mm). The size that may be tightly fit, but not forced, through the os is chosen. Over the next 8 to 12 hours the hygroscopic ("water-seeking") seaweed slowly expands (often three to five times its original diameter),[93] facilitating a slow and minimally traumatic dilatation. Often sufficient dilatation is accomplished by this method alone. If not, there is often little mechanical dilatation left to be done.[29] Concerns about an increased incidence of infection with the use of laminaria have proven unjustified.[93]

d) *Hysterotomy* may very rarely be indicated in failed dilatation or suction and curettage,[76] but not as a routine method for abortion.[69]

e) *Hysterectomy* may be indicated if there is concomitant uterine or other disease that, *of itself,* would warrant hysterectomy.[5,54,94] It is not a usual primary method of abortion.[83]

f) There are *no* routinely effective medical methods of first-trimester abortion.

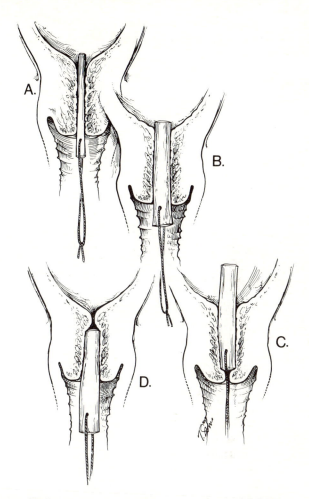

Figure 19–7. Insertion of laminaria. A. Laminaria immediately after being gently, but tightly placed such that the inner end is just past the internal os. B. The water-swollen laminaria and cervix that has been dilated as a result. C. Laminaria placed too far into the uterine cavity. Dangers here include inadvertent premature rupture of the membranes as well as difficulty in retrieval of the laminaria. D. Laminaria not inserted far enough to dilate the internal os. (From Pritchard J, McDonald P: Williams Obstetrics, 16th ed. New York, Appleton, 1980 p 604.)

g) If the patient is Rh-negative, anti-Rho immunoglobu-
lins should be given.[3,37,39,59,76,77]

h) Patients experiencing *recurrent spontaneous abortion*
should undergo vigorous evaluation, including couple
karyotyping, since the incidence of chromosomal
anomalies and other medical problems in this group is
higher than that of the general population.[18,34,75,90,96]

i) In many centers, *prophylactic antibiotics* (commonly
oral tetracycline) are given at the time of elective first-
trimester termination. The goal is to reduce the
incidence of postabortal endometritis and pelvic inflammatory disease and their possible effects on
fertility.[46,88]

j) *Elective first-trimester abortion* follows the same pre-
cepts as above. *Simultaneous sterilization* by tubal
ligation may be performed without increased risk
beyond that associated with the sterilization procedure itself.[22,83]

F. *Missed abortion*[29,76]

1. Defined as retention of a dead fetus for more than eight
weeks, during the first half of pregnancy.[76]

2. *Symptoms*

a) Initially the patient may "feel pregnant," often followed by an episode diagnosed as threatened abortion. Thereafter, amenorrhea may persist, but the
subjective signs of pregnancy may wane.[76]

b) Some patients have minimal vaginal spotting.

c) Other patients may have no symptoms and/or persist
in "feeling" pregnant.

3. *Physical examination*

a) Failure of fetus to grow in accordance with length of
amenorrhea, and often regression in uterine size as
the process progresses (absorption of amniotic fluid
plus fetal maceration).[76]

b) Rarely, minimal vaginal bleeding.

c) Cervix will not show signs of labor (effacement and/or
dilatation).

4. *Laboratory evaluation*
    a) *Pregnancy tests*
        (1) Urinary. May be negative initially or may progress from positive to negative
        (2) Radioimmunoassay for β-hCG. Falling titer, but usually positive
    b) *Ultrasonography*[17,23,80]
        (1) Disorganized cystic intrauterine sac with or without fetal pole or placental tissue identification. No fetal motion will be present.
        (2) To identify hydatidiform changes that mandate further measures.[29]
5. *Treatment*
    a) *Missed abortion will often terminate in a spontaneous incomplete abortion.*
    b) *If it does not, uterine evacuation is indicated.*
    c) Expectant management, because of the possible medical complications, as well as the emotional trauma to the patient, is no longer acceptable.
    d) Because there is often confusion about the diagnosis of pregnancy and then of in utero demise, patients are placed under great emotional strain. Emotional support and, often, expectant counseling are essential to complete therapy.[29]
G. *Criminal abortion*[29]
    1. *The diagnosis is entertained based on an index of suspicion raised by:*
        a) *Coherence and believability of the patient's history*
        b) Patient's emotional status
        c) Time and circumstances of presentation
        d) Appearance of patient and those who accompany her
    2. *Physical and laboratory examination*
        a) *Same as for incomplete abortion with the following additions:*
            (1) *Careful examination for trauma* of any kind, but especially as follows:
                (a) External genitalia

        (b) General body. Especially of abdomen and back/buttocks; watch for signs of acute abdomen associated with perforation of the uterus or viscera or of blunt trauma.

        (c) Vagina/perineum. Look especially for signs of perforation, laceration, and abrasion.

        (d) Cervix. Look especially for signs of trauma such as tenaculum puncture sites or other signs of instrumentation.

    (2) Gonorrhea, aerobic, and anaerobic *cultures* and *a Gram stain* should be taken from the endocervix.

    (3) *Supine anterior-posterior and lateral and standing* anterior-posterior *radiographs* of the abdomen and pelvis should be made to search for foreign objects or bowel perforation with a gas bubble under the diaphragm.

  3. *Treatment*

    a) *Uterine evacuation* and treatment as in incomplete abortion

    b) *Broad-spectrum antibiosis*

    c) Additional radiologic, and if necessary surgical, evaluation of any suspected trauma

    d) Whether to *report* a suspected criminal abortion depends on the philosophy of the individual physician, the rules of the health care facility, and the legal statutes governing criminal abortion.

H. *Septic abortion*[29,76]

  1. *Definition. Any infected abortion*

    a) Anaerobic and aerobic organisms are usually both involved, including streptococcus, staphylococcus, *Escherichia coli., Bacteriodies* species, *Proteus vulgaris, Neisseria gonorrhea,* and, rarely, *Clostridia* species.[13]

  2. May occur with any abortion, but more frequently seen in neglected incomplete abortion and criminal abortion.[13,76]

  3. Septic bacterial shock is a feared complication, that, if not treated vigorously, may prove fatal.

4. *Treatment.* Completion of the abortion as with incomplete abortion by appropriate means of evacuation, medical support as clinically indicated in cases of shock, culturing, and vigorous antibiosis.[13,76] Antibiosis should, if possible, be begun before evacuation. Many antibiotic regimens have proven effective, e.g., clindamycin and gentamicin. In any event, coverage for aerobic and anaerobic organisms is essential.

5. *The possibility of* Clostridia *species infection* must be especially kept in mind because of its rapid onset with septicemia, intravascular hemolysis, shock, and renal failure.[29]

6. Hysterectomy is seldom necessary unless indicated by extensive uterine damage,[76] absolute refractoriness to therapy, or worsening shock or septicemia.[29]

I. *Diagnosis and treatment of complications*[29,76,93,100]

1. *Incomplete abortion*
   a) Surgical completion of evacuation of uterine contents
   b) Appropriate culturing and antibiosis

2. *Uterine perforation*[67,97]
   a) Incidence. Estimated at 0.8 to 1.5/1000 abortions, as many perforations are either unrecognized or unreported.[7,49,66,76]
   b) Physician inexperience and severe anteflexion or retroflexion of the uterus are cited as the most common causes of uterine perforation.[76] Careful pre-procedure bimanual examination, appropriate use of the uterine sound to ascertain the exact direction of the endocervical canal, and careful, gentle dilatation and instrumentation will reduce these causes of error.[7,53]
   c) When perforation is suspected, prompt cessation of the procedure (if in progress) and evaluation of the possible perforation (site, maternal status) and gestation (abortion not begun, complete, incomplete) is made. *Table 19–2 suggests a clinical classification of*

TABLE 19–2. CLINICAL CLASSIFICATION AND TREATMENT OF UTERINE PERFORATION DURING ABORTION

Clinical Classification	Treatment
A. *Immediate recognition with cessation of the procedure* (suspected or actual perforation by any instrument including suction cannula with no suction applied)	
1. *Completed abortion.* Perforation after contents of uterus completely evacuated	Inhospital observation of clinical status, serial CBCs, for at least 48 hr.
2. *Intact sac.* Gestation undisturbed	As above, then readmit in about 2 weeks for repeat surgical evacuation.
3. *Incomplete abortion.* Perforation occurs during evacuation; uterus partially emptied.	Immediate diagnostic laparoscopy. Laparotomy and repair if needed. Completion of abortion, either transcervically under laparoscopic observation or, if laparotomy, via uterine rent if transcervical approach inappropriate.

B. *Delayed recognition after operative manipulation* (suction or curettage). No abdominal contents identified. Uterine evacuation may have been attempted before possible perforation was recognized.
   1. *Complete abortion*
   2. *Intact sac*
   3. *Incomplete abortion*

All require immediate diagnostic laparoscopy with laparotomy if indicated (bowel trauma, uncontrolled bleeding, etc.) B.2, B.3: Abortion may be completed as in case A.3.

C. *Perforation with identification of abdominal contents* (bowel, omentum, fat, etc.)
   1. *Completed abortion*
   2. *Intact sac*
   3. *Incomplete abortion*

All require immediate laparotomy and surgical repair as needed. C.2, C.3: Abortion may be completed as in case A.3.

(Adapted from Walden W, Birnbaum S: Contemp Obstet Gynecol 15:47, 1980. By permission.)

such perforations and their therapy. The use of diagnostic laparoscopy has reduced the need for laparotomy by more than one-half.[7,8,49,53,66,76,93,97]

3. *Infection*[29]
    a) *Endometritis/PID*[71]
        (1) Culture and appropriate antibiosis
        (2) Examine the patient for retained products of conception; when in doubt, repeat dilatation or suction and curettage is indicated after antibiosis is begun.
        b) *Chronic cervicitis.* Sometimes associated with cervical laceration
        c) *Sepsis.* An infrequent but serious complication, with a death-to-case rate for septic abortion estimated at about 0.5 deaths/100,000 legal and spontaneous abortions.[36A]

4. *Failure to recognize simultaneous ectopic pregnancy*
5. *Anesthetic reaction*
6. *Uterine synechiae* (Asherman's syndrome)
7. *Cervical incompetence*
8. *Cervical scarring and stenosis*
9. *Cervical laceration*[93]
    a) *External laceration.* Most commonly caused by a tearing action by a tenaculum. One or two hemostatic sutures usually suffice to repair this type of laceration.
    b) *Laceration of the internal os.* Felt to be associated with too vigorous or rapid dilatation, or dilatation at increased gestational age. The latter suggests that elective transcervical abortion should be performed at as early a gestational age as possible.[42,86]

10. *Postabortal syndrome*[29,67,93]
    a) Variously called postabortal syndrome, postabortal hematometra, postabortal uterine atony, and "redo syndrome."
    b) Although the cervix has remained open, blood clots collect within the uterine cavity (sometimes quickly, sometimes after several days) causing a swollen, tender uterus associated with fever and crampy pain.

Oxytocics may help,[81] but re-evacuation is the treatment of choice. Antibiosis is indicated. Hospitalization may be indicated.

11. *Failed abortion with continuation of pregnancy.*[93] A rare outcome. One series estimated an incidence of 0.071/100 cases (46 cases in a series of 65,045 elective first-trimester terminations).[33]

12. *Hemorrhage*[29]

13. *Uterine rupture*[74]

14. *Ureteral injury*[6]

15. *Amniotic fluid embolism and disseminated intravascular coagulation*[92]

16. *Failed abortion because of uterine anomalies*[63]

SECOND-TRIMESTER ABORTION

A. *Elective and therapeutic*

1. Because of the many problems associated with second-trimester termination of pregnancy, including medicolegal and psychosocial as well as purely medical, *such procedures are best done in facilities where they are performed routinely.* In such a setting an experienced staff will avoid many of the errors experienced by a staff exposed to these procedures on an intermittent basis.[42,71,75]

2. If second-trimester termination is considered, documentation of gestational age by ultrasound is a wise precaution.[70,93]

B. *Technique*[29,76,93]

1. *Dilatation and evacuation*[20]

a) In the United States one opinion has been that transcervical uterine evacuation should not be performed beyond 12 completed weeks of gestation.[19,29]

b) Many operators, however, disagree, suggesting that morbidity and mortality are much decreased with dilatation and evacuation as compared to other second-trimester techniques until 16 weeks of completed gestational age.[16,21A,38,40,45,93] The use of the technique is increasing steadily.[21A]

   c) The technique is similar to that in first-trimester dilatation and suction or curettage except that surgical forceps are usually needed to remove fetal parts, especially the calvarium.[93] Laminaria are used extensively, since greater cervical dilatation is usually required.

2. *Oxytocin infusion*
   a) Of little value until cervical dilatation has begun.[76]
   b) Potential problems[76] include failure of intended effect, water intoxication,[60,61] and rarely uterine rupture[74] (most often in grandmultiparas).
   c) Often used in conjunction with other methods to good effect.[9,14,82]

3. *Intraamniotic hyperosmotic solutions* (hypertonic saline, hyperosmolar urea)[14,29,48,71,76]
   a) In many centers, hypertonic saline has been shown to be especially effective[9,41] and is still popular, although the use of prostaglandins is supplanting its use.
   b) The procedures carry significant risks, however:[42,71,76,82]
      (1) Sepsis
      (2) Hyperosmolar crisis
      (3) Disseminated intravascular coagulation[12,58,81,89]
      (4) Water intoxication[55]
      (5) Fever
      (6) Myometrial necrosis (especially associated with inadvertent intramyometrial injection)[36,98]
      (7) Uterine rupture
      (8) Cervical and vaginal fistulae[36,62]
      (9) Retained placenta

4. *Prostaglandins*[29,76,93]
   a) *Intraamniotic prostaglandin $F_{2\alpha}$ ($PGF_{2\alpha}$)*[2,31,62]
      (1) A method often used for advanced second-trimester termination,[71] this route of administration for $PGF_{2\alpha}$ is successful in most cases within 48

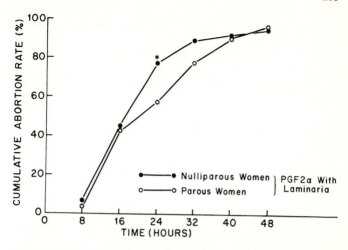

Figure 19-8. Cumulative abortion rate (percent) after the use of intraamnionic prostaglandin $F_{2\alpha}$ plus laminaria. (From Pritchard J, McDonald P: Williams Obstetrics, 16th ed. New York, Appleton, 1980, p 610.)

hours, with a mean time to abortion of 20 to 31 hours. One estimate suggests 86 percent will abort completely, 12.2 percent incompletely, and 1.8 percent will fail to abort.[57,71] (Fig. 19-8). In the event of the failure, uterine malformation may be the cause, and evaluation for it should be made so that appropriate therapy may be begun if indicated. Ultrasonography plays a key role in this evaluation.[57]

(2) Without augmentation (usually with oxytocin), about 15 to 20 percent of patients require a second injection.[93]

(3) Oxytocin administration, especially after membranes are ruptured, reduces evacuation time significantly. Great care must be taken, however, in the administration of this combination.[2,71]

(4) Use of laminaria also reduces evacuation time.

Whether they are inserted before or after injection varies with the operator and institution, but placement 12 to 24 hours before injections appears most efficacious.[31,62,71,93]

(5) Has been used in various multiple combinations, including intraamniotic urea,[50] oxytocin,[76] and laminaria.[76,91]

(6) To avoid transient fetal survival, combinations of $PGF_{2\alpha}$ and saline have been used to good effect. However, they do have the disadvantage of exposing the patient to some degree of the risks of hypertonic saline that are not inherent in the use of prostaglandins alone.[10,93]

(7) 15(S)-15-Methyl-prostaglandin F_2 (an artificial methylated analog of $PGF_{2\alpha}$) has been found useful, both as an intravaginal preparation and intramuscularly, in second-trimester termination and in the failed transvaginal second-trimester termination by other methods (intraamniotic prostaglandin, saline, etc.).[53A,56B]

b) *Prostaglandin E_2 (PGE$_2$) vaginal suppositories*

(1) Especially useful in missed abortions of advanced gestational age and in intrauterine fetal demise in advanced pregnancy.[2,4,25]

(2) Available in 10-mg suppositories, placed every two to four hours.

(3) Augmentation with oxytocin, especially after membrane rupture, is helpful in many cases. If used, careful monitoring of the severity of contractile activity is important.

(4) 15(S)-15-Methyl-prostaglandin E_2 (an artificial methylated analog of PGE_2) has been found useful, intravaginally and intramuscularly, in second-trimester termination.[56A]

c) *Adverse reactions common to prostaglandins*[42,71,76,93]

(1) Cervical or vaginal laceration and fistulae formation[62]

(2) Infection

      (3) Delayed or incomplete abortion (especially retained placenta)

      (4) Uterine rupture[81A]

      (5) Nausea, emesis, and diarrhea (prophylactic medication is indicated — prochlorperazine, diphenoxylate)

      (6) Hypotension

      (7) Tachycardia

      (8) Disseminated intravascular coagulation

      (9) Hemorrhage

    (10) Hyperthermia

  d) Asthma is a contraindication to the use of prostaglandins for abortion.[93]

  e) Since retention of fetal, or more commonly placental, tissue occurs, *a routine exploration of the vagina, cervix, and uterine cavity after completion of the procedure is indicated.* This allows identification and correction of complications in many of these areas.[36,49,62,71,93]

5. *Laminaria*[29,42,76]

  a) Technique previously discussed

  b) Often used in conjunction with other methods, both dilatation and evacuation and prostaglandin administration

6. *Hysterotomy*[29,69,76]

  a) Occasionally indicated when maternal status prohibits the use of other methods of abortion, but *outdated* as a primary method of abortion[69]

  b) Used in the event of failed transcervical abortion

  c) Because of the vertical uterine scar, *further pregnancies must be delivered by cesarean section*[76]

  d) A desire for permanent sterilization is not an indication to use hysterotomy as a primary method of abortion

  e) *Basic technique*

      (1) Following an appropriate preoperative evaluation and preparation, including determination of maternal blood type and Rh and the type and crossmatching of blood, the patient is brought to

the operating room and the anesthesia of choice is administered. The abdomen is then opened in the usual manner, exposing the uterus, ovaries, and fallopian tubes, which should be carefully inspected.

(2) Prior to uterine incision, a dilute oxytocin solution infusion is begun "piggyback" into the main IV line.

(3) A small vertical incision is made in the uterus. If there is a question of involving the bladder, a "bladder flap" may be created, although this is usually unnecessary. To avoid unnecessary additional blood loss, a small amount of oxytocin in sterile saline solution may be injected directly along the proposed incision line.

As small an incision as possible is made, and it is carried down slowly until the placenta and membranes are encountered. These should not be opened, if possible, so that the contents may be removed intact. The incision is then expanded as needed with scalpel or bandage scissors. The index finger is then carefully introduced between the products of conception and uterine wall, which are separated by blunt dissection until they are expelled through the uterine opening. The cavity should then be explored to ascertain that there is no remaining tissue. A sharp curette, or ring or ovum forceps may be used if needed (Figs. 19–9, 19–10).

The uterine incision is then closed in layers. Whether two or three layers are used depends on the depth of the incision wall, but the first layer should be of interrupted suture introduced about half-way between the endometrial and serosal surfaces and exiting just above the endometrial surface, being placed at about 0.5-cm intervals. The outer layer(s) may be closed at the operator's discretion (Fig. 19–11).

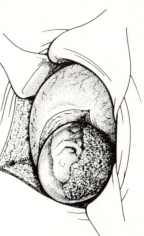

Figure 19–9. Abdominal hysterotomy. After careful vertical incision of the uterus such that the bag of waters has not been breeched, the index finger is used to perform a gentle blunt dissection of the products of conception from the uterine cavity. (From Quilligan EJ, Zuspan F: Douglas-Stromme Operative Obstetrics, 4th ed. New York, Appleton, 1982, p 207.)

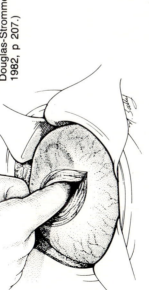

Figure 19–10. Abdominal hysterotomy. Following blunt dissection with the index finger, the products of conception may be expelled. Any remaining tissue should be bluntly or sharply curettaged or removed with an ovum or other forceps. (From Quilligan EJ, Zuspan F: Douglas-Stromme Operative Obstetrics, 4th ed. New York, Appleton, 1982, p 207.)

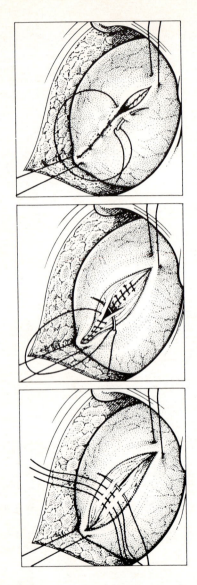

Figure 19–11. Abdominal hysterotomy. Repair of uterine incision in layers. (From Quilligan EJ, Zuspan F: Douglas-Stromme Operative Obstetrics, 4th ed. New York, Appleton, 1982, p 207.)

f) The *most common complications* are hemorrhage, infection, peritonitis, thrombophlebitis, and embolism.

g) This procedure has the highest morbidity and mortality rate of all abortion procedures, and should be used only when all other methods have been exhausted.[69]

7. *Hysterectomy*[5,29,54,76,83,94]

a) *Indications*

(1) Uterine or other gynecologic pathology that *by itself,* would have warranted the procedure

(2) Serious irreparable damage to the uterus

(3) Hemorrhage control following abortion by another method

b) *The technique* is that of cesarean hysterectomy. In the event that the operation is done for uterine trauma, careful attention to anatomy is imperative, especially the bladder and ureters.

c) The complications are those of hysterectomy, with increased risk of involvement of bladder and ureter.

8. Maternal blood type and Rh should be determined and Rh immunoglobulin administered if indicated.[3,37,39,59,76,77]

9. All tissues retrieved should be sent to the pathology lab for dating and for screening of trophoblastic changes.[24]

C. *Optimal setting*

1. Second-trimester termination is technically difficult and fraught with risk.

2. It should be performed only in medical facilities where the following are available:[93]

a) Staff experienced in the procedures and identification of the complications

b) Facilities to deal adequately and immediately with all possible complications

c) A well-organized pre- and postabortion counseling system[15]

d) A well-organized medical follow-up system

3. *Patients undergoing second-trimester termination procedures should never be left unattended, both for medical and psychosocial reasons.*

MORBIDITY AND MORTALITY

A. *Morbidity*
1. The *risk of morbidity* in all abortions is decreased by medical attention at an early gestational age by competent experienced staff in an approved facility.[15,42,76,93]
2. Present data suggest an *incidence of abdominal surgical procedures* coincident to abortion of about 3.9/1000 cases, including all causes, both related and unrelated to the abortion itself.[49]
3. *Suggested adverse effects on future pregnancies* after abortion (especially elective) include midtrimester spontaneous abortion, preterm delivery, infertility, and low-birth-weight infants. Controversy exists over these associations and their interpretation.[6,21,26,27,47,86,99]

B. *Mortality*
1. The *risk of mortality* from elective abortion is about *0.6 to 1.0/100,000* up to 8 weeks of gestation, doubling for each additional 2 weeks of gestation thereafter,[29,42,49,71,76] as compared to a present maternal mortality rate of 8 to 10/100,000 live births.[93] Thus, abortion and maternal mortality rates are probably equal at about 14 to 16 weeks of completed gestational age, with the value for abortion exceeding that for continued pregnancy thereafter.[49]
2. Dilatation or suction and curettage carries the lowest risk, followed by intraamniotic injection of $PGF_{2\alpha}$ or intravaginal PGE_2, and then hysterotomy/hysterectomy. Both the procedures and the gestational age determine the individual risk.[93]

MEDICOLEGAL AND SOCIAL ISSUES

Before the Supreme Court decision of *Roe* v. *Wade* in 1973, most abortions were "therapeutic," or presented as some type of incomplete abortion. Since then, elective abortion has become a major part of the reproductive control pattern in the United States. Great controversy presently exists about the many issues relating to abortion. The ultimate outcome of the deliberations over these is uncertain, but whatever decisions emerge will have a tremendous impact on women's health care in the years to come.[76,93]

Generally, state laws leave abortion decisions in the first trimester to the patient and her physician, whereas regulations of abortion in later pregnancy vary widely and are constantly changing.[76] Physicians who consider performing any elective abortions should fully review the regulations in their practice locality.[15]

When considering elective abortion, questions about gestational age should be answered by ultrasound examination if possible.[70,71,93] Further, pathologic examination of the retrieved products of conception to document the pregnancy and to rule out trophoblastic disease is indicated.[71]

REFERENCES

1. Alvior GT: Pregnancy outcome with removal of intrauterine devices. Obstet Gynecol 41:894, 1973

2. Anderson GG, Steege JF: Clinical experience using intraamniotic prostaglandin $F_{2\alpha}$ for trimester abortion in 600 patients. Obstet Gynecol 46:591, 1975

3. Ascari WQ: Abortion and maternal Rh immunization. Clin Obstet Gynecol 14:625, 1971

4. Bailey CD, Newman C, Ellinas SP, Anderson GC: Use of prostaglandin E_2 vaginal suppositories in intrauterine fetal death and missed abortion. Obstet Gynecol 45:110, 1975

5. Ballard C: Therapeutic abortion and sterilization by vaginal hysterectomy. Am J Obstet Gynecol 118:891, 1974

6. Barton J, Grier E, Mutchnik D: Uretero uterine fistulae as a complication of elective abortion. Obstet Gynecol (Suppl 1) 52:815, 1976

7. Ben-Baruch G, Menezek J, Shalev J, et al.: Uterine perforation during curettage. Perforation rates and postperforation management. Isr J Med Sci 16:821, 1980

8. Berek J, Stabblefield P: Anatomic and clinical correlates of uterine perforation. Am J Obstet Gynecol 135:181, 1979

9. Berger G, Edelman D, Kerenyi T: Oxytocin administration, instillation-to abortion time, and morbidity associated with saline instillation. Am J Obstet Gynecol 121:941, 1975

10. Bortman M: Use of combination prostaglandin $F_{2\alpha}$ and hypertonic saline for midtrimester abortion. Prostaglandins 12:625, 1976

11. Braunstein G, Karow W, Gentry W, Wade M: Subclinical spontaneous abortion. Obstet Gynecol (Suppl 1) 50:41S, 1977

12. Brown FD, Davidson E, Phillips LL: Coagulation changes after hypertonic saline infusions for late abortions. Obstet Gynecol 39:358, 1972

13. Burkman R, Atienza M, King T: Culture and treatment results in endometritis following elective abortion. Am J Obstet Gynecol 128:556, 1977

14. Burnette L, King T, Atienza M, Bell W: Intra-amniotic urea as a midtrimester abortifacient: clinical results and serum and urinary changes. Am J Obstet Gynecol 121:7, 1975

15. Burr W, Schultz K: Delayed abortion in an area of easy accessibility. JAMA 244:44, 1980

16. Cadesky K, Ravinsky E, Lyons E: Dilation and evacuation: a preferred method of midtrimester abortion. Am J Obstet Gynecol 139:329, 1981

17. Cadkin A, Sabbagha R: Ultrasonic diagnosis of abnormal pregnancy. Clin Obstet Gynecol 20:265, 1977

18. Carr DH: Cytogenetic aspects of induced and spontaneous abortions. Clin Obstet Gynecol 15:203, 1972

19. Conger S, Tyler C, Pakter J: A cluster of uterine perforations related to suction curettage. Obstet Gynecol 40:551, 1972

20. Cates W: D & E after 12 weeks: safe or hazardous? Contemp Obstet Gynecol 13:23, 1979

21. Cates W: Late effects of induced abortion. Hypothesis of knowledge? J Reprod Med 22:207, 1979

21A. Cates W, Grimes D: Deaths from second trimester abortion by dilatation and evacuation: causes, prevention, facilities. Obstet Gynecol 58:401, 1981

22. Cheng M, Rochat R: The safety of combined abortion-sterilization procedures. Am J Obstet Gynecol 129:548, 1977

23. Chilcote W, Asokan S: Evaluation of first trimester pregnancy by ultrasound. Clin Obstet Gynecol 20:253, 1977

24. Cohen B, Burkman R, Rosenshein N, et al.: Gestational trophoblastic disease within an elective abortion population. Am J Obstet Gynecol 135:452, 1979

25. Corson S, Bolognese R: Vaginally administered prostaglandin E_2 as a first and second trimester abortifacient. J Reprod Med 14:43, 1975

26. Daling J, Emanuel I: Induced abortion and subsequent outcome of pregnancy in a series of American women. N Engl J Med 297:1241, 1977

27. Daling J, Spadoni L, Emanuel I: Role of induced abortion in secondary infertility. Obstet Gynecol 57:59, 1981

28. Danforth D: Obstetrics and Gynecology, 3rd ed. Hagerstown, Md., Harper & Row, 1977, p 331

29. Douglas RG, Stromme WB: Operative Obstetrics, 3rd ed. New York, Appleton-Century-Crofts, 1976, Chap 6

30. Dreishpoon IH: Complications of pregnancy with an intra-uterine contraceptive device in situ. Am J Obstet Gynecol 121:412, 1975

31. Duenhoelter J, Grant N, Jimenez J: Concurrent use of prostaglandin $F_{2\alpha}$ and laminaria tents for induction of midtrimester abortion. Obstet Gynecol 47:469, 1976

32. Eriksen P, Philipsen T: Prognosis in threatened abortion evaluated by hormone assays and ultrasound scanning. Obstet Gynecol 55:435, 1980

33. Fielding W, Lee S, Friedman EA: Continued pregnancy after failed first trimester abortion. Obstet Gynecol 52:56, 1978

34. Genest P: Chromosome variants and abnormalities detected in 51 married couples with repeated spontaneous abortions. Obstet Gynecol Surv 35:368, 1980

35. Goldzieher JW: Double-blind trial of a progestin in habitual abortion. JAMA 188:651, 1964

36. Goodlin R, Newell J, O'Hare J, et al.: Cervical fistula, a complication of midtrimester abortion. Obstet Gynecol 40:82, 1972

36A. Grimes D, Cates W, Selik R: Fatal septic abortion in the United States, 1975–1977. Obstet Gynecol 57:739, 1981

37. Grimes D, Geary F, Hatcher R: Rh immunoglobulin after ectopic pregnancy. Am J Obstet Gynecol 140:246, 1981

38. Grimes D, Hulka J, McCutchen M: Midtrimester abortion by dilatation and evacuation versus intra-amniotic instillation of prostaglandin $F_{2\alpha}$: a randomized clinical trial. Am J Obstet Gynecol 137:785, 1980

39. Grimes D, Ross WC, Hatcher RA: Rh immunoglobulin utilization after spontaneous and induced abortion. Obstet Gynecol 50:261, 1977

40. Grimes D, Schultz K, Cates C, et al.: Midtrimester abortion by dilatation and evacuation: a safe and practical alternative. N Engl J Med 296:1141, 1977

41. Harlap S, Shiono P: Alcohol, smoking and incidence of spontaneous abortions in the first and second trimester. Obstet Gynecol 36:209, 1981

42. Harman C, Fish D, Tyson J: Factors influencing morbidity in termination of pregnancy. Am J Obstet Gynecol 139:333, 1981

43. Hartman CG: Uterine bleeding as an early sign of pregnancy in the monkey (*Macaca rhesus*) together with observation on fertile period of menstrual cycle. Bull Hopkins Hosp 44:155, 1929

44. Hertz J, Mantoni M, Svenstrup B: Threatened abortion studied by estradiol-17β in serum and ultrasound. Obstet Gynecol 55:324, 1980

45. Hodari A, Peralta J, Quiroga P, Gerbi E: Dilatation and curettage for second trimester abortions. Am J Obstet Gynecol 127:850, 1977

46. Hodgson J, Major B, Portmann K, et al.: Prophylactic use of tetracycline for first trimester abortions. Obstet Gynecol 45:574, 1975

47. Hogue CJR: Review of postulated fertility complications subsequent to pregnancy termination. In Sciarra JJ, Zatuchni GI, Speidel JJ (eds): Risks, Benefits, and Controversies in Fertility Control. Hagerstown, Md., Harper & Row, 1978, p 356

48. Herenyi T, Mandelman N, Sherman D: Five thousand consecutive saline inductions. Am J Obstet Gynecol 116:593, 1973

49. King T, Atienza M, Burkman R: The incidence of abdominal surgical procedure in a population undergoing abortion. Am J Obstet Gynecol 137:530, 1980

50. King TM, et al.: The synergistic activity and intra-amniotic prostaglandin $F_{2\alpha}$ and urea in the midtrimester election abortion. Am J Obstet Gynecol 120:704, 1974

51. Kline J, Stein Z, Shrout P, et al.: Drinking during pregnancy and spontaneous abortion. Obstet Gynecol Surv 36:209, 1981

51A. Laing F, Filly R, Marks W, Brown T: Ultrasonic demonstration of endometrial fluid collection unassociated with pregnancy. Ultrasound 137:471, 1980

52. Last PA: Pregnancy and the intrauterine contraceptive device. Contraception 9:439, 1974

53. Laufe L, Kreutner A: Vaginal hysterectomy: a modality for

therapeutic abortion and sterilization. Am J Obstet Gynecol 110:1096, 1971

53A. Lauersen N: A new abortion technique: intravaginal and intramuscular prostaglandin. Obstet Gynecol 58:96, 1981

54. Lauersen N, Birnbaum S: Laparoscopy as a diagnostic and therapeutic technique in uterine perforation during 1st trimester abortions. Am J Obstet Gynecol 117:522, 1973

55. Lauersen N, Birnbaum S: Water intoxication associated with oxytocin administration during saline-induced abortion. Am J Obstet Gynecol 121:2, 1975

56. Lauersen N, Conrad P: The effect of oxytocic agents on blood loss during first trimester suction curettage. Obstet Gynecol 44:428, 1974

56A. Lauersen N, Secher N, Wilson K: Midtrimester abortion induced by serial intramuscular injections of 15(S)-15-methyl prostaglandin E2 methyl ester. Am J Obstet Gynecol 123:665, 1975

56B. Lauersen N, Wilson K: The effects of intramuscular injections of 15(S)-15-methyl-prostaglandin $F_{2\alpha}$ in failed abortions. Fertil Steril 28:1044, 1977

57. Lauerson N, Wilson K, Zervoudakis K, et al.: Management of failed prostaglandin abortion. Obstet Gynecol 47:473, 1976

58. Lemkin S, Kattlove H: Maternal death due to DIC after saline abortion. Obstet Gynecol 42:233, 1973

59. Leong M, Duby S, Kinch R: Fetal-maternal transfusion following early abortion. Obstet Gynecol 54:424, 1979

60. Leventhal JM, Reid D: Oxytocin-induced water intoxication with grand mal convulsions. Am J Obstet Gynecol 102:310, 1968

61. Lilien AA: Oxytocin-induced water intoxication. A report of maternal death. Obstet Gynecol 32:171, 1969

62. Lowensohn R, Ballard C: Cervicovaginal fistula: An apparent increased incidence with prostaglandin $F_{2\alpha}$. Am J Obstet Gynecol 119:1057, 1974

63. McArdle C: Failed abortion in a septate uterus. Am J Obstet Gynecol 131:910, 1978

64. McDonough P, et al.: Overall evaluation of recurrent abortion. In Givens JR (ed): The Infertile Female. Chicago, Yearbook Medical, 1979, p 385

65. Matsunaga E, Shiota K: Threatened abortion, hormone therapy, and malformed embryos. Obstet Gynecol Surv 35:521, 1980

66. Nathanson BN: Management of uterine perforation suffered at elective abortion. Am J Obstet Gynecol 114:1054, 1972

67. Nathanson BN: The postabortal pain syndrome: a new entity. Obstet Gynecol 41:739, 1972

68. Newton BW: Laminaria tent: relic of the past or modern medical device? Am J Obstet Gynecol 113:442, 1972

69. Nottage B, Liston W: A review of 70 hysterotomies. Br J Obstet Gynecol 82:310, 1975

70. O'Brien G, Queenan J, Campbell S: Assessment of gestational age in the second trimester by real time ultrasound measurement of the femur length. Am J Obstet Gynecol 139:540, 1981

71. Palomaki J: Abortion techniques: what are their risks and complications. Contemp Obstet Gynecol 9:73, 1977

72. Parsons L, Sommers S: Gynecology, 2nd ed. Philadelphia, Saunders, 1978, Chap 27

73. Parsons L, Sommers S: Gynecology, 2nd ed. Philadelphia, Saunders, 1978, Chap 26

74. Peyser M, Toaff R: Rupture of uterus in the first trimester caused by high-concentration oxytocin drip. Obstet Gynecol 40:371, 1972

75. Poland B, Miller J, Jones D, Trimble B: Reproductive counseling in patients who have had a spontaneous abortion. Am J Obstet Gynecol 127:685, 1977

76. Pritchard J, MacDonald P: Williams Obstetrics, 16th ed. New York, Appleton-Century-Crofts, 1980, Chap 24

77. Queenan JT: Modern Management of the Rh Problem, 2nd ed. Hagerstown, Md., Harper & Row, 1977, p 256

78. Rasor J, Braunstein G: A rapid modification of the Beta-hCG radioimmunoassay. Obstet Gynecol 50:553, 1977

79. Rosal T, Saxena B, Landesman R: Application of a radioreceptorassay of human chorionic gonadotropin in the diagnosis of early abortion. Fertil Steril 26:1105, 1975

80. Sanders RJ, James AM: Ultrasound in Obstetrics and Gynecology. New York, Appleton-Century-Crofts, 1977

81. Sands R, Burnhill M, Hakim-Elahi E: Postabortal uterine atony. Obstet Gynecol 14:595, 1974

81A. Sawyer M, Lipshitz J, Anderson G, Dilts P: Third-trimester uterine rupture associated with vaginal prostaglandin E_2. Am J Obstet Gynecol 140:710, 1981

82. Schiffer M, Parter J, Clahr J: Mortality associated with hypertonic saline abortion. Obstet Gynecol 42:759, 1973

83. Schulman H: Major surgery for abortion and sterilization. Obstet Gynecol 40:738, 1972

84. Shine RM, Thompson JF: The in situ IUD and pregnancy outcome. Am J Obstet Gynecol 119:124, 1974

85. Simpson JL: What causes chromosomal abnormalities and gene mutations? Contemp Obstet Gynecol 17:99, 1981

86. Slater P, Davies A, Harlap S: The effect of abortion method of the outcome of subsequent pregnancy. J Reprod Med 26:123, 1981

87. Smith C, Gregori C, Breen J: Ultrasonography in treated abortion. Obstet Gynecol 51:173, 1978

88. Sonne-Holm S, Heisterberg L, Hebjorn S: Prophylactic antibiotics in first trimester abortions: a clinical controlled trial. Am J Obstet Gynecol 139:693, 1981

89. Stander RW, Flessa HC, et al.: Changes in maternal coagulation factors after intra-amniotic injection of hypertonic saline. Obstet Gynecol 37:660, 1971

90. Stenchever MA, Jarvis JA: Cytogenetic studies in reproductive failure. Obstet Gynecol 37:83, 1971

91. Strauss JH, Wilson M, Caldwell D, et al.: Laminaria use in midtrimester abortion induced by intra-amniotic prostaglandin $F_{2\alpha}$ with urea and intravenous oxytocin. Am J Obstet Gynecol 134:260, 1979

92. Stromme W, Fromke V: Amniotic fluid embolism and disseminated intravascular coagulation after evacuation of missed abortion. Obstet Gynecol (Suppl 1) 52:76S, 1978

93. Stubblefield P: Current technology for abortion. Curr Probl Obstet Gynecol 2(4), 1978

94. Stumpf P, Ballard C, Lowensohn R: Abdominal hysterectomy for abortion sterilization. Am J Obstet Gynecol 136:714, 1980

95. Tatum H, Schmidt F, Jain A: Management and outcome of pregnancies associated with copper T intrauterine contraceptive device. Am J Obstet Gynecol 126:809, 1976

96. Tsenghi C, Metaxoutou-Stavridaki C, Strataki-Benetou M, et al.: Chromosome studies in couples with repeated spontaneous abortions. Obstet Gynecol 47:463, 1978

97. Walden W, Birnbaum S: Classifying perforations that occur during abortion. Contemp Obstet Gynecol 15:47, 1980

98. Wentz AC, King T: Myometrial necrosis after therapeutic abortion. Obstet Gynecol 40:315, 1972

99. World Health Organization Task Force on Sequellae to Abortion: Gestation, birth-weight, and spontaneous abortion in pregnancy after induced abortion. Lancet 1:142, 1979

100. Wulff G, Friedman M: Primary diagnosis of complications by gestational age from LMP. Obstet Gynecol 49:351, 1977

20

Ectopic Pregnancy

Charles R.B. Beckmann, M.D.

PRACTICE PRINCIPLES

Ectopic pregnancy occurs when final implantation is outside the uterine cavity. In earlier eras, this was catastrophic, often leading to maternal mortality. With the advent of safe blood transfusion and better diagnostic methods allowing early diagnosis, maternal mortality has been drastically reduced, with attention now turning toward maximizing fertility after ectopic pregnancy.

GENERAL CONSIDERATIONS AND TUBAL ECTOPIC PREGNANCY

Demographics

A. *One in every 100 to 150 pregnancies (Fig. 20–1) is ectopic,* the majority (95 to 99 percent) being tubal ectopic pregnancies. Rare types include abdominal (0.03 percent), cervical (0.1 percent), and ovarian (0.05 percent) ectopic pregnancies,[6,47] as well as the even rarer combined intrauterine and ectopic pregnancy, occurring 1 in 30,000 pregnancies.[3,4,8,52a,56,75]

B. The usual maternal age distribution for pregnancy is seen in ectopic gestation.[5,7,9,22,28,40,42,61]

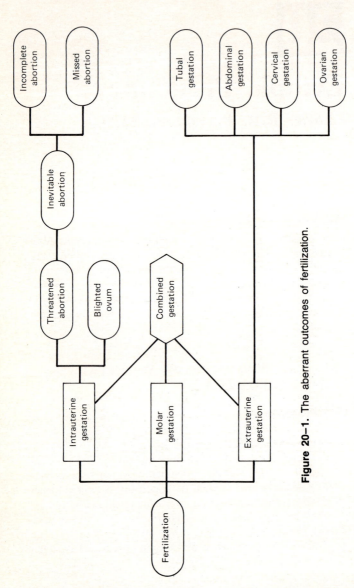

Figure 20–1. The aberrant outcomes of fertilization.

C. Subsequent fertility, compared to that for patients without history of ectopic pregnancy, is decreased (25 to 50 percent).[5,6,18,23,28,59,66,73]

D. Statistics on repetition are meaningful primarily in tubal ectopic pregnancy, where there is a 5 to 20 percent recurrence rate.[7,9,10,26]

Morbidity and Mortality

A. *Markedly decreased in the modern era,* largely for these reasons:[5,22,29]
   1. Earlier detection, often before rupture.
   2. Improved management of blood loss and shock.
   3. Improved treatment of infectious disease.

B. *Current mortality* in the United States is estimated at 5 to 6 percent of maternal deaths.[4,5,22,29,48,50a,58]

Etiology

A. *There are two possible categories of etiologic mechanisms:*
   1. *Alterations in transport*
      a) Delay or prevention of transport of ova, sperm, or fertilized ovum.
      b) Tubal dysfunction.
   2. *Alterations in implantation capability and implantation site receptiveness*[31]
      a) Increased invasiveness of human trophoblastic tissue.
      b) High decidualization capacity of the fallopian tube mucosae.

B. Many *specific factors* are cited, any of which may mediate its effect by either or both pathways described:[6]
   1. *Chronic pelvic inflammatory disease and chronic salpingitis are the most commonly discussed etiologic factors*[4,5,10,29,42,73]
      a) Mechanisms involved may include anatomic damage and the formation of pathologic entities, such as tuboovarian abscess and hydrosalpinx, and alteration in function.[14–16,36]

b) An exception is tuberculous salpingitis, where there is a definite increase in ectopic pregnancy rate to about 80 percent of pregnancies.[24,26]

2. *Previous history of infertility, especially if this includes previous infertility surgery.*[6,42]

3. The *intrauterine device (IUD)* has been associated with an increased rate of ectopic pregnancy, perhaps by causing a perisalpingitis/oophoritis, the risk evidently increasing with the duration of IUD use. *The risk of ectopic pregnancy with an IUD has been estimated at 5 percent.*[1a,4,10,27,36a,52a74,214,221–223]

4. *Abortion.*[53]

5. *Transperitoneal migration of sperm and/or ova.* Contralateral corpora lutea are convincing data supporting this agrument.[2,8,20,23,28,42,49,50,59]

6. Congenital diverticula of the fallopian tube.[54]

7. Fallopian tube spasm (as seen in some women during HSG).[6,23]

8. *Recanalization after tubal ligation,* whether partial or complete.[1a,20,30,34,76]

9. Tubal endometriosis.[52]

10. Salpingitis isthmica nodosa (which may be unilateral).[19,23,32,34]

Signs, Symptoms, and Historical Associations

A. Virtually every sign and symptom attributed to pregnancy or abdominal emergency has been associated with ectopic gestation. *Patients may be divided into two groups, those in whom the pregnancy is intact and still viable and those in whom the pregnancy has outgrown its implantation site, usually with resulting bleeding and pain.* In the latter situation, the findings are usually those of the acute surgical abdomen. Diagnosis is readily made, and surgical therapy is begun. When the gestation is viable or where the degree of nonviability is minimally apparent, the diagnosis may be difficult. *Three symptoms* (the classic triad) *and one physical finding are consistent in their relia-bility:*[1,4,5,9,22,28,29,36a,50a,66,73,83,98,113]

1. *Abdominal pain* — in 90 to 100 percent of patients.
2. *Amenorrhea* — in 75 to 85 percent of patients.
3. *Vaginal bleeding* — in 75 to 85 percent of patients.
4. *Palpable adnexal mass or fullness* — *in 45 to 55 percent of patients.*

B. *Other signs and symptoms:*

1. *Subjective symptoms of pregnancy* are seen in one half to three quarters of patients.[28,40,47]

2. *Abdominal pain* is characteristically unilateral but may be bilateral, is often colicky, and may be on the side opposite the ectopic gestation. The latter is often associated with a symptomatic corpus luteum.[5,8,50a]

3. *Referred shoulder pain* often results from the dia-phragmatic irritation caused by *hemoperitoneum* associated with ectopic pregnancy rupture,[5,8,40,50a,73] although there are other causes.[13,43] Fainting while straining at bowel movement is an often associated history.

C. *Physical findings:*

1. A *slight elevation in temperature* may be found, especially with any degree of hemoperitoneum, but rarely above 101F (38.3C) in a situation uncomplicated by concurrent infection.[40]

2. *Guarding and/or rebound* may be found in one or both lower quadrants, sometimes with distention and de-creased bowel sounds.[29]

3. *Pelvic examination*

   a) *The cervix* may be discolored (bluish), tender, and soft.[5,29] It may also be open, with passage of blood and occasionally tissue, the latter often being confused with an incomplete abortion. The tissue passed is usually a *decidual cast* formed by endometrial re-sponse to the hormonal influences of the developing gestation. It is passed, whole or in fragments, as the viability of the gestation wanes, although there may be several days delay between decreased gestational viability and the onset of decidual cast expulsion.[5,52]

    b) *The uterus* may be slightly soft, tender, and enlarged or may seem normal.

    c) *A discrete adnexal mass or fullness,* with or without tenderness, is found in nearly one half of patients.[50a]

D. When evaluating a patient for possible ectopic gestation, remember:

  1. Tubal ectopic pregnancy is slightly more common on the right side,[4,9,23,28] possibly due to appendiceal inflammatory effects.[5] The implantation site for tubal ectopic pregnancies is found more commonly as one moves distally along the tube.[4,9,23,28]

  2. Some ectopic gestations may be quite unusual (e.g., retroperitoneal and multiple ectopic pregnancy.[11,17,45,46,65]

  3. *Combined pregnancy* (also called conjoint, heterotropic, and coincident pregnancy), where there are simultaneous intra-uterine and extrauterine gestations, presents a difficult and often missed diagnosis.[12,56,75,77,94]

    a) *Incidence:* 1 in 30,000 pregnancies.[3,4,8,56,75]

    b) Possible *etiologic mechanisms* include twin gestation with abnormal development of one of the twins[64,69,75] and superfetation.[3,33,69] It is virtually impossible to establish etiology in any given case.[64,75]

    c) *Common errors in diagnosis*

      (1) Overlooking the intrauterine gestation upon diagnosis of the extrauterine gestation.

      (2) Overlooking the extrauterine gestation upon diagnosis of the intrauterine gestation.

      (3) Ignoring marked *unilateral* pain associated with a spontaneous abortion. This symptom should be viewed with great suspicion, since it was overlooked in some 40 percent of missed extrauterine components of combined pregnancies reported.[75]

      (4) Failure to appropriately evaluate when two corpora lutea are noted intraoperatively.[12]

      (5) Failure to be aware of unusual combinations.[3,21]

d) *Management*
   (1) Once the correct diagnosis is made, *a management for each pregnancy of the set must be formulated.*
   (2) The *fetal salvage rate for the intrauterine component* of the combined gestation is about one in three, the most likely termination being spontaneous abortion in the first trimester.[75] The possibility of diagnostic dilatation, suction, and curettage should be made available to the patient.

Special Examinations

A. When the clinical history and physical examination still leave controversy about the diagnosis of ectopic pregnancy, three examinations (pregnancy testing, culdocentesis, and ultrasound examination) and one minor surgical procedure (diagnostic laparoscopy) have proven of special value.
B. *Pregnancy testing*
   1. *Human chorionic gonadotropin (hCG)*
      a) Produced by the trophoblast, hCG (above certain levels) indicates a pregnancy but *does not by its presence indicate the location of the implantation site.* Since hCG levels may be low, the more sensitive the test, the higher the frequency of positive results. HCG concentrations, plotted individually or in a serial comparative manner against duration of amenorrhea, however, may have some diagnostic value, as abnormally implanted gestations and, ultimately, nonviable gestations (ectopic pregnancies and the various abortions) often produce less hCG than do normal gestations (Fig. 20–2). Of course, combined pregnancies, multiple ectopic pregnancies, or a viable ectopic pregnancy may not fit this pattern.[26,40,89,90,94,97a,98,99,101,103,105,112,113] Rarely, the situation may be confused by nonpregnancy-associated ectopic hCG production, most commonly associated with carcinoma of the bronchus, stomach, liver,

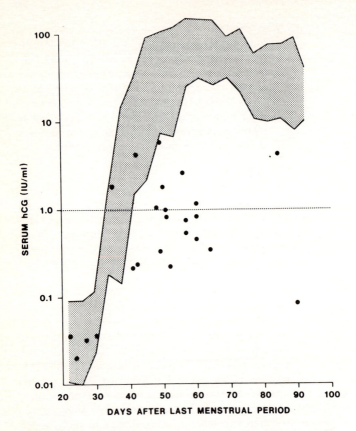

Figure 20–2. Serum β-hCG levels determined by radioimmunoassay (RIA) techniques in 24 women with ectopic pregnancies. The normal pattern of hCG secretion seen during the first trimester of uncomplicated pregnancy is indicated by the hatched area. Each point represents a single sample from a women with an ectopic pregnancy. The dotted line represents the level of detection of most commercial pregnancy tests. (Reprinted by permission of the publisher from: The rapid modification of the β-hCG radioimmunoassay: Use as an aid in the diagnosis of ectopic pregnancy, by Rasor JL and Brunstein GD. Obstet Gynecol 50:557. Copyright 1977 by American College of Obstetricians and Gynecologists.)

pancreas, and breast, and multiple myeloma and melanoma.[91]

b) *Urinary pregnancy tests*[82,106,107,112,113,115]

   (1) Urinary tests are hemagglutination inhibition or complement fixation tests, with sensitivities of 500 to 2,000 mIU/ml. They do not distinguish between hCG and luteinizing hormone (LH), which, because of physiochemical similarity, crossreact.

   (2) *These tests are positive in less than one half of cases of ectopic pregnancy. Hence, the test is useful only when positive.* When the test is negative, pregnancy (of any kind) is not excluded. Further, a positive test may be subject to suspicion if done in a time period coincident with an LH surge (and in the perimenopausal state).

c) *Radioimmunoassay for human chorionic gonadotropin using β-hCG antibodies* (RIA for β-hCG)[93,97a,103,105–107,113,114,117,124a]

   (1) *Specific for hCG* produced by trophoblastic tissue. Since the antibody is raised against the β-subunit of hCG, which is dissimilar to the β-subunit of LH, the test will discriminate between LH and hCG.

   (2) With a sensitivity of 0.5 to 10 mIU/ml of serum, the RIA for hCG using the β-hCG antibody can detect a gestation as early as 8 to 10 days postfertilization.

   (3) *A positive test indicates the presence of hCG-producing trophoblastic tissue* but does not give information about the implantation site. More than one determination, with titers, is needed to attempt any estimation of viability, especially if the initial titer is within the normal range. Rising titers are found in normal and abnormal pregnancy, while a falling titer usually indicates abnormality. To minimize interassay variability, 48-hour sampling intervals are recommended when the clinical situation permits.

(4) *A negative test virtually eliminates gestation at any site.*

d) *Radioreceptor assay for human chorionic gonadotropin (RRA for hCG)* [86-88,100,102,105,110-113]

(1) This test uses hCG-LH receptor from bovine corpus luteum instead of specific antibodies as the binding protein for hCG. Hence, it does not discriminate between LH and hCG, which is its main disadvantage.

(2) Approximately 90 to 95 percent accurate in detection of hCG-producing trophoblastic tissue, when the assay is set such that sensitivity is above the average midcycle LH surge of 174 mIU/ml. Theoretical sensitivities are 40 to 400 mIU/ml.

(3) *The main advantage of RRA is rapidity,* taking one to three hours, as compared to one half to three days for the RIA determinations.[105a]

2. Trophoblast-produced β-Glycoprotein behaves like β-hCG and may become a useful adjunct in the diagnosis of ectopic pregnancy, but presently it is not as useful as RIA for β-hCG.[92,93,95-98,104,108,109,114,115,116]

C. *Ultrasound examination*

1. Ultrasound is valuable in the evaluation of ectopic gestation if its capabilities and limitations are kept firmly in mind.[119,123,124]

2. *The bounds of ultrasound* (Table 20-1)

a) *Intrauterine pregnancy*

(1) With a positive pregnancy test and demonstration of an intrauterine gestational sac (especially when fetal heart motion is seen), intrauterine pregnancy is diagnosed, and ectopic pregnancy is effectively excluded[130a] (Fig. 20-3).

(2) This is suggested to correlate with a β-hCG above 6,000 mIU/ml. A range of 6,000 to 6,500 mIU has been suggested as a "discriminatory hCG zone," above which sonographic diagnosis of intrauterine pregnancy or ectopic pregnancy by the absence of

TABLE 20–1. THE BOUNDS OF ULTRASOUND

Normal Pregnancy	Possible Aberrant Pregnancy	No Pregnancy
Positive pregnancy test by any method	Pregnancy test: If urinary test, positive or negative; if RIA for β-hCG, positive	Negative pregnancy test by RIA for β-hCG
+	+	+
⇩	⇩	⇩
Intrauterine gestational sac on ultrasound	No clearly defined intrauterine gestational sac on ultrasound	Normal pelvic ultrasound
⇩	⇩	⇩
Diagnosis: intrauterine pregnancy; extrauterine pregnancy essentially excluded	*Diagnosis:* possible aberrant pregnancy; further evaluation indicated	*Diagnosis:* exclusion of pregnancy at any site

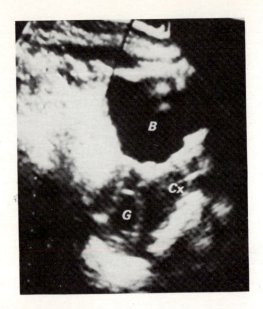

Figure 20–3. Sonogram showing an intrauterine gestational sac (**G**) in a retroverted uterus. **B,** bladder; **Cx,** cervix. (From Conrad M: In Sanders R, James A (eds): Ultrasonography in Obstetrics and Gynecology, 1977. Courtesy of Appleton-Century-Crofts.)

intrauterine findings is assured, and below which further (often serial) evaluations are indicated.[97a,124a]

   (3) The above does not, however, exclude the very rare combined pregnancy.[42,75,131]

 b) *No pregnancy*

   (1) A negative pregnancy test (by RIA for β-hCG) and a normal ultrasound make gestation, either intrauterine or extrauterine, very unlikely.

 c) *Between "pregnancy" and "no pregnancy" is a continuum of combinations of aberrant pregnancy.*

3. Essential to the ultrasonographic evaluation of ectopic pregnancy is the capability of recognizing normal and abnormal intrauterine gestation. *Intrauterine pregnancy, demonstrated as a prominent ring of echoes against the uniform density of the uterus, may be diagnosed as early as five and one half weeks gestational age,* when the chorionic sac is some 10 mm in size, and routinely by 7 weeks of completed gestation.[122]

   a) Fetal heart activity can be demonstrated as early as the seventh week of gestation and is easily detected by the ninth week.[122,125,127]

   b) A common differential diagnosis is a nonviable blighted ovum, characterized by a volume of less than 2.5 cc and absence of fetal echoes. Often only serial ultrasound examinations and clinical events will yield the correct diagnosis[121] (Fig. 20–4).

4. With a positive pregnancy test, a high clinical suspicion, and absence of a clearly defined intrauterine gestation, Kobayashi et al.[126] proposed the classic ultrasonographic criteria for ectopic pregnancy (Fig. 20–5).

   a) *Kobayashi's criteria for ectopic pregnancy*[123,126]
      (1) Uterine
         (a) Diffuse, amorphous uterine echoes.
         (b) Uterine enlargement.
         (c) Absence of intrauterine sac.
      (2) Extrauterine
      (a) Irregular, poorly defined mass containing some echoes.
      (b) Ectopic fetal head.

   b) These criteria provide a basis for diagnosis, but a *detailed differential consideration of the ultrasound findings is often required.* Table 20–2 provides such a differential review of the common findings.[43,119–121,123,124,125,128,128a,129,132,133]

   c) An important technical point is to provide *adequate bladder distention,* the distended bladder providing reference for other structures.[124]

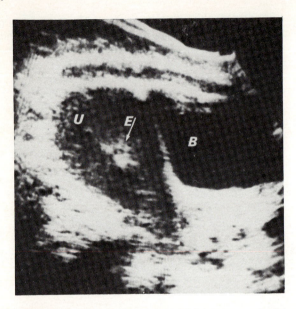

Figure 20–4. Longitudinal sonogram showing disorganized central intrauterine echoes due to residua of a blighted ovum, a finding easily confused with incomplete abortion, decidual reaction to ectopic gestation, or early intrauterine gestation. (From Conrad M: In Sanders R, James A (eds): Ultrasonography in Obstetrics and Gynecology, 1977. Courtesy of Appleton-Century-Crofts.)

    (1) Such distention may be provided by pushing fluids (either oral or intravenous) or by placing a Foley catheter and distending the bladder with sterile saline solution.

    (2) Care must be taken to neither overdistend nor underdistend the bladder. Overdistention is a common error, flattening and deforming pelvic structures and making analysis difficult. An exception is with a retroverted uterus, where overdistention aids in resolution.[121,132]

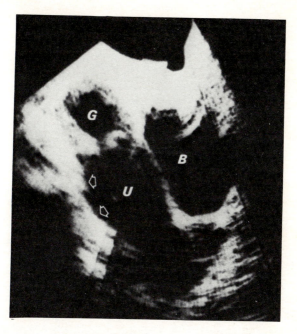

Figure 20–5. Midline logitudinal sonogram showing a tubal ectopic gestational sac (G) superior to the uterine fundus. Arrows demark posterior aspect of minimally enlarged uterus. **U,** uterus; **B,** bladder. (From Conrad M: In Sanders R, James A (eds): Ultrasonography in Obstetrics and Gynecology, 1977. Courtesy of Appleton-Century-Crofts.)

    5. False-negative and false-positive interpretations are made in 3 to 4 percent of patients.[118,120,125,126,128,130]

D. *Culdocentesis*

    1. Hemoperitoneum is an indication for early surgical intervention, yet at times the diagnosis is difficult. One of the easiest and most useful diagnostic procedures is the insertion of a needle through the posterior fornix (Fig. 20–6) into the posterior cul-de-sac (of Douglas), which

TABLE 20–2. DIFFERENTIAL DIAGNOSTIC CRITERIA FOR THE ULTRASOUND EVALUATION OF ECTOPIC PREGNANCY

Ultrasound Findings	Differential Considerations
Uterus	
Central linear band	Decidual band
	Abnormal intrauterine gestation (abortion, blighted ovum)
	Intrauterine pregnancy less than 5 to 6 weeks
Enlargement	Normal variant
	Myomas
	Adenomyosis
	Intrauterine pregnancy
Sac	Intrauterine pregnancy greater than 5 to 6 weeks
	Abnormal intrauterine gestation
	Intrauterine blood clot
	Gestational sac in a fallopian tube which has undergone muscular hypertrophy
	Fluid accumulation with endometritis
Adnexa	
Mass	Differential for solid adnexal masses
	Corpus luteum ($\pm$ bleeding)

Ring, dense shell echo	Tubo-ovarian abscess
	Appendiceal abscess
	Diverticulosis
	Ovarian cyst
	Bicornuate uterus with IUP in one horn
	Endometriosis (endometroma)
	Hydrosalpinx
	Gestational sac in hypertrophied fallopian tube
	Cornual pregnancy
	Intrauterine pregnancy in fundal leiomyoma
	Fluid-filled loop of small bowel
	Pedunculated uterine myoma
Fetal pole	Pregnancy, probably abnormal/ectopic
	Combined pregnancy
Pelvis	
Cul-de-sac echo	Blood (ruptured ectopic, tubal abortion, ruptured cyst, ruptured leiomyosarcoma, bleeding ulcer, and so on)
	Ascites
	Ovarian cyst

From Hallatt JG: Am J Obstet Gynecol 125:755, 1976.

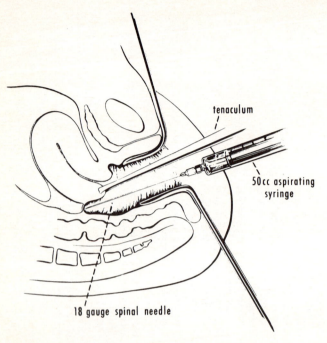

tenaculum

50 cc aspirating
syringe

18 gauge spinal needle

Figure 20–6. Culdocentesis. (From Mattingly R: Telinde's Operative
Gynecology, 1977. Courtesy of J.B. Lippincott.)

serves as a natural dependent drain for blood in the
abdominopelvic cavity. Because of the ease of access,
culdocentesis is more practical than paracente-
sis.[1,40,47,55,79]

2. *There are three possible outcomes — positive, negative,
and equivocal* — each of which is associated with a series
of clinical possibilities. These are reviewed in Table 20–
3.[43,79,81]

3. With good technique, culdocentesis may be considered
accurate in about two thirds of cases of hemoperitoneum,
the false-negative rate of about ten percent overshadow-

TABLE 20-3. EVALUATION OF CULDOCENTESIS DATA

Theoretical Outcomes	Clinical Possibilities
Positive Blood, nonclotting	**True Positive** Needle in abdominal cavity, easily drawn, nonclotting **False Positive** 1. Needle in vessel, blood clots, does not draw easily 2. Needle in abdominal cavity, easily drawn, nonclotting, but from other source (corpus luteum, other ovarian tumor, ruptured leiomyosarcoma, leiomyoma, punctured pelvic organ, such as pelvic kidney, and so on)
Negative Clear, serous fluid	**True Negative** Needle in abdominal cavity, easily drawn few milliliters **False Negative** 1. Needle in cyst, bladder, gestational sac (intrauterine or extrauterine) 2. *Unruptured ectopic pregnancy**
Equivocal Red-tinged fluid	1. Needle in abdominal cavity where there is minimal bleeding, draws easily 2. Needle in abdominal cavity, iatrogenic bleeding, draws easily 3. Needle in vessel, little fluid, draws poorly

*Negative culdocentesis *does not exclude* ectopic gestation.

ing the false positive rate of about two percent.[5,9,28,29,79,84,85]

4. Posterior colpotomy, a surgical approach through the
   posterior cul-de-sac with diagnostic and therapeutic
   capabilities, has been used to good result.[80] Its use is
   limited, however, by the surgical experience of the
   operator.[5,93]

E. Laparoscopy will be discussed in the Management section.

Management

A. Once the diagnosis of ectopic tubal gestation is made, *the
   choice of surgical approach*[62] depends on:
   1. *Competencies of the surgeon.*
   2. *Clinical status of patient*
      a) The arrest of hemorrhage, if occurring, or the preven-
         tion of hemorrhage is a primary objective.[73]
      b) When a patient is unstable, the minimal necessary
         surgery should be chosen.[50a]
   3. *Patient's desire for further reproductive capability*
      a) In general, elective sterilization in emergency situa-
         tions should be avoided, as *the quality of the patient's
         decision under emergent conditions is always suspect.*
      b) The incidence of repeat ectopic pregnancy, however,
         has suggested to some that sterilization is indicated if
         further pregnancy is not desired.[6,26]
   4. As a general rule, immediate surgical therapy is indicated
      once the diagnosis of ectopic gestation is made.
B. *Initial surgical options*
   1. *Dilatation and curettage (D & C)*
      a) The possibility of a viable intrauterine pregnancy
         should be discussed with the patient and dilatation
         and curettage avoided if the patient wishes to main-
         tain the intrauterine pregnancy.
      b) Examination of endometrial tissue has not been useful
         in diagnosis of ectopic pregnancy based on the Arias-
         Stella reaction, which is absent in about one half or
         three quarters of patients and, like the decidual

reaction, may be present in other situations.[52,73] *Absence of chorionic villi, however, is highly suspicious for ectopic gestation, requiring further investigation.*[135]

2. *Diagnostic laparoscopy*

   a) When the patient is stable and without evidence of hemoperitoneum, diagnostic laparoscopy allows direct evaluation via a minor procedure, often making it possible to avoid exploratory laparotomy.[10,28,29] When unruptured ectopic gestation is thereby discovered, conservative surgical procedures are more likely to be successful than when rupture has occurred.[66]

   b) Although there have been cases of excision of ectopic tubal pregnancies via laparoscope,[60a] most gynecologists feel laparotomy is safer and should be the approach of choice.[60,93]

3. *Laparotomy*

   a) The procedure of choice in the unstable patient where arrest of hemorrhage and stabilization of the patient are primary concerns.[93]

C. Choice of *procedures for ampullary and isthmic tubal ectopic pregnancy*[60a,61,62]

   1. *Ablative surgery*

      a) *Ipsilateral salpingectomy*[5,61,65,70]

         (1) The most common procedure—quick, simple, efficient.

         (2) *Management of the ipsilateral ovary*

            (a) Ipsilateral salpingo-oophorectomy remains a common management based on the argument that there is an increased incidence of ectopic pregnancy secondary to ovum transmigration of the peritoneal cavity with associated ovum pick-up delay.[2,6,38]

            (b) A more common view is that the ipsilateral ovary should be left if it is not itself seriously damaged and its blood supply is intact.[10,59]

      b) Laparoscopic ablation via electrocautery and/or segmental excision *is not recommended* because of the major disadvantages of poor visualization, excessive thermal tissue damage, increased incidence of adhesion formation, and increased risk of uncontrollable bleeding.

  c) *Cornual resection*

    (1) Recommended in the past as a procedure of choice to decrease the incidence of repeat ectopic pregnancy, especially isthmic.[8,20]

    (2) Presently *disclaimed as a primary management* because:

      (a) Questionably effective in reducing incidence of repeat ectopic pregnancy.

      (b) May lead to increased incidence of interstitial ectopic pregnancy and uterine rupture.[26,29]

2. *Nonablative surgery*

  a) *Manual expression of tubal abortion* (with or without associated hematosalpinx)[23,52,66,67]

    (1) Easily performed, often quickest procedure.

    (2) Risks include incomplete abortion, bleeding.

    (3) A major concern is that bleeding and/or any remaining trophoblastic tissue in the lumen may cause scars and adhesions and, thereby, an increased rate of repeat ectopic pregnancy and/or infertility.[6,71]

    (4) If attempted, major surgical goals are:

      (a) Removal of all gestational tissue.

      (b) Meticulous hemostasis by use of manual exposure, copious irrigation, and bipolar electrocoagulation. Dilute Pitressin injection has also been used.[62]

  b) *Reconstructive (plastic) tubal surgery*

    (1) Should be considered when patient wishes to preserve maximal reproductive capability.[6,26,57,66–68]

    (2) *Choice of procedure*

      (a) Most successful, as a class of operations,

when the ectopic pregnancy is unruptured but may be attempted when rupture has occurred depending on amount of damage and bleeding.[7,62,67] If repair is attempted, especially with rupture, ligation of the tubo-ovarian artery has been suggested as a means of decreasing bleeding.[72]

(b) In general, *the initial surgery should be restricted to removal of the ectopic gestation, and any extensive reconstructive surgery should be done at a second operation after tissue edema and hyperemia have resolved.*[62]

c) *Reconstructive surgery for ampullary tubal ectopic pregnancy* (about two thirds of tubal ectopic pregnancies)

(1) *Linear salpingostomy*

(a) Performed, if possible, on the antimesenteric border without closure.[7,10,40,41,66,72] Hemostasis is affected by bipolar electrocautery or suture of the cut edges.

(b) Some argue that incision of the fimbriae, if unaffected, is unnecessarily traumatic, and recommend a linear incision just proximal to the fimbriae with evacuation of the gestational products via that incision, often with the aid of a blunt curette.[6]

d) *Reconstructive surgery for isthmic tubal ectopic pregnancy.*

(1) *Linear salpingostomy with closure.*[25,37,40,41,61,67]

(2) *Segmental resection and subsequent midtube reanastomosis*[62,63,93]

(a) A major decision is whether to proceed with reanastomosis at the first operation or to perform an interval operation after tissue edema and hyperemia have resolved. Majority opinion supports the latter course.[93]

(b) There may be an increased risk of repeat

ectopic tubal pregnancy at the anastomosis
site, even if patency is achieved.[6] Intraoperative patency check is, nevertheless,
recommended, by the placement of a Bux-
ton clamp occluding the lower uterine segment and transfundal injection of a dilute
dye solution.[62]

e) *General procedural considerations for reconstructive
surgery*[7,34,44]

(1) *Minimize handling of tissues.*

(2) *Maximize use of gentle irrigation,* as blood clots
and retained tissue will cause scarring and adhesion formation, increasing the chances of infertility and repeat ectopic pregnancy.[23,44] Two types of
irrigation solution are recommended:

(a) Physiologic saline[23]

(b) A medicated solution. The initial irrigation is
with a solution whose composition is 1 gm
hydrocortisone and 500 units heparin in 1 liter
of lactated Ringer's solution. In final irrigation the same solution minus the heparin is
used.[44,93]

(3) *Meticulous attention to hemostasis.* Methods include ligation with fine suture, bipolar electrocautery, and injection and dilute Pitressin
solution.[6,62,66,67]

(4) *Medications*[44]

(a) Promethazine. Minimizes early inflammatory
reaction by histamine release blockage.

(b) Corticosteroids[10]

(c) Heparin. Prevents clotting and fibrin deposi-
tion, decreasing scarring and adhesion formation.

(d) Prophylactic antibiosis[73]

(e) A *suggested regimen* is ampicillin (or substi-
tute) 1 to 2 gm q6h for 48 to 72 hours,

Decadron 20 mg q4h IV for 12 to 18 doses,
Phenergan 25 mg IV q4h for 12 to 18 doses.

(5) Careful washing of all talc from gloves before operation.

(6) Choice of minimally reactive suture materials (polyglactin or nylon).

(7) Hydropertubation is recommended postoperatively by some authors.[73]

f) *Complications*

(1) Repeat ectopic pregnancy.[39,60a]

(2) Delayed hemorrhage.[39] Suture of mesosalpinx at tubal border along the implantation site has been suggested, interrupting the blood supply temporarily and thereby decreasing the risk.[57,72] The question is raised, however, concerning subsequent tubal function on the theoretical grounds of unnecessary, excessive interruption of fallopian tube blood supply.[62]

(3) Infertility

g) *Success rates*

(1) Values from 20 to 70 percent for subsequent intrauterine pregnancy are reported.[7,10,44,66]

(2) There is a greater chance for intrauterine pregnancy than repeat ectopic pregnancy, perhaps as much as six times.[26,60a]

h) *Management of the contralateral fallopian tube*

(1) While the tube often appears normal on gross inspection, as many as one half of contralateral tubes have significant microscopic abnormalities.[60a] Clinical judgment must be used in each situation.[61]

(2) Intraoperative tubal lavage has been recommended to exclude contralateral tubal occlusion.[6]

D. Rh immunoglobulin (RhoGAM)should be administered to all Rh-negative, unsensitized women who have an ectopic pregnancy.[23a]

INTERSTITIAL ECTOPIC PREGNANCY

A. Two to four percent of tubal ectopic gestations are interstitial. If the overall tubal ectopic pregnancy rate is taken at 1
in 100 live births, the interstitial tubal ectopic pregnancy rate
is *1 in 2,500 to 1 in 5,000 live births.*[135]

B. *Implantation site and natural history*
The interstitial implantation area provides more tissue into
which the gestation may develop and more vascular supply
for this development. Therefore, interstitial pregnancies,
relative to other tubal ectopic pregnancies, tend to develop
further, demonstrate delayed symptom presentation, and
rupture violently with more bleeding and a higher incidence
of shock.[137,138] They also develop higher hCG levels. The
evidence that interstitial pregnancy is more common following salpingectomy is equivocal.[134,136,140,141]

C. *Diagnosis*
  1. Like other tubal ectopic gestations, it is associated with
     the classic triad:
     a) Amenorrhea
     b) Lower quadrant pain
     c) Anomalous vaginal bleeding
     d) There are also the other signs and symptoms of tubal
        ectopic pregnancy.[144] The duration of amenorrhea
        may be longer than expected.[137]
  2. *Physical examination* is generally similar to that found in
     other types of tubal ectopic pregnancy. Specific to
     interstitial pregnancy, however, is *uterine asymmetry,*
     often with marked tenderness at the area of irregularity
     (usually irregular uterine enlargement).[135,144]
  3. The *laboratory diagnosis* is also similar except for the
     ultrasound examination, where an eccentric position of
     the gestational sac in the uterus is highly suspicious in a
     suggestive clinical setting [121](Fig. 20–7).
  4. *Differential diagnosis*[51,121,135,137a]
     a) Anomalous uterus
     b) Uterine myoma(s)

    c) Overdistended or underdistended bladder
    d) Abdominal or ovarian pregnancy
    e) Ovarian cyst
    f) Salpingitis isthmica nodosa
    g) Angular intrauterine pregnancy

5. Early diagnosis, especially with emergence of diagnostic laparoscopy, has greatly decreased the morbidity and mortality of interstitial pregnancy.[138] At operation, the key to the diagnosis is the uterine shape (usually regular in intrauterine pregnancy, except in angular intrauterine

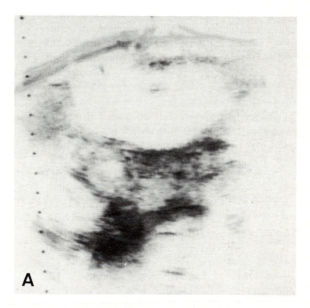

Figure 20–7. Longitudinal **(A)** and transverse **(B)** sonograms of an unruptured interstitial ectopic pregnancy, demonstrating a clearly defined gestational sac with its characteristic eccentric position. (Courtesy C.R.B. Beckmann, M.D., Department of Obstetrics and Gynecology, University of Illinois at the Medical Center, Chicago.)

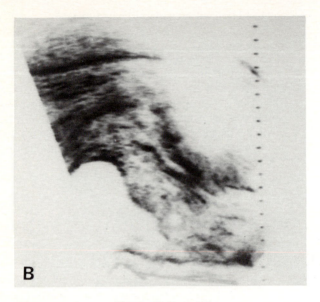

Figure 20-7. (cont.)

pregnancy) and the relationship of any irregular uterine enlargement to the round ligament. In intrauterine pregnancy, including the angular variety, the round ligament is lateral to the uterine enlargement, whereas in interstitial pregnancy the round ligament's point of insertion is medial to the enlargement, with the ligament coursing over the anterior aspect of the irregular uterine enlargement.[137,137a]

D. *Operative management*
   1. *Three questions are asked preparatory to surgical management:*
      a) Will conservative surgery (i.e., cornual resection) result in a *functional* uterus?
      b) How *stable* is the patient?

      c) Does the patient wish to maintain her *reproductive capability?*

2. Clinical judgment must be used in each situation, but *general guidelines* may be stated.

      a) With patient instability, minimal surgical intervention is best.

      b) In general, elective permanent sterilization in emergency situations should be avoided, as the quality of a patient's decision under emergency conditions is always suspect.

3. *Procedure selection*

      a) *Cornual resection with salpingectomy* is a common procedure, especially if reproductive capability is desired and uterine damage is minimal.[47] Extensive cornual resection may require cesarean section for subsequent intrauterine pregnancies.[131,139,144]

      b) *Hysterectomy* is generally reserved for situations where uterine damage is so severe that the remaining portion of uterus will not be functional. If there has been severe uterine damage and the patient is unstable, this may be one of the rare indications for supracervical hysterectomy.

      c) *Conservative tubal surgery with tubal conservation* is difficult surgery best limited to surgeons specializing in tubal surgery.[142,143]

ABDOMINAL PREGNANCY

Definitions

A. *Abdominal pregnancy results from implantation on the peritoneal surfaces of the abdominopelvic cavity.*[145,151,151a,153,197] *Implantation may occur anywhere in the abdominopelvic cavity. The most common sites are adnexae, broad ligaments, sigmoid colon, and uterine fundus. Involvement of the ureters and great vessels is rare.*[166a]

B. *Primary abdominal pregnancy*[151,151a,153,164.195,197,205]

   1. *Definition: primary implantation of the fertilized ovum on a peritoneal surface,* with otherwise normal uterus, ovaries, and fallopian tubes.

   2. *Proposed etiologies*[151a,164,197]

     a) *Müllerian tract anomalies.*[52,145,150,155,173,188,191,204]
A few pregnancies in a rudimentary uterine horn have progressed to term, with surgical delivery of a viable child. Commonly, however, these rupture in the first or early second trimester. Because normal intrauterine pregnancies may follow in patients in whom there is a normal anatomic component within the anomaly, every attempt should be made to preserve any normal structures.

     b) *Delayed ovulation* with extrusion of a postmature ovum which is subsequently fertilized in the peritoneal cavity.[164]

     c) *Endometriosis,* which provides a preferred implantation site on the peritoneum because of decidual reaction of the endometrial implant.[164,186]

     d) *Reflux transport of a fertilized ovum* or postmature ovum during menstruation.[171]

     e) *Failure of the fallopian tube to pick up a fertilized ovum,*[158,160,161,167] an etiology supported by the preponderance of abdominal pregnancies implanting in the dependent cul-de-sac, where fallopian tube activity is thought to be maximal.

     f) *Pelvic inflammatory disease*[208,211]

C. *Secondary abdominal pregnancy*[145,151,151a,153,164,175]

   1. *Definition: reimplantation on a peritoneal surface following separation from a primary implantation site.*

   2. *Proposed etiologies and comments*

     a) *Tubal abortion* is probably the most common cause.[52,151,151a,163,175,195]

     b) *Ruptured tubal ectopic pregnancy,* either into the

abdomen or into the mesosalpinx, with subsequent intraligamentous pregnancy.[210]

c) *Ruptured uterus.*[146,163,200] Not all uterine ruptures are violent, leading to abdominal crisis and fetal demise. In some cases the rent in the uterus opens slowly with extrusion of the fetoplacental unit and its reimplantation outside the uterus. Predisposing factors include previous cesarean section, previous myomectomy, previous difficult forceps delivery, previous cornual resection, previous uterine perforation during abortion or dilatation and curettage, uterine perforation during elective abortion, and subtotal hysterectomy.[185,195]

d) *Pelvic inflammatory disease*[211]

e) *An association with IUDs has been suggested.*[203]

f) *Hysterectomy*[185]

Demographic Statistics

A. Abdominal pregnancy is *rare*,[164] occurring approximately 1 *in 3,300 pregnancies.*[145–147,151a,152,153,157,164,175,195,208,211] Preoperative diagnosis is made in less than one half of patients.[154,169]

B. The *age distribution* is that common to normal pregnancy[163,211] or slightly older.[151,208]

C. *Subsequent pregnancy*
   1. Normal pregnancy is well documented following abdominal pregnancy.[176]
   2. Repeat abdominal pregnancy is rare, but several cases have been documented.[166,179,200]
   3. As with intrauterine gestation, malignant trophoblastic disease can follow abdominal pregnancy.[172]
   4. Heterotrophic pregnancy is seen in abdominal pregnancy[187,209] as well as in more uncommon situations, such as twin abdominal pregnancy.[147]

D. *Morbidity and mortality* for the mother have improved for the same reasons as found in tubal ectopic pregnancy.[195,208]

Evaluation

A. *Symptoms*
   1. Virtually every sign and symptom associated with pregnancy and aberrant gestation has been discussed in connection with abdominal pregnancy.[153,157,195,211] *A few symptoms are of special value:*
      a) Persistent, severe nausea and emesis, more than expected in normal pregnancy.[151,153,195]
      b) Anomalous vaginal bleeding.[151,163,208]
      c) Unusually painful fetal movements.[147,153,163,184,195,211]
      d) Abrupt cessation of fetal movement (abrupt fetal demise).[211]
      e) Severe abdominal cramping, not characteristic of round ligament pain in either quality or severity,[146,151,152,153,184,195,196,208,211] especially if interpreted as acute abdominal crisis in early pregnancy,[211] although some feel this is overly stressed.[157]
      f) No Braxton Hicks contractions.[151,175,195,208,211]
   2. *Failure of response to oxytocics* has been used as a diagnostic maneuver. Historically, it is often at such failure that the suspicion of abdominal pregnancy is first raised.[151,151a,157,195,210,211]

B. *Physical findings*
   1. *Abnormal fetal presentation* is quite characteristic,[146,151,153,156,159,163,195] especially *transverse or oblique lie* and *high position*.[146,157,208,211]
   2. *Palpation of the uterus, separate from the fetal parts,* is considered diagnostic,[151,151a,153,154,159] although it is often difficult and thus considered an uncommon finding.[157,195]
   3. *Cervical displacement* is considered a major finding.[147,154,157,163,196,209,211]
   4. *Abnormalities of the uterine souffle* are noted, from absence[153] to increased vascular sounds.[159]
   5. *Unusually loud fetal heart sounds* are prized as a finding

by many authorities,[146,151,195,211] although they are discounted in value by others.[157,208]

6. *Easy palpation of fetal parts,* which often feel closer to the surface of the abdominal wall than usual.[151,154]

C. *Laboratory examination*

1. *Pregnancy testing*—as under General considerations.

2. *Radiologic evaluation*

   a) After 16 weeks of gestation, fetal ossification allows direct visualization of the fetus.[55] Weinberg and Sherwin[207] and others[147,151,151a,153,159,174,195,208,210] have suggested the *radiologic signs of advanced abdominal pregnancy.*

      (1) Eccentric position of the fetus from the mid-coronal plane of the pelvis.

      (2) Malposition of the fetus, usually oblique or transverse lie, with the back cephalad (also seen in placenta previa).

      (3) Lack of visualization of the uterine wall as a soft shadow about the fetus.

      (4) Unusual clarity of the fetal parts.

      (5) Maternal intestinal gas shadows overlying or *caudad* to the fetus.

      (6) *Fetal parts posterior to the lumbar spine in a true lateral x-ray of the pelvis,* a finding considered diagnostic.

   b) Several conditions may cause some of these findings, including uterine sacculation,[147] bicornuate uterus or other Müllerian anomalies, and intraligamentary pregnancy.[210]

   c) Intravenous *aortography* and percutaneous transfemoral retrograde *arteriography* have been suggested, although the value of these studies is questionable.[147,162,174,193]

   d) *Hysterosalpingography* has been discussed as very useful,[146,147,151a,153,175,210,211] of minimal value,[151,195] misleading, [208] and contraindicated.[159] Although dramatic when diagnostic, Weinberg's comment that it is "seldom justified" seems appropriate.[207]

    e) Thermography[149]
3. *Ultrasound*[165,177,189,190,195]
    a) *Diagnosis is made by demonstration of a fetal head outside of the uterus.* This is sometimes difficult when the uterus is deformed and displaced.
    b) Placental localization is difficult in abdominal pregnancy because of lack of chorionic plate formation and multiplicity of implantation site echoes. Nevertheless, it is an important and useful procedure.

Management

A. There are *two great debates in the management of abdominal pregnancy.* First, *when to operate,* second, *when and what to do with the placenta.* In all cases, careful clinical judgment of each individual case is the key to successful management.
B. *If the fetus is alive:*
    1. *Many authors argue for operative intervention as soon as the diagnosis is made,* regardless of fetal status. They argue that the possible risks of hemorrhage and shock and the incidence of abnormal pregnancies outweigh the possible benefits of awaiting fetal viability.[146,147,151,153,154,168,175,181,195,196,210]
    2. *Others argue that if the risks are explained to and understood by the patient, surgery may be postponed to fetal viability* (not term) *if the patient is continuously hospitalized during the period.*[151a,159,163,178,179,196,199,208]
C. *If there is fetal demise:*
    1. *Immediate operation* is advised by some authors,[151,181] who suggest that delay causes[146,157,211] an increased incidence of infection, an increased risk of spontaneous intraabdominal hemorrhage, and no decrease in hemorrhage at operative attempt to remove the placenta.
    2. *Waiting one to eight weeks* is advocated by others, who suggest that placental circulation decreases markedly

during this time, decreasing the risk of intraoperative hemorrhage.[55,146,151a,157,159,181,208]

3. Care should be taken to avoid cutting into the placenta at the time of initial abdominal incision, making preoperative localization of the implantation site important.[147,152,154,181]

D. *Management of the placenta*

1. *The greatest risk in removal of the placenta is hemorrhage,* which is usually extremely brisk and difficult to control.

2. Decision about placental management must be individualized,[154,211] *with great care taken not to begin placental manipulation if there is significant reason to suspect hemorrhage.[208] The availability of large amounts of blood for transfusion is the single most important preoperative preparation.[168,211]*

3. The variables to consider in operative decision about the placenta are[165,195] placental location, placental blood supply, placental shape, placental viability, and patient condition.

4. *Options*

   a) *If the placenta and its implantation site can be removed in block dissection without disruption of the implantation, such removal is optimal management*[147,148,151,151a,153,154,159,168,195,208] *(provided unwished sterilization is not incurred).*

   b) *If the placenta and its implantation bed cannot be removed in block dissection, it is best left in situ without manipulation. The placenta then undergoes spontaneous resorption.[146,147,151a,153,157,163,184,195,196,206,208]*

   Membranes should be dissected away and the umbilical cord cut and ligated as close to the placenta as possible.[157,181] Left in situ the placenta will function for some time, with demonstrable hCG production for three to six weeks.[192]

   c) *Management of retained intraabdominal placenta*

   (1) The placenta undergoes spontaneous resorption, either complete or to the formation of a small

calcified mass. Further therapy may not be needed.[146,147,151a,153,157,163,184,195,196,206,208] In other cases, the retained placenta is symptomatic and/or interferes with normal abdominopelvic function. Further therapy is then indicated.[146,157,182,201,202,211]

(2) *Methotrexate* has been used to shorten the life and vascularity of the retained placenta, both as a primary management and as a preoperative therapy.[163,169,170,178] The hCG levels have been used to monitor this therapy,[192] as have various radiographic and ultrasonographic techniques.[183]

d) If removal of the placenta, at any time, is attempted and hemorrhage ensues, hemostasis must be effected surgically. Direct pressure on the bleeding site or on the aorta (temporary) has helped, as has the application of Gelfoam and heated laparotomy tapes.[195,211]

e) Ureteral obstruction is rare.[180]

Fetal Outcome[199]

A. *Most abdominal pregnancies do not survive.* The natural history of these gestations is fertilization, implantation, survival, intrapartum demise, maceration, suppuration, mummification, calcification, and lithopedion formation.[52,154] About 1.5 to 3 percent form actual lithopedia, which are classically diagnosed by one of three events:

1. Discovery at laparotomy
2. Percutaneous extrusion of bones.
3. Observation on radiographs taken for other reasons.[52,175,208]

B. The overall *fetal salvage* for abdominal pregnancy is estimated at *10 to 20 percent*,[153,159,196] although this may increase to 25 percent in cases where the diagnosis of a viable pregnancy is made past the fifth month.[151,198] Of surviving infants, one third to one half will have some degree of deformity.[151,195,198,208,211]

OVARIAN PREGNANCY

Demographics and Natural History

A. One in 25,000 to 1 in 50,000 pregnancies are ovarian and are usually single.[220]

B. Ovarian pregnancy usually terminates spontaneously in the first trimester.[215,223,225,226]

Definition and Etiology

A. *Criteria for ovarian pregnancy*[52,55,212–214,223]
   1. Fallopian tube
      a) Must be intact, including fimbria.
      b) Must be clearly separate from ovary.
      c) Must be microscopically free of gestational tissue.[224]
   2. Gestational sac
      a) Must occupy normal position in ovary.
      b) Must be connected to uterus by ovarian ligament.
      c) Unquestioned ovarian tissue in the wall of the gestational sac.
B. *Definitions*[52,213,214]
   1. *Primary ovarian pregnancy* — *initial implantation on/in ovary.*
   2. *Secondary ovarian pregnancy* — reimplantation of a gestation which has separated from its initial implantation site.
C. *Possible etiologies*
   1. *Intrauterine device*[214,216,217,221–223]
      a) Because of the difference in the ratio of ovarian pregnancy to other ectopic pregnancies with an IUD (1 in 9) and without an IUD (1 in 2,000), it has been suggested that IUDs increase the incidence of ovarian pregnancy.
      b) Boronow et al.[214] suggest that IUDs act by, in some

manner, reducing implantation capability, having the
greatest effect (99.5 percent implantation decrease)
on the uterus, next greatest effect (95 percent) on the
tubes, but no effect on the ovary. According to this
analysis, IUDs do not cause an actual increase in the
ovarian pregnancy rate but rather a change in the
ovarian pregnancy/overall ectopic pregnancy ratio.

2. *Obstructed ovulation*[214]
3. *Ineffective tubal function*[214]
4. *Surface phenomena favorable to implantation*[214]

Diagnosis

A. The *history and physical findings* are similar to that of tubal
ectopic pregnancy with two exceptions.
  1. Continued *menses,* which may appear normal, seem to be
  relatively common with ovarian implantation.[213,225]
  2. An *adnexal mass* is felt more often (80 to 90 percent) than
  in tubal ectopic pregnancy.[214]
B. *Diagnosis* of ovarian pregnancy is usually a pathologic one,
the preoperative diagnosis usually being tubal ectopic pregnancy.
C. An actual fetus is identified in less than one half of cases.[218]

Management

A. When ovarian gestation is *obvious,* wedge resection of the
ovary or removal of the ovary is indicated.[214]
B. When an ovarian lesion is noted and ovarian pregnancy is
suspected, a generous wedge resection is indicated combined
with a careful abdominopelvic examination to avoid missing
an abdominal pregnancy. Any material (blood, clots, tissue)
found in the abdominal cavity should also be sent for
pathologic evaluation.[219,223]

CERVICAL PREGNANCY

Demographics, Definitions, Etiology, and Natural History

A. *Incidence*

   Occurring *between 1 in 10,000 and 1 in 20,000* pregnancies.[223]

B. *Definition*

   Cervical pregnancy occurs when the ovum implants primarily in the cervical mucosae below the level of the histologic cervical os.[235,240]

C. The *criteria* for cervical pregnancy are those of Rubin[228,231,233,235,237,240]

   1. Cervical glands opposite placental attachment
      a) Chorionic villi in cervical canal.
      b) No chorionic villi in corpus.
   2. Intimate attachment of placenta to cervix.
   3. All or part of placenta must be situated below:
      a) Entrance of uterine vessels.
      b) Anterior/posterior uteroperitoneal reflections.
   4. No fetal elements in corpus uteri.
   5. Cervical os
      a) Internal os closed.
      b) External os open or closed.

D. *Etiology*

   No clear etiology has been established. Several items have been associated with it, however, including rapid transport of fertilized ovum,[240] previous curettage,[235,239] and abnormal timing of fertilization.[232]

E. *Cervical pregnancy rarely progresses beyond the first trimester, with painless vaginal bleeding heralding the onset of gestational wastage.*

   1. Cervical pregnancy rarely continues[234] to term.

F. *Violent hemorrhage is the rule,* sometimes at the start of wastage, almost always at the time of manipulation, whether at digital examination or instrumental at the time of attempted evacuation.[227,229,237] It is the hemorrhage that caused the 40 to 50 percent mortality reported by Rubin in 1911 and which still maintains *maternal mortality at about 5 percent.*

Diagnosis

A. Patients with cervical pregnancy demonstrate the common *signs and symptoms* of pregnancy.[227,235,238,240] Of the classic triad of symptoms associated with other types of ectopic pregnancy, they have amenorrhea, but *the vaginal bleeding they experience, unlike that in tubal or ovarian ectopic pregnancy, is without pain.*

B. *Physical examination*
   1. *Abdominal examination* is usually unremarkable. Acute abdomen and hemoperitoneum are rare.
   2. The *cervix* is soft, thin-walled, round rather than conical, and disproportionally large — equal or larger than the uterine corpus. The examination is often confusing, with the complex referred to as an *"hourglass-shaped" uterus.* The cervical pregnancy is often mistaken for the uterine corpus, pregnant or nonpregnant, and the actual uterine corpus is mistaken for a pedunculated myoma or solid adnexal mass.
      a) A crucial distinction is that the *internal os* is *snug* and *closed,* whereas the *external os* may be *open or closed.*

C. *Differential diagnosis*[235]
   1. Cervical phase of spontaneous abortion.
   2. Cervical abortion.
   3. Placenta previa with extension of placental portion into cervical canal.
   4. Uterine malignancy.
   5. Prolapsed pedunculated myoma or polyp.

D. *Diagnosis of cervical pregnancy is usually made at the time of curettage for "incomplete abortion."*[227a]

Management

A. *Surgical management is determined by the gestational age*[227,228,237,238]

1. If the gestational age is *less than 12 weeks* and:
   a) There is *no desire for conservation of reproductive potential,* abdominal hysterectomy is indicated.
   b) There is a *desire for conservation of reproductive potential,* an attempt may be made at vaginal removal of the products of conception. Cervical packing is sometimes helpful to control the bleeding that will ensue, as the cervical tissue cannot undergo contraction like the uterine tissue to affect mechanical hemostasis. If the bleeding cannot be controlled, abdominal hysterectomy is indicated. Hypogastric arterial ligation is usually not helpful. Emergency cerclage, to occlude the cervical branches of the uterine artery, has been suggested, both as a temporizing measure to reduce blood loss before hysterectomy and as an alternate conservative procedure.[227a]

2. If the gestational age is *greater than 12 weeks,* abdominal *hysterectomy* is indicated. If the fetus is of viable age, a cesarean hysterectomy should be performed. Whether to observe a patient in the hospital if the gestation is near viability is an open question. Considering the violence of hemorrhage, this option is probably not appropriate.

3. Full preparation for massive hemorrhage must be made prior to any intervention, to include at least two intravenous lines and the availability of at least 6 units of whole blood.

4. If vaginal evacuation is successful, care must be taken to observe for recurrent hemorrhage, which commonly occurs one to six weeks after evacuation. This hemorrhage is usually uncontrollable, hysterectomy being needed to avoid exsanguination.

B. Reports of cervical pregnancy without hemorrhage at evacuation usually represent cases of *cervical abortion* misdiag-
nosed as cervical pregnancy.[237] Cervical abortion occurs
when an intrauterine gestation is extruded through the
internal os into the cervical canal but retained by a tight
external os (the opposite of the findings in cervical
pregnancy).[230]

REFERENCES

Ectopic Pregnancy

1. Armstrong J, Sweard H, Willis H, Moore J, Lauden A: Ectopic
   pregnancy, a review of 481 cases. Am J Obstet Gynecol 77:364,
   1959
1a. Beral V: An epidemiological study of recent trends in ectopic
   pregnancy. Br J Obstet Gynaecol 82:775, 1975
2. Berlund M: The contralateral corpus luteum — an important factor
   in ectopic pregnancies. Obstet Gynecol 16:51, 1960
3. Bisca B, Felder M: Coexistent intestinal and intrauterine pregnancy following homolateral salpingo-oopherectomy. Am J Obstet
   Gynecol 79:263, 1960
4. Bobrow ML, Bell HG: Ectopic pregnancy: a 16 year survey of 905
   cases. Obstet Gynecol 20:500, 1962
5. Breen J: A 21 year survey of 654 ectopic pregnancies. Am J Obstet
   Gynecol 106:1004, 1970
6. Bronson RA: Tubal pregnancy and infertility. Fertil Steril 28:226,
   1977
7. Bukovsky I, Lnager RB, Herman A, Caspi E: Conservative
   surgery for tubal pregnancy. Obstet Gynecol 53:709, 1979
8. Chez RA, Moore JG: Diagnostic errors in the management of
   ectopic pregnancy. Surg Gynecol Obstet 117:589, 1963
9. Crawford E, Hutchinson C: A decade of reports on tubal pregnancies condensed from the literature plus three hundred consecutive
   cases without a death. Am J Obstet Gynecol 67:568, 1954
10. DeCherney A, Kase N: The conservative surgical management of
    unruptured ectopic pregnancy. Obstet Gynecol 54:451, 1979
11. Demick P, Cavanagh D: Unilateral tubal twin pregnancy. Am J
    Obstet Gynecol 76:533, 1978

12. DeVoe RW, Pratt JH: Simultaneous intrauterine extrauterine pregnancy. Am J Obstet Gynecol 56:1119, 1948

13. Disaia P, Morrow C, Townsend D: Synopsis of Gynecologic Oncology. New York, Wiley, 1975

14. Doyle JB: Exploratory culdotomy for observation of tuboovarian physiology at ovulation time. Fertil Steril 2:475, 1951

15. Doyle JB: Ovulation and effects of selective uterotubal denervation: Direct observation by culdotomy. Fertil Steril 5:105, 1954

16. Doyle JB: Tubo-ovarian mechanism: observation at laparotomy. Obstet Gynecol 8:686, 1956

17. Fill L, Ross CV: Unilateral tubal twin pregnancy. Obstet Gynecol 9:358, 1957

18. Franklin E, Zeiderman A, Laemmle P: Tubal ectopic pregnancy: etiology and obstetrics and gynecologic sequelae. Am J Obstet Gynecol 117:220, 1973

19. Freakley G, Normal WJ, Ennis JT: Diverticulosis of the fallopian tubes. Clin Radiol 25:535, 1974

20. Fulsher R: Tubal pregnancy following homolateral salpingectomy. Am J Obstet Gynecol 78:355, 1959

21. Funderburk AG: Bilateral ectopic pregnancy with simultaneous intra-uterine pregnancy. Am J Obstet Gynecol 119:274, 1974

22. Gilstrap LC III, Harris RE: Ectopic pregnancy: a review of 122 cases. South Med J 69:604, 1976

23. Grant A: The effect of ectopic pregnancy on fertility. Clin Obstet Gynecol 5:861, 1962

23a. Grimes D, Geary F, Hatcher R: Rh immunoglobulin after ectopic pregnancy. Am J Obstet Gynecol 140:246, 1981

24. Halbrecht I: Genital tuberculosis. Fertil Steril 13:371, 1962

25. Hallatt JG: Ectopic pregnancy in perspective. Postgrad Med 44:100, 1968

26. Hallatt JG: Repeat ectopic pregnancy: a study of 123 consecutive cases. Am J Obstet Gynecol 122:520, 1975

27. Hallatt JG: Ectopic pregnancy associated with the intra-uterine device. A study of seventy cases. Am J Obstet Gynecol 125:754, 1976

28. Halpin TF: Ectopic pregnancy: the problems of diagnosis. Am J Obstet Gynecol 106:227, 1970

29. Helvacioglu A, Long EM, Yang SL: Ectopic pregnancy: an eight year review. J Reprod Med 22:87, 1979

30. Hernandez F: Tubal ligation and pregnancy: mechanism of recanalization after tubal ligation. Fertil Steril 26:393, 1975

31. Hertig AT, Mansell H: Atlas of Tumor Pathology, Washington, D.C., Armed Forces. Institute of Pathology, 1956, Section IX, Fascicle 33, Part 1

32. Honore L: Salpingitis isthmic nodosa in female infertility and ectopic tubal pregnancy. Fertil Steril 29:164, 1978

33. Honore LH, Nickerson KG: Combined intrauterine and tubal ectopic pregnancy: a possible case of superfetation. Am J Obstet Gynecol 127:885, 1977

34. Honore LH, O'Hara K: Failed tubal sterilization as an etiologic factor to ectopic tubal pregnancy. Fertil Steril 29:509, 1978

35. Horne H: Prevention of postoperative pelvic adhesions following conservative operative treatment for human infertility. Int J Fertil 18:109, 1973

36. Horne HW, Thibault JP: Sperm migration through the human female reproductive tract. Fertil Steril 13:135, 1962

36a. Hughes G: The early diagnosis of ectopic pregnancy. Br J Surg 66:789, 1979

37. Jarvinen PA, Nummi S, Pietila K: Conservative operative treatment of tubal pregnancy with postoperative daily hydrotubations. Acta Obstet Gynecol Scand 51:169, 1972

38. Jeffcoate TNA: Salpingectomy or salpingo-oophorectomy. J Obstet Gynaecol Br Emp 62:214, 1955

39. Kelly R, Martin S, Strickler R: Delayed hemorrhage in conservative surgery for ectopic pregnancy. Am J Obstet Gynecol 133:225, 1979

40. Kistner RW: Gynecology, 3rd ed. Chicago, Year Book, 1979

41. Kistner RW, Patton GW: Atlas of Infertility Surgery. Boston, Little, Brown, 1975, pp 152-159

42. Kleiner GJ, Roberts TW: Current factors in causation of tubal pregnancy—a prospective clinicopathologic study. Am J Obstet Gynecol 99:21, 1967

43. Lazaro N, Batts J, Rishi A, Matseoane S, Chauhan P: Rupture of leiomyosarcoma uteri with hemoperitoneum clinically simulating ruptured ectopic pregnancy. J Reprod Med 24:174, 1980

44. Levinson C, Swolin K: Postoperative adhesions: etiology, prevention and therapy. Clin Obstet Gynecol 23:1213, 1980

45. Livant E, Scommegna A: A bilateral ureteral obstruction in ruptured chronic ectopic pregnancy. Am J Obstet Gynecol 127:330, 1977

46. Loh W, Loh H: Unilateral tubal twin pregnancy with intraperitoneal rupture. Obstet Gyencol 19:267, 1962
47. Mattingly RF: Telinde's Operative Gynecology. Philadelphia, Lippincott, 1977
48. May WJ, Miller J, Greiss F: Maternal deaths from ectopic pregnancy in the South Atlantic region, 1960 through 1976. Am J Obstet Gynecol 132:140, 1978
49. Metz K, Mastronianni L: Tubal pregnancy distal to complete tubal occlusion following sterilization. Am J Obstet Gynecol 131:911, 1978
50. Metz K, Mastroianni L: Tubal pregnancy subsequent to transperitoneal migration of spermatoza. Obstet Gynecol Surv 34:554, 1979
50a. Niswander K: Manual of Obstetrics. Boston, Little, Brown, 1980, Chap 17, Ectopic pregnancy
51. Novak E, Jones S, Jones H: Textbook of Gynecology, 9th ed. Baltimore, Williams & Wilkins, 1975
52. Novak E, Woodruff J: Gynecologic and Obstetric Pathology. Philadelphia, Saunders, 1979
52a. Ory H: Ectopic pregnancy and intrauterine contraceptive devices: new perspectives. Obstet Gynecol 57:137, 1981
53. Panayotou PP, et al.: Induced abortion and ectopic pregnancy. Am J Obstet Gynecol 114:507, 1972
54. Peraup V: Etiology of tubal ectopic pregnancy. Obstet Gynecol 36:257, 1970
55. Pritchard J, MacDonald P: Williams Obstetrics, 16th ed. New York, Appleton-Century-Crofts, 1980
56. Reeves C, Savarese M: Simultaneous intra- and extrauterine pregnancies. Obstet Gynecol 4:492, 1954
57. Rosenbaum J, Davling R, Barnes A: Treatment of tubal pregnancy. Am J Obstet Gynecol 80:274, 1960
58. Schneider J, Berger CJ, Cattell C: Maternal mortality due to ectopic pregnancy: a review of 102 deaths. Obstet Gynecol 49:557, 1977
59. Schoen J, Novak R: Repeat ectopic pregnancy. Obstet Gynecol 45:542, 1975
60. Shapiro H, Adler D: Excision of an ectopic pregnancy through the laparoscope. Am J Obstet Gynecol 117:290, 1973
60a. Siegler A, Wang C, Westhoff C: Management of unruptured tubal pregnancy. Obstet Gynecol Surv 36:599, 1981

61. Skulj V, Pavlic Z, Stoiljkovic C: Conservative operative treatment of tubal pregnancy. Fertil Steril 15:634, 1964

62. Stangel J, Gomel V: Techniques in conservative surgery for tubal gestation. Clin Obstet Gynecol 23:1221, 1980

63. Stangel JJ, Reyniak JV, Stone ML: Conservative surgical management of tubal pregnancy. Obstet Gynecol 48:241, 1976

64. Steadman HE: Combined intrauterine and extrauterine pregnancy. Obstet Gynecol 2:277, 1953

65. Storch M, Petrie R: Unilateral tubal twin gestation. Am J Obstet Gynecol 125:1148, 1976

66. Stromme WB: Conservative surgery for ectopic pregnancy: a twenty year review. Obstet Gynecol 41:215, 1973

67. Stromme WB, McKelvey JL, Adkins D: Conservative surgery for ectopic pregnancy. Obstet Gynecol 19:294, 1962

68. Stromme WB: Salpingotomy for tubal pregnancy. Obstet Gynecol 1:472, 1953

69. Studdiford WE: Is superfetation possible in the human being? Am J Obstet Gynecol 31:845, 1936

70 Tait L: Pathology and treatment of extrauterine pregnancy. Br Med J 2:317, 1884

71. Timonen S, Nieminen U: Tubal pregnancy: choice of operative method of treatment. Acta Obstet Gynecol Scand 46:327, 1967

72. Tompkins P: Preservation of fertility by conservative surgery for ectopic pregnancy. Fertil Steril 7:448, 1956

73. Webster H, Barclay D, Fischer C: Ectopic pregnancy: a seventeen year review. Am J Obstet Gynecol 92:23, 1965

74. Wei P: Occurrence of ectopic pregnancy in women with IUD's and consideration of the contraceptive mechanism of the IUD. Am J Obstet Gynecol 101:776, 1968

75. Winer AE, Beigman WD, Field C: Combined intra- and extrauterine pregnancy. Am J Obstet Gynecol 74:170, 1957

76. Wolf G, Thompson N: Female sterilization and subsequent ectopic pregnancy. Obstet Gynecol 555:17, 1980

77. Zarou G, Sy A: Combined intrauterine and extrauterine pregnancy progressing to term. Am J Obstet Gynecol 64:1338, 1952

Culdocentesis

79. Bobbrow M, Winkelstein L: The value of centesis and diagnostic procedure in ruptured ectopic gestations. Am J Obstet Gynecol 69:101, 1955

80. Draa CC, Baum HC: Posterior colpotomy: An aid in the diagnosis and treatment of ectopic pregnancy. Am J Obstet Gynecol 61:300, 1951

81. Grant M, Gordon T, Issaq E, Shabtai M: Accidental puncture of pelvic kidney: a rare complication of culdocentesis. Am J Obstet Gynecol 138:233, 1980

82. Halpin TF: Ectopic pregnancy: the problems of diagnosis. Am J Obstet Gynecol 106:227, 1970

83. Lacas C, Hassem A: Place of culdocentesis in the diagnosis of ectopic pregnancy. Br Med J 1:200, 1970

84. Schifter MA: A review of 268 ectopic pregnancies. Am J Obstet Gynecol 86:264, 1963

85. Webster H, Barclay D, Fischa C: Ectopic pregnancy—a seventeen year review. Am J Obstet Gynecol 92:23, 1965

Pregnancy Testing

86. Berry C, Thompson J, Hatcher R: The radioreceptor assay for hCG in ectopic pregnancy. Obstet Gynecol 54:43, 1979

87. Boyko WL, Russell H: Application of the radioreceptor assay for human chorionic gonadotropin in pregnancy testing and management in trophoblastic disease. Obstet Gynecol 50:324, 1977

88. Boyko WL, Russell H: Evaluation and clinical application of the quantitative radioreceptor assay for serum hCG. Obstet Gynecol 54:737, 1979

89. Braunstein GD: Grodin JM, Vaitukaitis JL, Roso GT: Secretory rates of human chorionic gonadotropin by normal trophoblast. Am J Obstet Gynecol 115:447, 1973

90. Braunstein GD, Karow WG, Gentry WD, et al.: Subclinical spontaneous abortion. Obstet Gynecol 50:41-S, 1977

91. Braunstein GD, Vaitukaitis JL, Carbone D: Ectopic production of human chorionic gonadotropin by neoplasms. Am Intern Med 78:39, 1973

92. Cohen HP, Braunstein GD, Van de Belde R, Van de Velde S: In vitro production of pregnancy-specific β_1-glycoprotein and ovarian cystadenocarcinoma line. Abstracts, Endocrine Society, 61st National Meeting, No. 882

93. Dawood MY: Laboratory Investigation of Fetal Disease.

94. Dhont M, Serreyn R, Vanderkerchkhove D, et al.: Serum chorionic gonadotropin assay and ectopic pregnancy. Lancet 1:559, 1978

95. Grudzinskas J, Evans D, Gordon Y, Jeffrey D, Chard T: Pregnancy-specific β_1-glycoprotein in fetal and maternal compartments. Obstet Gynecol 52:43, 1978

96. Grudzinskas JG, Gordon YB, Jeffrey D, et al.: Specific and sensitive determination of pregnancy-specific β_1-glycoprotein by radioimmunoassay. Lancet 1:333,1977

97. Ho P, Jones W: Pregnancy-specific β_1-glycoprotein as a prognostic indicator in complications of early pregnancy. Am J Obstet Gynecol 138:253, 1980

97a. Kadar N, Caldwell B, Romero R: A method of screening for ectopic pregnancy and its indications. Obstet Gynecol 58:162, 1981

98. Kauppila A, Rantakyla P, Huhtaniemi I, Ylikorkala O, Seppala M: Trophoblastic markers in the differential diagnosis of ectopic pregnancy. Obstet Gynecol 55:560, 1980

99. Kosasa T, Taymor M, Goldstein D, Leveque L: Use of radioimmunoassay specific for human chorionic gonadotropin in the diagnosis of early ectopic pregnancy. Obstet Gynecol 42:868, 1973

100. Landesman R, Saxena BB: Results of the first 100 radioreceptor assays for the determination of human chorionic gonadotropin: a new, rapid reliable and sensitive pregnancy test. Fertil Steril 27:357, 1976

101. Lin-t M, Halbert AP: Placental localization of human pregnancy-associated plasma proteins. Science 193:1249, 1976

102. Lorenz RP, Work BA, Menon KMJ: A radioreceptor assay for human chorionic gonadotropic in normal and abnormal pregnancies. A clinical evaluation. Am J Obstet Gynecol 134:471, 1979

103. Lundstrom V, Bremme K, Eneroth P, Nygard I, Sundvall M: Serum beta-human chorionic gonadotropin levels in the early diagnosis of ectopic pregnancy. Obstet Gynecol Surv 35:261, 1980

104. Mandelin M, Rutanen EM, Keikinheimo M, et al.: Pregnancy-specific beta$_1$-glycoprotein and chorionic gonadotropin levels after first trimester abortions. Obstet Gynecol 52:314, 1978

105. Milwidsky A, Adoni A, Miodovnik M, Segal S, Palti Z: Human chorionic gonadotropin (β-subunit) in the early diagnosis of ectopic pregnancy. Obstet Gynecol 51:725, 1978

105a. Pelosi MA: Use of the radioreceptor assay for human chorionic gonadotropin in the diagnosis of ectopic pregnancy. Surg Gynecol Obstet 152:149, 1981

106. Rasor JL, Braunstein GD: A rapid modification of the beta-hCG

radioimmunoassay: use as an aid in the diagnosis of ectopic pregnancy. Obstet Gynecol 50:553, 1977

107. Rosal TP, Saxena BB, Landesman R: Application of a radioreceptor assay of human chorionic gonadotropin in the diagnosis of early abortion. Fertil Steril 26:1105, 1975

108. Rosen S, Kaminska J, Calvert I, Aaronson S: Human fibroblasts produce "pregnancy-specific" beta$_1$-glycoprotein in vitro. Am J Obstet Gynecol 134:734, 1979

109. Rosen S, Kaminska J, Calvert I, Nelson E, Aaronson S: Ectopic production of "pregnancy-specific" beta$_1$-glycoprotein in vitro: discordance with three other placental proteins. Am J Obstet Gynecol 137:525, 1980

110. Roy S, Klein T, Scott J, Kletzky O, Mishell D: Diagnosis of pregnancy with radioreceptor assay for hCG. Obstet Gynecol 50:401, 1977

111. Saxena BB, Hasan SJ, Haour F, Gollwotzer M: Radioreceptor assay of chorionic gonadotropin in early detection of pregnancy. Science 184:793, 1974

112. Saxena B, Landesman R: The use of a radioreceptor assay of human chorionic gonadotropin for the diagnosis and management of ectopic pregnancy. Fertil Steril 26:397, 1975

113. Schwartz R, DiPietro D: β-hCG as a diagnostic aid for suspected ectopic pregnancy. Obstet Gynecol 56:197, 1980

114. Seppala M, Venesmaa P, Rutanen EM: Pregnancy-specific beta$_1$-glycoprotein in ectopic pregnancy. Am J Obstet Gynecol 136:189, 1980

115. Seppala M, Rutanen EM, Heikinhei M, et al.: Detection of trophoblastic tumor activity by pregnancy-specific beta$_1$-glycoprotein. Int J Cancer 21:265, 1978

116. Tatarinov YS: Trophoblast-specific beta-glycoprotein as a marker for pregnancy and malignancies. Gynecol Obstet Invest 9:65, 1978

117. Vaitukaitis JL, Braunstein GD, Ross GT: A radioimmunoassay which specifically measures human chorionic gonadotropin in the presence of human luteinizing hormone. Am J Obstet Gynecol 113:751, 1972

Ultrasound

118. Blackwell RJ, Shirley I, Farnan D, Michael CA: Ultrasonic B-scanning as a pregnancy test after less than 6 weeks amenorrhea. Br J Obstet Gynecol 83:108, 1975

119. Brown T, Filly R, Laing F, Barton J: Analysis of ultrasonographic criteria in the evaluation for ectopic pregnancy. Am J Roentgenol 131:967, 1978

120. Cadkin A, Bezjian A, Sebbagha R: Ectopic pregnancy. In Sabbagha R(ed): Diagnostic Ultrasound Applied to Obstetrics and Gynecology. New York, Appleton-Century-Crofts, 1977, pp 21

121. Cadkin A, Sabbagha R: Ultrasonic diagnosis of abnormal pregnancy. Clin Obstet Gynecol 20:265, 1977

122. Chilcote W, Asokan S: Evaluation of first trimester pregnancy by ultrasound. Clin Obstet Gynecol 20:253, 1977

123. Conrad M, Johnson J, James A: Sonography in ectopic pregnancy. In Sanders R, James AE (eds): Ultrasound in Obstetrics and Gynecology New York, Appleton-Century-Crofts, 1977, pp 114–121

124. Fleischer A, Boehm F, James AE: Songraphic evaluation of ectopic pregnancy. In Sanders RC, James AE (eds): Ultrasonography in Obstetrics and Gynecology. New York, Appleton-Century-Crofts, 1980, Chap 24

124a. Kadar N, DeVoe G, Romero R: Discriminatory hCG Zone: Its use in the sonographic evaluation for ectopic pregnancy. Obstet Gynecol 58:156, 1981

125. Kelly MT, Santos-Ramos R, Duenhoelter J: The value of sonography in suspected ectopic pregnancy. Obstet Gynecol 53:703, 1979

126. Kobayashi M, Hellman L, Fillisti L: Ultrasound: an aid in the diagnosis of ectopic pregnancy. Am J Obstet Gynecol 103:1131, 1969

127. Kukard R, Coetzee M: A comparison between ultrasonic and clinical diagnostic reliability in early pregnancy complications. S Afr Med J 49:2109, 1974

128. Lawson TL: Ectopic pregnancy: criteria and accuracy of ultrasonic diagnosis. Am J Roentgenol Radium Ther Nucl Med 131:153, 1978

128a. Laing, FC, Filly R, Marks W, Brown TW: Ultrasonic demonstration of endometrial fluid collections unassociated with pregnancy. Ultrasound 137:471, 1980

129. Levi S: Abnormalities in early pregnancy. In Handbook of Clinical Ultrasound. New York, Wiley, 1978

130. Maklad N, Wright C: Grey scale ultrasonography in the diagnosis of ectopic pregnancy. Radiology 126:221, 1978

130a. Marks WM, Filly RA, Cullen PW: The decidual cast of ectopic pregnancy: a confusing ultrasonographic appearance. Radiology 133:451, 1979

131. Pardanai N, Amalkin M: Combined intrauterine and extrauterine pregnancy diagnosed by ultrasound. N Engl J Med 301:841, 1979

132. Queenan JT, Kubarych SF, Douglas LD: Evaluation of diagnostic ultrasound in gynecology. Am J Obstet Gynecol 123:453, 1975

133. Varma T: The value of ultrasonic B-scanning in diagnosis when bleeding is present in early pregnancy. Am J Obstet Gynecol 14:607, 1972

Interstitial Ectopic Pregnancy

134. Bisca B, Felder M: Coexistent interstitial and intrauterine pregnancy following homolateral salpingo-oophorectomy. Am J Obstet Gynecol 79:263, 1960

135. Chandra P, Kownigsberg M, Romney S, Koren Z, Schulman H: Unruptured Interstitial pregnancy (diagnosis and treatment). Obstet Gynecol 52:612, 1978

136. Fara FJ, Varga A: Interstitial twin pregnancy with cornual rupture. Obstet Gynecol 10:579, 1957

137. Felmus LB, Pedowitz P: Interstitial pregnancy. Survey of 45 cases. Am J Obstet Gynecol 66:1271, 1953

137a. Jansen R, Elliott P: Angular intrauterine pregnancy. Obstet Gynecol 58:167, 1981

138. Makii M, Evans M, Yang S: Interstitial twin pregnancy. Obstet Gynecol 55:23-S, 1980

139. Pedowitz P, Felmus LB: Obstet Gynecol Surv 7:305, 1952

140. Simpson J, Alford P, Miller A: Interstitial pregnancy following homolateral salpingectomy. Am J Obstet Gynecol 82:1173, 1961

141. Steadman H: Ruptured interstitial pregnancy following homolateral salpingectomy. Obstet Gynecol 7:572, 1956

142. Stromme WB, McKelvey JL, Adkins D: Conservative surgery for ectopic pregnancy. Obstet Gynecol 19:254, 1962

143. Stromme WB: Conservative surgery for ectopic pregnancy: a twenty year review. Obstet Gynecol 41:215, 1973

144. Toongswan S: Interstitial tubal pregnancy. Aust NZ J Obstet Gynecol 9:62, 1969

Abdominal Ectopic Pregnancy

145. Baldwin WF: Abdominal pregnancy: discussion, classification and case presentation. Obstet Gynecol 4:435, 1954

146. Beacham WD, Beacham DW: Abdominal pregnancy. Obstet Gynecol Surv 1:777, 1946
147. Beacham WD, Hernquist WC, Beacham DW, Webster HD: Abdominal pregnancy at Charity Hosptial in New Orleans. Am J Obstet Gynecol 84:1257, 1962
148. Beck AC: Treatment of extrauterine pregnancy after the fifth month. JAMA 73:962, 1919
149. Beck P, Birnbaum SJ: Thermographic and hormone studies of the placenta in abdominal pregnancy. Am J Obstet Gynecol 99:29, 1967
150. Bourgeois G, Shapiro M: Abnormal pregnancy secondary to rupture of accessory uterus with survival of mother and infant. N Engl J Med 247:84, 1952
151. Bright AS, Maser AH: Advanced abdominal pregnancy. Obstet Gynecol 17:316, 1961
151a. Cavanagh D: Primary peritoneal pregnancy. Am J Obstet Gynecol 76:523, 1958
152. Clark JFJ, Bourke J: Advanced ectopic pregnancy. Am J Obstet Gynecol 78:340, 1959
153. Clark JFJ, Guy R: Abdominal pregnancy. Am J Obstet Gynecol 96:511, 1966
154. Clark J, Jones S: Advanced ectopic pregnancy. J Reprod Med 14:30, 1975
155. Cohn F, Goldenberg R: Term pregnancy in an unattached rudimentary uterine horn. Obstet Gynecol 48:234, 1976
156. Crawford J, Ward J: Advanced abdominal pregnancy. Obstet Gynecol 10:549, 1957
157. Cross JB, Lester WM, McCain JR: The diagnosis and management of abdominal pregnancy. Am J Obstet Gynecol 62:303, 1951
158. Decker A, Decker WH: A tubal function test. Obstet Gynecol 4:35, 1954
159. Dixon HG, Stewart OB: Advanced extrauterine pregnancy. Med J 2:1103, 1960
160. Doyle JB: Tubo-ovarian mechanism: observation at laparotomy. Obstet Gynecol 8:686, 1956
161. Doyle JB: Exploratory culdotomy for observation of tuboovarian physiology at ovulation time. Fertil Steril 2:425, 1951
162. Eisenman J, Markowitz J, Thompson WB: Pelvic angiography in retained placenta of abdominal pregnancy. Obstet Gynecol 28:637, 1966

163. Foster H, Moore D: Abdominal pregnancy. Obstet Gynecol 30:249, 1967

164. Friedrich EG, Rankin CA: Primary peritoneal pregnancy. Obstet Gynecol 31:649, 1968

165. Garrett WD, Crowe PH, Robinson DC: The interpretation of ultrasonic echograms in abdominal pregnancy. Aust NZ J Obstet Gynecol 9:26, 1969

166. Hazlett WH: Repeated term abdominal pregnancy. Obstet Gynecol 1:313, 1953

166a. Hibbard L: The management of secondary abdominal pregnancy. Am J Obstet Gynecol 74:543, 1957

167. Horne H, Thibault J: Sperm migration through the human female reproductive tract. Fertil Steril 13:135, 1962

168. Hreschchyshyn M, Borgen B, Loughran C: What is the actual present day management of the placenta in late abdominal pregnancy? Am J Obstet Gynecol 81:302, 1961

169. Hreschchyshyn, M, Grahm J, Holland J: Treatment of malignant trophoblastic growth in women with special reference to amethopterin. Am J Obstet Gynecol 81:688, 1961

170. Hreschchyshn MM, Naples JD, Randall CL: Amethopterin in abdominal pregnancy. Am J Obstet Gynecol 93:286, 1965

171. Iffy L: Contribution to the aetiology of ectopic pregnancy. J Obstet Gynaecol Br Emp 68:441, 1961

172. Jackson RL: Pure malignancy of the trophoblast following primary abdominal pregnancy. Am J Obstet Gynecol 79:1085, 1960

173. Johansen K: Pregnancy in rudimentary horn. Obstet Gynecol 34:805, 1969

174. Jones S, Clark J, Anderson J: X-ray diagnosis of advanced extrauterine pregnancy. Obstet Gynecol 34:578, 1969

175. King G: Advanced extrauterine pregnancy. Am J Obstet Gynecol 67:712, 1954

176. Kirkland, JA, Glover JB: Normal intrauterine pregnancy following previous abdominal pregnancy. Am J Obstet Gynecol 99:911, 1967

177. Kobayashi M, Hellman L, Fillisti L: Ultrasound, an aid to the diagnosis of ectopic pregnancy. Am J Obstet Gynecol 103:1113, 1969

178. Lathrop JC, Bowles GE: Methotrexate in abdominal pregnancy: report of a case. Obstet Gynecol 32:81, 1968

179. Lester WM, Fish J: Two successive abdominal pregnancies

associated with uterus bicornes unicolis. Am J Obstet Gynecol 65:411, 1953

180. Levitt CA, Ingram JM: Abdominal pregnancy with complete ureteral obstruction. Am J Obstet Gynecol 120:203, 1974

181. Lull CB: Abdominal pregnancy. Am J Obstet Gynecol 40:194, 1940

182. Millen RS: The fate of the placenta left in site following the delivery of a fetus in abdominal pregnancy. Am J Obstet Gynecol 71:1348, 1956

183. Nelson J, Bernstine R, Huston J, Garcia N, Garenlaub C: Percutaneous retrograde femoral arteriography in obstetrics and gynecology. Obstet Gynecol Surv 16:1, 1961

184. Nethey RA: Abdominal pregnancy with survival of mother and normal child. Am J Obstet Gynecol 69:435, 1955

185. Niebyl JR: Pregnancy following total hysterectomy. Am J Obstet Gynecol 119:512, 1974

186. Norenberg D, Gundersen J, Janis J, Gundersen A: Early pregnancy on the diaphragm with endometriosis. Obstet Gynecol 49:620, 1977

187. Nylandar P, Akanoe E, Ogunbode O: Simultaneous advanced extrauterine and intrauterine pregnancy. Int J Gynecol Obstet 9:102, 1971

188. O'Leary JL, O'Leary JA: Rudimentary horn pregnancy. Obstet Gynecol 23:371, 1963

189. Sabbagha R: Diagnostic Ultrasound. Hagerstown, Md., Harper & Row, 1980, pp 253–255

190. Sanders RC, James AE: Ultrasonography in Obstetrics and Gynecology, 2nd ed. New York, Appleton-Century-Crofts, 1980, p 285

191. Schultz M: Full-term pregnancy in rudimentary horn. J Obstet Br Comm 58:293, 1951

192. Siegler AH, Zeichner J, Robenstein L, Wallace E, Canter AC: Endocrine studies in two instances of term abdominal pregnancy. Am J Obstet Gynecol 78:369, 1959

193. Smulewicz JJ, Tafreshi M, Cagan SH, Hedjaz M: Retained placenta following term abdominal pregnancy—diagnosis by angiography. Am J Obstet Gynecol 109:1220, 1971

194. Steadman H: Combined intrauterine and extrauterine pregnancy. Obstet Gynecol 2:277, 1953

195. Strafford J, Ragan W: Abdominal pregnancy. Obstet Gynecol 50:548, 1977

196. Stromme WB, Reed SC, Haywa EW: Abdominal pregnancy: early diagnosis and delivery of a surviving infant. Report of a case. Obstet Gynecol 13:109, 1959
197. Studdiford WE: Primary peritoneal pregnancy. Am J Obstet Gynecol 44:487, 1942
198. Suter M, Wichsu C: The fate of the living viable babies in extrauterine pregnancy. Am J Obstet Gynecol 55:489, 1948
199. Tan K, Goon S, Wee J: The pediatric aspects of advanced abdominal pregnancy. J. Obstet Gynaecol Br Comm 76:1021, 1969
200. Tan K, Vergadasalm D, Leon T: Recurrent abdominal pregnancy. J Obstet Gynaecol Br Comm 78:1044, 1971
201. Thompson LR: Abdominal pregnancy at term. Am J Surg 98:625, 1959
202. Thompson L: Abdominal pregnancy at term with late removal of the placenta. Am J Surg 111:272, 1966
203. Tisdall L, Nichols R, Sicuranza B: Abdominal pregnancy associated with an intrauterine contraceptive device. Am J Obstet Gynecol 106:937, 1970
204. Wahlen T: Pregnancy in non-communicating rudimentary uterine horn. Acta Obstet Gynecol Scand 51:155, 1972
205. Walker J: Ein Fall von primaerer abdominalsch Wangerschaft. Arch Gynaek 111:342, 1919
206. Ware HH: Observations on thirteen cases of later extra uterine pregnancy. Am J Obstet Gynecol 55:561, 1948
207. Weinberg A, Sherwin AS: A new sign in roentgen diagnosis of advanced ectopic pregnancy. Obstet Gynecol 7:99, 1956
208. Yahia C, Montgomery G: Advanced extrauterine pregnancy. Obstet Gynecol 8:68, 1956
209. Zarou G, Sy A: Combined intrauterine and extrauterine pregnancy progressing at term. Am J Obstet Gynecol 64:1338, 1952
210. Ziel HK, Miyazki FS, Baker TH, White JD: Advanced intraligamentary pregnancy. Obstet Gynecol 31:643, 1968
211. Zuspan FP, Quilligan EJ, Rosenblum JD: Abdominal pregnancy. Am J Obstet Gynecol 74:259, 1957

Ovarian Ectopic Pregnancies
212. Baden W, Heins O: Ovarian pregnancy. Am J Obstet Gynecol 64:353, 1952
213. Bobrow M, Winkelstein L: Intrafollicular ovarian pregnancy. Am J Surg 91:991, 1956

214. Boronow R, McElin T, West R, Buchingham J: Ovarian pregnancy Am J Obstet Gynecol 91:1095, 1965
215. Breuer R: Pregnancy—ovarian pregnancy. Am J Obstet Gynecol 79:255, 1960
216. Campbell JS, et al.: Acute hemoperitoneum, IUD, and occult ovarian pregnancy. Obstet Gynecol 43:438, 1974
217. Duckman, S, Suarez J, Tantakesem P: Ovarian pregnancy and the intrauterine contraceptive device. Am J Obstet Gynecol 118:570, 1974
218. Gerin-Lajoie L: Ovarian pregnancy. Am J Obstet Gynecol 62:920, 1951
219. Helde MD, Campbell JS, Himaya A, et al.: Detection of unsuspected ovarian pregnancy by wedge resection. Can Med Assoc J 106:237, 1972
220. Kalfayan B, Gundersen J: Ovarian twin pregnancy. Obstet Gynecol 55:255, 1980
221. Lehfeldt H, Tietze C, Gorstein F: Ovarian pregnancy and the intrauterine device. Am J Obstet Gynecol 108:1005, 1970
222. Levin S, Caspi E, Hirsch H: Ovarian pregnancy and intrauterine devices. Am J Obstet Gynecol 113:843, 1972
223. McMorries K, Lofton R, Stinson J, Cummings R: Is the IUD increasing the number of ovarian pregnancies? Contemp Obstet Gynecol 13:165, 1979
224. Norris CC: Primary ovarian pregnancy, report of a case combined with intrauterine pregnancy. Surg Gynecol Obstet 9:123, 1909
225. Tan KK, Yeo OH: Primary ovarian pregnancy. Am J Obstet Gynecol 100:240, 1968
226. Williams JW: Obstetrics. New York, D. Appleton and Company, 1903, p 537

Cervical Ectopic Pregnancy

227. Baptisti A: Cervical pregnancy. Obstet Gynecol 1:353, 1953
227a. Bernstein D, Holzinger M, Ovadia J, Frishman B: Conservative management of cervical pregnancy. Obstet Gynecol 58:741, 1981
228. Clark CL: Cervical pregnancy. A review of the literature and report of a case. Obstet Gynecol 16:454, 1960
229. Duckman S: Cervical pregnancy. Am J Obstet Gynecol 62:1381, 1951
230. Duckman S, Amico J: Cervical abortion. Obstet Gynecol 10:240, 1957

231. Jauchlex GW, Baker RL: Cervical pregnancy. Review of the literature and a case report. Obstet Gynecol 35:870, 1970

232. Mortimer C, Aitken D: Cervical pregnancy. J Obstet Gynaecol Br Comm 75:741, 1968

233. Paalman RJ, McElin TW: Cervical pregnancy. Am J Obstet Gynecol 77:1261, 1959

234. Pisarski L: Cervical pregnancy. J Obstet Gynaecol Br Comm 67:759, 1960

235. Rothe DJ, Birnbaum SJ: Cervical pregnancy: diagnosis and mangagement. Obstet Gynecol 42:675, 1973

236. Schneider P: Distal ectopic pregnancy. (Implantation of the ovum in the cervical mucosae). Am J Obstet Surg 72:526, 1946

237. Schneider P, Dreizin DH: Cervical pregnancy. Am J Surg 93:27, 1957

238. Sherwin A, Berg F: Cervical pregnancy. Am J Obstet Gynecol 79:259, 1960

239. Shinagawa S, Nagagama M: Cervical pregnancy as a possible sequela of induced abortion. Am J Obstet Gynecol 105:282, 1969

240. Studdiford WE: Cervical pregnancy. Am J Obstet Gynecol 49:169, 1945

21

Normal and Abnormal Sexual Differentiation and Development

Edra B. Weiss, M.D.
Ira M. Rosenthal, M.D.

PRACTICE PRINCIPLES

Problems of abnormal sexual differentiation and development are uncommon in the general physician's practice. As a result the physician may be unfamiliar with the appropriate evaluation and therapy of these disorders. A thorough knowledge of the developmental anatomy and physiology and pathophysiology of the various disorders facilitates such evaluation and treatment.

NORMAL SEXUAL DEVELOPMENT AND PHYSIOLOGY

A. *Normal female differentiation*
1. *Ovarian development.* In the female fetus, the indifferent gonad develops into an ovary during the thirteenth to sixteenth week of gestation. Two X chromosomes are necessary for normal fetal ovarian development. The

absence of one chromosome (i.e., 45,X) results in the deterioration of ova, with resultant streak gonads.

2. *Müllerian duct differentiation.* The Müllerian ducts form most of the internal reproductive tract of the female, i.e., oviducts, fallopian tubes, uterus, and a small portion of the vagina. Most of the vagina, however, is formed from the urogenital sinus. The Wolffian ducts degenerate in the female except for the small caudal portion which forms the Gartner duct and a small cranial portion which forms the epöophoron.

3. *External genitalia.* The external genitalia change little from the indifferent gonad stage of fetal life. The clitoris is formed from the genital tubercle, the labia minora develop from the urethral folds, and the labia majora develop from the genital swellings.

B. Normal male differentiation

1. *Testicular development.* In the male infant (46,XY) there is coding for H-Y antigen, a histocompatibility antigen. This antigen results in the differentiation of the indifferent fetal gonad into a testis by the seventh week of gestation.

2. *Müllerian duct regression.* The fetal testis produces two hormones, anti-Müllerian hormone (AMH) and testosterone. Anti-Müllerian hormone, probably a large polypeptide, causes regression of the müllerian ducts except for the most cranial portion, which persists as the appendix testes.

3. *Wolffian duct differentiation.* Testosterone is responsible for the differentiation of the Wolffian ducts into epididymis, vas deferens, and seminal vesicles. Five enzymes are necessary for the synthesis of testosterone from cholesterol. Three of these enzymes (cholesterol 20,22-desmolase, 3-β-hydroxysteroid dehydrogenase, and 17-α-hydroxylase) are present in the adrenal as well as in the testes. Therefore, a deficiency in any one of these enzymes results in a defect of glucocorticoid and/or mineralocorticoid production, as well as in the produc-

tion of sex hormones. Two of the enzymes necessary for testosterone synthesis (17,20-desmolase and 17-β-hydroxysteroid oxidoreductase) are present primarily in the testes.

4. *External genitalia.* Testosterone is also necessary for fusion of the genital swellings to form the scrotum. The prostatic bud, an outpocketing of the urogenital sinus, develops into the prostate. Testosterone is reduced in the genital tubercle and urogenital sinus by 5-α-reductase to dihydrotestosterone. The reduced form is necessary for male differentiation of these tissues (i.e., penile and prostatic development).

C. *Role of pituitary gland in sexual development*

1. *Function of FSH and LH in gonadal development.* The hypothalamic-pituitary-gonadal axis begins functioning during fetal life. FSH (follicle-stimulating hormone), LH (luteinizing hormone), and hCG (human chorionic gonadotropin) play important roles in sexual differentiation by stimulating gonadal growth and by helping to maintain sex steroid synthesis and secretion by the gonads. FSH plays a synergistic role with LH in the development of LH receptors on Leydig cells. The stimulation of hCG-LH receptors on Leydig cells is necessary for the fetal testis to produce testosterone.

2. *Function of FSH and LH at puberty.* FSH and LH are elevated at birth, but by 2 years of age low values characteristic of prepubertal children are reached. Gonadotropin secretion is regulated by a complex interaction of the central nervous system, the hypothalamus, the pituitary, and the feedback regulation of these centers by both estrogens and androgens.

When puberty begins, there is increased secretion from the hypothalamus of gonadotropin-releasing hormone (GnRH). The event or events that trigger increased GnRH secretion remain unknown. LH is first produced in nocturnal surges followed by smaller episodic increases in FSH production. An adult pattern of LH release (pulsatile throughout the 24-hour period) is reached late in puberty. In females, FSH rises during the early stages of puberty until a plateau is reached at about the time of menarche (Tanner stage III). LH values remain lower than FSH values until about a year before menarche, when higher values are present. In the female, FSH stimulates follicle development and, along with LH, is part of the ovulatory surge. LH also supports corpus luteal function.

3. *Function of DHA and DHAS.* About two years before the GnRH surge begins, adrenal androgen secretion — dehydroepiandosterone (DHA) and its sulfate (DHAS) — begins. This plays a role in the development of pubic and axillary hair. The exact control of this process is incompletely understood at this time. However, it is believed that ACTH plays a role in the production of DHA and DHAS.

D. *Nutrition and sexual development.* Nutrition is important in the onset of puberty. The trend toward earlier menarche in our country since 1850 probably reflects better nutrition. For at least three decades, the critical weight of 46 kg has been associated with menarche. This usually corresponds to a child between 12.5 and 13 years of age.

INTERSEXUALITY

Abnormalities of sexual differentiation may result from virilization of a genetically female fetus, incomplete masculinization of a genetically male fetus, a chromosome abnormality (i.e., 45,X/46,XY) or from the presence of both ovarian and testicular tissue in the same individual. Prompt diagnosis is necessary both to designate the sex of rearing and to institute appropriate therapy.

A. *Virilization of a genetic female. Female pseudohermaphroditism* occurs when the genitalia are partially masculinized, but the gonads are ovaries, and the chromosomes are 46,XX.

1. *Congenital adrenal hyperplasia* (CAH). These are auto-somal recessive inherited abnormalities. Affected females have varying degrees of virilization of external genitalia. A urogenital sinus is usually present. The virilization results either from excessive testosterone production (21- and 11-hydroxylase deficiencies) or from increased DHA production (3-β-ol-dehydrogenase defect). Normal Müllerian elements are present. The patients have potential for normal fertility if treated properly. Virilization will continue if proper therapy is not instituted and maintained.

   a) *21-hydroxylase deficiency.* Over 90 percent of all patients with congenital adrenal hyperplasia have a 21-hydroxylase enzymatic defect. These patients have elevated levels of 17-α-hydroxyprogesterone and elevated levels of testosterone. The clitoris is enlarged at birth, and there is usually a urogenital sinus. Occasionally, there may be a clitoral urethra. In about half the patients, there is an associated lack of aldosterone production, with resultant electrolyte disturbance characterized by a low serum sodium and elevated serum potassium. This is usually manifested by day 4 to day 10 of life with symptoms of vomiting and lethargy and signs of dehydration. Hypoglycemia may also be present in the neonate.

      (1) *Diagnosis* is suspected from the clinical presentation. Confirmation of the diagnosis is obtained from a markedly elevated plasma 17-hydroxy-progesterone level. Serum testosterone is usually elevated. In those patients with associated sodium loss, the serum sodium is decreased and the serum potassium is increased. Urinary 17-ketosteroids and pregnanetriol are also elevated. However, pregnanetriol may not be elevated in the first weeks of life.

      (2) *Therapy.* Patients with no associated electrolyte disturbance are treated with glucocorticoids from

the time of diagnosis. The dose must be increased as the child becomes older. In case of stress, this medication should be increased further.

Patients with associated electrolyte disturbance require intravenous fluids with sodium chloride and glucose. In addition, they require mineralocorticoid treatment with DOCA (desoxycorticosterone acetate). Later, this can be replaced by monthly injections of DCTMA (desoxycorticosterone pivalate) or oral fludrocortisone acetate. Extra oral sodium chloride is required in the diet. The blood pressure of these patients should be carefully monitored, and if it is elevated, the amount of mineralocorticoids should be decreased appropriately.

b) *11-hydroxylase deficiency.* This is a rare disorder affecting less than 3 percent of the patients with congenital adrenal hyperplasia. It is associated with hypertension in most cases due to the excessive synthesis of desoxycorticosterone.

(1) *Diagnosis* is confirmed by increased urinary excretion of compound S and its metabolites and mild elevation of serum 17-hydroxyprogesterone.

(2) *Therapy* consists of glucocorticoid replacement. The hypertension usually disappears with proper therapy.

c) *3-β-ol-dehydrogenase deficiency.* The virilization of female infants with this condition is usually mild. However, the electrolyte disturbance is usually severe, since there is impairment of mineralocorticoid as well as glucocorticoid production.

(1) *Diagnosis* is confirmed by elevated serum levels of pregnenolone and dehydroepiandrostenedione and very low 17-hydroxyprogesterone.

(2) *Therapy* is similar to that for 21-hydroxylase deficiency with electrolyte disturbance. Prognosis is guarded in severe cases.

d) *Virilizing maternal tumor.* The *arrhenoblastoma* is the most common virilizing tumor occurring in women during pregnancy. The infant may be born with an enlarged clitoris. Virilization of the infant is not progressive.

(1) *Diagnosis* is usually obtained from history and maternal blood samples.

(2) *Therapy.* The infant may require no therapy as some regression of the virilization may occur after delivery. In occasional cases, however, surgery is required.

e) *Ingestion of virilizing medication during pregnancy.* The physical findings indicate enlargement of the clitoris and some fusion of the labia.

(1) *Diagnosis.* A history of ingestion of virilizing substances during early pregnancy is obtained. A number of progestational agents have been implicated.

(2) *Therapy.* Virilization is not progressive. Female sex should be assigned. Plastic surgery is required in some cases.

B. *True hermaphroditism* is characterized by the presence of ovarian and testicular tissue in the same individual. An ovotestis may be present on each side of the body. There may be an ovotestis on one side and a testis on the other, an ovary on one side and a testis on the other, or an ovotestis on one side with no gonad on the other. The karyotype is usually 46,XX. Mosaicism, 46,XX/46,XY, is not uncommon. It is unusual to have a 46,XY pattern. All individuals with true hermaphroditism appear to be HY antigen positive. Although almost all cases have been sporadic, there have been a few reports of familial true hermaphroditism.

1. *Diagnosis* is suspected from the clinical presentation. The degree of male differentiation depends on the capacity of the fetal testicular tissue to secrete testosterone and anti-Müllerian hormone. There is considerable variation in the development of the phallus and in the configuration

of the external genitalia. A uterus and vagina are usually present, but the fallopian tube is generally absent on the side with testicular tissue. Sexual maturation at puberty is dependent on the functional capacity of the ovarian and testicular tissue.

2. *Therapy* depends upon the sex assignment. After diagnostic studies focused on the functional capacity of the genitalia for sexual activity, a decision is made regarding sex assignment. Fertility is not a consideration since these patients are almost always sterile. Consideration must be given to gender identification in older children when sex assignment is considered. In most cases female sex is assigned. Testicular tissue is removed, and reconstructive surgery of the genitalia is done. True hermaphrodites usually require replacement sex hormones at the time of puberty.

C. *Incomplete Masculinization of a genetic male.* Patients with male pseudohermaphroditism have testes, but male differentiation of the external genitalia is incomplete or there is persistence of internal müllerian structures. The basic causes include an abnormality of fetal testicular formation, an unresponsiveness of the fetal Leydig cells to hCG and LH, an inborn error in testosterone biosynthesis, a deficiency of 5-α-reductase, the enzyme necessary for peripheral conversion of testosterone to dihydrotestosterone, end organ unresponsiveness to testosterone, or an abnormality in the production or action of anti-Müllerian hormone. The karyotype of these patients is 46,XY.

1. *Inborn errors of testosterone biosynthesis.* Of the five enzymes necessary for the synthesis of testosterone from cholesterol, three are present in both the adrenal gland and the testes and affect the production of glucocorticoid and mineralocorticoids. In all five enzyme defects, the degree of intersexuality present varies considerably and is dependent upon the extent of deficiency (Fig. 21–1). Müllerian duct development does not occur in these patients. Testes are usually underdeveloped and fre-

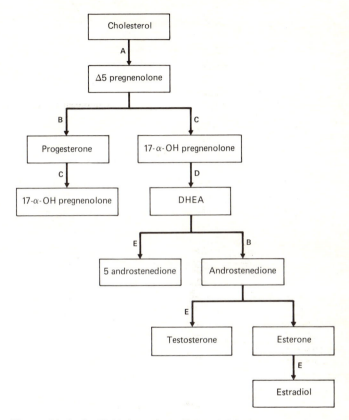

Figure 21–1. A, 20,22-desmolase; **B,**3-β-ol-dehydrogenase; **C,** 17-alpha-hydroxylase; **D,** 17,20-desmolase; **E,** 17-β-ol-oxidoreductase.

quently intraabdominal. The defects are inherited in an autosomal recessive manner.

a) *20–22-desmolase deficiency.* In 46,XY infants with this condition, also known as congenital lipoid adrenal hyperplasia, the external genitalia are female with a blind vaginal pouch. Since neither glucocorticoids nor mineralocorticoids are synthesized, there is severe electrolyte disturbances and early Addisonian crisis. Most patients have a severe deficiency with a high mortality rate.

(1) *Diagnosis.* Very low or absent urinary 17-ketosteroids and 17-hydroxycorticosteroids.

(2) *Therapy* consists of glucocorticoids and mineralocorticoid replacement. Appropriate sex hormone substitution would be necessary at puberty if the patient survives.

b) *3-β-ol-dehydrogenase deficiency.* Male pseudohermaphrodites with this condition are only partially masculinized due to the weak androgenic action of dehydroisoandrosterone and the lack of testosterone. The electrolyte disturbance is severe in patients with this defect, and the mortality rate is high despite therapy.

(1) *Diagnosis.* Serum dehydroisoandrosterone is elevated along with its urinary metabolites. Serum cortisol and aldosterone are low or not detectable.

(2) *Therapy.* These patients require glucocorticoids and mineralocorticoids. In partially affected patients, normal puberty may occur. Plastic surgery is generally needed to correct the hypospadias if the child is reared as a male or to reduce the phallic enlargement and create a vagina if the sex of rearing is female.

c) *17-α-hydroxylase deficiency.* Patients with a complete defect have external genitalia of a female phenotype. In partial deficiency, there may be variable degrees of phallic development with hypospadias. These patients may demonstrate some signs of spontaneous secondary sex development and gynecomastia has occasionally been seen. In complete deficiency, secondary sex development does not occur, and the patients, regardless of the genotype, have normal-appearing female external genitalia. Hypertension and hypokalemia are common in the older patient due to the excessive production of desoxycorticosterone (DOC).

(1) *Diagnosis.* Elevated serum levels of pregnenolone, progesterone, DOC, and corticosterone are present with low serum levels of cortisol and aldosterone. Renin is also quite low. Serum gonadotropins are elevated.

(2) *Therapy.* Sex of rearing is dependent upon the ability to function sexually as an adult. Glucocorticoid replacement usually lowers the blood pressure to normal. Appropriate sex hormone replacement at the time of puberty is necessary.

d) *17,20-desmolase deficiency.* Since this enzyme is not present in the adrenals, neither mineralocorticoid nor glucocorticoid deficiencies occur. There are variable abnormalities of phallic development and hypospadias in this condition.

(1) *Diagnosis.* Increased urinary pregnenetriol and 11-ketopregnenetriol are found. Serum and urinary testosterone levels are extremely low, and no rise in testosterone occurs following hCG injection. Plasma gonadotropins are elevated.

(2) *Therapy.* Replacement sex hormones are needed at the time of puberty. Surgery to produce external genitalia appropriate to the sex assignment may be necessary. If the sex assignment is female, orchiectomy is indicated.

e) *17-β-hydroxysteroid oxidoreductase deficiency.* Patients with this deficiency are seldom identified until puberty. Because of the limitation of this enzyme to the testes, neither salt loss nor addisonian crisis occurs. The external genitalia are usually that of a female, with a blind vaginal pouch. However, testes may be palpated in the inguinal canal.

At the time of puberty both feminization (i.e., breast development) and masculinization (i.e., phallic growth and hirsutism) may occur.

(1) *Diagnosis.* At puberty, serum testosterone and

estradiol levels are much lower than the precursor values of androstenediol and estrone. The ratio of precursor to product is important in establishing the diagnosis.

In prepubertal subjects, daily hCG administration for five days with subsequent measurement of serum testosterone, androstenediol, estradiol, and estrone aids in establishing the diagnosis. In either pubertal or prepubertal subjects, gonadotropins are elevated. There is little increase in testosterone or estradiol, but levels of androstenediol and estrone increase. In either pubertal or prepubertal subjects, gonadotropins are elevated.

(2) *Therapy*. Similar to that employed for 17,20-desmolase deficiency.

2. *Inborn errors of testosterone metabolism*

   a) *5-α-reductase deficiency*. There is inadequate conversion of testosterone to dihydrotestosterone in this condition. Dihydrotestosterone is necessary for normal penile and prostate development as well as for facial hair. It is related to male-pattern baldness and acne. Patients with 5-α-reductase deficiency lack Müllerian structures and have a blind vaginal pouch, with varying degrees of phallic development. Severe hypospadias is present. Virilization occurs at the time of puberty with penile growth and formation of spermatozoa. This defect is inherited as an autosomal recessive condition.

   (1) *Diagnosis*. Laboratory values include a high serum testosterone:serum dihydrotestosterone ratio. This may be found in prepubertal patients after hCG administration. Gonadotropins are not elevated. Definitive diagnosis is established by demonstration of decreased 5-α-reductase activity in genital skin obtained by biopsy.

   (2) *Therapy*. If good phallic development is present,

the sex of rearing should be male, since virilization occurs at the time of puberty. Surgical repair
of the hypospadias is necessary. If the phallus is
poorly developed, sex assignment should be
female. Orchiectomy followed by plastic surgery
and treatment with female sex hormones at the
time of puberty are indicated.

3. *End organ insensitivity to androgens.* There is considerable variation in the syndrome of end organ resistance to androgens. The more complete form was
previously referred to as the "feminizing testes syndrome." The external genitalia are female in appearance.
There is a blind vagina with absence of uterus and
fallopian tubes. The Wolffian ducts are also underdeveloped. Testes usually are normal in size and may be
located in the labia, the inguinal canals, or in the
abdomen. At puberty there is breast development but
pubic and axillary hair development is scanty.

a) There are also *incomplete forms of androgen insensitivity.* In these patients there is some phallic enlargement, hypospadias, and partial labial fusion. At
puberty some degree of virilization occurs in association with development of gynecomastia. *Reifenstein's
syndrome* is considered an example of partial androgen resistance. These conditions are believed to be
inherited as X-linked recessive.

b) In *pseudovaginal perineoscrotal hypospadias* there
may be either a biochemical defect involving synthesis
of testosterone or a partial defect of androgen sensitivity. In some patients, a biochemical abnormality
cannot be identified. It is possible that such cases may
be related to late development of testosterone synthesis by the fetus.

c) *Diagnosis.* High serum LH values are present. In
affected adults, serum testosterone levels are the same
as those found in normal adult men.

d) *Therapy.* In the complete form, patients should be

reared as females. In the partial types, male sex assignment may be made consistent with genital development. Repair of hypospadias as well as orchiopexy is required if the sex of rearing is male.

In patients with a female sex assignment as well as in males in whom the testes cannot be brought into the scrotum, orchiectomy is indicated due to the possibility of gonadal malignancy following puberty.

4. *Testicular unresponsiveness to hCG and LH.* As mentioned earlier in the chapter, hCG with the synergistic effort of LH is necessary for the Leydig cells to produce testosterone.

   The physical examination demonstrates variation of sexual development dependent on amount of functional Leydig cells present. More severely affected individuals show lack of breast tissue, a female pattern of pubic hair, normal sized clitoris, partial fusion of the labia, and short vaginal pouch. No Müllerian structures are present.

   a) *Diagnosis.* Definitive tests include a 46,XY karyotype, elevated serum LH, and gonadal biopsy with absent Leydig cells.

   b) *Therapy.* Sex of rearing depends upon the age of diagnosis and the degree of Leydig cell agenesis present. Appropriate replacement hormones are necessary at the time of puberty to induce appropriate secondary sexual characteristics. Plastic surgery is necessary in the patient with female sex assignment in order to enlarge the vaginal orifice and to produce a functional vagina.

5. *Persistence of Müllerian duct derivatives.* In rare cases, phenotypic males are found to have a uterus and fallopian tubes, probably due to an abnormality of anti-Müllerian hormone produced by the fetal testes. It is possible that, in some cases, there may be end organ resistance of this hormone. The patients may present with apparently routine inguinal hernias. In some patients,

bilateral undescended testes are present. These patients virilize normally at puberty.

a) *Diagnosis.* Demonstration at surgery of Müllerian duct derivatives in otherwise normal males.

b) *Therapy.* Since the vas deferens is frequently found on the posterior surface of the uterus, to prevent damage to the vas deferens it is recommended that the uterus not be removed in order to preserve the potential for fertility. Orchiopexy should be performed, and if not technically feasible, orchiectomy should be done.

6. *Abnormalities of fetal testicular formation*

a) *Pure gonadal dysgenesis, (46,XY).* This condition is also known as Swyer syndrome. Patients are phenotypic female, of normal stature, who lack secondary sex characteristics. Minimal phallic development may be present. Müllerian derivatives are present. This condition is believed to have an X-linked recessive inheritance pattern. Abnormality of synthesis of H-Y antigen itself and a lack of receptors to H-Y antigen are the postulated causes for this condition.

(1) *Diagnosis.* Streak gonads are present bilaterally. Patients may be either positive or negative for H-Y antigen.

(2) *Therapy.* Most patients have inadequate male differentiation and should be reared as females. The streak gonads should be removed due to the high potential for tumor formation, especially if the patient is H-Y antigen positive. Replacement sex hormones are necessary at the time of puberty.

b) *Mixed gonadal dysgenesis (45,X/46,XY).* Patients with 45,X/46,XY karyotype usually combine features of Turner's syndrome with male pseudohermaphroditism. These patients are understatured. A streak gonad is frequently found on one side with a testis on the other. The fallopian tube is usually present on the side with the streak gonad. There is considerable variation in the sexual phenotype, with varying degrees of male differentiation depending on the capacity of the fetal testicular structure to synthesize and secrete testosterone.

(1) *Diagnosis.* Chromosomes from peripheral lymphocytes demonstrate 45,X/46,XY mosaicism. At laparotomy a streak gonad along with testicular tissue is found.

(2) *Therapy.* Female sex assignment with removal of gonads is recommended for most of these patients. Replacement sex hormones are necessary at the time of puberty. If the phenotype is definitely male, sex assignment in accord with the phenotype sex is recommended.

D. *Abnormalities of the Y chromosome.* The pericentromeric region of the short arm of the Y chromosome apparently contains genes related to testicular differentiation, probably through coding for the synthesis of H-Y antigen. Loss of the short arm of the Y chromosome will result in H-Y antigen-negative phenotypic females. Gonadal dysgenesis occurs in these patients. Thus, no signs of masculinization are found in cases of 46,X,i(Yq). Male differentiation, however, does occur with deletion of the long arm of the Y.

1. *Diagnosis.* Failure of sexual maturation. Demonstration of streak gonads. Abnormal karyotype with deletion of the short arm of the Y chromosome.

2. *Therapy.* Removal of streak gonads is indicated. Replacement therapy with estrogens and, later, progestational agents is also required.

PRECOCIOUS PUBERTY

Precocious puberty may be defined as the development of secondary sexual characteristics before the age of 8 years. Precocious puberty has been classified into true precocious puberty and pseudoprecocious puberty. In *true precocious puberty,* the hypothalamic-pituitary-gonadal axis has been activated. In *pseudoprecocious puberty,* the secondary sexual characteristics arise from either an exogenous source or from spontaneous endogenous sex hormone production without activation of the hypothalamic-pituitary-gonadal system.

Precocious pubertal development is classified as *isosexual,* i.e., in accordance with the phenotypic sex, or *heterosexual,* i.e., discordant with the phenotypic sex. Precocious thelarche and precocious adrenarche are benign conditions that mimic precocious puberty.

A. *True precocious puberty*

In females, true precocious puberty is usually idiopathic. An underlying cause is found in only about 15 percent of patients. The etiology in this 15 percent may be familial, secondary to trauma or infection, or due to other systemic illnesses. In all patients, physical examination should include a complete neurologic examination with careful funduscopic evaluation. The patient is usually tall for age (greater than 90th percentile) when plotted on a standard height curve.

1. *Idiopathic precocious puberty* is the presumptive diagnosis if the conditions mentioned below can be ruled out.

   a) *Diagnosis* by exclusion. Bone age is advanced. Serum FSH and LH values may be in the range of adult levels. However, since overlap in values occurs, a urinary gonadotropin determination (12-hour collection) is recommended. Computerized axial tomography (CAT) scanning of the head is a useful noninvasive procedure.

   b) *Therapy.* In idiopathic true precocious puberty, therapy with medroxyprogesterone acetate may be used in selected cases. Menstruation does not occur during treatment, and breast development may regress. However, bone advancement is usually not affected, and regardless of therapy, the child develops premature epiphyseal closure with some loss of adult stature. In general, treatment includes education and acceptance by the patient and her family. Modest

clothing should be worn to discourage sexual molestation. It should be stressed that although the child is
advanced in physical appearance, she behaves according to her chronologic age mentally and psychologically, and should be so treated.

2. *Familial precocious puberty* can occur as a dominant trait.
The family history of time of menarche of mother, aunts,
and female siblings in cases of precocious puberty is
important.
   a) *Diagnosis.* Same as Section 1a.
   b) *Therapy.* Same as Section 1b.

3. *Trauma, infection, or tumor as cause.* A history of head
trauma, encephalitis, meningitis, hydrocephalus, or previous brain surgery is important to obtain because any of
these conditions may predispose the child to precocious
puberty. It is also important to look for neurologic signs
and symptoms that indicate the possibility of a brain
tumor.
   a) *Diagnosis.* Bone age is advanced. Gonadotropins are
   elevated. If LH is elevated more that the FSH value,
   the cross reactivity of hCG with LH should be
   considered and an hCG-secreting tumor (e.g.,
   hepatoma, teratoma, choriocarcinoma) sought. CAT
   scanning of the head is useful if a tumor mass is
   identified, and further studies, such as pneumoencephalography or angiography, may be required.
   b) *Therapy.* If brain tumor is diagnosed, therapy is
   directed toward removal, if possible. An appropriate
   shunting procedure should be done if the child has
   hydrocephalus. In general, treatment includes education and acceptance by the patient and her family.

4. *Systemic illness* associated with precocious puberty
   a) *Tuberous sclerosis* and *von Recklinghausen* disease,
   transmitted as autosomally dominant traits, can be
   associated with precocious puberty. Careful examination of the parents may reveal stigmata of these
   conditions. However, spontaneous mutations do occur.

(1) *Diagnosis.* Bone age is advanced. Elevated gonadotropins with characteristic neurologic and dermatologic findings are pathognomonic for these conditions.

(2) *Therapy* is directed at educating the child and her family. Occasionally medroxyprogesterone acetate is indicated.

b) *Silver syndrome* is associated with understature and hemihypertrophy. Sexual precocity often occurs.

(1) *Diagnosis.* Clinical picture plus the advanced bone age and adult level gonadotropins point to this diagnosis.

(2) *Therapy* consists of support, education, and possibly medroxyprogesterone acetate.

c) *Hypothyroidism* is occasionally associated with precocious puberty. These patients are usually understatured. Breast development is present, although pubic and axillary hair is absent or sparse. Menstruation occurs, and galactorrhea may be present.

(1) *Diagnosis.* Delay in bone age is present. Skull x-ray may indicate an enlarged sella. A low serum thyroxine associated with elevated serum TSH, prolactin, FSH, and LH is diagnostic.

(2) *Therapy.* Appropriate thyroid replacement, preferably levothyroxine, results in dramatic improvement. Galactorrhea usually subsides within two to three weeks, and the serum thyroxine level also falls within the normal range. However, the elevated TSH value may not return to normal for six months or longer after therapy is started.

d) *McCune-Albright syndrome,* characterized by pigmented skin lesions and polyostotic fibrous dysplasia, is also associated with endocrine dysfunction. The most common abnormality is sexual precocity with a strong female predilection. The precocious puberty may be either true precocious puberty of hypothalamic origin or pseudoprecocious puberty of ovarian origin.

(1) *Diagnosis.* Elevated urinary gonadotropins as well as elevated serum FSH and LH point to a hypothalamic origin. If these values are low, an active ovarian cyst should be sought and can often be demonstrated by ultrasound. Advanced bone age is present regardless of the underlying pathogenesis.

(2) *Therapy* is dependent upon the cause. If central in origin, management as described above is appropriate. If an ovarian cyst is present, surgical removal should be considered.

B. *Pseudoprecocious puberty*

Pseudoprecocious puberty must be considered in any case of early sexual development.

1. *Isosexual pseudoprecocity.* Before extensive investigation of isosexual pseudoprecocity is undertaken, a careful history should be obtained to rule out exogenous sources of estrogens, such as oral contraceptives, contaminated foods, and cosmetics.

a) *Ovarian and adrenal causes.* Functional ovarian and adrenal tumors are quite rare in children. The most common tumor that produces isosexual change is the *granulosa cell* tumor. Physical examination may reveal an abdominal mass. Other less common ovarian tumors to be considered are *luteomas, thecomas, teratomas,* and *choriocarcinomas.* Rarely, adrenal neoplasms cause isosexual pseudoprecocity.

(1) *Diagnosis.* Evaluation of these patients reveals advanced bone age and tall stature. Vaginal smear for estrogen effect is positive. Serum and urinary estrogens as well as their metabolites are increased. Serum LH may be elevated, reflecting a high hCG level in patients with choriocarcinoma. Except for this condition, serum FSH and LH values as well as urinary gonadotropins are low. Urinary 17-ketosteroids are low unless an adrenal tumor is present. Sonograms may be helpful, as well as abdominal CAT scanning.

    (2) *Therapy.* Surgical extirpation is indicated. After surgery, treatment is dependent upon the type of tumor present. If all tumor tissue is removed, some regression of secondary sexual characteristics may occur. Menarche follows bone age, occurring when the bone age reaches 12.7 years.

2. *Heterosexual pseudoprecocity* is occasionally due to the ingestion or local application of androgens. A careful history should be obtained.

  a) *Adrenal and ovarian causes.* Aberrant adrenal function, either tumor or *adrenal hyperplasia,* is the usual cause. Patients with congenital adrenal hyperplasia usually have 21-hydroxylase deficiency. Occasionally, 11-hydroxylase deficiency is found associated with hypertension. *Ovarian causes* are very rare in young children. These include *arrhenoblastoma, lipoid cell tumor,* and *hyperthecosis.*

    Evaluation of patients with heterosexual pseudoprecocity should include careful family history, since some cases are familial. Physical examination may reveal increased muscularity, deep voice, acne, receding hairline, enlarged clitoris, and hirsutism.

    (1) *Diagnosis.* Bone age is advanced. Initial laboratory tests include serum testosterone, FSH, LH, 17-α-hydroxyprogesterone, and cortisol. Urinary 17-ketosteroids, 17-hydroxysteroids, and pregnanetriol should be obtained. To distinguish virilizing congenital adrenal hyperplasia from adrenal tumor or ovarian tumor, dexamethasone suppression may be employed. Dexamethasone causes a marked reduction in excretion of urinary 17-ketosteroids in patients with congenital adrenal hyperplasia. Sonograms and body CAT scanning may also be useful in detection of tumors. Angiography may be helpful in localization.

    (2) *Therapy.* Adrenal or ovarian tumors should be removed surgically. Some regression of viriliza-

tion may be anticipated, i.e., reduction in size of clitoris, improvement in acne, and scalp hair growth. Congenital adrenal hyperplasia should be treated medically with adrenocorticoid steroids. Patients with salt loss in addition to the glucocorticoids also require additional sodium chloride and fludrocortisone acetate or parenteral desoxycorticosterone pivalate.

C. *Precocious thelarche,* isolated breast development, may be due to enhanced estrogen receptor activity in the breast anlage.
   1. *Diagnosis.* Bone age is not advanced. Urinary gonadotropins are not elevated. Serum FSH and LH levels are prepubertal, and sexual hair and menarche do not appear early. If the condition presents before two years of age, the breasts may decrease in size with time.
   2. *Therapy.* Reassurance is the only therapy required. Follow-up is recommended every six months.

D. *Precocious adrenarche,* the presence of pubic hair with or without axillary hair, is due to early adrenal activation and production of DHEA and its sulfate. Clitoral enlargement is not present.
   1. *Diagnosis.* Bone age may be slightly advanced. Height and weight percentile rankings are not abnormal. Serum FSH and LH are prepubertal. Serum testosterone is also normal. Urinary 17-ketosteroids and 17-hydroxysteroids are normal for age, as are urinary gonadotropins. Serum DHEA by radioimmunoassay may be elevated.
   2. *Therapy.* No therapy is required, but evaluation every six months is recommended.

INCOMPLETE SEXUAL DEVELOPMENT
AT ADOLESCENCE

A phenotypic female who has not shown any secondary sexual characteristics by age 14 years or has not had her menarche by age 16 years should be investigated for pathologic cause.

A. *Delayed adolescence*

The most common cause of sexual infantilism is delayed adolescence. Understature is a frequent component, with a growth spurt occurring at the time of puberty. A family history of other female family members following the same course may be obtained. The age of menarche of female family members should be established.

 1. *Diagnosis* is based on clinical findings, a normal karyotype, a slightly delayed bone age, and normal hypothalamic, pituitary, and gonadal function. Serum FSH and LH values are compatible with those found in the preadolescent child.

 2. *Therapy.* Prognosis is good. No drug therapy is indicated. Reassurance and explanation to the patient and her parents is essential.

B. *Systemic disease*

Serious systemic disease can result in delayed adolescence. Among the conditions to be considered are Crohn's disease, ulcerative colitis, and celiac disease. Severe renal disease, cardiac disease, liver disease, hypothyroidism, sickle cell disease, and thalassemia may cause delayed adolescence. Short stature is frequently found in these conditions, and bone age may be delayed.

 1. *Diagnosis* of a systemic disease should be the initial consideration as the cause for delayed adolescence.

 2. *Therapy* should be directed at the underlying condition. If systemic disease is not present, diagnostic studies are indicated to identify dysfunction at the hypothalamic, pituitary, or gonadal level.

C. *Hypothalamic dysfunction*

Patients with delayed adolescence associated with hypothalamic dysfunction may also have labile temperature control, abnormal appetite, and behavioral problems. Gonadotropin levels are prepubertal. A rise is FSH and LH is found by stimulation with GnRH.

 1. *Prader-Willi* syndrome is characterized by varying degrees of hypogonadism, hyperphagia with marked obes-

ity, hypotonia, understature, mental retardation, and small hands and feet. A history of feeding difficulties in infancy is frequently obtained. The exact etiology is unknown, but hypothalamic dysfunction has been postulated. The condition occurs sporadically in both males and females. There is evidence for an autosomal chromosome abnormality involving chromosome 15.

   a) *Diagnosis* is primarily based on clinical findings. Chromosomal studies are indicated.

   b) *Therapy* consists of dietary control with sex hormone replacement, if necessary.

2. *The Laurence-Moon-Biedl syndrome.* This disease is transmitted as an autosomal recessive trait. It is believed to have a hypothalamic component. The syndrome is characterized by hypogonadism, understature, polydactyly, obesity, retinitis pigmentosa, and mental retardation.

   a) *Diagnosis* is based on clinical findings.

   b) *Therapy.* Sex hormone replacement, if indicated. Glucose intolerance may be present and usually responds to dietary management.

3. *Kallman's syndrome* (anosomia or hyposomia and hypogonadism) is familial, possibly autosomal dominant. Midline facial defects, such as cleft lip and palate, as well as other congenital anomalies, have been reported in these patients.

   a) *Diagnosis* is based on clinical findings and evaluation of olfactory function.

   b) *Therapy* with either hCG or clomiphene may induce fertility in some patients. Appropriate sex hormone replacement may be required.

4. *Isolated gonadotropin deficiency.* This condition is usually hypothalamic in origin. Patients have normal stature but remain sexually infantile.

   a) *Diagnosis.* Serum and urinary gonadotropins are low and remain low as the child reaches the late teenage years. Response to GnRH shows an appropriate rise.

b) *Therapy.* Replacement therapy with sex hormones is indicated. Clomiphene therapy may be tried if pregnancy is desired.

5. *Isolated HGH deficiency* is characterized by sexual infantilism and delayed bone age. Secondary sexual characteristics and menarche may not appear until the third decade of life.

   a) *Diagnosis.* Failure of growth hormone release using at least two provocative stimuli (i.e., sleep, exercise, L-dopa, arginine, and insulin).

   b) *Therapy.* Should be limited to replacement of growth hormone only, since the addition of sex hormone causes increased advancement of bone age above linear growth achievement. At a bone age of 13.7 years, menarche usually occurs.

D. *Pituitary dysfunction*

   Craniopharyngiomas are the most common cause of *panhypopituitarism* as a cause of delayed sexual maturation. Other causes include *trauma* and *histiocytosis X.*

   1. *Diagnosis.* Patients have low serum FSH and LH values with no response to GnRH. TSH is often low with no response to TRH. Serum cortisol levels obtained under stress are low. There is no rise in HGH with provocative tests.

   2. *Therapy.* Replacement with thyroid and hydrocortisone is indicated. Growth hormone and replacement sex hormone administered at the appropriate age may also be used.

E. *Gonadal dysfunction*

   Gonadal disorders associated with delayed or absent secondary sexual development include *Turner syndrome, 46,XY pure gonadal dysgenesis (Swyer syndrome), 46,XX pure gonadal dysgenesis,* or *damaged gonads* as a result of trauma, surgery, or irradiation.

   1. *Turner syndrome.* Patients with this condition often have pterygium colli, short fourth metacarpals, edema of the hands and feet, or congenital heart disease (primarily

coarctation of the aorta) in addition to understature. Patients with 45,X/46,XX mosaicism usually demonstrate short stature. Other features of Turner syndrome are less common than in patients with a 45,X karyotype.

a) *Diagnosis.* Bone age is slightly delayed. Serum FSH and LH values are elevated, even in infancy. Buccal smear is usually chromatin negative. The karyotype is diagnostic. Chromosome determinations are indicated in females with understature and delayed sexual maturation.

b) *Therapy* consists of appropriate sex hormone replacement beginning with low doses of estrogens at 12 years of age, followed by cyclic therapy with estrogens and progestational agents when Tanner stage III of sexual development is achieved. On rare occasions, spontaneous menarche and even pregnancy have occurred in patients with a 45X/46XX karyotype. In these cases, serum FSH and LH values are within normal range, and no therapy is required.

2. *46,XX pure gonadal dysgenesis.* Patients with this condition are of normal stature, and normal müllerian duct differentiation occurs. Lack of secondary sexual characteristics and primary amenorrhea are the usual reasons for seeking medical assistance. Family history may be helpful in establishing the diagnosis since the disorder is autosomal recessive.

a) *Diagnosis.* Elevated gonadotropins, a 46,XX karyotype, and the demonstration of streak gonads at the time of laparotomy are diagnostic.

b) *Therapy* is similar to that used in patients with Turner syndrome.

3. *Rokitansky syndrome.* This syndrome is characterized by failure to achieve menarche and absence of the vagina. Uterine elements are hypoplastic. There may be associated renal, skeletal, and cardiac anomalies. Secondary sexual characteristics are normal.

a) *Diagnosis.* Physical findings are diagnostic. Karyotype is 46,XX.

b) *Therapy.* Surgical construction of a vagina.

BIBLIOGRAPHY

Rosenthal IM, Weiss EB: Precocious puberty and sexual immaturity. In

Gold JJ (ed): Textbook of Gynecologic Endocrinology, 3rd ed. New York, Harper, 1980, pp 625-641

Wachtel SS: Immunogenetic aspects of abnormal sexual differention. Cell 15:691, 1979

Wilson JD: Sexual differentiation. Ann Rev Physiol 40:279, 1978

22

Disorders of Menstruation

Frank W. Ling, M.D.

PRACTICE PRINCIPLES

As with all dysfunctions, a basic understanding of the normal serves as the foundation for the approach to the abnormal. Far too intricate to review in detail here, menstrual physiology, in brief, rests on the *delicate balance of the hypothalamic-pituitary-ovarian — endometrial axis* to cyclically discharge blood, cellular debris, and mucus from the endometrium. This occurs from puberty until menopause, with physiologic exceptions during pregnancy and lactation.

THE MENSTRUAL CYCLE

Certain key hormonal relationships aid in the rudimentary understanding of the menstrual cycle (Fig. 22–1). Central to the cyclic nature of these events is the level of circulating estrogen. The menstrual cycle can be divided into preovulatory, ovulatory, and postovulatory phases.

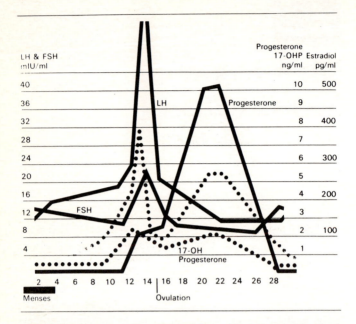

Figure 22–1. Blood levels of gonadal steroids and gonadotropins in the normal menstrual cycle (From Speroff L, Glass RH, Kase NG: Clinical Gynecologic Endocrinology and Infertility, 2nd ed, 1978, p. 21. © 1978 The Williams and Wilkins Co., Baltimore.)

A. *Preovulatory phase*
  1. *Ovary*—follicular phase
  2. *Endometrium*—proliferative phase
  3. *Predominant hormone*—*estrogen, which promotes endometrial growth and prepares the endometrium for progesterone-induced maturation.*
  4. Rise of follicle-stimulating hormone (FSH)
     a) Began in previous cycle as steroidogenesis decreased.
     b) Responsible for follicular growth and lutenizing hormone (LH) receptors.[1]

5. Rise of estradiol
    a) Increase of FSH receptors.
    b) Enhance induction of LH receptors by FSH.
    c) Gonadatropin feedback mechanisms
        (1) FSH—negative inhibitory.
        (2) LH—low levels: negative inhibitory, high levels: positive inhibitory.
6. Rapid rise of estradiol
    a) Suppression of FSH
        (1) Dominant follicle has increased sensitivity to circulating FSH.
        (2) Regression of other follicles due to FSH levels.
    b) Induction of midcycle LH surge by a positive stimulatory feedback.

B. *Ovulation*
    1. *Ovary*—rupture of follicle within 24 hours of LH peak.
    2. Estradiol triggers gonadotropin surge.
        a) LH positive feedback mechanism.
        b) FSH surge due to a common gonadatropin-releasing hormone.
    3. LH drop
        a) Etiology unclear.
        b) Pituitary LH depletion (less LH available).
        c) Hypothalamic suppression via negative LH feedback.
        d) Plasma estrogens decrease (loss of positive feedback). Luteinization of the follicle: theca cell dominance (estrogen secreting) becomes granulosa cell dominance (progesterone secreting).
        e) Plasma progesterone increases (negative feedback to block LH centrally).[2]

C. *Postovulatory phase*
    1. *Ovary*—luteal phase
    2. *Endometrium*—secretory phase
    3. *Predominant hormone*—progesterone. *Progesterone withdrawal produces normal uterine bleeding.*
    4. Corpus luteum produces estrogen and progesterone
        a) Negative feedback to suppress FSH and LH.

   b) Regression of corpus luteum 9 to 11 days after
      ovulation unless pregnancy ensues.
5. Possible role of estrogen in corpus luteum regression.

MENSTRUAL TERMINOLOGY

Different terms are used to describe variations from the norm.
Among them are the following commonly used terms.

A. *Normal menstrual cycle:* 22 to 34 days in length, 2 to 7 days
   duration, less than 80 cc blood loss.
B. *Abnormal uterine bleeding:* any uterine bleeding other than
   that of the normal menstrual cycle.
C. *Dysfunctional uterine bleeding (DUB):* abnormal uterine
   bleeding for which a specific organic etiology cannot be
   identified.
D. *Menorrhagia (hypermenorrhea):* regular uterine bleeding,
   excessive in amount and duration.
E. *Hypomenorrhea:* regular, scant uterine bleeding.
F. *Polymenorrhea:* regular uterine bleeding at intervals of 21
   days or less.
G. *Oligomenorrhea:* infrequent, often irregular uterine bleeding at intervals greater than 35 days.
H. *Metrorrhagia:* irregular uterine bleeding independent of the
   menstrual period.
I. *Intermenstrual bleeding:* uterine bleeding at times other than
   the normal menstrual flow.
J. *Amenorrhea:* absence of menstruation.

MENSTRUAL DYSFUNCTION — ORGANIC ETIOLOGIES

*The key to diagnosis in all abnormal uterine bleeding is thorough
history.* Since dysfunctional uterine bleeding (DUB) is a diagnosis of exclusion, the astute clinician must efficiently rule out all
possible organic causes of menstrual dysfunction before treating
DUB. Both gynecologic (inflammation, tumor, pregnancy) and

nongynecologic (trauma, blood dyscrasia, systemic diseases, iatrogenic) etiologies must be excluded. The history must, therefore, eliminate a large number of potential causes of abnormal uterine bleeding each of which would require its own separate work-up.

A. *Extragenital bleeding*
   1. Urinary tract (cystitis, urethritis, etc.).
   2. Gastrointestinal tract (hemorrhoids, etc.).

B. *Pregnancy*
   In the reproductive age group, assume that there is a complication of pregnancy until proven otherwise.
   1. Trophoblastic disease.
   2. Ectopic pregnancy.
   3. Abortion (spontaneous or induced).

C. *Tumor*
   In the menopausal or perimenopausal age group, assume cancer until proven otherwise.
   1. Vulva (varices, condylomata, malignancy, etc.).
   2. Vagina (malignancy, adenosis, etc.).
   3. Cervix (polyp, cervical intraepithelial neoplasia [CIN], malignancy, ectopy, condylomata, etc.).
   4. Uterine fundus (leiomyomata, sarcoma, endometrial polyps, endometrial malignancy, adenomyosis).
      a) Only 10 percent of perimenopausal abnormal bleeding is due to cancer, but this is the most important category.
      b) Twenty-five percent of postmenopausal bleeding is due to cancer.
      c) *Hormone replacement is the most frequent cause of postmenopausal bleeding.* The presence of estrogen replacement or genital atrophy *does not* negate the need to rule out malignancy in postmenopausal bleeding patients.
      d) In the patients beyond perimenopausal age, endometrial sampling is *mandatory*.
   5. Fallopian tube (malignant neoplasm is a rare cause of abnormal uterine bleeding).

     6. Ovary (granulosa and theca cells tumors). Other types of "nonfunctioning ovarian tumors can have a hormonal effect due to hyperactive stroma cells.

     7. Endometriosis

D. *Infection*
    1. Vaginitis
    2. Cervicitis
    3. Endometritis
    4. Salpingitis

E. *Systemic disease*
    1. Thyroid
    2. Liver
    3. Adrenal gland
    4. Kidney[3,4]
    5. Diabetes
    6. Starvation, debilitation
    7. Heart failure

F. *Blood dyscrasias*[5]
    1. Idiopathic throbocytopenic purpura
    2. Leukemia
    3. Aplastic anemia
    4. Von Willebrand's disease

G. *Iatrogenic*
    1. Contraceptives
       a) Oral contraceptives
       b) Intrauterine devices
    2. Other medications
       a) Steroids
       b) Androgens
       c) Psychotropic drugs
       d) Anticholinergic agents
       e) Anticoagulants

H. *Trauma*
    1. Foreign body (especially in the premenarchal patient)
    2. Coital injury
    3. Tampon, pessaries

DYSFUNCTIONAL UTERINE BLEEDING

A. Diagnosis

In addition to ruling out organic etiologies of abnormal uterine bleeding, a careful history can identify specific details of the menstrual cycles that will aid greatly in the final definitive diagnosis and appropriate treatment. It must be kept in mind that there is no specific history, physical examination, or laboratory test to make the diagnosis of dysfunctional uterine bleeding. A good history should begin to rule out organic causes of bleeding and determine if this is in addition to predictable ovulatory cycles or associated with anovulation. Therapy will be individualized to fit the concerns of the patient — both short term (cessation of the acute episode) and long term (prevention of recurrences and reproductive potential).

1. *Associated symptoms.* Predictability, weight gain, dysmenorrhea, breast tenderness, and emotional changes imply ovulatory cycles. *Since up to 90 percent of DUB is anovulatory,* the history of predictable menses aids in differentiating this type of bleeding.

2. *Nature of bleeding.* Interval, duration, amount, number of pads used, passage of clots or tissue all help to determine the ovulatory nature of cycles. Menstrual blood usually does *not* clot due to fibrinolysin. If clotting does occur, excessive bleeding must be considered.

3. *Comparison to "the norm."* The patient can identify bleeding episodes which are similar to or completely unlike her regular ovulatory periods.

4. *Age.* Dysfunctional bleeding tends to occur at the extremes of the reproductive age. Anovulatory cycles are more common at these times, caused at menarche by hypothalamic-pituitary-ovarian axis immaturity and at menopause by waning ovarian function. It is during these anovulatory cycles that the endometrium is subjected to

prolonged estrogen stimulation without the intervening progesterone effect resulting from ovulation.

5. *Predisposing emotional factors.* Psychogenic or emotional stress can induce ovulatory dysfunction and thus menstrual irregularity. A history of similar episodes in the past is also helpful.

6. *Reproductive history,* including pregnancy exposure, number and outcome of pregnancies, contraception and ages of children, will not only help in putting menstrual irregularity in proper perspective but also aid in the long-term management of these patients.

7. *Nutritional disturbances,* such as rapid weight loss or obesity, can be associated with abnormal uterine bleeding.

B. *Ovulatory bleeding*
   History and physical examination alone may be sufficient to diagnose ovulatory dysfunctional bleeding. Extremely helpful data would be derived from the basal body temperature chart (BBT) and/or endometrial sampling at the time of bleeding.

   1. *Bleeding at ovulation*
      a) Due to estrogen withdrawal at midcycle (Fig. 22–1).
      b) Correlation with BBT temperature shift.
      c) Association with Mittelschmerz.
      d) Endometrial biopsy shows late proliferative or early secretory endometrium.
      e) Rarely needs treatment.

   2. *Polymenorrhea*
      a) BBT identifies follicular (early rise) versus luteal (early decline) shortening.
      b) Endometrial biopsy timing based on BBT.
      c) Treatment based on the type of dysfunction.
         (1) Follicular
             (a) Low-dose estrogen early in cycle, e.g., ethinyl estradiol, 0.2 mg qd day 1 to 13.
             (b) Clomiphene citrate.

      (2) Luteal — progesterone suppository 25 mg bid.

      (3) Oral contraception if fertility not desired.

  3. *Oligomenorrhea*

    a) Prolonged proliferative phase.

    b) BBT shows a late rise.

    c) Endometrial biopsy confirms normal luteal phase.

    d) Decreased follicular response to gonadotropins.

      (1) Ovarian failure.

      (2) Infrequent ovulation, e.g., polycystic ovary disease (PCOD).

    e) Treatment

      (1) Watchful expectation if process is self-limited.

      (2) Clomiphene citrate 50 mg qd days 5 through 9 if fertility desired.

      (3) Oral contraceptives if fertility not a concern.

  4. *Persistent corpus luteum (Halban's syndrome).*

    a) Etiology undetermined.

    b) Must be differentiated from ectopic pregnancy.

    c) No specific treatment needed.

C. *Anovulatory bleeding*

  Approximately 90 percent of DUB is anovulatory.[6] This is a relatively frequent event, occurring in up to 15 percent of gynecologic patients with DUB, accounting for up to one fourth of all gynecologic surgery in some series.[7] Again, treatment should be individualized, specifically dealing with various age groups into which a patient might fit. It is during the extremes of reproductive age that anovulation is more prevalent. *Regardless of age, the basic abnormality causing the menstrual dysfunctions is persistent estrogen stimulation of the endometrium without cyclic progesterone influence.*

  1. *Childhood*[2]

    a) Less than 1 percent of DUB.

    b) More likely: trauma, foreign bodies.

    c) Consider the rare feminizing tumor or precocious puberty.

2. *Adolescence*
   a) Most periods in the first two to three years after menarche are anovulatory.
   b) Consider hypothalamic-pituitary-ovarian axis immaturity and psychogenic etiologies. In one study, 50 percent of teenagers with a psychic conflict were hyperestrogenic, as opposed to 13 percent of control patients.[8]
   c) Treatment depends on individual needs.
      (1) In absence of clinical symptoms, use watchful expectation. Maturity will correct this problem.
      (2) Correction of stress factors.
      (3) Provera 10 mg qd days 21 through 25 of cycle to induce controlled withdrawal bleeding of estrogen-deprived endometrium.
      (4) Birth control pills if contraception also needed.
3. *Reproductive age.* The basic premise in this age group must be to *rule out a complication of pregnancy. Then the attention may be turned to the choice of several hormonal modalities* available to arrest the acute bleeding episode. Subsequent long-term management will also depend on the individual desires for contraception and/or fertility.
   a) Acute excess bleeding[9]
      (1) Estrogen and progestin (outpatient management)
         (a) Oral contraceptive (with $\geq$ 50 µg estrogenic substance) qd for five to seven days.
         (b) Lack of proper response (12 to 24 hours) requires further investigation (e.g., dilatation and curettage) into possible organic etiologies.
      (2) Estrogen intravenously (in prolonged bleeding or hypoestrogenic conditions)
         (a) Conjugated estrogens (Premarin) 20 to 25 mg IV q four to six hours until bleeding stops.
         (b) Consider dilatation and curettage if response is not prompt. (Provera 10 mg qd for five to

seven days may be added to induce controlled withdrawal bleeding.)
- (3) Estrogen and progestin sequentially
    - (a) Premarin 10 mg PO qd for 21 days followed
      by Provera 10 mg PO qd on days 17 through
      21.
    - (b) If bleeding persists beyond the first two days,
      double Premarin dose, then continue for 21
      days with Provera added as above.
    - (c) If no response, dilatation and curettage.
- b) Chronic management
    - (1) Birth control pills if fertility is not a concern.
    - (2) Endometrial biopsy proliferative
        - (a) Periodic withdrawal using Provera 10 mg first
          five to seven days every month.
        - (b) Clomid induction of ovulation.
    - (3) Endometrial biopsy secretory. Consider organic
      etiology. Possible hysterosalpingogram or hys-
      teroscopy.[10]
    - (4) Dilatation and curettage for repeated episodes (30
      to 40 percent recurrence rate after dilatation and
      curettage in true DUB). This may remove the
      bleeding fragments and further reveal endome-
      trial pathology (e.g., infection, pregnancy compli-
      cations). Indeed, suction curettage with its
      minimal dilatation requirement may be just as
      effective as dilatation and curettage.[11]
    - (5) Hysterectomy *only* in those patients resistant to
      conservative management (including dilatation
      and curettage and hormonal therapy).
4. *Perimenopause and menopause.* The *mandatory endometrial sampling must not be forgotten* in this age group.
Though cancer is not the most frequent etiology of
bleeding, it is the most important. As ovarian function
wanes, so does the predictability of menstrual cycles.
Prolonged estrogen stimulation and potential malignancy

or its precursor lesions become more likely as the patient's age increases.

a) Endometrial sampling to rule out cancer.
b) Observation: once cancer has been ruled out, perimenopausal bleeding may be self-limited by the impending menopause.
c) Hormonal therapy, short-term only
    (1) Low-dose estrogen to treat atrophic conditions.
    (2) Provera to treat hyperestrogenic conditions not considered premalignant.
d) Hysterectomy is used only when all conservative management has failed. More likely to be used in this age group because of lack of desire to maintain childbearing potential and other concurrent problems.

AMENORRHEA

Amenorrhea is defined as *the absence of menstruation in a woman during her reproductive age.* The term *primary amenorrhea* applies to those who have never menstruated, while *secondary amenorrhea* implies that the menses have ceased for over six months after their initial appearance. *The most common etiologies are pregnancy and menopause.*

A. *Primary amenorrhea*
  1. Indications for evaluation
    a) Amenorrhea at age 16.
    b) Amenorrhea at age 14 in the absence of secondary sexual development.
    c) Amenorrhea despite three-year lapse from thelarche.
    d) Patient or parental concern.
  2. Classification
    a) Central lesion
      (1) Pituitary — tumors, congenital defects.
      (2) Hypothalamus — stress, psychosis, anorexia, post-pill, Kallman syndrome.
      (3) Organic disease — trauma, infection, and so on.

    b) Peripheral lesion

        (1) Ovary — Turner syndrome, mosaicism, agenesis, tumors.

        (2) Uterus and vagina — imperforate hymen, vaginal septum, congenital absence or malformation, cervical and/or vaginal stenosis, Asherman syndrome.

    c) Systemic lesion

        (1) Nutritional—obesity, malnutrition.

        (2) Chronic disease — tuberculosis, leukemia, or other.

        (3) Metabolic — thyroid, adrenal, renal, juvenile diabetes, and so on.

    d) Pregnancy

3. Diagnosis. In addition to a careful history:

    a) With secondary sexual development

        (1) Vaginal defect: consider septum, imperforate hymen, congenital absence.

        (2) Uterus absent: obtain buccal smear

            (a) If positive, congenital absence.

            (b) If negative, testicular feminization.

        (3) Uterus and vagina normal

            (a) Ovaries enlarged — PCOD, tumor.

            (b) Ovaries not enlarged

                (i) Gonadotropins elevated—ovarian dysgenesis, or insensitivity.

                (ii) Gonadotropins normal or low—end organ defect (cervix or uterus). If no response to estrogen stimulation, consider delayed puberty versus central origin if estrogen stimulation causes bleeding.

    b) Without secondary sexual development

        (1) Karyotype — Turner, mosaic, 46,XY.

        (2) Gonadotropins

            (a) High: ovarian dysgenesis versus premature failure.

        (b) Low: delayed puberty, pituitary tumor, or dysfunction.
     (3) Bone age
   4) *Treatment.* As seen above, the treatment is sometimes straightforward based on a clear history and physical examination. If the diagnosis is in doubt, treatment may include further observation to differentiate the physiologic delayed puberty.

B. *Secondary amenorrhea*

The differential diagnosis of these women must include many of those previously discussed in primary amenorrhea. Less laboratory evaluation is needed, and greater dependence is placed on the history and physical examination. *Diagnostic considerations must include ruling out pregnancy* (positive pregnancy test), *pituitary tumor* (elevated serum prolactin, and possibly abnormal polytomography), and *menopause* (elevated gonadotropins).

  1. History must include:
    a) Careful menstrual review
    b) Sexual and contraceptive histories
    c) Medications
    d) Emotional stress
    e) Symptoms of climacteric
    f) Symptoms of systemic disease
    g) Galactorrhea
  2. Physical examination should include:
    a) Signs of early pregnancy
    b) Estrogenic cervical mucus
    c) Atrophic vagina with no cervical mucus
    d) Nipple discharge
  3. Diagnosis (Fig. 22–2)
    a) If *serum prolactin* is elevated, polytomography of the sella turcica is required. A significant percentage of patients with secondary amenorrhea may have pituitary tumor. The possibility of tumor increases even further with galactorrhea,[12,13] although hyperprolactinemia can be present without galactorrhea.

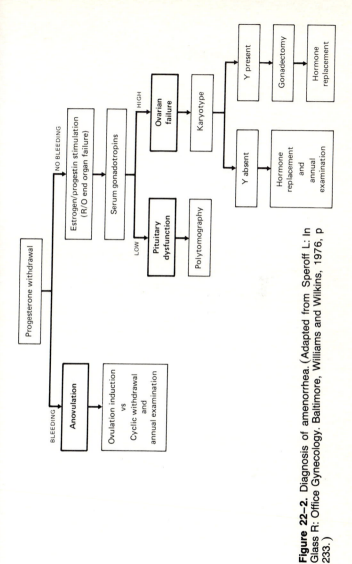

Figure 22-2. Diagnosis of amenorrhea. (Adapted from Speroff L: In Glass R: Office Gynecology. Baltimore, Williams and Wilkins, 1976, p 233.)

b) Progesterone withdrawal test.[14] Progesterone in oil 100 to 200 mg IM or Provera 10 mg daily for five days should induce withdrawal bleeding in one week or less. This withdrawal bleeding implies:

   (1) The endometrium is estrogen-stimulated.

   (2) The gonadotropins have adequately stimulated the ovaries.

   (3) The amenorrhea is due to ovulation failure. This should *not* be used as a test for pregnancy.

c) Estrogen/progestin stimulation. If no withdrawal bleeding occurs in b, stimulation of the endometrium with Premarin 1.25 mg to 2.5 mg daily for 21 days with Provera 10 mg daily on days 17 through 21 can differentiate whether the endometrium can successfully be primed and shed. Failure to bleed to this stimulation would indicate anatomic lesions, such as Asherman syndrome (endometrial scarring), cervical stenosis, and so on.

d) Serum gonadotropins. If the patient does not have withdrawal bleeding, ovarian failure (high gonadotropins) versus pituitary dysfunction (low gonadotropins) must be differentiated.

   (1) Low: polytomography to evaluate pituitary. If normal, the etiology for the secondary amenorrhea is probably hypothalamic. This is the most common etiology of secondary amenorrhea.

   (2) High: ovarian failure — rule out the presence of a Y chromosome if patient is under 35 years old

      (a) Karyotype normal — annual follow-up with hormonal replacement.

      (b) Presence of Y chromosome — gonadectomy to remove potentially malignant tumor. A blood assay for the H-Y antigen might also be considered.

4. Treatment is based on the etiology of amenorrhea and the patient's specific needs

a) Fertility desired — ovulation induction if not contraindicated.

b) Fertility not desired
  (1) Watchful expectation.
  (2) Periodic progesterone-induced withdrawal to prevent endometrial hyperplasia.
  (3) Contraception (patient may spontaneously ovulate.)

REFERENCES

1. Kammerman S, Ross J: Increase in numbers of gonadotropin receptors on granulosa cells during follicle maturation. J Clin Endocrinol Metab 41:546, 1975

2. Vorys N, Norias, Boutselis JG: Menstrual dysfunction. In Gold JJ (ed): Gynecologic Endocrinology, 2nd ed. Hayes & Row, 1975, p 213

3. Rice GG: Hypermenorrhea in the young hemodialysis patient. Am J Obstet Gynecol 116:539, 1973

4. Perez RJ, et al.: Menstrual dysfunction of patients undergoing chronic hemodialysis. Obstet Gynecol, 51:552, 1978

5. Quick AJ: Menstruation in hereditary bleeding disorders. Obstet Gynecol 28:37, 1966

6. Kupperman HS: Human Endocrinology. Philadelphia, Davis, 1963.

7. Wallach EE: Physiology of menstruation. Clin Obstet Gynecol 13:336, 1970

8. Frisk M, et al.: "Hyperestrogenism" — psyche and gama in teenagers. Acta Psychother 12:284, 1964

9. March CM: Management of dysfunctional bleeding. Female Patient October 1977, pp 54–59

10. Siegler AM, et al.: Hysteroscopic procedures in 257 patients. Fertil Steril 27:1267, 1976

11. Hamilton JV, Knab DR: Suction curettage: therapeutic effectiveness in dysfunctional uterine bleeding. Obstet Gynecol 45:47, 1975

12. Nader S, et al.: Galactorrhea, hyperprolactinemia and pituitary tumors in the female. Clin Endocrinol 5:245, 1976

13. Franks, et al.: Incidence and significance of hyperprolactinemia in women with amenorrhea. Clin Endocrinol 4:597, 1975

14. Kupperman, Lekovics SC: Progesterone in problems in sterility, diagnostic and therapeutic use. Fertil Steril 8:131, 1957

23

Contraception

John C. Jarrett II, M.D.

PRACTICE PRINCIPLES

The world is facing ever increasing demands on its food, energy, and geographic resources as the population continues to increase. Efficient and safe contraception is one of the more urgent medical and public health issues of our times. Many methods of contraception are available, each with its particular risks, benefits, and side effects. It is incumbent on every physician in this field to be able to provide informed and accurate contraceptive counseling.

NATURAL METHODS

A. *Rhythm methods (natural family planning techniques)*
  1. This is the contraceptive choice of 5 percent of American couples.[1] The basic principle of all rhythm methods is abstinence during the fertile period.
  2. *Techniques*[2]
    a) *Calendar method.* The lengths of twelve consecutive menstrual cycles are recorded. The beginning of the fertile period is estimated by subtracting 18 days from the shortest cycle length. The end of the fertile period is estimated by subtracting 11 days from the length of the longest cycle.

b) *Temperature method.* Daily basal body temperatures are recorded using a basal body thermometer. Abstinence is practiced from the beginning of menses until three days after the rise in temperature associated with ovulation.

c) *Cervical mucus or ovulation method*
   (1) Depends upon the ability of the woman to recognize the increased and clearer cervical mucus associated with rising estrogen levels.
   (2) Abstinence is practiced from the first sensation of increased mucus until four days after maximal mucus secretion. Abstinence is required during menses as mucus cannot be properly evaluated. Intercourse may not occur on consecutive days in the early preovulatory period as mucus cannot be properly evaluated for 24 hours after intercourse.

d) *Symptothermal method.* Combines the cervical mucus method with either the calendar or temperature method, with abstinence required from the earliest day indicated by either method to the latest day indicated by either method.

3. *Effectiveness.* Rates vary widely, and depend on the patient population and method used. The overall rate is about *20 to 30 pregnancies per 100 woman years of use.*[2]

4. *Advantages and disadvantages*
   a) *Advantages*
      (1) May be used by couples who object to other forms of contraception.
      (2) Is free and universally available.
   b) *Disadvantages*
      (1) Long periods of abstinence from vaginal intercourse are required, as are extensive user education and motivation.
      (2) There are concerns over the aging of gametes and the incidence of spontaneous abortion and congenital anomalies.

B. *Withdrawal (coitus interruptus)*

  1. Withdrawal of the penis from the vagina prior to ejaculation, which must occur outside of the vagina and away from the immediate perivaginal area. Practiced frequently in Europe, but by only 3 percent of American couples.[1]

  2. *Effectiveness*[4]

    a) Method — 9 to 15 pregnancies per 100 woman years of use.

    b) User — 20 to 25 pregnancies per 100 woman years of use.

  3. *Advantages.* Withdrawal requires no mechanical or chemical devices, may be practiced under any circumstances, and is free.

  4. *Disadvantages.* Withdrawal demands a high level of self-control. May markedly decrease the enjoyment of intercourse, and is associated with a high failure rate even if it is adhered to because of the occasional unnoticed release of sperm.

BARRIER METHODS

A. *Spermicides*

  1. Primary form of contraception of about 4 percent of American women.[1]

  2. *Effectiveness*[5]

    a) Method — two to four pregnancies per 100 woman years of use.

    b) User — reported rates vary from 2 to 40 pregnancies per 100 woman years of use. This is highly dependent upon the degree of professional instruction, population tested, and user motivation. There does not seem to be a significant difference among the various forms of spermicides.

  3. *Types.* Spermicides are available as creams and jellies, foams, foaming tablets, and suppositories.

4. *Composition.* All contain an inert base or vehicle and an active ingredient, most commonly a surfactant, such as nonoxynol 9, which disrupts the integrity of the sperm membrane.

5. *Advantages.* Spermicides are associated with few side effects or user risks, are inexpensive and easily available, and are convenient when intercourse is infrequent. Some protective effect against the transmission of veneral disease is also offered.

6. *Side effects.* Spermicides can cause local irritative responses on rare occasions. There are some concerns over the systemic effects of transvaginal absorption of the active ingredients, but no good studies have as yet demonstrated any specific adverse effects.

B. *Condoms*

1. Condoms are thin sheaths, most commonly made of latex, which prevent the transmission of sperm from the penis to the vagina. They are the most widely used form of contraception in the world but are the primary form of contraception of only about 11 percent of American couples.[1]

2. *Effectiveness*

   a) *Method*—2 to 3 pregnancies per 100 woman years of use.[6]

   b) *User*—6 to 30 pregnancies per 100 woman years of use.

   c) Failures are due to nonuse, inadequate application, vaginal penetration prior to application, failure to withdraw the penis from the vagina while still erect, or tears or breaks.

3. *Advantages*

   a) Condoms are easy to use, inexpensive, easily available, and offer protection against venereal disease transmission.

   b) Condoms are the most nonpermanent form of male contraceptive currently available.

    c) Condoms can be used as effective adjuncts to other forms of contraception.

  4. *Disadvantages.* Use of condoms necessitates interruption of love-making for application and may decrease tactile sensation.

  5. *Side effects.* Rare allergic reactions have been reported, in which case natural skin condoms may be employed.

C. *Diaphragms*

  1. Diaphragms are shallow rubber cups with flexible metal rims that are placed in the vagina so as to cover the cervix. They function both as mechanical barriers and as receptacles for spermicidal agents, which must be used in conjunction with diaphragms. They are *the primary form of contraception of about 3 percent of American women.*[1]

  2. *Effectiveness*

    a) *Method* — 2 to 3 pregnancies per 100 woman years of use.

    b) *User* — 10 to 15 pregnancies per 100 woman years of use.[7]

  3. *Types*

    a) *Arcing spring*

      (1) The rim is very sturdy with firm spring strength.

      (2) Is the first choice of many physicians for routine use.

      (3) Firm construction allows use in cases of cystocele, rectocele, mild pelvic relaxation, and uterine retroversion.

      (4) Insertion may be easier due to the flexibility of the rim.

    b) *Coil spring*

      (1) The rim is spiral-coiled and sturdy.

      (2) Best suited for women with good vaginal tone and no uterine displacement.

    c) *Flat spring*

      (1) The rim is flat and more rigid than the other types.

  (2) Best suited for women with good vaginal tone and a shallow symphyseal arch or long, posterior cervix.
4. *Fitting*
   a) Most diaphragms are available in sizes ranging from 55 mm to 105 mm.
   b) *Should fit snugly* between the posterior fornix, pubic symphysis, and lateral vaginal walls, *yet cause no discomfort.*
      (1) If it is too small, it may slip out during sexual excitation with the resultant vaginal elongation.
      (2) If it is too large, it may buckle and cause discomfort or even vaginal ulceration.
5. *Advantages and disadvantages*
   a) May be inserted up to six hours prior to intercourse.
   b) Some protective effect against transmission of certain venereal diseases.
   c) Effective form for women who have infrequent intercourse.
   d) May be associated with an increased incidence of urinary tract infections.

INTRAUTERINE DEVICES (IUDs)

A. Introduced in the early 1900s, IUDs are used today by 6 to 7 percent of American women.[8]
B. *Types of IUDs*
   1. *Lippes loop*
      a) Serpentine-shaped devices composed of inert polypropylene plastic, available in sizes A through D.
      b) The most widely used type of IUD.
      c) It does not require replacement at regular intervals.
   2. *Saf-T-Coil*
      a) Inert polypropylene devices in a T configuration with helical-shaped arms, available in two sizes.
      b) Does not require replacement at regular intervals.

3. *Copper-bearing devices*
   a) Available in both T and 7 configurations, they are polypropylene devices with a small copper wire wrapped around the ascending arm which releases a systemically insignificant amount of copper per day.
   b) Smaller, and may be more appropriately suited for nulliparous women.
   c) *Require replacement every three years,* as their effectiveness is markedly diminished upon complete dissolution of the copper.

4. *Progestasert*
   a) T-shaped polypropylene device with progesterone impregnated in the ascending arm, which releases 65 μg of progesterone per day.
   b) Must be replaced yearly.
   c) Smaller, and may be more appropriate for nulliparous women.

C. *Mechanism of action*
   1. *Inert devices*
      a) Evoke a sterile inflammatory response in the endometrium consisting of mononuclear cells, foreign body giant cells, plasma cells, and macrophages. These may engulf the sperm or ovum or inhibit implantation of the blastocyst.
      b) Increase prostaglandins and immunoglobulins.
      c) Produce asynchronous development of the endometrium.
   2. *Copper-bearing devices*
      a) Produce an inflammatory response which is accentuated by the presence of the copper. Cupric ions may also interfere with several enzyme systems in the endometrium which are important in implantation.[9]
      b) Prostaglandin synthesis is increased further.
   3. *Progestasert.* The response to the local levels of progesterone maintains the endometrium in a decidualized state.

D. *Insertion*
   1. *Timing*
      a) *Usually recommended during menses* to avoid pregnancy but, under appropriate circumstances, may be inserted at any time.
      b) Most commonly inserted only after complete uterine involution has occurred following pregnancy or abortion.
   2. *Technique*
      a) Obtain informed consent.
      b) The results of a Pap smear and GC culture should be available.
      c) Bimanual examination to exclude pelvic abnormalities and pregnancy and to determine the axis and position of the uterus.
      d) Wash the ectocervix with an antiseptic solution.
      e) Place a tenaculum on the anterior lip of the cervix.
      f) Paracervical anesthesia may be administered if desired.
      g) Sound the uterus.
      h) Using sterile technique, load the IUD into its applicator.
      i) Insert applicator into the cervical canal using mild traction on the tenaculum.
         (1) Plunge technique. The inner plunger pushes the IUD into the uterine cavity once the outer sheath is past the internal os.
         (2) Withdrawal technique. The outer barrel is inserted to the fundus of the uterus and then withdrawn with the inner plunger in place.
      j) Leave the strings long—they may be cut later.
      k) Repeat bimanual examination.
E. *Effectiveness.* IUDs have a failure rate of three to five pregnancies per 100 woman years of use.[10]
F. *Lost IUD*
   1. *Differential diagnosis*
      a) Pregnancy

      b) Spontaneous expulsion

      c) Perforation

      d) Presence within the uterus with the strings retracted up

  2. *Localization*

      a) Pregnancy should be excluded.

      b) The uterus may be gently probed for the presence of the string or IUD.

      c) Ultrasonography may be used.

      d) Anterior-posterior (AP) and lateral pelvic x-rays may be obtained after placing a different type of IUD, uterine sound, or radiopaque catheter in the uterus, for use as a reference point.

  3. *Removal*

      a) If the strings are visible, simple traction with a forceps will usually suffice.

      b) If demonstrable in the uterine cavity, an IUD hook or Novak curette may be used if removal is indicated. Occasionally, dilatation and curettage or hysteroscopy will be necessary.

      c) If the IUD is outside the uterine cavity, it should be removed by laparoscopy or laparotomy, as it may induce the formation of significant adhesions.

G. *Complications*

  1. *Infection*

      a) Users of IUDs are twice as likely as users of no contraceptive method to develop pelvic inflammatory disease. They are 4.5 times as likely to develop inflammatory disease as users of oral contraceptives and 3.3 times as likely as users of barrier methods.[11]

      b) Women under age 25, those with multiple sexual partners, and those with a history of prior pelvic inflammatory disease are at increased risk.

      c) Risk is greatest during the first month after insertion.

  2. *Ectopic pregnancy* occurs in 2.9 to 8.9 percent of women who conceive with an IUD in place.[12]

3. *Perforation* occurs in about 1 out of every 1,000 patients, most commonly at the time of insertion.[12]

4. *Bleeding*
   a) Menstrual blood loss may be increased by as much as 90 percent.[12] (It may actually be diminished with a Progestasert.)
   b) Intermenstrual bleeding is not uncommon.
   c) About 15 percent of women will request removal because of bleeding problems.
   d) Menstrual blood loss can be effectively reduced by the use of prostaglandin synthetase inhibitors.

5. *Expulsion.* There is a 10 percent spontaneous expulsion rate during first year of use.

6. *Pregnancy*[13]
   a) *Spontaneous abortion*
      (1) If the IUD is not removed, the incidence is 55 percent.
      (2) If the IUD is removed, the incidence is reduced to 20 to 25 percent.
   b) *Second trimester loss*
      (1) If the IUD is left in place, the risk is 10 times greater than that of a control population.
      (2) If it is removed during the first trimester, there is no increased risk.
   c) *Septic complications.* Septic second trimester fetal loss in increased 26-fold if an IUD is left in place.

7. *Dysmenorrhea.* IUD use (except the Progestasert) is commonly associated with some increase in dysmenorrhea, which may be relieved by prostaglandin synthetase inhibitors.

H. *Contraindications*
   1. *Absolute*
      a) Active pelvic infection.
      b) Pregnancy.
      c) Cervical or uterine malignancy or unresolved abnormal Pap smear.
   2. *Relative*
      a) History of pelvic infection or gonorrhea.

b) History of ectopic pregnancy.
c) Uterine anomalies or leiomyomata.
d) Hypermenorrhea and dysmenorrhea (the Progestasert may be therapeutic).
e) Valvular heart disease.
f) Impaired immunity.
g) *Concern for future fertility.*

HORMONAL METHODS

A. *Combination oral contraceptives (the pill)*
   1. The most widely used form of contraception in the United States, accounting for an estimated 33 percent of all contraceptive methods used in 1976.[1]
   2. *Effectiveness.* The *failure rate is less than 1 pregnancy per 100 woman years of use.* It is the most effective of all nonpermanent forms of contraception. Effectiveness is reduced if the estrogen content is less than 30 μg.
   3. *Steroid components*
      a) There are currently 25 different combination pills available in the United States (Table 23–1). Many of these are available in both 21-day packets and 28-day packets, which contain seven inert tablets to facilitate remembering to start the next cycle on time. They are formulated from synthetic estrogens and progestins and administered for 21 days, with a seven-day hiatus to allow for withdrawal bleeding.
      b) *Estrogens*
         (1) Ethinyl estradiol.
         (2) Mestranol—hepatic conversion of mestranol to ethinyl estradiol accounts for its metabolic activity.
         (3) These two compounds may be considered equipotent.[14]
      c) *Progestins*
         (1) The five currently available progestins are all derivatives of 19-nortestosterone. The removal of

TABLE 23–1. ORAL CONTRACEPTIVES

Trade Name	Estrogen	Estrogen (μg per tablet)	Progestogen	Progestogen (mg per tablet)
Brevicon	Ethinyl estradiol	35	Norethindrone	0.5
Demulen	Ethinyl estradiol	50	Ethynodiol diacetate	1.0
Enovid-E	Mestranol	100	Norethynodrel	2.5
Enovid 5 mg	Mestranol	75	Norethynodrel	5.0
Loestrin 1.5/30	Ethinyl estradiol	30	Norethindrone acetate	1.5
Loestrin 1/20	Ethinyl estradiol	20	Norethindrone acetate	1.0
Lo/Ovral	Ethinyl estradiol	30	Norgestrel	0.3
Modicon	Ethinyl estradiol	35	Norethindrone	0.5
Norinyl 2 mg	Mestranol	100	Norethindrone	2.0
Norinyl 1 + 80	Mestranol	80	Norethindrone	1.0
Norinyl 1 + 50	Mestranol	50	Norethindrone	1.0
Norlestrin 2.5 mg	Ethinyl estradiol	50	Norethindrone acetate	2.5

Norlestrin 1 mg	Ethinyl estradiol	50	Norethindrone acetate	1.0
Ortho-Novum 10 mg	Mestranol	60	Norethindrone	10.0
Ortho-Novum 2 mg	Mestranol	100	Norethindrone	2.0
Ortho-Novum 1 + 80	Mestranol	80	Norethindrone	1.0
Ortho-Novum 1 + 50	Mestranol	50	Norethindrone	1.0
Ortho-Novum 1 + 35	Ethinyl estradiol	35	Norethindrone	1.0
Ovcon-50	Ethinyl estradiol	50	Norethindrone	1.0
Ovcon-35	Ethinyl estradiol	35	Norethindrone	0.4
Ovral	Ethinyl estradiol	50	Norgestrel	0.5
Ovulen	Mestranol	100	Ethynodiol diacetate	1.0
Zorane 1/50	Ethinyl estradiol	50	Norethindrone acetate	1.0
Zorane 1.5/30	Ethinyl estradiol	30	Norethindrone acetate	1.5
Zorane 1/20	Ethinyl estradiol	20	Norethindrone acetate	1.0

the 19-carbon from testosterone alters the major
metabolic effect from androgenic to proges-
togenic.

   (2) The available progestins, their relative potencies,
and their estrogenic and androgenic effects are
listed in Table 23–2. The differences in these may
be useful to consider when managing some of the
minor side effects of the pill.

4. *Mechanism of action*
  a) *Progestational component*
    (1) Suppresses LH secretion by a negative feedback
effect on the hypothalamus and/or pituitary.
    (2) Produces a decidualized endometrium which is
not receptive to implantation.
    (3) Produces thick cervical mucus.
    (4) May alter tubal motility.
  b) *Estrogen component*
    (1) Enhances the negative feedback of the progestin
on LH.
    (2) Suppresses FSH secretion.
    (3) Stabilizes the endometrium to prevent irregular
bleeding.

5. *Contraindications*
  a) *Absolute*
    (1) Thrombophlebitis, thromboembolic disorders,
cerebral vascular disease, coronary arterial disease, or a history of these conditions.
    (2) Undiagnosed abnormal genital bleeding.
    (3) Impaired liver function.
    (4) Pregnancy.
    (5) Known or suspected malignancy of the breast or
reproductive system.
  b) *Relative.* Require a thorough consideration of the
risk:benefit ratio and informed consent.
    (1) Diabetes.
    (2) Hypertension.
    (3) Migraine headaches.

TABLE 23–2. ORAL CONTRACEPTIVE PROGESTOGENS

Progestogen	Ratio of Progestational Potency*	Relative Estrogenic Potency†	Relative Antiestrogenic Effect‡	Relative Androgenicity§
Norethindrone	1	0.3	2.5	1.6
Norethynodrel	1	2.1	0.0	0
Norethindrone acetate	2	0.9	25.0	2.5
Ethynodiol diacetate	15	0.4	1.0	1.0
Norgestrel	30	0.0	18.5	7.6

Note: Different results may be obtained depending upon the assay employed. Some of these values are based on animal studies. They should, therefore, be used only as approximations.
*From Greenblatt RB: Med Sci, May 1967, pp 37–49.
†Relative to ethinyl estradiol-100. From Jones RC, Edgren RA: Fertil Steril 24:284, 1973.
‡From Dickey RP: ACOG Sem Fam Plan p 32, 1974. As cited in Hatcher.[4]
§From Tausk M, deVisser J: International Encyclopedia of Pharmacology and Therapeutics, Section 28, Pergamon Press, 1973, Chap. 28. As cited in Hatcher.[4]

     (4) Hemoglobinopathies, e.g., sickle cell or sickle C
         disease.
     (5) Congenital hyperlipidemia.
     (6) Cholestatic jaundice during pregnancy.
     (7) Varicose veins.
     (8) Epilepsy.
     (9) Uterine leiomyomata.
   (10) Cigarette smoking, especially in women over 30.
   (11) Women over age 35.
   (12) Elective surgery. The pill should be discontinued
         four weeks prior to any elective surgery.
   (13) Breast feeding. The pill decreases the quantity
         and quality of lactation, and some drug crosses
         over to the fetus.

6. *Administration*
  a) *The low-dose pills, i.e., those with 30 or 35 μg of
     estrogen should be used for all women.*
  b) If the pill is begun on the fifth day of the menstrual
     cycle, contraceptive protection is afforded during the
     first cycle. Some pills are packaged so as to encourage
     starting them on Sunday.
  c) *Should be taken at the same time every day.* Taking the
     pill at bedtime will often decrease any nausea which
     might occur.
  d) If a patient misses one pill, she should take it as soon
     as possible and take the next pill on schedule.
  e) If two pills are missed, the pills should be discontinued
     for seven days and another form of contraception used
     in the interim. Alternatively, two pills may be taken
     each of the two following days. Another form of
     contraception should be used for the remainder of
     that cycle.
  f) *There is no good rationale for recommending routine
     pill-free intervals.*
  g) If an abortion has occurred at less than 12 weeks
     gestation, the pill can be started immediately. If an
     abortion of greater than 12 weeks occurs, wait 1 week.

h) Following delivery after 28 weeks in a nonnursing patient, wait 2 weeks.

7. *Follow-up*

a) Patients should be seen six to eight weeks after the initial visit. Blood pressure should be checked. Evidence of side effects should be sought. Proper use can be confirmed.

b) Yearly visits thereafter are appropriate in the absence of complicating factors.

c) Laboratory evaluation of glucose or lipid levels may be indicated in patients at particular risk for these problems.

8. *Clinical problems*

a) *Breakthrough bleeding*

(1) Occurs as a result of insufficient estrogen to stabilize the endometrium and is, therefore, more common with the low-dose pills.

(2) Will abate after two or three cycles in most patients. Reassurance may be the only treatment needed.

(3) If the bleeding persists at a problematic level, a seven-day course of conjugated estrogens or ethinyl estradiol may be administered around the time of bleeding in conjunction with the pill. Alternatively, change to a pill with a higher estrogen:progestin ratio.

b) *Amenorrhea*

(1) Occurs in about 1 percent of patients and is more common with the low-dose pills.

(2) It is a result of insufficient estrogen stimulation to endometrial growth, resulting in inadequate endometrium for withdrawal bleeding to occur.

(3) There is no evidence that prolonged amenorrhea while on the pill has any adverse effects. This will often be adequate assurance for the patient who is taking the pill properly and in whom, therefore, there is virtually no chance of pregnancy. If the

amenorrhea is of concern to the patient, the
estrogen content may be increased.

c) *Weight gain.* Some minor weight gain is frequently
reported, but usually responds to dietary restriction.

d) *Chloasma.* A rare problem with low-dose pills, which
in some cases may be permanent.

e) *Androgenic effects.* Acne, oily skin, and mild hirsutism may occur. Use of a less androgenic pill may
alleviate this problem.

f) *Depression* is usually a mild problem which can be
alleviated by the administration of vitamin B_6.

g) *Postpill amenorrhea*
   (1) Defined as amenorrhea of six months or more
   duration following discontinuation of the pill, it
   occurs in less than 1 percent of patients.[15]
   (2) More common in women with a prior history of
   menstrual irregularity. For this reason, the pill
   should be used with caution in young women who
   have not established regular menses.
   (3) Not related to the type of pill or the duration of
   pill use.
   (4) Most likely related to hypothalamic suppression.
   (5) The incidence of pituitary adenomas is increased
   in this group of patients.

9. *Side effects*
   a) *Vascular thrombosis.* The major risk factor associated
   with pill use, accounting for virtually all of the
   increased risk of mortality in pill users. *Smoking* and
   aging are significant determinants of the risk for
   vascular complications. *Virtually all of the increased
   risk is concentrated in patients who smoke, particularly
   after the age of 30, and in nonsmokers after the age of
   35*[16] (Table 23–3).
   (1) *Deep venous thrombophlebitis and pulmonary
   embolism*
      (a) Risk increased 5.7-fold by pill use.
      (b) The risk is estrogen related. The incidence in

one series was decreased from 25.9 to 7.2
cases per 100,000 by lowering the estrogen
content from 75 μg to 50 μg or less.[17]
  (2) *Myocardial infarction*
    (a) The risk is proportionate to the estrogen dose.
    (b) The dosage and type of progestin may be
significant factors.[18]
    (c) The presence of other risk factors, such as
obesity, hypertension, and hyperlipidemia,
increases the risk.
    (d) The increased risk may persist even after
discontinuation of the pill.[19]
  (3) *Cerebrovascular accidents*
    (a) Usually heralded by headaches, which must,
therefore, be evaluated in pill users.
    (b) The risk of thrombotic stroke is increased
threefold to fourfold and that of hemorrhagic stroke by twofold.[14] The incidence in
pill users is 1 in 10,000 woman years.[20]
b) *Lipid metabolism*[21]
  (1) Plasma triglycerides and cholesterol are elevated,
as are low density lipoproteins. High density
lipoproteins are lowered. These effects may be
related to the increased incidence of vascular
phenomena in pill users. A decrease in the
amount of progestin, as in some of the low dose
pills, may decrease the significance of these effects.
  (2) The type and the amount of progestin may be the
determining factors of the lipoprotein-cholesterol
changes.
c) *Carbohydrate metabolism.* Estrogens and progestins
produce an increased peripheral resistance to insulin.
Fifteen to fifty percent of women on the pill will
develop an impaired glucose tolerance. A recent
study, however, has shown no impairment of glucose
tolerance in a group of women taking a pill containing

TABLE 23-3. BIRTH-RELATED, METHOD-RELATED, AND TOTAL DEATHS PER 100,000 WOMEN PER YEAR, BY AGE

Regimen	Age in Years					
	15–19	20–24	25–29	30–34	35–39	40–44
No control						
Birth-related	5.3	5.8	7.2	12.7	20.8	21.6
Abortion only						
Method-related	1.0	1.9	2.4	2.3	2.9	1.7
Oral contraceptives only/nonsmokers						
Birth-related	0.1	0.2	0.2	0.4	0.6	0.4
Method-related	0.6	1.1	1.6	3.0	9.1	17.7
Total deaths	0.7	1.3	1.8	3.4	9.7	18.1

Oral contraceptives only/smokers						
Birth-related	0.1	0.2	0.2	0.4	0.6	0.4
Method-related	2.1	4.2	6.1	11.8	31.3	60.9
Total deaths	2.2	4.4	6.3	12.2	31.9	61.3
IUDs only						
Birth-related	0.1	0.2	0.2	0.4	0.6	0.4
Method-related	0.8	0.8	1.0	1.0	1.4	1.4
Total deaths	0.9	1.0	1.2	1.4	2.0	1.8
Barrier methods only						
Birth-related	1.1	1.5	1.9	3.3	5.0	4.0
Barrier methods plus abortion						
Method-related	0.1	0.3	0.4	0.4	0.4	0.2

From Tietze C, Lewitt S: In Keith LG, Kent PR, Berger GS, Brittain JR (eds): The Safety of Fertility Control, 1980. Courtesy of Springer Publishing Company.

35 μg of ethinyl estradiol and 0.4 mg of norethin-drone.[22] The clinical significance of the elevated blood sugar in normal women is unclear but may be of importance in women with latent, subclinical, or gestational diabetes.

d) *Hypertension.* Five percent of pill users develop significant hypertension after five years of use.[16] This is thought to involve alterations in the renin-angiotensin system, as there is an eightfold increase in angiotensinogen in pill users.[14] Sodium retention may also be a factor.

e) *Liver adenomas*[23] are benign solitary or multiple tumors that are extremely vascular and prone to hemorrhage. They are a rare but recognized side effect of pill use. Fifty percent of patients present with right upper quadrant or epigastric pain, and 40 percent have a palpable mass. The principal danger is hemorrhage. They may regress upon discontinuation of the pill.

f) *Gallbladder disease.* The risk of gallstones and cholecystitis is increased twofold in pill users[16] and is probably related to increased cholesterol saturation.

g) *Neoplasms*
   (1) *Cervix.* An association between oral contraceptives and cervical neoplasia has not been established.
   (2) *Uterus.* Oral contraceptives are associated with a decreased risk of endometrial carcinoma.[24]
   (3) *Breast.*[16] *There appears to be no association between breast cancer and pill usage.* The pill affords some protection against the development of benign breast disease.

h) *Pregnancy complications*
   (1) Congenital anomalies of the VACTERL type (anomalies of the vertebral column, anal, cardiac, tracheal, esophogeal, and renal tissues, and limb reduction) are increased if the pill is taken through the first trimester.

    (2) The incidence of spontaneous abortion or still birth after discontinuation of the pill is not increased.[25]

    (3) There is a twofold increase in twinning in patients who become pregnant soon after discontinuing the pill.[25]

    (4) *Patients should be encouraged to wait two or three cycles after discontinuing oral contraceptives before attempting pregnancy.*

B. *Progestin only pills (minipills)*

  1. Contain 350 μg of norethindrone or 75 μg of norgestrel only. The contraceptive effect depends on alterations in the endometrium and cervical mucus. LH suppression is incomplete, and a significant number of women will ovulate. Irregular bleeding is common and frequently results in discontinuation of this method.

  2. The failure rate is 2.5 percent.[14]

  3. They may be used in patients for whom estrogens are contraindicated.

  4. The incidence of ectopic gestations is increased if pregnancy does occur.

  5. They must be taken continuously.

C. *Depomedroxyprogesterone acetate (DMPA, Depo-Provera)*

  1. Not yet FDA approved although widely used throughout the world since 1963. The recommended dose is 150 mg IM every three months. The contraceptive effect of 150 mg is maintained for four months, so some margin of safety is provided.[26]

  2. The *failure rate* is less than 1 pregnancy per 100 woman years.[27]

  3. *Mechanism of action.* It blocks the LH surge and alters the endometrium and cervical mucus.

  4. *Advantages*

    a) Infrequent administration is required.

    b) Provides an extremely effective means of contraception for women in whom other forms are contraindicated.

    c) Estrogen levels are maintained at an early follicular

phase level. There are no hypoestrogenic side effects.

d) Produces amenorrhea. This is a highly desirable in some women and, in others, e.g., the mentally retarded, may be beneficial.

5. *Concerns and disadvantages*

a) Unpredictable vaginal bleeding may occur, especially during the first treatment cycle. Short courses of estrogens are therapeutic.

b) There is evidence of breast tumorogenesis in beagle dogs, but there has been no substantiation of this effect in women or other mammals.

c) Because of the long-acting nature of the preparation, there may be some delay in return of menses and fertility upon discontinuation. However, these effects do not appear to persist beyond 8 or, at most 12 months.

d) Weight gains of 5 to 10 pounds are not uncommon.

D. *Postcoital contraception* entails the use of agents to prevent pregnancy following an episode of unprotected intercourse during the fertile phase of the cycle.

1. *Indications*

a) Rape.

b) Condom breakage or diaphragm displacement during intercourse.

c) Failure to use adequate protection, especially common among young women during their first sexual experience.

2. *Available methods*

a) *Hormonal methods* must be initiated as soon as possible after coitus, preferably within 24 hours but no later than 72 hours. They must be administered for five consecutive days.[28]

(1) Diethylstilbestrol 25 mg bid (FDA approved).

(2) Ethinyl estradiol 2.5 mg bid.

(3) Conjugated estrogens 10 mg tid.

(4) Ethinyl estradiol 0.2 mg and norgestrel 2.0 mg, given as two divided doses 12 hours apart.

b) *Mechanical.* Copper-bearing IUDs inserted within five days are effective.

3. *Mechanism of action of hormonal methods* include asynchronous development of endometrium, alteration of tubal motility, and direct, or indirect, luteolysis.

4. *Effectiveness.* Most studies report failure rates of less than 1 percent.[28] Most failures are due to delay in treatment, poor patient compliance, or repeated unprotected intercourse.

5. *Side effects and cautions*
   a) Nausea and vomiting are frequent. Antiemetics should be prescribed.
   b) If pregnancy does occur, the incidence of ectopic gestation is increased.
   c) Because of concerns over possible teratogenic effects of the high doses of estrogen, abortion should be considered if pregnancy occurs.
   d) Preexistent pregnancy must be excluded prior to therapy.
   e) Contraindications to the use of high dose estrogens must be excluded.
   f) The possibility of infectious complications with respect to the use of an IUD must be considered.
   g) *Patients must have adequate short-term folow-up to exclude complications and failures. This also provides the opportunity for contraceptive counseling.*

E. *Abortion* is thoroughly discussed elsewhere in this book.

F. *Sterilization of female*

1. In 1976, 14 percent of all married women had undergone sterilization.[1] There are estimated to be over 11,000,000 sterilized adults in the United States, and for couples over 30, sterilization may be the most commonly used form of contraception.

2. *Approaches and techniques*
   a) *Laparotomy* is most commonly used for puerperal sterilization. The use of the minilaparotomy as a means of achieving interval sterilization is gaining

increasing favor. Various techniques include:

(1) *Madlener.* A loop of tube is elevated, and the base is crushed with a clamp. The crushed area is then ligated using nonabsorbable suture.

(2) *Pomeroy.* A loop of tube from the middle third of the tube is elevated, ligated with plain gut, and excised.

(3) *Irving.* The tube is divided, and the proximal stump is buried in the wall of the uterus. The distal stump is buried in the leaves of the broad ligament.

(4) *Cook.* Similar to the Irving, but the proximal stump is buried in the round ligament.

(5) *Kroener.* The fimbriated portion of the tube is excised.

(6) *Aldridge.* The fimbriated end of the tube is buried in the broad ligament.

(7) *Uchida.* The mesosalpinx is injected with a saline-epinephrine solution. It is then incised so as to expose the tube itself. The serosa of the proximal end is stripped off, and the majority of the proximal segment is removed, the stump ligated with nonabsorbable suture and placed back in the broad ligament. The distal end is ligated, and the broad ligament is closed, with the stump left outside the broad ligament.

(8) *Partial or total salpingectomy.* A part or all of the tube is removed.

(9) *Cornual resection.* The tube is ligated 1 cm from the cornua and excised from the cornua. The distal end can be buried in the broad ligament, and the proximal wound may be covered with the round and broad ligaments.

b) *Laparoscopy.* In 1976, 38 percent of all female sterilizations were performed laparoscopically.[29]

(1) *Electrical methods*

(a) *Unipolar.* A low voltage, high frequency current is passed from the laparoscopic instrument through the patient to a ground plate from which it returns to the generator. This carries the serious risk of inadvertent burns to bowel, bladder, or skin in 0.2 percent of cases.[30] For this reason, unipolar cautery has been largely replaced by other techniques, and its use should no longer be encouraged.

    (i) *Coagulation, transection, and recoagulation.* The addition of transection, recoagulation, or even biopsy does not decrease the failure rate[31] and may lead to an increased rate of complications.

    (ii) *Coagulation and transection.*

    (iii) *Coagulation only* may be performed at one or several sites on the tube.

  (b) *Bipolar.* The current passes from one jaw of the instrument to the other jaw. It is used for coagulation only techniques and carries less risk of accidental burns.

  (c) *Thermocoagulation.* Low voltage electricity heats the instrument, which then actually sears the tube.

(2) *Silastic bands.* With the use of a special applicator, a knuckle of tube is elevated, and a small Silastic band is placed around the bases of knuckle. Tears in the mesosalpinx, especially if the tubes are thickened or scarred, may occur in up to 3 percent of patients.[32] Greater immediate and late postoperative pelvic pain may occur with this technique.

(3) *Spring-loaded clips.* The clip is placed across the tube and occludes the lumen with minimal tissue destruction.

c) *Colpotomy.* An incision is made in the posterior fornix, the tube is delivered and then ligated by one of the above techniques, often fimbriectomy. This carries a higher morbidity rate than other techniques and is used infrequently.

   c) *Culdoscopy.* A special instrument is inserted into the posterior cul-de-sac, the tube is visualized, grasped, and delivered into the vagina and ligated as above. This is a technically difficult procedure and is rarely used.

   e) *Hysteroscopy.* The techniques of thermocoagulation and electrocoagulation, as well as mechanical occlusion with sclerosing agents or tubal plugs, have been attempted through the hysteroscope. Unacceptable failure and complication rates have been encountered. At present, these techniques must be considered experimental.

3. *Timing*

   a) *At the time of cesarean section,* the techniques most commonly used are the Pomeroy and Irving.

   b) *Postpartum*

     (1) Can be performed through a minilaparotomy.

     (2) If performed within 48 hours, there is no increase in infectious morbidity.

     (3) Adds little time to the hospital stay and avoids the need for a second hospitalization.

   c) *Interval*

     (1) Should wait at least eight weeks postpartum for an abdominal approach, six months for a vaginal.

     (2) Best done during the proliferative phase to avoid luteal phase pregnancies, although a concomitant dilatation and curettage obviates this.

     (3) Requires good contraceptive counseling in the interim.

4. *Sequelae*

   a) There is some evidence of altered pituitary-ovarian function after tubal ligation.[33] The incidence of menstrual irregularity may be increased.[34] This has been postulated to be due to an alteration in ovarian blood supply.

   b) The incidence of dysmenorrhea may be increased.[34]

c) Subjective complaints of decreased sexual enjoyment, a worsening of general health status, and depression are not uncommon.

5. *Reversal*[35,36]

a) *Approximately 1 percent of sterilized women will request reversal of the procedure, and 3 to 4 percent will regret their decision.* Of those requesting reversal, 89 percent are less than 30 at the time of sterilization. Unstable marital relationships are present at the time of sterilization in 50 percent of those requesting reversal.

b) *Reasons for requesting reversal*
   (1) Change in marital status—63 percent.
   (2) Crib death—17 percent.
   (3) Desire more children—10 percent.
   (4) Tragedies—4 percent.
   (5) Psychologic reasons—6 percent.

6. *Failure rates*

Pregnancy occurring after tubal ligation may be ectopic in anywhere from 10 to 60 percent of cases.[32] *Any post-sterilization pregnancy should be considered ectopic until proven otherwise.*

a) Madlener[37]—14/1,000
b) Pomeroy[37]—4/1,000
c) Cornual resection[37]—29/1,000
d) Irving[37]—less than 1/1,000
e) Kroener[38]—18/1,000
f) Uchida[39]—0/1,000
g) Cautery[31]—1 to 4/1,000
h) Silastic band[40]—3.3/1,000
i) Spring clip[41]—2 to 25/1,000

G. *Sterilization of male*

1. Vasectomy is the surgical interruption of the vas deferens in its scrotal portion. Male sterilization accounts for about 14 percent of all contraceptive methods.[1] Approximately 250,000 vasectomies are performed each year in the United States.[3]

2. *Effectiveness. The failure rate is less than 1 per 100.*

Azospermia does not occur immediately and must be documented prior to resumption of unprotected intercourse.

3. *Complications*

   a) Minor postoperative pain and swelling are common, but serious complications are rare. Sperm granulomas may occur in as many as 20 percent of males.[42]

   b) Sperm immobilizing and agglutinating antibodies have been demonstrated in a significant percentage of males after vasectomy.[43]

   c) The relationship between vasectomy and long-term sequelae, such as altered immune status, changes in coagulation status, and atherosclerosis, is currently under investigation.

4. *Reversibility.* Silber has reported the presence of sperm in the ejaculate in 90 percent, and pregnancy in 70 percent, of patients undergoing reversal.[44]

H. *The future*

The perfect contraceptive has not yet been developed. It would be one that could be used for long periods of time without significant side effects. It should be 100 percent effective and 100 percent reversible. There are several avenues of investigation.

1. *Barrier methods.* More effective and less displeasurable methods are being developed. Long-acting spermicides and spermicidally impregnated condoms and diaphragms and sponges hold promise.

2. *IUDs.* IUDs that are impregnated with antifibrinolyic substances or prostaglandin synthetase inhibitors, as well as ones that can be inserted immediately postpartum are being tested.

3. *Hormonal methods.* Much of the work in this area is being directed toward the use of agonists and antagonists of LRH. Hormonally impregnated vaginal rings may soon be available. Agents are also being sought which will specifically block hormonal action at a given level, e.g., endometrium, ovum, or blastocyst.

4. *Vaccines*. Vaccines which would produce immunity to implantation hormones, e.g., hCG, or to sperm, are under investigation.

5. *Sterilization*. Many techniques that would allow easier and more effective reversibility are being developed for both males and females.

REFERENCES

1. Ford K: Contraceptive use in the United States, 1973-1976. Fam Plan Perspect 10:265, 1978

2. Liskin LS, Fox G: Periodic abstinence: how well do new approaches work? Population Rep, Series I, Number 3, September, 1981

3. Ogino K: Ovulationstermin and konzeptionstermin. Zentralbl Gynakol 54:464, 1930

4. Hatcher RA, Stewart GK, Stewart F, Guest F, Schwartz DW, Jones SA: Contraceptive Technology 1980–1981. New York, Irvington, 1980, Chap 13

5. Coleman S, Piotrow PT: Spermicides—simplicity and safety are major assets. Population Rep, Series H, Number 5, September, 1979

6. Tietze C: Ranking of contraceptive methods by levels of effectiveness. Adv Plan Parentage 6:117, 1970

7. Vaughan B, Trussell J, Mencken J, Jones EF: Contraceptive failure among married women in the United States, 1970–1973. Fam Plann Perspect 9:251, 1977

8. Piotrow PT, Rinehart W, Schmidt JC: IUDs— update on safety, effectiveness and research. Population Rep, Series B, Number 3, May 1979

9. Oster G, Salgo MP: The copper intrauterine device and its mode of action. N Engl J Med 9:432, 1975

10. ACOG Technical Bulletin: The intrauterine device. Number 40, June, 1976

11. Burkman RT, The Women's Health Study: Association between intrauterine device and pelvic inflammatory disease. Obstet Gynecol 57:269, 1981

12. Mishell DR: Intrauterine devices. Clin Obstet Gynecol 6:1, 27, 1979

13. Foreman H, Stadel BV, Schlesslman S: Intrauterine device usage and fetal loss. Obstet Gynecol 58:669, 1981
14. Speroff L, Glass RH, Kase NG: Clinical Gynecologic Endocrinology and Infertility, 2nd ed. Baltimore, Waverly Press, 1978
15. Shearman RP, Smith ID: Statistical analysis of relationship between oral contraceptives, secondary amenorrhea, and galactorrhea. J Obstet Gynecol Br Comm 79:654, 1972
16. Royal College of General Practitioners: Oral Contraceptives and Health. New York, Pitman, 1974
17. Bottiger LE, Boman G, Eklud G, Westerholm B: Oral contraceptives and thromboembolic disease: effects of lowering estrogen content. Lancet 1:1097, 1980
18. Meade TW, Greenberg G, Thompson SG: Progestogens and cardiovascular reactions associated with oral contraceptives and a comparison of the safety of 50 μg and 30 μg oestrogen preparations. Br Med J 1:1157, 1980
19. Royal College of General Practitioners: Further analysis of mortality in oral contraceptive users. Lancet p 541, March, 1981
20. ACOG Technical Bulletin: Oral Contraception. Number 41, July 1976
21. Larson-Cohn V, Fahraeus L, Wallentin L, Zador G: Lipoprotein changes may be minimized by proper composition of a combined oral contraceptive. Fertil Steril 35:172, 1981
22. Spellacy, WN, Buhi WC, Birk SA: Carbohydrate metabolism prospectively studied in women using a low-estrogen oral contraceptive for six months. Contraception 20:137, 1979
23. Kent DR, Nissen ED: Liver tumors and oral contraceptives. In Keith LG, Kent DR, Berger GS, Brittain JR (eds): The Safety of Fertility Control. New York, Springer, 1980
24. Kaufman DW, Shapiro S, Slone D, et al.: Decreased risk of endometrial cancer among oral-contraceptive users. N Engl J Med 303:1045, 1980
25. Rothman KJ: Fetal loss, twinning and birth weight after oral contraceptive use. N Engl J Med 297:468, 1977
26. Nash HA: Depo-Provera: A review. Contraception 12:377, 1975
27. Schwallie PC: Experience with Depo-Provera as an injectable contraceptive. J Reprod Med 13:113, 1974
28. Blye RP: The use of estrogens as postcoital contraceptive agents. Am J Obstet Gynecol 116:1044, 1973
29. King TM, Zabin LS: Sterilization: efficacy, safety, regret, and reversal. Fem Pat Nov. 1, 1981 (Suppl) p 3

30. Loffer FD, Pent D: Pregnancy after laparoscopic sterilization. Obstet Gynecol 55:643, 1980

31. Loffer FD, Pent D: Indications, contraindications and complications of laparoscopy. Obstet Gynecol Surv 30:407, 1975

32. Phillips JM, Hulka J, Hulka B, Keith D, Keith L: American Association of Gynecologic Laparoscopists' 1976 membership survey. J Reprod Med 21:3, 1978

33. Alvarez-Sanchez F, Segal SJ, Brache V, Adejuwon CA, Leon P, Faundes A: Pituitary-ovarian function after tubal ligation. Fertil Steril 36:606, 1981

34. Madrigal V, Edelman DA, Goldsmith A, Brenner WE: Female sterilization via laparoscopy. Int J Gynaecol Obstet 13:268, 1975

35. Thomson P, Templeton A: Characteristics of patients requesting reversal of sterilization. Br J Obstet Gynaecol 85:161, 1978

36. Gomel V: Profile of women requesting reversal of sterilization. Fertil Steril 30:39, 1978

37. Garb AE: A review of tubal sterilization failures. Obstet Gynecol Surv 12:291, 1957

38. Metz KGP: Failures following fimbriectomy. Fertil Steril 28:66, 1977

39. Uchida H: Uchida's abdominal sterilization technique. Proc Third World Congress Obstet Gynecol 1:26, 1961

40. Chi I, Mumford SD, Gardner SD: Pregnancy risk following laparoscopic sterilization in nongravid and gravid women. J Reprod Med 26:289, 1981

41. Hulka JF, Mercer JP, Fishburne JI, et al.: Spring clip sterilization: one year follow-up of 1,079 cases. Am J Obstet Gynecol 125:1039, 1976

42. Davis JE: Risk and benefits of vasectomy. In Keith LG, Kent DR, Berger GS, Brittain JR (eds): The Safety of Fertility Control. New York, Springer, 1980

43. Ansbacher R: Sperm-agglutinating and sperm-immobilizing antibodies in vasectomized men. Fertil Steril 22:629, 1971

44. Silber SJ: Vasectomy and vasectomy reversal. Fertil Steril 29:125, 1978

24

Dysmenorrhea

Roger P. Smith, M.D.

PRACTICE PRINCIPLES

It has been estimated that of the 35 million women of childbearing age in the United States, 30 to 50 percent suffer from painful menstrual periods, or dysmenorrhea. Ten to fifteen percent have such discomfort that they are forced to miss work, school, or family life. This loss from the work force accounts for about 140 million work hours lost annually. For many years, this disorder presented a frustrating dichotomy between severe, incapacitating symptoms and an often normal physical examination. Treatment was equally frustrating by its lack of effectiveness. It has only been in the last decade that several lines of research have come together to delineate the pathophysiology of this symptom complex. With this new understanding, rational and effective treatment is finally becoming a reality.

CLASSIFICATION OF DYSMENORRHEA

Secondary dysmenorrhea is menstrual pain caused by pelvic pathology, such as infection, tumors, endometriosis, and polyps. These causes should be readily identifiable through history and physical examination. *Primary dysmenorrhea* is menstrual pain in which clinical examination does not reveal any noteworthy cause and is due to factors intrinsic to the uterus itself. Primary dysmenorrhea is further divided into *congestive* and *spasmodic*.

This separation is important because of differences in etiology and treatment.

A. *Secondary dysmenorrhea*

Secondary dysmenorrhea is painful menstruation due to an identifiable pathologic or iatrogenic condition. These conditions should be readily separated and identified on the basis of history and physical examination.

1. Etiology. The following is a list of frequent causes of secondary dysmenorrhea that should be considered:

   a) *Extrauterine*
      (1) Endometriosis
      (2) Tumors
         (a) Fibroids (subserosal or intraligamentous)
         (b) Malignancies (primary or metastatic)
      (3) Inflammation
         (a) Pelvic inflammatory disease
         (b) Tuberculosis (rare)
      (4) Adhesions
      (5) Psychogenic

   b) *Intrauterine*
      (1) Adenomyosis
      (2) Fibroids (intramural or pedunculated)
      (3) Polyps
      (4) Intrauterine contraceptive devices
      (5) Cervical stenosis/cervical lesions

2. Treatment. While secondary dysmenorrhea may be improved by using pain relievers, *treatment should always be directed to its cause.* For therapy, see chapters devoted to these specific problems.

B. *Primary dysmenorrhea*

Primary dysmenorrhea is painful menstruation without identifiable causes. Primary dysmenorrhea is divided into congestive and spasmodic types based upon symptom, cause, and treatment differences. Correct separation of these types is essential for effective treatment.

1. *Congestive dysmenorrhea* While a strict definition of dysmenorrhea includes only pain at the time of menstrua-

tion, the prodromal symptoms of premenstrual tension are generally included in most discussions of dysmenorrhea. These symptoms are attributed to general and localized edema along with pelvic venous congestion.

a) Symptoms. Congestive dysmenorrhea generally presents with one or more of the following symptoms:

   (1) Irritability and depression
   (2) Tension and nervousness
   (3) A feeling of exhaustion
   (4) Backaches
   (5) Headaches
   (6) Constipation
   (7) Bloating
   (8) Weight gain
   (9) Breast tenderness
 (10) Continuous dull aches

These symptoms generally appear prior to the onset of menstrual flow. The consistency of these symptoms from month to month is such that many women with congestive dysmenorrhea will state "I know that my period is coming without looking at the calendar."

b) *Treatment* of congestive dysmenorrhea is mainly symptomatic and frequently lacks complete effectiveness. Fortunately, the discomfort of congestive dysmenorrhea is usually less debilitating than is that of the spasmodic type. Thus, mild symptomatic improvement is often sufficient to allow partial or complete return to normal activities. Treatments employed are as follows.

   (1) *Analgesics.* Aspirin and aspirin compounds, acetaminophen and acetaminophen combinations (Tylenol), propoxyphene and propoxyphene combinations (Darvon, Darvocet), and synthetics (Ponstel, Motrin) all may be of some use. Potent analgesics, such as codeine or narcotic analogs, are seldom required. Their need should suggest the possibility of incorrect diagnosis.

   (2) *Diuresis.* Effective treatment of general and lo-

calized edema is often obtained by sodium restriction during the 7 to 10 days prior to menstruation, combined with fluid restriction or mild loading. When further diuresis is needed, natural diuretics (tea, coffee, or alcohol in small amounts) or mild agents, such as the thiazides (Hydrodiuril 50 mg per day), may be useful but should be used sparingly.

(3) *Hormones.* The use of hormones for congestive dysmenorrhea has been limited to *oral contraceptives.* These agents may be of some benefit but should only be used when birth control is desired or other methods are ineffective. Low estrogen, progesterone-dominant types appear to be most effective.

(4) *Physical*

   (a) *Heat.* A heating pad or hot water bottle may give some comfort and, through increased blood flow, may lessen local venous engorgement and edema.

   (b) *Exercise.* Physical activity and exercise have been reported to be helpful in reducing pelvic congestion and edema. Their role in treating congestive dysmenorrhea should be tailored to the needs, desires, and symptoms of the patient. Inactivity during menstruation is unnecessary and should not be recommended.

   (c) *Orgasm.* Orgasm, through masturbation or coitus, has been reported to give relief of congestive symptoms. Sexual arousal without orgasmic release may make symptoms worse. While this may not be a practical therapy, patients should be reassured that sexual activity is permissible and possibly advantageous.

(5) *Emotional.* While counseling, relaxation therapy, and even hypnosis have been advocated, these methods appear useful only when other distinctly

emotional factors are contributing to the problems of menstruation. However, emotional support and understanding by the patient's family and physician should not be overlooked.

2. *Spasmodic dysmenorrhea.* Spasmodic dysmenorrhea often causes the most debilitating symptoms found with menstrual discomforts. The pain of spasmodic dysmenorrhea often accounts for between one and three days of inability to work, attend school, or be active within the family. This may amount to more than 36 days per year, representing a significant personal and social loss.

a) *Symptoms.* Women with spasmodic dysmenorrhea are acutely ill, frequently appearing shocklike with hypotension, pallor, diaphoresis, restlessness, nausea, and diarrhea. They are in extreme pain. Presenting symptoms include the following:

(1) *Recurrent pain*
    (a) Abdominal pain
    (b) Pelvic cramping
    (c) Severe backache
(2) *Nausea*
(3) *Diarrhea*
(4) *Weakness*
(5) *Dizziness* (especially postural)

b) *Etiology.* Research has shown that women with primary spasmodic dysmenorrhea produce elevated levels of prostaglandins E_2 and $F_{2\alpha}$ in the endometrium prior to and at menstruation. These prostaglandins cause uterine contractions. The combination of increased prostaglandins and an increased myometrial sensitivity that these women also demonstrate produce uterine contractions of tremendous intensity (Fig. 24–1). These contractions can produce intrauterine pressures as high as 400 mm Hg. The contractions may last 60 to 90 seconds, with rest periods of only 15 to 20 seconds. Resting pressures

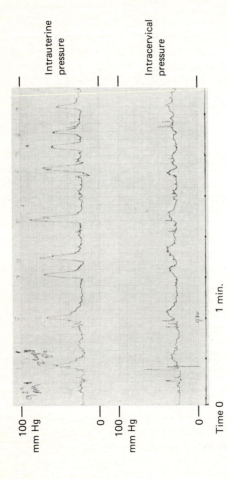

Figure 24–1. Intrauterine pressure recorded by dual channel microtransducer in a 19-year-old women with primary spasmodic dysmenorrhea. The upper tracing shows intrauterine pressure and the lower tracing intracervical pressure, with a pressure range of 0 to 100 mm Hg. Peak pressures of 80 to 100 mm Hg are seen. Pressures may range as high as 400 mm Hg in these women.

vary from 20 to 80 mm Hg. These pressures create uterine ischemia and the intense spasmodic pain characteristic of this disease.

c) *Treatment.* Traditionally, the treatment of spasmodic dysmenorrhea has fallen into two types: modification of the menstrual period or cycle and modification of pain. Studies that demonstrated the causative role of prostaglandins also pointed the way to specific therapy with *prostaglandin synthetase inhibitors* or *prostaglandin antagonists.* These agents offer the possibility of pain prevention through interruption of the process by which the pain is created.

(1) *Modification of periods.* Because spasmodic dysmenorrhea is almost exclusively found in ovulatory menstrual cycles, hormonal suppression of ovulation has been frequently employed. In women with mild dysmenorrhea, this approach may be very effective, but in women with severe pain or in those who do not want or need birth control, this approach may not be ideal. When used, low dose combination type oral contraceptive agents appear to be the best. The use of progesterone-containing intrauterine contraceptive devices (Progestasert) has been advocated for dysmenorrhea, but controlled studies have not demonstrated their effectiveness.

(2) *Modification of pain.* Pain relievers have been the mainstay of dysmenorrhea therapy in the past. For mild pain, aspirin, acetominophen, propoxyphene, or their compounds have found wide use. Unfortunately, the pain of spasmodic dysmenorrhea is generally of sufficient magnitude that these agents are less than fully effective. Potent analgesics are often required. Useful agents and their compounds are *butalbital* (Fiorinal 1 or 2 q4h), *oxycodone* (Percodan 1 q6h), *pentazocine* (Talwin 1 q3 to 4h), *pro-*

methazine (Syanlgos 2 q4h), *codeine* (30 to 60 mg q4h) or *meperidine* (Demerol 50 to 100 mg q4 to 6h). While these agents, adjusted to the needs of the individual, may give good pain relief, their potential side effects may still render the patient unable to function normally. The use of these potent drugs should be limited, and care must be exercised.

(3) *Pain prevention.* By suppressing uterine activity, it is possible to interrupt the process by which spasmodic dysmenorrhea pain is created (Fig. 24–2). Drugs such as calcium antagonists (Nifedipine), spasmolytic agents (Isoxuprine, Papaverine, Ritodrine), and hormones (Lututrin) may suppress uterine activity in the laboratory, but their side effects limit their clinical usefulness. The most practical method of suppressing uterine activity has been by reducing the level of prostaglandin through prostaglandin synthetase inhibitors and/or reducing the sensitivity of the myometrial receptors. The agents that can produce these effects are the nonsteroidal antiinflammatory (NSAI) drugs often employed in arthritis treatment.

(a) *Aspirin (650 mg q3 to 4h)* is a poor synthetase inhibitor which requires high doses and one to two days of preperiod treatment to obtain results. It is useful for mild discomfort in women with regular periods and no possibility of pregnancy.

(b) *Indomethacin (Indocin 25 mg tid).* As a potent inhibitor of the prostaglandin synthetase system, this drug has been very useful. It is generally started one to two days prior to flow but may give some relief if started only at the onset of pain. Its potential side effects, especially in the gastrointestinal

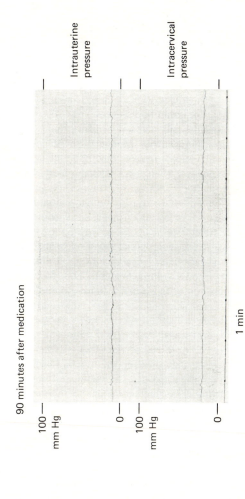

Figure 24–2. Intrauterine and intracervical pressures in the same patient recorded 90 minutes after medication (mefenamic acid, 250 mg by mouth). Complete loss of uterine contractile activity is seen, which correlates with the subjective relief of pain. Resting pressures are approximately one fourth those found prior to treatment.

447

tract and eye, along with its contraindication in possible pregnancy and nursing mothers, has limited its use.

(c) *Phenylbutazone (Butazolidin 100 mg qid).* While phenylbutazone is an effective antiin-flammatory agent with the ability to reduce prostaglandin synthesis, its poor tolerance by many patients has limited its use in dys-menorrhea. Few studies of this drug in dys-menorrhea have been done, and it is seldom used for this indication.

(d) *Arylalkanoic acids (propionic acid deriva-tives): Ibuprofen* (Motrin 400 to 600 mg q4 to 6 h), *fenoprofen* (Nalfon 300 to 600 mg qid), *naproxen* (Naprosyn 250 mg bid) Though effective synthetase inhibitors, only ibupro-fen and naproxen have been used to any extent in the treatment of dysmenorrhea. Clinical studies have confirmed the efficacy of these agents, but almost all of the studies to date have involved 24 to 72 hours of premenstrual medication. This limits their usefulness in women with irregular periods or those who might become pregnant. Recent work indicates that these agents may be useful when started at the onset of pain. A lag time of two to three hours from dose to effect may be expected, while synthetase inhibition reduces production and previously formed prostaglandins are metabolized.

(e) *Anthranilic acids (fenamates): mefenamic* acid (Ponstel 250 mg q4 to 6h), *meclofenamic acid* (Meclomen 50 to 100 mg tid), *flufenamic acid* (not available in the United States). The fenamates are potent prostaglandin synthet-ase inhibitors which also have the ability to block the myometrial prostaglandin receptors. Only indomethacin shares the latter ability. This dual action permits these drugs to be used at the onset of pain, without preloading. The lag time is reduced to between 30 minutes (meclofenamic acid) and 90 minutes (mefenamic acid). Blockade of the myometrial receptors gives more rapid and complete uterine relaxation, which, by improved blood flow, contributes to rapid metabolism of previously formed prostaglandins. These drugs are effective and well tolerated with side effects similar to aspirin and the arylalkanoic acid derivatives.

(f) Care should be used when prescribing any of these NSAI drugs. All of them have the potential for interaction with other drugs, such as anticoagulants, and all of them may aggravate existing medical conditions, such as asthma or gastrointestinal bleeding. Use of any of these agents should be limited to the time of pain only, if possible, to minimize total dosage and possible adverse reactions.

(g) With proper selection of patients and the careful use of one or more of these drugs, primary spasmodic dysmenorrhea is a readily treatable problem. If a patient does not respond, careful reconsideration of the original diagnosis should be undertaken, and further testing should be carried out when indicated.

BIBLIOGRAPHY

Textbook

Novak ER, Jones GS, Jones HW: Textbook of Gynecology, 9th ed. Baltimore, Williams & Wilkins, 1975, pp 721-730

Journals

Acta Obstet Gynecol Scand (Suppl 87), 1979 (complete issue devoted to dysmenorrhea)

Dawood MY: Primary Dysmenorrhea, part one: etiology and diagnosis. Female Patient 4:80, 1979

Dawood MY: Primary dysmenorrhea, part two: treatment. Female Patient 4:68, 1979

Ylikorkala O, Dawood MY: New concepts in dysmenorrhea. Am J Obstet Gynecol 130:833, 1978

25

Endometriosis and Adenomyosis

M. Yusoff Dawood, M.B., Ch.B., M.D.

PRACTICE PRINCIPLES

Endometrial tissue on sites other than the uterine cavity results in disease states whose symptoms and effects may vary widely but not always proportionally to the physical dimensions of the disease. This degree of disparity and poor understanding of the precise etiologic mechanism have led to the difficulties in diagnosis and treatment of the various types of endometriosis.

Endometriosis is the presence of endometrial tissue in sites other than the uterine cavity and can be subdivided into two types.

A. *Endometriosis externa (endometriosis)* is the presence of endometrial tissue outside of the uterus.
B. *Endometriosis internal (adenomyosis)* is the presence of endometrial tissue within the myometrium.

ENDOMETRIOSIS EXTERNA (ENDOMETRIOSIS)

A. *Theories of pathogenesis*
   1. *Retrograde menstruation* (Sampson's theory). This results in the menses flowing out of the fallopian tubes into the pelvis. Retrograde menstruation has been observed in women and in rhesus monkeys. It accounts for the frequent sites of endometriosis in the posterior aspects of the pelvis. However this theory does not explain the extrapelvic sites of endometriosis.
   2. *Direct implantation.* Endometrial tissues are displaced into and implant in the new sites. This theory is supported by endometriosis seen in scars. Implantation of menstrual fluid into peritoneum results in endometriosis in animals. Implantation occurs after retrograde menstruation. Ovarian estrogens are necessary for successful implantation. However, this theory does not explain endometriosis in the limbs and thorax.
   3. *Celomic metaplasia.* All tissues in which endometriosis arise can be traced embryologically to celomic epithelium. Metaplasia of such epithelial derivatives can result in endometrial tissue. This theory can account for all the sites of endometriosis so far described.
   4. *Lymphatic and hematogenous spread.* This theory attempts to account for distant sites of endometriosis but is not well supported.
   5. *Genetic.* There is a 5.8 percent familial incidence among immediate female siblings, an 8.1 percent risk if the mother has endometriosis,[1] and a 7 percent risk of endometriosis if the female sibling or mother has endometriosis. This is probably polygenic and multifactorial inheritance. It does not account for the majority without family history.
   6. *Prostaglandins.* Preliminary evidence in women and animals show that prostaglandin F2α is increased in the endometrial tissue, in the peritoneal washings, and in

the endometrial implants.[2] It may partially account for the dysmenorrhea.

B. *Pathology*

1. *Sites.* Most frequent sites are in structures in the pelvis, particularly posterior to the uterus: (1) ovaries, (2) cul-de-sac, (3) rectovaginal septum, (4) uterosacral ligaments, (5) uterovesical peritoneum, (6) fallopian tubes, (7) bladder dome, (8) broad ligament, and (9) umbilicus. Other less frequent sites include (1) bowel, (2) bladder, (3) cervix, (4) vagina, (5) upper limbs, (6) thorax, and (7) even the head.

2. *Appearance*

   a) Macroscopically, the lesions appear as small nodules of 1 to 2 mm to large cystic collections which are usually in the ovary and are referred to as "chocolate cysts," but more correctly "endometriotic ovarian cysts." The small nodules resemble a matchstick head with either bright red, rust, or silvery powder burns.

   b) Histologically, lesions demonstrate endometrial tissue with menstrual type blood, hemosiderin, and organization at different stages. Both endometrial glands and stroma are present.

C. *Classification*

1. Several methods of classification have been introduced. These include the classifications by Acosta-Sisson, Andrews, and Behrman. Currently it is probably best to adopt the classification recommended by the American Fertility Society, which is given in Table 25–1.

2. The purpose of classification is to be able to stage the extent and severity of disease and, secondly, to be able to compare the results of therapy on a much more objective and comparable basis.

D. *Clinical features*

1. Endometriosis usually occurs:

   a) In the *second and third decades* of life.

   b) In women with *"striving" personalities,* and thus usually higher socioeconomic groups.

TABLE 25–1. CLASSIFICATION AND STAGING OF ENDOMETRIOSIS

PERITONEUM			
Endometriosis	< cm	1–3 cm	> 3 cm
Points Scored	1	2	3
Adhesions	Filmy	Dense with partial cul-de-sac obliteration	Dense with complete cul-de-sac obliteration
Points Scored	1	2	3
OVARY			
Endometriosis	< 1 cm	1–3 cm	> 3 cm or ruptured endometrioma
Points Scored			
Right (R)	2	4	6
Left (L)	2	4	6
Adhesions	Filmy	Dense with partial ovarian enclosure	Dense with complete ovarian enclosure
Points Scored			
R	2	4	6
L	2	4	6

TUBE	< 1 cm	> 1 cm	Tubal occlusion
Edometriosis			
Points Scored			
R	2	4	6
L	2	4	6
Adhesions	Filmy	Dense with tubal distortion	Dense with tubal enclosure
Points Scored			
R	2	4	6
L	2	4	6

STAGE I	Mild	Total Points Scored: 1-5
STAGE II	Moderate	Total Points Scored: 6-15
STAGE III	Severe	Total Points Scored: 16-30
STAGE IV	Extensive	Total Points Scored: 31-54

*Assigned at laparoscopy or laparotomy aparotomy.
(After American Fertility Society.)

455

    c) In *infertile women and often nulliparous women.*

    d) In teenagers as early as the menarche.

    e) In blacks more frequently than previously suspected.

2. *Symptoms*

    a) *Asymptomatic*

    b) *Infertility.* The longer the duration of endometriosis, the higher the incidence of infertility. Seventy-one percent of the associated infertility is primary infertility, and 29 percent is secondary infertility.[3]

    c) *Dysmenorrhea* starts one to three days before menses and is often worse on the first one or two days of menses. Often difficult to distinguish from primary dysmenorrhea in the absence of positive signs. *Occurs in 63 percent of patients with endometriosis.*[3] *Severity of dysmenorrhea is not directly related to severity of endometriosis.*

    d) *Dyspareunia.* Usually deep-seated, particularly on deep to and fro thrust of the penis. Occurs in 27 percent of endometriosis patients and is only partially related to severity of endometriosis.[3]

    e) *Pelvic pain* that may be *localized or vague* and *not related to any phase of menstrual cycle.* The pelvic pain and dysmenorrhea are not directly related to the amount and extent of the endometriosis. Often the degree of pain is inversely proportional to the size or extent of the lesions.

    f) *Symptoms of ovarian cyst or its complications* when chocolate cyst is present.

    Less frequent symptoms include:

    g) Gastrointestinal symptoms. Diarrhea, intestinal obstruction, melena, and perforation of the gut—when the bowel is involved.

    h) Urinary symptoms. Dysuria, hematuria, and recurrent urinary infections—when the urinary tract is involved.

    i) Menstrual dysfunction. Secondary to anovulation or oligo-ovulation. Includes oliogomenorrhea or amenorrhea. Occurs in 10 percent of pelvic endometriosis.[4]

j) Catamenial hemothorax, when endometriosis occurs in the chest.

k) Cyclical bleeding from umbilicus or limbs where the endometriosis may be present.

3. *Physical findings.* A complete examination to look for extrapelvic endometriosis in other parts of the body is mandatory. *A rectovaginal examination is a sine qua non in order not to miss small nodules, thickening, or induration. More common physical findings may include:*

a) Negative general and pelvic examinations.

b) Unequal enlargement of the ovary, which is tender.

c) Nodules and/or thickenings which are usually tender and in the cul-de-sac, uterosacral ligaments, and the rectovaginal septum.

d) Fixed retroversion of the uterus.

e) Obvious prune- or rust-colored nodules or deposits on distant parts of the body, such as the umbilicus or limbs.

f) Deposits (rust or prune colored) in the cervix and/or vagina.

g) Thickenings in the area of the fallopian tubes.

Less frequent signs include:

h) Those of intestinal obstruction.

i) Hemoperitoneum from rupture of an ovarian endometriotic cyst.

j) Those of torsion of an ovarian endometriotic cyst.

k) Positive findings in the chest examination.

E. *Differential diagnosis*

1. *Primary dysmenorrhea.* Differentiation can be difficult and laparoscopy may be necessary to distinguish between the two.

2. *Pelvic inflammatory disease.* Usually pyrexic, elevated blood sedimentation rate, leukocytosis, and generally bilateral adnexal tenderness with a hot vagina on bimanual examination.

3. *Salpingitis isthmica nodosa.* Rarely, the nodularities on the tubes may be felt, but often only laparoscopy or laparotomy will distinguish the two.
4. *Ovarian cyst.* Cannot be distinguished until at surgery, which is needed for both.
5. *Pelvic adhesions.* Past history with regard to appendicitis, pelvic inflammatory disease, and previous pelvic surgery is an important clue.
6. *Adenomyosis.* Occurs in older age group, menorrhagia is usually present (85 percent of patients), dysmenorrhea is present in 30 percent, the uterus is usually somewhat symmetrically enlarged, hysterogram can sometimes be useful.
7. *Gastrointestinal lesion.* Often difficult to distinguish from if the endometriosis involves bowel. Unusually, intestinal obstruction may occur. Often diagnosed at laparotomy. Sigmoidoscopy and biopsy may assist if lesion is visible.
8. *Urinary tract lesion.* Endometriosis of this tract uncommon but may occur. Cystoscopy may be useful, as may intravenous urography.

F. *Laboratory investigations*
1. Complete blood count, blood sedimentation rate, RPR, and VDRL, endocervical cultures for gonorrhea, routine urinalysis, and Pap smear of the cervix.
2. Pelvic sonogram is useful if a palpable pelvic mass is felt.
3. Intravenous pyelogram and cystoscopy may be needed if urinary tract is involved and symptoms are present.
4. Upper gastrointestinal series and/or barium enema is necessary if bowel involvement is suspected. Sigmoidoscopy and biopsy if the lesion is visible.
5. *Laparoscopy is almost always essential to confirm or rule out pelvic endometriosis.*
6. *Biopsy of lesion* should preferably be done when readily accessible, as on the abdominal wall, limbs, vagina, and cervix. Laparascopic biopsy of pelvic endometriosis *should be done when the lesions are not located over critical sites with potential dangers* (such as near ureter,

blood vessels in the broad ligament, and so on). Biopsy is helpful in establishing histologic diagnosis prior to initiating therapy.

G. *Management*

1. *Prophylactic measures*

a) Avoid hysterosalpingograms, tubal insufflation, and manipulative procedures during menstrual flow and until after complete cessation of menstrual flow.

b) Preferably avoid tampon use. There is some consideration, not proven, that use of tampon may account for increased endometriosis seen. Certainly prudent to avoid in high-risk woman, such as those with family history of endometriosis.

c) Shorten unnecessary prolonged deferment of pregnancy. Particularly helpful in women with family history of endometriosis.

2. *Therapeutic measures*

a) *Nonoperative therapy is essentially hormonal therapy or pregnancy. It is indicated in patients who have small depostis of endometriosis and those who do not have ovarian endometriotic cysts.*

(1) *Pregnancy* will suppress endometriosis and usually result in complete eradication of the disease. The gestational hormones induce pseudodecidual or decidual changes within the endometriotic deposits and cause glandular atrophy and eventual scarring.

(2) *Hormonal therapy*[5] is aimed at (1) suppressing ovarian function and thus reducing the growth-promoting effects of ovarian estrogens, (2) directly inhibiting endometrial growth, and (3) converting the endometrium to a secretory or pseudodecidual type of tissue with resultant glandular atrophy. Three main types of hormones have been used: *oral contraceptives, progestagens,* and *androgens.*

(a) Oral contraceptives. Any combined oral contraceptive can be used, but one with a higher progestogen content, such as Enovid, is preferable. A pseudopregnancy condition is desired, i.e., the patient is given the oral contraceptive agent continuously so as to render her amenorrheic. The effect of continuous exposure to a combined estrogen-progesterone preparation is to suppress endometrial growth (including the endometriosis) and produce an inactive and atrophic endometrium. This is then resolved by macrophage activity and engulfed in fibrosis. The oral contraceptive pill will also suppress pituitary gonadotropins and thus inhibit ovarian function and ovulation. Treatment is usually continued for nine months. If pain or dysmenorrhea is not relieved or if there is breakthrough bleeding, the dose of the pill may be increased to two tablets or more per day. Side effects are those usually seen in oral contraceptive therapy.

(b) *Progestin therapy.* With this therapy, a progestogen is given by itself. The progestogens that are commonly used include norethindrone or medroxyprogesterone acetate. Both are given orally. The initial dose of norethindrone is 5 mg PO bid. It is increased at one- to two-weekly intervals until symptoms are relieved or the patient is intolerant of the dose. The dose is then reduced by 5 mg per day. Usually a daily dose of 20 to 30 mg is required. The usual dose of medroxyprogesterone acetate (Provera) is 30 to 40 mg per day.[6] If depo-medroxyprogesterone acetate is used, the usual dose is 100 mg every two weeks for four doses and then 200 mg every month. Treatment is usually for six to nine months, and pseudopregnancy is induced. Besides inhibiting pituitary gonadotropin secretion, progestogens induce excessive secretory and pseudodecidual changes of the endometrium, including the endometriosis, resulting in glandular atrophy, increased macrophage activity, and fibrosis. Side effects of progestogen therapy include water retention and weight gain, oily skin, acne, and infrequently mild hirsutism. Breakthrough bleeding may occur if the dose is inadequate.

(c) *Androgen therapy.* Testosterone and methyltestosterone have been widely used and are effective in relieving the pain of endometriosis. The usual dose of methyltestosterone is 5 to 10 mg daily sublingually. Testosterone probably inhibits the endometriotic lesions directly, since ovulation may not be inhibited by these doses. With these doses, side effects are infrequent but may include facial hair growth, acne, and infrequently jaundice. Remissions tend to be transient.

(d) *Danazol.* This is probably the most effective hormonal therapy for endometriosis, but it is expensive compared to the other hormones used. It is a modified androgen and is an antigonadotropin. The usual dose is 800 mg daily given orally, although preliminary data suggest that 600 mg daily may also be effective. Danazol inhibits pituitary gonadotropin release and thus ovulation. It may have a direct effect on the endometrium and on the ovary by interfering with gonadotropin action. It induces an atrophic endometrium similar to that of postmenopausal women. Thus, danazol therapy has been referred to as *"pseudomenopause therapy."* Treatment is continued for at least three months but usually for six to nine months. It is very effective for relieving pain and dysmenorrhea, with success rates of up to 61 percent.[7] Pregnancy rates after danazol therapy are also claimed to be higher than with other forms of hormone therapy, with success rates of 72 percent.[7] Side effects of danazol therapy includes nausea, vomiting, weight gain, breakthrough bleeding with lower doses (below 600 mg per day), acne, oily skin, and infrequently hirsutism and hyperlipidemias. Other reported side effects include decrease in libido (6 percent of patients), decrease in breast size, and hot flashes (8 percent).

b) *Indications for surgical therapy* in patients with endometriosis are:

(1) To relieve intractable pain during the reproductive years when associated with nodularities, a fixed uterus, and symptoms of dysmenorrhea, dyspareunia, and menometrorrhagia.

(2) Endometrioma of 2 cm or more in size.

(3) To improve fertility

(4) In patients with known endometriosis having palpably increasing lesions and symptoms.

(5) For definitive treatment of endometriosis in women who have completed childbearing.

(6) When there is obstruction, such as intestinal obstruction, and in patients with endometriosis who develop an acute abdomen.

c) *Conservative surgery. Surgery should be conservative when fertility potential is to be preserved.*

(1) *Excision and/or cauterization* of the endometriotic implants can be done through the laparoscope or at laparotomy to avoid injury to adjacent structures. Only lesions that are a few millimeters in

size and located over nonstrategic sites may be cauterized. The laser is being evaluated for this purpose.

(2) *Lysis of adhesions* is necessary when pelvic adhesions are present and additional pelvic surgical procedures are required for the endometriosis. Lysis of pelvic, peritubal, and periovarian adhesions may be the only procedure in the absence of active endometriosis when enhancement of fertility is required in the infertile woman with endometriosis.

(3) *Ovarian cystectomy* is indicated if there is ovarian endometrioma 2 cm or more in size. If ovarian cystectomy is technically difficult, wedge resection of the endometrioma or even an oophorectomy will become necessary. If the endometrioma ruptures during surgery or prior to it, the pelvis should be carefully cleaned of all visible chocolate material to reduce the chance of subsequent peritoneal implantation from such spillage.

(4) *Cervical dilatation* should be performed in conjunction with the pelvic surgical procedures mentioned. Cervical dilatation will enhance antegrade menstrual flow and thus reduce likelihood of retrograde menstruation.

d) *Radical surgery and other forms of surgery*

(1) *Abdominal hysterectomy* is performed when childbearing is no longer required or is completed and pain cannot be relieved by hormonal therapy. Usually both ovaries and tubes need to be removed so that endometriosis in other sites will not be subject to the stimulatory effects of ovarian estrogens. When the uterus is extensively fixed to the bowel, bladder, and important pelvic structures and cannot be easily dissected free without injury to these adjacent structures, a bilateral oophorectomy may be sufficient.

(2) *Presacral neurectomy* is indicated if pelvic pain is

severe and the pelvic endometriotic lesions are minimal.

(3) *Ventral suspension of the uterus* is indicated when lysis of pelvic adhesions is performed and the uterus is found to be fixed and retroflexed, or when there is extensive dissection and considerable amounts of raw peritoneal surface that cannot be satisfactorily peritonealized.

(4) *Extrapelvic endometriosis*. These lesions usually require excision.

(5) *Postoperative hormonal therapy*. If the surgery has removed the endometriotic lesions completely, postoperative hormonal therapy is not necessary, since conception appears to be highest in the first 12 months after surgery. If there is pelvic pain or dysmenorrhea, postoperative hormonal therapy is generally required.

H. *Prognosis*

1. *Pregnancy rates*. With pseudopregnancy therapy, pregnancy rates of 47 to 55 percent have been obtained.[8] With conservative surgical therapy, pregnancy rates of 33 to 79 percent have been obtained, while surgery combined with pseudopregnancy therapy has produced about 20 percent fertility rates.[9] With danazol therapy, pregnancy rates of up to 76 percent or more have been reported,[10] but recent analysis gives rates of 50 percent.[11] More than 50 percent of the pregnancies occurred within the first year of treatment.

2. *Relief of symptoms*. With danazol therapy, relief of dysmenorrhea was achieved in 97 percent of patients, relief of pelvic pain in 86 percent, and relief of dyspareunia in 47 percent.[9] The improvement was more marked with doses of 800 mg/day than of 600 mg/day.

3. *Recurrence rate*. With conservative surgery, there is a 30 to 36 percent chance of recurrence of the endometriosis requiring reoperation.[9] With long-term follow-up of danazol therapy, recurrence rate of symptoms is 33 percent but usually less severe than before treatment.[11]

4. *Prognosis for female siblings or offspring*. Since there is a 7 percent chance of a female sibling or offspring having endometriosis when there is a first-degree female relative with endometriosis, such siblings or offspring should be carefully looked at for endometriosis, especially if there are symptoms. Such relatives should also be told not to postpone pregnancies too long after marriage.

ADENOMYOSIS (ENDOMETRIOSIS INTERNA)

A. *Definition*
   Presence of endometrial tissue in the myometrium.
B. *Pathogenesis*
   Ingrowth and pinching off within the muscular wall of the uterus of islands of normal endometrial tissue from the endometrial cavity. Probably secondary to traumatic and disruptive effect of pregnancy or vigorous curettage on the uterine wall.
C. *Pathology*
   Occurs in 21.5 percent of all hysterectomy specimens. May be localized, when it is referred to as *adenomyomata* or *localized adenomyosis*. Accompanied by varying degrees of cystic and adenomatous hyperplasia in 35 to 50 percent of patients.
   1. *Appearance*
      a) *Macroscopic*
         (1) Diffuse and uniform involvement of entire uterine wall, with the myometrium having a trabeculated appearance when cut and sometimes blood-filled cystic spaces. Myometrial hypertrophy and symmetrical uterine enlargement present.
         (2) If localized adenomyosis, it appears as a localized tumor that may be indistinguishable from a fibroid tumor or may protrude into the uterine cavity as an adenomatous polyp.
      b) *Microscopic*
         (1) Endometrial tissue is present within the myome-

trium, and sometimes the connection to the
endometrial tissue within uterine cavity is present.
Both glands and stroma are present and, occasionally, decidual transformation.

(2) Less than half the patients show cyclic hormonal
effects.

(3) Myometrial cells show hypertrophy and hyperplasia.

(4) Blood and hemosiderin may be present.

D. *Clinical features*
   1. Estimated to occur in 15 to 25 percent of all women.
   2. More common in older women, with peak incidence in
      fifth decade of life.
   3. Usually multiparous women.
   4. *Symptoms*
      a) May be asymptomatic in many women.
      b) Usually *menorrhagia,* which is heavier and more
         prolonged menstrual flow.
      c) Heavy dragging suprapubic discomfort or feeling of
         weight in the pelvis, which is worse premenstrually.
      d) Congestive *dysmenorrhea* (secondary dysmenorrhea).
      e) *Dyspareunia.*
      f) *Infertility* if associated with endometriosis or recurrent
         early pregnancy wastage in those who are trying to
         have children.
      g) Secondary *bladder or bowel irritation* from the en-
         larged uterus.
   5. *Physical signs*
      a) *Symmetrical enlargement of the uterus* if the adenomy-
         osis is diffuse, usually seldom larger than 12 weeks'
         gestation size, firm and globular and typically *tender*
         to palpation.
      b) *If localized adenomyosis, uterine enlargement is asym-
         metrical* and may resemble a myoma but is usually
         tender.

E. *Differential diagnosis*
   1. *Myoma.* Uterine enlargement is irregular with myoma

but *symmetrical* with adenomyosis. *Tenderness* is a key feature of adenomyosis but present in myoma only when a complication or degeneration occurs.

   2. *Endometriosis* may coexist with adenomyosis in as many as 10 to 20 percent of patients.

F. *Management.* Unlike endometriosis, treatment is almost exclusively by surgery.

   1. *Total hysterectomy.* If childbearing is completed, total hysterectomy is the treatment of choice. The ovaries may be left in situ in premenopausal women if there is no associated endometriosis.

   2. *Resection.* If childbearing is desired and the adenomyosis is localized, resection of the affected area with preservation of the uterus is the treatment.

   3. Unlike the situation with endometriosis, hormonal therapy is of no value, and estrogens may certainly increase menorrhagia.

REFERENCES

1. Simpson JL, Elias S, Malinak LR, Buttram VC Jr: Heritable aspects of endometriosis. I. Genetic studies. Am J Obstet Gynecol 137:327, 1980
2. Weed JC: Prostaglandins as related to endometriosis. Clin Obstet Gynecol 23:895, 1980
3. Buttram VC Jr: Conservative surgery for endometriosis in the infertile couple: a study of 206 patients with implications for both medical and surgical therapy. Fertil Steril 31:117, 1979
4. Dmowski WP, Cohen MR, Wilhelm JL: Endometriosis and ovulatory failure: does it occur? In Greenblatt RB (ed): Recent Advances in Endometriosis. Amsterdam, Excerpta Medica, 1976, pp 129–136
5. Hammond CB, Harvey AF: Conservative treatment of endometriosis. Fertil Steril 30:497, 1978
6. Moghissi KS, Boyce CR: Management of endometriosis with oral medroxyprogesterone acetate. Obstet Gynecol 47:265, 1976
7. Dnowski WP, Cohen MR: Antigonadotropin (danazol) in the treatment of endometriosis. Am J Obstet Gynecol 130:41, 1978

8. Kistner RW: Endometriosis and infertility. In Behrman SJ, Kistner RW (eds): Progress in Infertility. Boston, Little, Brown, 1975, pp 345–366

9. Behrman SJ: The surgical management of endometriosis. In Greenblatt RB (ed): Recent advances in Endometriosis. Amsterdam, Excerpta Medica, 1976, pp 60–67

10. Freidlander RL: Experiences with danazol in therapy of endometriosis. In Greenblatt RB (ed): Recent Advances in Endometriosis. Amsterdam, Excerpta Medica, 1976, pp 100–107

11. Greenblatt RB, Tzingounis V: Danazol treatment of endometriosis: long-term follow-up. Fertil Steril 32:518, 1979

26

Infertility

Edward L. Marut, M.D.

PRACTICE PRINCIPLES

The magnitude of the problem of infertility is difficult to define exactly, but conventional wisdom states that *10 to 15 percent of couples actively attempting conception fail to do so in one year.*[64] The elements that confound statistics are such things as inadequate coital technique, poor coital timing, intermittent contraception, multiple partners, and failure to seek medical aid. *Before committing a couple to a time-consuming infertility work-up, several basic prerequisites should be fulfilled:*

A. 12 consecutive months of unprotected intercourse.
B. Successful insemination at least every two to three days.
C. No inadvertent chemical barriers, such as lubricating substances or douching.

If these apparent reasons for infertility exist, they should be corrected and attempts continued for several months prior to initiating a work-up. Approximately 25 percent of fertile couples will conceive in the first cycle and 75 percent by the sixth cycle, with only another 10 percent conceiving in the next six months. Of the 15 percent remaining, probably 5 percent may spontaneously conceive over the next year, but because the likelihood of conception declines with time, the one year time constraint is used to begin infertility investigation. Less than one year of unsuccessful attempts at conception will result in unnecessary diagnostic and therapeutic measures, and much more than a year would result in unnecessary delays. The latter becomes especially important in the face of the natural infertility imparted by increasing maternal and possibly paternal age.

ELEMENTS OF SUCCESSFUL CONCEPTION

A. Before undertaking an infertility work-up, it is appropriate to consider the framework of *the elements of successful conception.* Briefly, an adequate number of motile sperm with fertilizing capacity must be deposited in the vagina at the time of the menstrual cycle that permits transport through the female reproductive tract to fertilize a mature ovum which has been released from an ovarian follicle. The conceptus must be transported at an appropriate time to the endometrial cavity, where the environment has been adequately prepared for implantation.

B. Thus, the *steps involved in conception* are (1) *insemination,* (2) *transportation,* (3) *ovulation,* (4) *fertilization,* (5) *implantation.* Defects in each of these areas may be further broken down into *the usual categories of factors pertaining to fertility.*

1. *Male* (insemination or fertilization defect).
2. *Ovarian* (ovulation, fertilization, or implantation defect).
3. *Cervical* (transportation defect).
4. *Tubal* (transportation defect).
5. *Peritoneal* (transportation or ovulation defect).
6. These categories have often been assigned certain frequencies of occurrence as possible etiologies of a couple's infertility, but traditional figures have not stood up well with time. One problem is the fact that *multiple etiologies occur in up to 35 percent of couples.* In addition, criteria used for making specific diagnoses have changed through the years, through new developments in understanding of reproductive physiology as well as increased use of laparoscopy.

GENERAL APPROACH TO THE INFERTILE COUPLE

A. *A systematic approach to the possible etiologies of a couple's infertility must be undertaken in a logical and economical fashion. The discovery of one factor must not preclude continued investigation at an appropriate schedule of the other aspects of reproductive physiology.*

B. *Initial investigation* obviously includes a *complete history and physical examination* of the male and female partners, *with attention to elements of each that may point to specific etiologic aspects.*[69]

1. The *common sense questions* must not be taken too lightly, and the obvious is not to be assumed. How long have the man and woman been trying to achieve a pregnancy without contraception? Have they wavered in their decision to have a baby? Have there been other partners? How frequently do they have intercourse? Does the male partner ejaculate intravaginally each time?

2. *Timing* is critical if midcycle insemination does not occur or if intercourse is always concentrated on weekends. Ova have a fertilizable life of no more than 18 hours, and sperm can live in the female reproductive tract while maintaining their fertilizing ability for about 72 hours. Thus the *conception window* is generally less than four days.

3. *Other initial habits,* such as *extravaginal ejaculation* and *excessive frequency of coitus,* will also lower the chances of fertility. Personal habits including *use of lubricants and douching* can also interfere with normal access of sperm to the upper tract. *Frequent vaginal infections* as well as the use of *topical vaginal medications* may change the favorable vaginal environment to a hostile one. An apparently unrelated *illness of one partner* or the other may result in failure to conceive because weeks or months passed with reduced frequency of coitus. Use of certain *drugs in the male* can result in ejaculation failure or

outright reduction in sperm output. *Alcohol* is an offender in this way, and heavy intake can influence subsequent spermatogenesis for over two months. The same is true for *viral infections,* especially when fevers occur, since spermtogenesis is heat sensitive. This information is important in the assessment of a semen analysis and shows why a diagnosis of abnormal semen requires multiple samples over time to rule out an intermittent effect of exogenous substances or infection on the sperm cycle. *Tightly fitting underwear* that brings the testes in closer proximity to the body may reduce sperm production in certain men, especially in those with borderline analyses. This group is probably the most difficult to deal with — while there are really adequate numbers of motile sperm, there is not enough reserve to survive insults as mentioned above and still have the potential to fertilize an ovum.

C. *Once these functional aspects of infertility are eliminated, a systematic approach to discovering a possible etiology for the infertility should be undertaken.*[62] Primary infertility refers to no previous conception, while *secondary infertility* follows a previous pregnancy. An abnormality in each area must be ruled out by showing evidence for the normal function.
   1. Detect ovulation and normal luteal function:
   2. Demonstrate normal semen.
   3. Show compatability of sperm and cervical mucus.
   4. Prove tubal patency.
   5. Visualize a normal pelvis.

OVULATION DETECTION

A. *Basal body temperature*
   1. The simplest, cheapest way to detect ovulation is by *charting the basal body temperature* (BBT). The temperature is taken daily before rising, and an elevation of 0.5F or more from the postmenstrual baseline followed by a

fall with the ensuing menses is strongly suggestive of ovulation within a day or two of the temperature shift.[47] If accompanied by premenstrual molimina (bloating, breast tenderness, mood changes) which abate with the menses and there is mild dysmenorrhea, there is excellent correlation with other means of assessing ovulation. Of course, the only definite proofs of ovulation are pregnancy or recovery of an ovum from the reproductive tract or peritoneal cavity. Short of these, *a biphasic BBT* accompanied by the signs of premenstrual progesterone withdrawal on a regular basis (25 to 35 days), especially if the temperature shift is heralded by ovulatory pain (Mittelschmerz), is sufficient *evidence of presumptive ovulation for initial evaluation.*

   a) The exception is the *luteinized unruptured follicle,* where all endocrine parameters point to ovulation, but rupture of the follicle and extrusion of the ovum do not occur. This is relatively unusual and would be a late consideration if all other aspects of the work-up prove normal.[15]

B. *Progesterone levels*

   1. If the symptothermal detection of ovulation is unclear or inconsistent, further evaluation is indicated. The simplest test is a serum progesterone, drawn to coincide with the peak of corpus luteum function (that is, a week prior to the next expected menses).

   2. While many formulae have been put forth to decide if a certain level is diagnostic of the luteal function, including serial samples, *a serum progesterone over 4 ng/ml is reasonable to confirm ovulation,* although "the higher the better," *with 10 ng/ml being generally used as unequivocal proof of normal luteal function.* Progesterone levels have replaced urinary pregnanediol excretion as the routine hormonal means to diagnose ovulation.

C. *Evaulation of the endometrium* (and corpus luteum function)

   1. More invasive, but not without the value of further information, is the *endometrial biospy.*[66]

a) Well-described *histologic changes in the endometrium* obtained from the fundal portion of the cavity occur in the presence of progesterone, and this has been the most common method of ovulation detection prior to routine availability of progesterone radioimmunoassay. The estrogen-primed proliferative endometrium undergoes secretory changes indicative of cumulative effects of progesterone (levels and duration), so that the endometrium can be dated according to the traditional criteria plus or minus one day.

b) Because there is usually patient discomfort, and risks of cervicouterine injury or infection do exist, although infrequent, routine endometrial biopsy is not always recommended. However, *if serum progesterone levels are inconclusive, especially if a range of cycle lengths occurs unpredictably in an individual, an endometrial biopsy even on day 1 of the next menses usually shows secretory changes undergoing menstrual sloughing.*

2. In a woman with persistently short or long cycles as well as in apparently normal cycles, *abnormal corpus luteal function* may be present and be responsible for infertility.[5]

a) *The endometrial biopsy, correlated with the BBT, provides the best means of diagnosing luteal dysfunction.*

b) Luteal dysfunction is manifest in at least two forms.

(1) *The short luteal phase,* where menses occur less than 10 days following ovulation, as manifest by the temperature shift.

(2) The *inadequate luteal phase,* which may be normal in length but reflect lower than normal serum progesterone levels and be diagnosed by a discrepancy of at least two days between the histologic dating of the endometrium and the actual postovulatory day on two consecutive cycles. Thus, an endometrial biopsy done as late as possible in the luteal phase (i.e., day 12 or 13 postovulation) would have the best chance of

showing a lag in the cumulative secretory effect of luteal progesterone.

c) Luteal dysfunction also accounts for up to 15 percent of repeated spontaneous abortions due to abnormal implantation.[44] Further, the use of the drug clomiphene in the induction of ovulation is associated with a high rate of subsequent luteal abnormality.

d) The importance of noting two consecutive abnormal cycles, in terms of either a short luteal phase or an inadequate luteal phase, lies in the fact that sporadic luteal dysfunction may occur in fertile individuals[2] and indeed is a normal part of the evolution and deterioration of of cyclic ovarian function in postmenarchal and premenopausal women.

D. *Follicle observation by ultrasound*

1. The latest means of detecting ovulation is by *ultrasonographic examination,* which has been used mostly for observing follicular development and subsequent rupture during ovulation induction but may also be used to visualize growth of the dominant preovulatory follicle and subsequent collapse and transformation into the corpus luteum in a spontaneous ovulation.[17]

E. *Laparoscopy*

1. This use of laparoscopy, when a luteinized unruptured follicle is suspected, is reserved for the situation where all other aspects of the work-up are normal.[15] Visualization of the postovulatory stigma on the surface of the corpus luteum is evidence that ovum extrusion has occurred.

2. These patients may also manifest delayed luteinization, and endometriosis may play a role in this ovulatory defect of unknown frequency.

ANOVULATION

A. When it is apparent from history alone that regular ovulatory cycles are not occurring, as in amenorrhea or oligomenorrhea, diagnosis of the cause of the anovulation must be made, followed by appropriate therapy.[65] A *first step* in this diagnosis is determination of the *gonadotropin levels, FSH and LH, the prolactin level, if the women is hirsute or virilized, serum testosterone, and an index of adrenal function. If a woman is having spontaneous uterine bleeding* on any schedule, has adequate support of secondary sexual characteristics, and while amenorrheic has estrogenic cervical mucus (ferning, good Spinnbarkeit), there is then evidence of ovarian function, and the gonadotropin level will be normal. Often in the case of the polycystic ovarian syndrome, the LH level itself or the LH:FSH ratio will be elevated and confirm the diagnosis.[23,32] These measurements may be thought to be academic by some, but their value in diagnosis and therapy is immense. *If there is no bleeding* at all, no cervical mucus, and possibly decreased estrogenic effects on the breast and reproductive tract, the gonadotropins will discriminate *ovarian failure* (with high FSH and LH) from *hypothalamic-pituitary dysfunction* (FSH and LH low or normal). The latter general category also encompasses the high estrogen anovulatory state, with there being a difference in degree of ovarian stimulation. The exception to the rule is the *resistant-ovary syndrome,* where because of abnormal ovarian receptors for gonadotropins, LH and FSH are elevated in the face of a normal estrogenic milieu and the presence of follicles in the ovaries (diagnosed by ovarian biopsy at laparoscopy). *If anovulation, oligo-ovulation, or even normal menses is accompanied by galactorrhea,* spontaneous or expressible, the serum *prolactin must be determined.*

B. *Hyperprolactinemia*
   1. *The possibility of hyperprolactinemia* when amenorrhea and galactorrhea coexist is up to 75 percent with amenorrhea alone up to 50 percent and with oligo-ovulation and galactorrhea up to 40 percent. Moreover, the frequency of an elevated prolactin in any form of ovulatory dysfunction, including luteal abnormalities, is high enough to warrant the determination.[53]

2. Elevated prolactin levels may *cause* infertility by direct effects on ovarian steroidogenesis, pituitary response to gonadotropin-releasing hormone (GnRH, LRF), or hypothalamic secretion of the releasing factors.[52]

3. The development of hyperprolactinemia may follow the full spectrum from normal ovulatory cycles, through luteal dysfunction, anovulation, and finally amenorrhea.[7] *The finding of persistently elevated prolactin on multiple samples requires detailed endocrinologic and neuroradiologic evaluations.*[68]

   a) *Thyroid function* tests must be done, since hyperprolactinemia may be due to primary hypothyroidism.

   b) *Exogenous elements* which raise prolactin spuriously are many *psychoactive drugs* or *inordinate breast stimulation. Oral contraceptives* may also raise prolactin levels, but a patient complaining of infertility would not be taking these compounds.

4. If the prolactin is truly elevated above the normal for the individual (usually > 20 to 25 ng/ml), a *pituitary adenoma* must be ruled out before instituting any other therapy.

   a) The advent of *hypocycloidal polytomography* has permitted detection of minimal changes in the sella turcica suggestive of microadenoma (less than 10 mm), while large tumors (including macroadenomata and extrapituitary tumors) may often be demonstrated on plain skull films or coned views of the sella. The current practice is to perform at least a coned view of the sella in the presence of an abnormal prolactin. Polytomography or a CAT scan should be performed over a defined prolactin level (50 or 100 ng/ml). When pregnancy is to be attempted, polytomography or a CAT scan should probably be performed irrespective of the degree of hyperprolactinemia.

   b) Tumors larger than 10 mm must also be evaluated for extrasellar extension. Detailed *visual field examination* by an ophthalmologist is necessary in every instance of elevated prolactin, since optic chiasmal compression by a growing tumor is an early sign of expansion.

c) The use of new high resolution CT scanning may avoid some of the pitfalls of conventional neuroradiology, since the pituitary itself and not just bony structures may be visualized and examined. CT scans may eventually replace polytomography — abnormal tomography may exist in normal individuals due to anatomic variations, so the diagnosis of a microadenoma may be questionable.

5. Controversy currently exists regarding *surgical or medical management of hyperprolactinemia.*

a) In the absence of a demonstrable tumor, pregnancy may be attempted, although an undetected tumor must be suspected and watched for during a pregnancy by at least serial visual fields. Prolactin levels normally rise during gestation so that measurement becomes useless.

b) Induction of ovulation has been successful on rare occasions with clomiphene but more so with exogenous gonadotropins in the face of an elevated prolactin.

c) The use of *2-bromo-α-ergocryptine* is highly successful in restoring fertility to hyperprolactinemic women [65] and has been approved recently for use in this country during the cycle of conception. There are many reports of pregnancy occurring with the use of this drug with no untoward effects, except the rare expansion of a tumor.[14,22,40,59]

d) *If a macroadenoma* or extrapituitary tumor is present (e.g., craniopharyngioma) or if there are neurologic signs, radiation or surgical treatment by either *frontal craniotomy or transsphenoidal adenectomy* is the therapy of choice.[34,36,50]

e) The *microadenoma* is most controversial in deciding between surgical and medical management. *Transsphenoidal microadenectomy* is relatively safe in experienced neurosurgical hands and has resulted in cures and subsequent fertility. However, side effects and recurrences are frequently reported. The use of *2-bromo-α-ergocryptine* has been shown to lower prolactin levels and restore ovulatory function in women with microadenomata and even result in achieving pregnancy.[63] The drug bromocryptine has been used to treat recurrence and expansion of both microadenomata and macroadenomata with good success, often with evidence of tumor shrinkage. This has been done during pregnancies with preexisting prolactinomas with no ill effects on the fetus. Thus, in terms of elevated prolactin and inducing ovulation for the purpose of conception, both surgical and medical therapy have their place, with bromocryptine being most useful.

C. *With normal prolactin levels, the women who do not ovulate tend to fall into two categories — the one who has sufficient estrogen priming of the endometrium to allow progestin withdrawal bleeding and the one who has not.*

1. The most common etiology of the estrogenic anovulatory state is *polycystic ovarian syndrome* (PCO), which is well described clinically, histologically, and endocrinologically but not fully understood.[23,32] Often seen in the setting of a high androgenic state due to ovarian and/or adrenal sources, *the possibility of an ovarian or adrenal tumor must be ruled out,* especially when hirsutism is excessive or there are signs of virilization (clitoromegaly, temporal balding, deepening of the voice) or rapid onset of the disease. In its benign state, hyperandrogenism tends to manifest itself peripubertally and gradually. Attenuated or incomplete forms of enzyme deficiencies, notably, *21-α-hydroxylase,* have been described in individuals who otherwise appear to have PCO.[10,39] As initial evaluation, in addition to FSH, LH, and prolactin, serum testosterone and either serum dehydroepiandrosterone sulfate or urinary 17-ketosteroids should be determined to rule

out ovarian or adrenal neoplasia. All of these are generally high normal or slightly elevated in PCO, but marked elevation of androgens should point to possible tumors.

2. If signs and symptoms of Cushing's syndrome are present, urinary free cortisol and diurnal serum cortisols should be determined and the patient further evaluated if any of these are normal. In addition, a 17-OH progesterone level drawn one hour after ACTH stimulation is appropriate to detect a 21-hydroxylase deficiency, since women thus affected would more likely be treated with corticosteroids than those with no adrenal component.

3. The *progesterone withdrawal test* is part of the initial evaluation of any suspected anovulatory patient — *100 to 200 mg progesterone in oil intramuscularly should induce some sort of withdrawal bleeding,* which correlates well with a prevailing estradiol level of more than 40 pg/ml. *Failure to withdraw suggests that ovulation induction will be difficult.*

4. *If amenorrhea is primary,* steps must be taken to rule out a *müllerian abnormality* involving atresia or agenesis of the uterus or vagina. Clinical examination may be misleading. If *secondary amenorrhea* followed uterine curettage (postpartum or postabortal), *intrauterine synechiae* may be present — *Asherman's syndrome* — which would further not respond to exogenous priming and withdrawal (sequential estrogen and progestin, e.g., 50 to 100 μg ethinyl estradiol for 25 days, and 10 mg medroxyprogesterone acetate the last 10 days). The diagnosis should be confirmed by hysterosalpingography and/or hysteroscopy. These two reasons for amenorrhea are probably the only types of uterine factors leading to infertility, the rest relating to recurrent spontaneous abortions.

5. A nonprolactin-secreting pituitary or hypothalamic tumor may result in a hypogonadotropic state and failure of progesterone withdrawal due to inadequate ovarian steroidogensis and endometrial priming. Thus, a skull

film is indicated. Withdrawal failure suggests a more severe pituitary or hypothalamic abnormality.

D. *Treatment of anovulation*

1. The initial treatment of anovulation in a woman who responds to a progesterone challenge with withdrawal bleeding is *clomiphene citrate.*[30]

   a) The drug is given for five-day courses, usually starting the fifth day after bleeding, although with induced menses this is not crucial except to establish a pattern. The initial dose is 50 mg a day for the five days, with gradual increments of 50 mg per day if ovulation is not achieved in one or two cycles at any given dose. The patient must keep a BBT chart to assess ovulatory function and to be used in timing of further tests. The patient would expect to ovulate approximately one week after the last pill and have subsequent menses in two more weeks. Thus if a period occurs, ovulation induction has been successful if other parameters hold true (BBT shift, premenstrual symptoms), and the same dosage is administered after a pelvic examination during the next cycle.

   b) The risks of clomiphene usage include ovarian cysts and twinning, and if an ovarian cyst is detected postmenstrually, clomiphene therapy should be withheld until the cyst regresses.

   c) If no menses occur by day 35, the patient should be seen and examined for estrogenic mucus and ovarian cysts, and her BBT chart should be analyzed. If there is no evidence of a pregnancy (persistent elevation of BBT, soft globular uterus) or delayed ovulation (BBT shift late in cycle) or cyst, withdrawal with progesterone should again be done and clomiphene reinstituted. Progesterone in oil is preferable to synthetic progestins because of the possible teratogenic effects of the latter on an unsuspected pregnancy and the failure of women in some cases to respond to the oral medication.

d) Clomiphene acts by interrupting the negative feed-back of estrogens on the hypothalamus and by inducing follicular development via FSH and LH release, resulting in an endogenous estradiol elevation and ovulatory LH/FSH surge. It is nonsteroidal attenuated estrogen which acts as an antiestrogen on estrogenic receptors. In polycystic ovarian syndrome, there is a steady state of noncyclic LH secretion and elevated total estrogen by virtue of peripheral conversion of ovarian (or adrenal) androgens to estrone.

e) It has been shown that the highest success of ovulation induction with clomiphene is achieved by using an individualized graduated method. When 200 mg per day is reached, an ovulating dose of hCG (5,000 to 10,000 IU intramuscularly) is given if follicular development is occurring (rising serum estradiol levels, cervical mucus changes, or evidenced by sonography) without ovulation. If this is unsuccessful, the maximum dose of 250 mg daily is used first without, and then with, hCG. If the maximum regimen fails to effect ovulation after several months, the patient is considered a clomiphene failure and must undergo further evaluation and therapy.

f) Although the high estrogenic milieu of PCO makes it most amenable to clomiphene therapy, failure to successfully induce ovulation may be weight-related or due to excessively high androgen levels. These patients would be candidates for *exogenous gonado-tropin therapy or wedge resection of the ovary*. Wedge resection has fallen from favor due to the risks of major surgery (although laparoscopic ovariotomy has been done) and subsequent adhesive disease. The underlying defect in the ovary, excess intraovarian androgen production, presumably temporarily corrected by removal of the androgen-producing tissue, will recur in the future. These patients should be evaluated (if not done previously) for adrenal contribution to the androgen pool by *ACTH stimulation or suppressive tests.* Addition of small doses of cortico-steroids (e.g., dexamethasone 0.25 mg daily) may be useful in these patients. Indeed, controversy exists about the use of corticosteroids rather than clomiphene as primary therapy in PCO, with successful ovulation induction.[1]

g) The *pregnancy rate with clomiphene is not identical to the ovulation rate* — at best, 85 percent ovulate and 65 percent become pregnant. This discrepancy is first explained by other undiagnosed factors — the presence of a luteal defect while taking clomiphene, antiestrogenic effects on cervical mucus precluding sperm penetration, the luteinized unruptured follicle, or possibly deleterious antiestrogenic effects on the preovulatory follicle. The pitfalls may be minimized by carefully continuing the remainder of the infertility investigation including laparascopy, if conception has not occurred in six months. The possibility exists that clomiphene may be administered in too high or too low a dosage and may require titration of the dose in 25 mg increments. The optimal dosage which results in ovulation with normal luteal function may or may not lie between the dosage causing inadequate luteal function and that causing overstimulation (multiple ovulation, cysts). In some patients, a lower dose, rather than a higher dose, may be most effective. Luteal dysfunction may often be due to prior abnormal follicular development.[18]

2. The *luteal phase defect,* either clomiphene induced or spontaneous, may be dealt with in several ways.

a) *Supplementary progesterone* in the form of vaginal suppositories, 25 mg bid following ovulation as determined by BBT, has been shown to be useful. *Menses will occur* if conception does not take place. Although the trophoblastic tissue takes over progesterone production sufficiently by the fifth to sixth week after conception, and the corpus luteum is not necessary for pregnancy maintenance, continued use of the progesterone suppositories through the first trimester is usually advised.

b) Spontaneous luteal dysfunction has been successfully treated with clomiphene, probably because of augmented follicular stimulation.[29] However, a clomiphene-induced luteal defect may respond to either a lower or higher dose of drug, as well as progesterone supplementation. It is noteworthy that *although synthetic progestins have been associated with teratogenesis, no such association has been noted with native progesterone.*

c) Luteal dysfunction related to hyperprolactinemia is treatable with *bromocryptine.*

3. *Hypothalamic-pituitary dysfunction* resulting in anovulation may be treatable with clomiphene depending on the estrogenic milieu. Reasons for this type of anovulation can range from psychic stress, simple weight loss, exercise, or thyroid disease to systemic illness, and it may manifest itself in the full spectrum of ovulatory dysfunction from luteal dysfunction to amenorrhea. The most severe form is *anorexia nervosa,* where drastic weight loss and psychopathology coexist with a return to prepubertal reproductive function. *Psychiatric therapy* is the primary mode of treatment. The other forms (idiopathic probably being most common) should first be treated with clomiphene as described previously. However, the hypoestrogenic forms usually do not respond. *Destruction of the hypothalamus or pituitary* by infiltrative disease or tumor, or Sheehan's syndrome (postpartum ischemic necrosis) virtually mandates treatment with exogenous gonadotropins.

4. *Human menopausal gonadotropins (HMG, Pergonal)* are available in ampules each containing 75 IU FSH activity and 75 IU LH activity. Because of the time, cost, and risks involved, the rest of the infertility work-up including laparoscopy *must be completed* prior to HMG/HCG therapy institution.

a) While ovulation induction occurs in up to 95 percent of women treated, pregnancy is achieved in about 50 percent of those treated.[55] *Multiple pregnancy* occurs in 20 percent of patients and *hyperstimulation* syndrome in 1 percent, with attendant risk of mortality.[54] *Ovarian cysts* are common, due to large and multiple follicles, and must be detected, so the ovulating dose of hCG is not given.

b) Gradual increments of HMG are used and/or folliculogenesis is detected by daily clinical examination of the cervical mucus, ovarian size, sonography, and estradiol determination.[60] The cervical mucus will become copious as estrogen levels rise, so that it is a rough bioassay of the prevalant estradiol level. The same dose of HMG is given daily during the estradiol rise until the 500 to 1,000 pg/ml level is reached. If the optimal estradiol level is attained too rapidly, exceeds 1,000 pg/ml, or ovarian enlargement is detected, the hCG is withheld, the patient is withdrawn with progesterone in 7 to 10 days, and retreatment is begun again in the next cycle with modification of the dosage. *Hyperstimulation cannot occur unless the ovulating dose of hCG is given.* At the time of hCG administration, a postcoital test is performed to assess sperm-mucus interaction. *The use of both clinical and hormonal parameters* is absolutely necessary.

5. *Bromocriptine,* as previously mentioned, is now approved for use in hyperprolactinemic states without an adenoma. It is extremely useful in lowering prolactin, with virtually no serious side effects,[35] and can be given continuously or only in the follicular phase.[8] Administered in a dosage of 2.5 to 7.5 mg daily, bromocriptine can lower prolactin levels often even in the presence of a detectable tumor. An ensuing pregnancy must then be monitored for possible tumor expansion.

6. *Gonadotropin-releasing hormone (GnRF, LRF)* has been used experimentally in ovulation induction with an intact

pituitary when clomiphene fails. Pulsatile administration seems to be most efficacious and without the risks of HMG/hCG.[27]

THE MALE FACTOR AND SEMEN ANALYSIS

A. The vagaries of assessing the adequacy of semen were alluded to earlier. *The parameters of semen analysis* that are generally considered to be the lower limits of normal are:
1. A *volume* of 2.5 ml.
2. A *concentration* of 20,000,000 sperm/ml.
3. A total *count* of 50,000,000.
4. 60 percent progressive *motility*.
5. 60 percent normal *morphology*.

Males with *proven fertility* often have semen analyses *far below* these criteria. Some feel that at least *six semen analyses* must be obtained at intervals so as to overlap at least two sperm cycles (74 days per cycle) before a diagnosis of inadequate semen can be made.[56] Indeed, the *count* is probably *secondary* to motility and morphology in determining ability to achieve fertilization.[3] This has been further put forth by numerous groups who utilize an in vitro system of zona-free hamster ova and their penetration by human spermatozoa to correlate fertility.[51] Concentrations in the 5,000,000/ml range were found in men who had fathered children and whose sperm penetrated the zona-free egg. Conversely, high counts were found in men who were infertile in vivo and in vitro.

B. The evaluation in the great majority of cases will prove to be endocrinologically normal. Many feel that when presence of a *varicocele* is associated with an abnormal semen analysis, surgical correction is indicated. This is not uniformly accepted. Numerous empirical treatments of idiopathic oligospermia have resulted in apparent improvement and resultant fertility, but again these are suspect due to the normal fluctuations in sperm quality.
1. *Aside from obstructive disease and endocrinopathies, the*

truly abnormal semen analyses are rarely amenable to improvement. Primary testicular disease, either genetic or acquired, is virtually untreatable.

2. The only recourse for many of these couples is *artificial insemination* with *donor* semen (AID).

3. *Artificial insemination* with the *husband's* sperm (AIH) is only useful if intravaginal insemination does not occur due to:

   a) Psychologic or physical reasons (e.g., hypospadias).

   b) Such cervicovaginal anatomic abnormality that deposited semen does not come in contact with the cervical mucus.

   c) Mucus-sperm incompatability in certain situations.

   d) Low concentration semen with high volume, where the first portion of a split ejaculate is used due to its superior quality.[4]

C. *In short, male infertility is probably much less frequent than generally thought, usual criteria are too strict, and severe dysfunction in spermatogenesis has poor prognosis.*

   1. The assessment of the male factor by the serial examination of semen samples should take place simultaneously with the full work-up of the female partner. The exception would be a delay in invasive procedures if azospermia, severe oligospermia, or a motility disorder is apparent and the couple refuses artifical donor insemination.

   2. Many cases of male infertility are probably *undiagnosed subtle abnormalities* in the *female* partner. Others go undetected due to sperm abnormalities not evident in conventional semen analysis.

CERVICAL FACTOR AND SPERM-MUCUS INTERACTION

A. *The role of the cervix in transportation of the spermatozoa* is to provide a sufficient, nonhostile, cascade of mucus in the preovulatory interval which will permit the sperm to reach

the upper reproductive tract from the vaginal pool.[16,46]
Anatomic, physiologic, and immunologic abnormalities may
interfere with this role.

1. *Malposition* due to severe uterine retroversion may make
   the mucoid stream inaccessible to the sperm.
2. *Congenital and acquired malformations:*
   a) *DES-associated* changes.
   b) *Stenosis* due to operative, inflammatory, or obstetric
      injury.
   c) Other malformations.
3. Abnormal endocervical crypts may not produce adequate
   mucus under estrogenic stimulation, or they may be
   absent due to prior deep conization or cautery.

B. The cervical mucus undergoes physiologic cyclic changes,
   with scant, cellular mucus in the early follicular phase
   undergoing progressive estrogen-induced changes.

1. In the immediate preovulatory interval when estradiol is
   peaking, the mucus is clear, acellular, and copious as it
   cascades from a pouting external os. The *Spinnbarkeit,* a
   measurement of the thin threads of mucus that may be
   stretched between two surfaces, should be in excess of 10
   cm, and the crystallization pattern of high sodium
   chloride content, *ferning,* is at its peak.
2. Following ovulation, progesterone causes rapid loss of
   ferning and Spinnbarkeit, and an influx of white cells
   occurs as the mucus becomes *tacky* and *sparse.* These
   physical characteristics reflect the ability of the sperm
   to traverse the mucus bridge in the few days before
   ovulation and no other time. If the preovulatory mucus is
   not of the quality described, a *cervical factor* responsible
   for infertility may be present.

C. This is determined by the *Sims-Huhner or postcoital test* [48];
   using previous BBT records to predict the day or two prior
   to ovulation (peak mucus), the couple is instructed to have
   intercourse the morning of the examination but not the night
   before. The closer coitus occurs to the time of the examination the better, since an inordinate delay may be responsible

for an abnormal test because of semen loss or ascent of a greater proportion of normal sperm. A speculum examination is performed on the woman, and several slides are prepared.

1. The *vaginal pool* of semen is sampled to confirm ejaculation and presence of *motile sperm.*

2. Mucus from the *endocervical canal* is aspirated in a 14- or 16-gauge polyethylene catheter and placed on another slide to be covered by a coverslip. By touching the drop of mucus with the slip and picking it up, the *Spinnbarkeit* can be measured.

3. Another slide is used to detect ferning so more mucus is smeared on another slide and allowed to dry. It is important to *avoid contamination* of the mucus with *blood* or *vaginal secretion,* since these can alter the findings.

4. Microscopic examination of the covered drop of mucus will demonstrate the *cellularity* of the mucus. White cells would be evidence of a cervical or vaginal *infection* which may alter the mucus. *Reexamination* should be done following treatment of the infection. Using the high-dry objective, the mucus is examined in multiple fields to count:

   a) *Total sperm* per field.

   b) *Number* of *progressively motile* sperm (moving across the field).

   c) Number of *partially motile* sperm.

   d) Number of *immotile* sperm.

   e) *Clumping* of sperm heads or tails is suggestive of presence of *antisperm antibodies.*

   f) *Immotile* sperm in the *mucus* with motile sperm in the vaginal pool also suggest *hostile mucus* due to either biophysical or immunologic factors.

   g) *While texts note that more than 20 motile sperm per high power field correlates with a normal sperm count, the presence of any motile sperm speaks strongly against a cervical factor.*

h) If the mucus is of poor quality or immotile sperm only are seen, repeat testing must be done, since improper timing is the most common reason for an abnormal test.

5. *The problem of poor quality mucus* is treated by small doses of estrogen ($\sim$ 20 μg ethinyl estradiol) for the week prior to ovulation in an attempt to augment the estrogenic effect and improve the quality.

   a) If there is no mucus production with increasing dosages of estrogen, as in a cervix previously operated upon, *intrauterine insemination of the semen* may be useful on the day prior to ovulation.[49] A small volume (no more than 0.3 ml) of semen or washed sperm is injected directly into the uterine cavity, and the patient is observed for cramping, vasovagal, or allergic symptoms. This same technique may be used when sperm *clumping* or *immotility* in the mucus is present, suggesting immune factors. However, the same antibodies, if present, possibly exist in the upper reproductive tract as well, rendering intrauterine insemination useless.

   b) This opens *the question of immunologic factors,* which have also been treated by condom therapy (removal of antigenic stimulus) or immunosuppression of the female, with varied results.[12,31,45,46] In addition, some *circulating* antibodies have been detected in both fertile and infertile women, and the contribution of these antibodies to sperm *agglutination* or *immobilization* and their relevance is an ongoing *controversy.*

6. Detection of factors that block motility of sperm can be done by placing a drop of *semen* next to a drop of *mucus* on a slide, allowing contact and *observing movement* of sperm into the mucus and through it. However, it remains uncertain what this information will add. *Repeated testing* must be done to confirm the diagnosis. *Completion of the remainder of the work-up including laparoscopy should be achieved regardless of the post-coital test results,* since there is the chance of multiple

etiologies and the relatively small frequency of the cervical factor being solely responsible for infertility.

TUBAL FACTOR AND PERITONEAL FACTOR

As previously mentioned, the *uterine* factor in *infertility,* as opposed to recurrent abortion, is *limited* to congenital or acquired malformation, or Asherman's syndrome, and will not be discussed separately. The tubal and peritoneal factors will be considered within the same section.

A. *The tube* functions as more than a conduit for sperm and ovum to meet and then be transported into the uterine cavity. It is a *dynamic organ* with these functions:
   1. To *capture* the freshly ovulated ovum.
   2. To *harbor* it prior to fertilization.
   3. To *move* the conceptus through the uterotubal junction in a *timely fashion* for it to arrive at the *proper time* in endometrial maturation for *implantation.* (It responds to *neutral* and *hormonal* stimuli in varying degrees during the menstrual cycle and must aid in transporting *spermatozoa retrograde* while the *ovum* and subsequently the *zygote* are moved *antegrade.*)

B. *Tubal dysfunction* may range from complete obstruction to subtle abnormalities in ovum pick-up. Pathology may be *congenital* or *acquired.* Acquired tubal dysfunction may be *iatrogenic, infectious, neoplastic,* or *endometriotic.*
   1. *Congenital pathology* would include such developmental abnormalities as agenesis, hypoplasia, or atresia of portions of the tube or the entire tube, especially in association with other müllerian defects, such as uncornuate uterus or one with rudimentary horn. Abnormalities associated with DES exposure in utero have been noted and related to infertility.[28,33] Unilaterality of the tube does not seem to lower the fertility rate when it is normal and is often unsuspected unless the lone tube becomes damaged.
   2. *The acquired forms of tube pathology* are significantly

more frequent. *Iatrogenic obstruction* is typified by tubal ligation, fulguration, or resection for purposes of sterilization. Iatrogenic dysfunction may be considered also to be *secondary* to other *gynecologic procedures,* such as ovarian cystectomy or myomectomies, where postoperative adhesions involve the tube.

3. *Neoplasms* of the tube are rare and even rarer bilaterally. However, *pelvic masses* of either uterine or ovarian origin can *distort* the relationship between tube and its ovary and thus *prevent normal pick-up* and/or *transport* of the ovum. Neoplasms may also provoke peritoneal reaction and increase fluid in the cul-de-sac that may interfere with normal tube function.

4. The specific *obstructive aspects of tubal disease* are broken down into *distal* and *proximal* disease:

   a) The most common is distal tubal disease secondary to salpingo-oophoritis. Depending on the severity of the disease, rapidity and success of treatment, organisms involved, and number of episodes, inflammatory tubal disease due to infectious agents can result in anything from peritubal adhesions to complete bilateral distal occlusion manifest as hydrosalpinges. *Thirteen percent of women will become infertile following one episode of tubal infection, 35 percent after two episodes, and 75 percent after three or more.*[67] The obvious acute gonococcal salpingo-oophoritis and secondary anaerobic invasion is the most likely initiating event, but subtle infections, such as silent IUD-associated endometritis or postabortion infection, can also do serious damage.

   b) *Obstruction* at the *cornua* or *isthmus* can result from inflammatory disease. *Proximal obstruction* can also result from *salpingitis isthmica nodosa* which is thought to be a sequela of inflammation. It is generally *bilateral* and has been associated with *ectopic pregnancy.*

   c) The gray zone between tubal patency with normal function and subtle dysfunction due to incomplete blockage or adhesive disease provides the infertile women with a higher risk of ectopic pregnancy. The even higher recurrence risk of an ectopic pregnancy following one ectopic pregnancy is probably due to bilateral disease or adhesive disease following surgery for the initial ectopic pregnancy.

d) *Pelvic tuberculosis* is an unusual cause of tubal disease but must be considered in anyone with a history of tuberculosis or who has come from a geographical area where tuberculosis is more common. The tubal changes tend to be diffuse and generally confer a diagnosis of sterility on the woman. Diagnosis is made by endometrial biopsy and culture. Even more unusual granulomatous disease may have similar effects.

5. *Endometriosis*

Endometriosis can cause infertility by *directly* or *indirectly* affecting the tube. As previously mentioned, ovarian endometriosis may affect *ovulation* as well, but it is with dual capacity of *inflammatory* and *hormonal* effects that *tubal dysfunction* may result. *Implants* on the tube itself or in the area of the fimbriae can cause *scarring* and *retraction* so as to mimic inflammatory disease, even to appear as a tubo-ovarian complex. However, it is the cases of *nontubal endometriosis*, expecially with minimal disease on the peritoneal surfaces, where a *hormonal effect* on the tube has been postulated in the form of *excessive prostaglandin production* by the *implants* in the pelvis. Either fimbrial *pick-up* of the egg or *tubal motility* may be affected so as to preclude conception. *While up to 30 percent of infertile women have endometriosis, pregnancy occurs in women with untreated endometriosis as well, so that correlation is not 100 percent. In the absence of other factors, even minimal disease should be treated.*

C. *Diagnosis*

The mainstays of diagnosis of tubal and peritoneal disease are *hysterosalpingography* (HSG)[57,58] and *laparoscopy*.[20]

1. *The hysterosalpingogram* is performed during the post-

menstrual follicular phase, to avoid forcing menstrual effluent into the pelvis, as well as to avoid radiation to a possible conceptus. It is performed by injecting a radiopaque dye through the cervical canal so that the *uterine cavity* is visualized, as are the *mucosal surfaces* of the tubes. *Free spill* from the ends of the tubes confirms *patency.* The procedure is performed under sterile conditions with fluoroscopy and an image intensifier. A small *risk* of cervico-uterine *damage* and *infection* exists, but the latter may be further reduced by prophylactic *treatment* with antibiotics in patients who have a history of recurrent inflammatory disease. The procedure should be postponed at least three months after an acute exacerbation and treatment and obviously not done if any question of active disease exists.

2. *False-negative and false-positive HSG studies are common.* Apparent proximal tubal obstruction can be due to *technique, tubal spasm,* or *distortion* by relatively minor adhesive disease that kinks the tubes at the cornua. An apparently normal HSG may lead the examiner into believing no abnormality exists when actually *severe adhesions* are present. *Adhesions* often can be surmised by *loculations of dye* or failure of the dye to settle in the cul-de-sac and shift with motion. Except in the case of obvious bilateral distal obstruction with ampullary dilatation, *laparoscopy* is mandatory to confirm the abnormality as well as to confirm a normal pelvis if no other etiology for the infertility is found. *The discordance between findings on HSG and laparoscopy can be as high as 50 percent.*[69]

D. *Treatment*

The development of microsurgery in gynecology has resulted in higher pregnancy rates following repair in every category of tubal disease, with *anastomosis* following *previous tubal ligation* being the most successful.[71]

1. The pregnancy rate depends on:
   a) Type of sterilization procedure done.
   b) The portion of the tube damaged.

    c) The length of the remaining functional tube after reconstruction.[70]

Attention to detail in hemostasis, use of fine suture, and atraumatic tissue handling are the key points of microsurgery. In the series reported, *pregnancy rates up to 75 percent have been reported with midtubal anastomasis. The integrity of the ampulla lends to greatest success,* and *tubal length over 4 cm is most conductive to pregnancy.*

2. Proximal destruction of the tube, as in laparoscopic fulguration, has probably the poorest prognosis, since a large portion of the remaining tube is damaged, including in many cases, the interstitial portion, and an anastomosis is difficult if not impossible. When the interstitial (intramural) tubal lumen is obliterated due to fulguration or inflammation, a microsurgical or macrosurgical approach is used with *implantation* of the healthy part of the tube (often ampulla) into the cornual portion of the endometrial cavity by incising the myometrium or in a posterior fundal incision. Pregnancy rates of up to 50 percent have been reported.

3. The isthmic applications of *clips,* Silastic *bands,* or *suture* as in a *Pomeroy* procedure, preserve the most functional tube and have the best prognosis for restoration of function. Irving or Uchida procedures which may resect a portion give less good results.

4. The *Kroener* procedure, or *fimbriectomy,* has been considered irreversible, mainly because a hemisalpingectomy is performed, losing the entire ampulla, which is critical for fertility. Retention of the ampulla may allow distal salpingostomy to be done with a reasonable chance at pregnancy.

5. *The overall pregnancy rate with inflammatory disease tends to be much lower than with anastomosis.*[25] The heterogeneity of disease — hydrosalpinges, fimbrial agglutination, proximal obstruction, peritubal adhesions, chronic tuboovarian complex, and combinations of these — make it difficult to quote success rates. However, in the best of hands, a microsurgical salpingostomy of

pure hydrosalpinges results in intrauterine pregnancies in up to 30 percent, but ectopic pregnancies occur in up to 10 percent of the patients. When adhesions are present, the statistics are worse, and *in extensive inflammatory disease adhesions are the rule rather than the exception.* When adhesions alone are present or fimbriae are agglutinated but relatively normal, the pregnancy rate is much better, probably in the 50 to 75 percent range. When proximal or midtubal disease is present, it is resected, and anastomosis or implantation is performed as with poststerilization procedures.[43]

6. *Pregnancies following anastomosis* tend to occur within a year, although late pregnancies are reported. For distal disease, the consensus is that early pregnancy is more likely, since reformation of adhesions or occlusion may recur with time. However, if patency is retained, regeneration of tubal mucosa may be necessary before a pregnancy can occur. After a year, hysterosalpingography and laparoscopy should be performed to assess the tubes and to decide on further therapy. Reoperation is even less promising than is a primary procedure.[24]

7. *The use of adjunct therapy* is a topic of intense discussion.[38] Prophylactic antibiotics, systemic antihistamines and corticosteroids, peritoneal lavage with antibiotics, steroids, or low or high weight dextran have all been used in some combination without well-controlled studies. The same is true for postoperative hydrotubation — theorectically a good idea to disrupt adhesions but unproven. The best means of preventing adhesion formation is by meticulous technique.

8. *Endometriosis,* when associated with adhesions, scarring, and obstruction, must be dealt with surgically as in infectious inflammatory disease.[41,42] The diagnosis of endometriosis can only be made at laparoscopy[13] or laparotomy, and while surgical therapy alone has resulted in pregnancy rates up to 75 percent, some minimal cases of endometriosis are more amenable to medical therapy

with less risk to the patient.[6] Medical therapy is also advisable following surgical resection of endometriosis due to unseen remnants. *The attenuated androgen, danazol, is currently the drug of choice in causing a pseudomenopause to effect regression of active endometriotic implants, with pregnancy rates also approaching 75 percent.*[19,26,37] Danazol is effective at a dose of 800 mg a day orally in split doses for up to six months, but recent studies suggest lower dosages to be as successful with less side effects and less cost to the patient.[9] Previous medical therapy was restricted to continuous oral contraceptive or progestin therapy, which as pseudopregnancy had more side effects and risks.

9. *The use of laparoscopy* to diagnose the unsuspected minor adhesive disease or minimal endometriosis has reduced the category of unexplained infertility to only a few cases in a hundred.[20] It is this fact that mandates the performance of laparoscopy sooner rather than later in the work-up of a couple with all parameters normal or when a certain therapeutic regimen (e.g., clomiphene) does not result in pregnancy within six months of the desired effect (e.g., ovulation).

WHAT IF EVERYTHING IS NORMAL?

If the diagnostic tests—semen analysis, ovulation detection (BBT, serum progesterone), postcoital test, hysterosalpingo-gram, laparoscopy—are all unequivocally normal, less likely aspects should be investigated, such as further luteal phase evaluation, even with normal menstrual cycles, BBT, and progesterone. Repetition of the semen analysis more than two or three times may uncover a cyclic oligospermia. *Hysteroscopy* has been put forth as an important part of the infertility work-up.[58] However, uterine factors (except for Asherman's syndrome discussed earlier), especially those not seen during HSG, are not related to infertility as much as recurrent spontaneous abortion. Nonetheless, given a completely normal couple, *they may be considered as possible spontaneous aborters.* Late luteal β-hCG levels in several cycles may uncover preclinical pregnancies, so that the emphasis may be shifted.[44] In the same way, *Mycoplasma* and *Ureaplasma infections of the cervix and uterus have been associated with infertility.* Culturing for these agents may be considered as a later procedure.[21]

Occult hyperprolactinemia, thyroid dysfunction, or glucose intolerance should also be sought, although the association with infertility may be tenuous. Finally, after a rest of several months with no testing or therapy, reevaluation from point one can begin again depending on the patient's wishes.

THE FUTURE

The promise of new hope for infertile couples is continually being sought. While over 95 percent of infertile couples will be given a diagnosis for their infertility, only one half of them will achieve a liveborn baby. Some of the noncorrectible aspects have been mentioned, such as true male infertility. This can be overcome by artificial donor insemination. Others may have ovulation dysfunction and either be refractory to therapy or achieve ovulation without conception. The freer use of bromocryptine in hyperprolactinemic states should permit many more pregnancies, and the use of pulsatile GnRH either by injection or automated pump may fill the need of clomiphene failures or supplant the use of exogenous gonadotropins. The most emotionally charged issue is that of in vitro fertilization and embryo transfer[11,61], which has well-publicized successes but provides a small fraction of pregnancies from the initial number of couples who enter such a program. This is not a panacea, but unfortunately it is seen by many to be just that. However, continued interest and research in this and other aspects of reproductive physiology hopefully will increase the likelihood of an infertile couple achieving a pregnancy. The unknown etiologies lying within the nucleus and cytoplasm of sperm and ovum have yet to be uncovered.

REFERENCES

1. Abraham GE: Role of the adrenal cortex in female infertility. In Givens JR (ed): The Infertile Female. Chicago, Year Book, 1979, p 213

2. Aksel S: Sporadic and recurrent luteal phase defects in cyclic women: comparison with normal cycles. Fertil Steril 33:372, 1980

3. Amelar RD, Dubin L, Schoenfeld C: Sperm motility. Fertil Steril 34:197, 1980

4. Amelar RD, Hotchkiss RS: The split ejaculate, its use in the management of male infertility. Fertil Steril 16:46, 1965

5. Andrews WC: Luteal phase defects. Fertil Steril 32:501, 1979

6. Andrews WC: Medical versus surgical treatment of endometriosis. Clin Obstet Gynecol 23: 917, 1980

7. Bahamondes L, Saboya W, Tambasoia M, Trevisan M: Galactorrhea, infertility, and short luteal phases in hyperprolactinemic women: early stage of amenorrhea-galactorrhea? Fertil Steril 32:476, 1979

8. Bennink RJTC: Intermittent bromocriptine treatment for the induction of ovulation in hyperprolactinemic patients. Fertil Steril 31:267, 1979

9. Biberoglu KO, Behrman SJ: Dosage aspects of danazol therapy in endometriosis: short-term and long-term effectiveness. Am J Obstet Gynecol 139:645, 1981

10. Birnbaum MD, Rose LI: The partial adrenocortical hydroxylase deficiency syndrome in infertile women. Fertil Steril 32:536, 1979

11. Blandau RJ: In vitro fertilization and embryo transfer. Fertil Steril 33:3, 1980

12. Chen C: Immunological infertility—management and prognosis. Clin Obstet Gynecol 6:403, 1979

13. Cohen MR: Laparoscopic diagnosis and pseudomenopause treatment of endometriosis with danazol. Clin Obstet Gynecol 23:901, 1980

14. Corenblum B: Successful outcome of ergocryptine-induced pregnancies in twenty-one women with prolactin-secreting pituitary adenomas. Fertil Steril 32:183, 1979

15. Craft I, Shelton K, Yovich J, Smith D: Ovum retention in the human. Fertil Steril 34:537, 1980

16. Davajan V: Cervical factor. In Givens JR (ed): The Infertile Female. Chicago, Year Book, 1979, p 377

17. de Crespingny LC, O'Herlihy C, Robinson HP: Ultrasonic observation of human ovulation. Am J Obstet Gynecol 139:636, 1981

18. diZerega GS, Hodgen GD: Luteal phase dysfunction infertility: a sequel to aberrant folliculogenesis. Fertil Steril 35:489, 1981

19. Dmowski WP, Cohen MR: Treatment of endometriosis with an antigonadotropin, danazol: a laparoscopic and histologic evaluation. Obstet Gynecol 46:2, 1975

20. Drake TS, Grunert GM: The unsuspected pelvic factor in the infertility investigation. Fertil Steril 34:27, 1980

21. Friberg J: Mycoplasmas and ureaplasmas in infertility and abortion. Fertil Steril 33:351, 1980

22. Gemzell C, Wang CF: Outcome of pregnancy in women with pituitary adenomas. Fertil Steril 31:363, 1979

23. Goldzieher JW: Polycystic ovarian disease. Fertil Steril 35:371, 1981

24. Gomel V: Causes of failure of reconstructive infertility microsurgery. J Reprod Med 24:139, 1980

25. Gomel V, Swolin K: Salpingostomy: microsurgical technique and results. Clin Obstet Gynecol 23:1243, 1980

26. Greenblatt RB, Borenstein R, Hernandez-Ayup S: Experiences with danazol (an antigonadotropin) in the treatment of infertility. Am J Obstet Gynecol 118:783, 1974

27. Hammond CB, Wiebe RH, Haney AN, Yancy SG: Ovulation induction with luteinizing hormone-releasing hormone in amenorrheic, infertile women. Am J Obstet Gynecol 135:924, 1979

28. Haney AF, Hammond CB, Soules MR, Creasman WT: Diethylstilbestrol-induced upper genital tract abnormalities. Fertil Steril 31:142, 1979

29. Hensleigh PA, Fainstat T: Corpus luteum dysfunction: serum progesterone levels in diagnosis and assessment of therapy for recurrent and threatened abortion. Fertil Steril 32:396, 1979

30. Huppert LC: Induction of ovulation with clomiphene citrate. Fertil Steril 31:1, 1979

31. Jones WR: Immunologic infertility—fact or fiction. Fertil Steril 33:577, 1980

32. Judd HL, Lasley BL: Ovarian disorders. In Givens JR (ed): The Infertile Female. Chicago, Year Book, 1979, p 181

33. Kaufman RH, Binder GL, Gray PM, Adam E: Upper genital tract changes associated with exposure in utero to diethylstilbestrol. Am J Obstet Gynecol 128:51, 1977

34. Kenan PD: Surgical approaches for pituitary tumors. Clin Obstet Gynecol 23:413, 1980
35. Kinch RA: The use of bromocriptine in obstetrics and gynecology. Fertil Steril 33:463, 1980
36. Kramer RS: Prolactin-producing pituitary tumors: surgical therapy. Clin Obstet Gynecol 23:425, 1980
37. Lauersen NH, Wilson KH, Birnbaum S: Danazol: an antigonado-tropin agent in the treatment of pelvic endometriosis. Am J Obstet Gynecol 123:747, 1975
38. Levinson CJ, Swolin K: Postoperative adhesions: etiology, prevention, and therapy. Clin Obstet Gynecol 23:1213, 1980
39. Lobo RA, Goebelsmann U. Adult manifestation of congenital adrenal hyperplasia due to incomplete 21-hydroxylase deficiency mimicking polycystic ovarian disease. Am J Obstet Gynecol 138:720, 1980
40. Magyar DM, Marshall JR: Pituitary tumors and pregnancy. Am J Obstet Gynecol 132:739, 1978
41. Malinak RL: Management of endometriosis in the infertile female. In Givens JR (ed): The Infertile Female. Chicago, Year Book, 1979, p 359
42. Malinak RL: Infertility and endometriosis: operative technique, clinical staging and prognosis. Clin Obstet Gynecol 23:925, 1980
43. McComb P, Gomel V: Cornual occlusion and its microsurgical reconstruction. Clin Obstet Gynecol 23:229, 1980
44. McDonough PG, Tho PT, Byrd JR: Overall evaluation of recurrent abortion. In Givens JR (ed): The Infertile Female. Chicago, Year Book, 1979, p 385
45. Menge AC, Behrman SJ: Immunologic infertility. Clin Obstet Gynecol 22:231, 1979
46. Moghissi KS: The cervix in infertility. Clin Obstet Gynecol 22:27, 1979
47. Moghissi KS: Prediction and detection of ovulation. Fertil Steril 34:89, 1980
48. Moghissi KS, Sacco AG, Borin K: Immunologic infertility. I. Cervical mucus antibodies and postcoital test. Am J Obstet Gynecol 136:941, 1980
49. Nachtigall RD, Faure N, Glass RH: Artificial insemination of husband's sperm. Fertil Steril 32:141, 1979
50. Noell KT: Prolactin- and other hormone-producing pituitary tumors: radiation therapy. Clin Obstet Gynecol 23:441, 1980

51. Overstreet JW, Yanagimachi R, Katz DF, Hayashi K, Hanson FW: Penetration of human spermatozoa into the human zona pellucida and the zona-free hamster egg: a study of fertile donors and infertile patients. Fertil Steril 33:534, 1980

52. Pepperell RJ: Prolactin and reproduction. Fertil Steril 35:267, 1981

53. Quigley MM, Haney AF: Evaluation of hyperprolactinemia: clinical profiles. Clin Obstet Gynecol 23:337, 1980

54. Schenker JG, Yarkoni S, Granat M: Multiple pregnancies following induction of ovulation. Fertil Steril 35:105, 1981

55. Schwartz M, Jewelewicz R: The use of gonadotropins for induction of ovulation. Fertil Steril 35:1, 1981

56. Sherins RJ, Brightwell D, Sternthal PM: Longitudinal analysis of semen of fertile and infertile men. In Troen P, Nankin H (eds): New Concepts of the Testis in Normal and Infertile Men: Morphology, Physiology and Pathology. New York, Raven Press, 1977, p 473

57. Siegler AM: Hysterosalpingography, 2nd ed. New York, Medcom Press, 1974

58. Siegler AM: Hysterosalpingography and hysteroscopy. In Givens JR (ed): The Infertile Female. Chicago, Year Book, 1979, p 453

59. Skrabanek P, McDonald D, Meagher D, et al.: Clinical course and outcome of thirty-five pregnancies in infertile hyperprolactinemic women. Fertil Steril 33:391, 1980

60. Smith DH, Picker RH, Sinosich M, Saunders DM: Assessment of ovulation by ultrasound and estradiol levels during spontaneous and induced cycles. Fertil Steril 33:387, 1980

61. Soupart P: Current status of in vitro fertilization and embryo transfer in man. Clin Obstet Gynecol 23:683, 1980

62. Speroff L, Glass RH, Kase NG: Clinical Gynecologic Endocrinology and Infertility, 2nd ed. Baltimore, Williams & Wilkins, 1978, p 311

63. Vaughn TC, Hammond CB: Prolactin- producing pituitary tumors: medical therapy. Clin Obstet Gynecol 23:403, 1980

64. Wentz AC: An overview of female infertility. In Givens JR (ed): The Infertile Female. Chicago, Year Book, 1979, p 15

65. Wentz AC: Initial assessment of menstrual disorders. In Givens JR (ed): The Infertile Female. Chicago, Year Book, 1979, p 129

66. Wentz AC: Endometrial biopsy in the evaluation of infertility. Fertil Steril 33:121, 1980

67. Westrom L: Effect of acute pelvic inflammatory disease on fertility. Am J Obstet Gynecol 121:707, 1975

68. Wiebe RH: Endocrine evaluation of hyperprolactinemia. Clin Obstet Gynecol 23:349, 1980

69. Wilson EA: The infertile couple: interview and physical examination. In Givens JR (ed): The Infertile Female. Chicago, Year Book, 1979, p 27

70. Winston RML: Reversal of tubal sterilization. Clin Obstet Gynecol 23:1261, 1980

71. Winston RML: Microsurgery of the fallopian tube: from fantasy to reality. Fertil Steril 34:521, 1980

27

Hirsutism, Defeminization, and Virilization

Gretajo Northrop, M.D., Ph.D.

PRACTICE PRINCIPLES

Women with hyperandrogenism, elevated blood levels of male sex steroid hormones, represent a wide clinical spectrum, with their presentation from mild to severe hirsutism rarely accompanied by defeminization and virilization (masculinization). Female hairiness, *hirsutism,* in the male face and body distribution is almost always associated with increased androgen production but not necessarily increased androgen concentration in the blood. *Virilization,* characterized by amenorrhea, temporal hair recession, lowering of voice pitch, and clitoral hypertrophy, results when exposure to androgen is excessive due to either high blood concentrations for a relatively short time or moderately high blood levels for a longer duration. *Defeminization* is the loss of female body characteristics, such as decreased breast size and female body fat distribution, with increased muscle mass. A clear difference between virilization and defeminization is not made. Virilization is considered all inclusive. Hypertrichosis is the abnormal growth of hair usually considered to be nonandrogen-dependent on places such as ears, forehead, and interphalangeal joints.

HISTORICAL INFORMATION

Women most frequently present with varying amounts of excessive body and/or facial hair, often accompanied by acne (face, shoulders, or chest) and/or hyperhidrosis. Important historical information is:

A. *Age of onset*
   Knowledge of onset of hyperandrogenation may supply a clue as to etiology (Table 27–1).
B. *Progression and duration of symptoms*
   Progression from a few facial hairs to generalized hirsutism over 3 to 12 months is suggestive of possible tumor, as is virilization at anytime. Women are very knowledgeable

TABLE 27–1. ETIOLOGY OF HYPERANDROGENATION BY AGE GROUP

Age	Causes of Hyperandrogenation
Birth to puberty	Genetic syndromes: Congenital adrenal hyperplasia Leprechaunism Gangliosidosis Precocious puberty: tumor or physiologic Tumors: pituitary, ovaries or adrenal glands Drugs
Puberty to menopause	Polycystic ovary disease (PCOD) including Stein-Leventhal and adult adrenogenital syndromes Pregnancy: luteoma Tumors: ovaries or adrenal glands Intersex disorders Drugs
Menopause to death	Ovary: biochemical changes associated with menopause Tumors: ovaries or adrenal glands Drugs

about their facial and body hair, and any report of change should be respected and investigated.

C. *Associated symptoms, diseases, factors*
   1. *Amenorrhea, oligomenorrhea, menorrhagia, and menometrorrhagia.* About 50 percent of women with polycystic ovary disease (PCOD) report normal, regular menses. Oligomenorrhea is the most commonly reported menstrual abnormality, with menorrhagia and menometrorrhagia reported less frequently. Primary amenorrhea is rarely reported. When plasma androgen levels are greater than two times normal, as frequently associated with tumor, secondary amenorrhea is more likely.
   2. *Infertility, abortions, and miscarriages.* Excessive androgen may be associated with relative infertility. In general the higher the plasma testosterone (T) concentration, the more likely the woman is to be infertile. Fetal loss is rarely associated with excessive androgen.
   3. *Obesity and increased muscle mass.* Obesity is commonly (50 percent) associated with PCOD. Androgens are anabolic steroids that stimulate appetite, which results in positive nitrogen balance, and increased muscle mass may also be noted.
   4. *Libido and aggressiveness.* Excessive androgen production is often accompanied by excessive aggressiveness and dominance. These attitudes are also expressed in sexual desire and activity.
   5. *Nongonadal endocrine, metabolic, and other disorders associated with hirsutism*
      a) *Cushing's syndrome or disease* frequently results in elevation of blood androgens as well as cortisol.
      b) *Hypothyroidism* leads to decreased 5-α-reductase with build-up of biologically active precursors including testosterone.

$$\uparrow \text{Testosterone} \xrightarrow[\text{Blockade}]{\text{5-}\alpha\text{-reductase}} \downarrow \text{Androsterone}$$

c) *Malnutrition,* including *anorexia nervosa,* is associated with the low T_3 (triiodothyronine) syndrome. T_4 (thyroxine) and TSH (thyroid-stimulating hormone) are normal with low T_3 blood levels. Decreased 5-α-reductase (see above) and other enzyme changes involving cortisol and estrogen metabolism occur.

d) *Liver disease,* porphyria cutanea tarda, results in decreased 5-α-reductase.

e) *Skin disease other than hirsutism*

   (1) *Hyperhidrosis,* excessive sweating, is caused by androgen-stimulated proliferation of sweat glands, resulting in excessive sweating and odor.

   (2) *Acne* is caused by dihydrotestosterone (DHT) stimulation of the sebaceous glands, which results in increased sebum production and alteration of keratinization with obstruction of the pilosebaceous unit, which subsequently becomes infected. Enzymes in the sebaceous glands convert preandrogens to testosterone, and 5-α-reductase reduces T to DHT.

f) *Race* is associated with body hair patterns. Women of several racial backgrounds, including peri-Mediterranean and Middle Eastern countries and India, have more body and facial hair than do women from northern Europe and America. American Indian and Oriental women have the least body and facial hair as a group.

g) *Heredity* plays a known role in hirsutism and virilism in some diseases, such as congenital adrenal hyperplasia (CAH) and hyperthecosis. The specific genetics of PCOD is unknown, but the association of hirsutism, infertility, obesity, and menstrual problems in different combinations in family members is well established.

PHYSICAL FINDINGS

Some or all of the following physical findings may be present in a woman with excessive blood androgen concentration.

A. *Skin*
   1. *Hair.* To the female pattern of terminal hair (eyebrows, axillary and pubic hair) may be added that of the male (face, neck, chest, back, shoulders, abdomen, presacral, heavy on forearm with extension to the dorsum of the hand, thighs, and heavy on the legs with extension to the dorsum of the feet). Recession or thinning of frontal or temporal scalp hair is evidence of hyperandrogenation.
   2. *Acne.* The face, chest, shoulders, and back may have acne. Increased frequency of boils and abscesses may be noted in the inguinal and other skin fold areas.
   3. *Hyperhidrosis.* Excessive development and secretion of the sweat glands particularly in the axilla and inguinal areas.
   4. *Acanthosis nigricans.* Black velvet-like pigmentation predominantly found in flexor skin folds, e.g., neck, axilla antecubital, inguinal.
B. *Breasts*
   Size of the breasts may diminish with exposure to androgens.
C. *Clitoris*
   Enlargement of the clitoris is accompanied by increased sensitivity following exposure to high levels of androgen.
D. *Ovary*
   Enlarged ovaries are frequently (approximately 50 percent) noted in hirsute women. These enlarged ovaries frequently (approximately 50 percent) are not diagnosed on pelvic examination for one or more of the following reasons.
   1. *Virginal introitus.* Poor cooperation by the patient may make palpation of the ovaries impossible.
   2. *Obesity.* A thick abdominal wall prevents palpating a 2 to 3 cm ovary.
   3. *Adhesions.* Chronic pelvic inflammation may distort pelvic anatomic relationships.
   4. *Location.* Large ovaries may be high and out of reach of the examiner. Beware the phrase "adnexa negative" as it may mean that the ovaries are normal or that the ovaries are not palpated by the examiner!

E. *Muscle*

Increased muscle mass is occasionally present in virilized women.

F. *Obesity*

More than half the patients with hirsutism exceed their ideal weight by 20 percent. (Ideal weight is estimated in women as 100 pounds for 60 inches, plus addition of 5 pounds for every additional inch in height.)

PATHOPHYSIOLOGY

Exposure of a hair follicle to any of the androgenic steroids (testosterone T, androstenedione A, androstenediol A'diol, dihydrotestosterone DHT, DHEA, or DHEAS) results in increased hair growth. Enzymatic conversion of less biologically active steroids (A, A'diol, DHEA, DHEAS) to steroids of high activity (T and DHT) may occur at the hair follicle. Thus, elevated levels of T and DHT in the blood may not always be present, and testing for precursors, A, A'diol, DHEA, and DHEAS is frequently required for diagnosis of excessive androgen. Once a hair follicle is stimulated for a significant time (longer than one year), the hair will continue to grow in the absence of excessive androgen stimulation. Destruction of the follicle is the only known method of terminating this hair growth (Fig. 27–1).

A. *Diseases of the ovary*

1. *Polycystic ovary disease.* Excessive androgen production is frequently associated with polycystic ovaries. Polycystic ovary disease may occur any time chronic anovulation is accompanied by adequate pituitary function. Excessive androgenic steroids are secreted by the ovaries and/or adrenal glands with subsequent conversion, partly in the ovary but predominantly peripherally in liver cells, fat cells, etc., to estrogens. The acyclic, continual conversion of excessive androgen to estrogen results in persistently increased estrogen levels which cause elevation of

luteinizing hormone (LH) and lowering of follicle-stimulating hormone (FSH) via positive and negative, respectively, feedback mechanisms with the hypothalamic-pituitary axis.

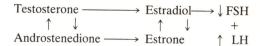

Inhibin generated from the ovary (granulosa cells) has recently been implicated in altering FSH levels in animals and may play some as yet undetermined role in the development of PCOD in women.

Polycystic ovaries may be from normal to four or five times normal in size, surrounded by a thickened white capsule, with prominent, numerous capillaries and multiple cysts of varying size which may protrude through the capsule or remain subcapsular in location. Microscopic alterations observed are multiple small follicular cysts surrounded by hyperplastic theca interna cells and hypertrophy of the ovarian stroma. Evidence of ovulation, a corpus luteum, or corpora albicantia may be present. Thus, morphology corroborates the biochemical findings of increased androgen production by the theca cells due to elevated LH with decreased aromatization of the androgen to estrogen in the ovary by the FSH-sensitive granulosa cells because of a decreased concentration of this gonadotropin. Peripheral conversion of androgen to estrogen results in relatively high, slightly fluctuating estrogen levels which perpetuates the gonadotropin pattern of an LH:FSH ratio greater than 2.

Stein and Leventhal described the syndrome that bears their name based on eight women who had hirsutism, obesity, irregular menses with infertility, and enlarged polycystic ovaries. Most physicians do not use these rigid criteria but consider the Stein-Leventhal syndrome as one of several diseases resulting in PCOD, which includes

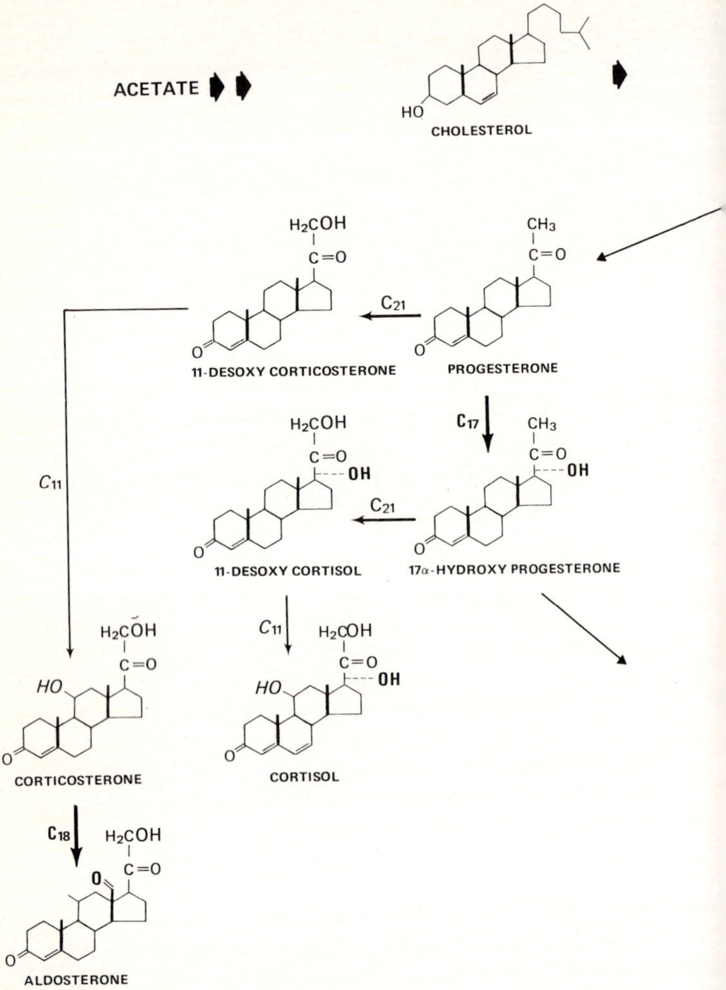

Figure 27-1. Common steroid metabolic pathways in the ovaries, testes, and adrenal glands. Enzymatic steps (arrows) and sites of hydroxylation or reduction on the steroid molecule are labeled for ease in recognition as follows: C_{17}, 17-α-hydroxylation; C_{21}, 21-

hydroxylation; C_{11}, 11β-hydroxylation; C_{18}, 18-dehydrogenation; C_5, 5 = α-reduction. Molecules of cyclopentanophenanthrene rings (box at lower right) exhibit varying degrees of androgen activity in the human female (i.e., DHEAS, DHEA, androstenediol, androstenedione, testosterone, dihydrotestosterone).

most but not necessarily all of the above criteria in a given woman.

2. *Ovarian hyperthecosis.* Ovarian hyperthecosis cannot be distinguished from PCOD as a specific disease except by ovarian biopsy. Microscopically, nests of luteinized cells are seen in the hyperplastic ovarian stroma that otherwise appears as classic PCOD. Hyperthecosis may be familial. Women with hyperthecosis may be refractory to treatment with clomiphene as well as to wedge resection of their ovaries.

3. *Luteoma of pregnancy and stromal luteoma.* Lutenized thecal cells may become hyperplastic and develop into nodular masses during pregnancy, luteoma of pregnancy, or at other times, particularly menopause, stromal luteoma, probably due to elevation of chorionic gonadotropin or luteinizing hormone, respectively. Hirsutism or virilization usually resolves with termination of pregnancy. Lesions found at menopause are benign.

B. *Neoplasms of the ovary*

1. *Granulosa-theca cell tumor.* These tumors may be composed of granulosa or thecal cells or contain both cell types. Most tumors secrete estrogens, but some secrete androgen and progestogens.

2. *Sertoli-Leydig cell tumor (arrhenoblastoma).* These tumors predominantly produce androgenic steroids in adult women.

3. *Gynandroblastoma.* Androgen-secreting tumors composed of granulosa-theca or Sertoli-Leydig cell patterns.

4. *Lipid cell tumors* ("adrenal rests," hilum cell tumors). Most of these tumors secrete androgens. However, about 10 percent of the patients have Cushing's syndrome.

5. *Gonadoblastoma.* These tumors arise in dysgenetic gonads, predominantly containing a Y chromosome. This tumor can produce androgens or estrogens.

6. *Dysgerminoma.* These tumors occur primarily in young adult women. They are malignant and secrete androgens or chorionic gonadotropin.

7. *Rare androgen-secreting tumors*
    a) Mucinous and serous cystadenomas.
    b) Brenner's tumors (more commonly secrete estrogens but can, on occasion, secrete androgens).
    c) Krukenberg tumors (reported as a source of androgen in pregnancy).
C. *Diseases of the adrenal glands*
    1. *Congenital adrenal hyperplasia (CAH).* Hereditary diseases, which have in common low plasma cortisol levels due to inadequate enzyme concentrations in the cortisol pathway, result in excessive ACTH stimulation of adrenal steroid synthesis. Cortisol precursors accumulate behind the blockade caused by the compromised enzyme, which results in predictable abnormal steroid profiles in the blood and urine. *Both 21- and 11-hydroxylase deficiency may be associated with hirsutism and virilization* (Fig. 27–1). Ambiguous genitalia and female pseudohermaphroditism occur in female infants with exposure to excessive androgen prior to the twelfth week of gestation. Inadequate mineralocorticoid synthesis occurs when blockade is relatively severe and is associated with potassium retention and sodium loss, *salt losing.* HLA typing may be used to identify both homozygous and heterozygous states in 21-hydroxylase deficiency, as this deficiency is closely related to HLA-B in both nonsalt-losing and salt-losing types.
    2. *Adult adrenal hyperplasia (adult adrenogenital syndrome).* There is no question that some hirsute women with mild 21- or 11-hydroxylase deficiencies may be first identified during adulthood by demonstration of increased urinary pregnanetriol and other urinary steroid metabolites, following either prolonged or short ACTH stimulation tests. The question of whether most of the women encountered with hirsutism, irregular menses, PCOD, and so on have excessive androgen exposure due to an ovarian or an adrenal gland source remains unanswered. Some investigators feel that the rule of

thirds best explains this dilemma. One third of these women have only an adrenal gland source, one third have only an ovarian source, and one third have both an ovarian and an adrenal gland source of excessive androgen production. Almost all physicians who investigate these unfortunate women report excessive androgen production even when blood androgen concentrations are normal. A clinical fact is that a decreased rate of hair growth, regularity of menstrual cycles, improved fertility, and resolution of acne and oily skin accompanied by decreased blood levels of DHEA and DHEAS as well as testosterone and/or androstenedione may follow adrenal cortex suppression with prednisone or dexamethasone in physiologic (low) doses. It is important to realize that 90 percent of DHEA and its sulfate, DHEAS, arises from the adrenal glands. Thus, elevation of these precursors serves as a clue that adrenal cortical suppression will most likely be effective therapy. These women should not be confused with patients with Cushing's syndrome or disease because plasma cortisol as well as urinary free cortisol concentrations are normal.

3. *Cushing's syndrome and Cushing's disease.* Adrenal cortical hyperplasia may be associated with hirsutism or virilization. However, loss of diurnal variation in cortisol secretion and/or elevation of plasma cortisol as well as elevation of urinary free cortisol and 17-hydroxycorticosteroids are almost always present. Cushing's syndrome may be due to autonomous adrenal cortical hyperactivity (hyperplasia, adenoma, or carcinoma) or to an ectopic ACTH-secreting tumor. In contrast, Cushing's disease is due to excessive ACTH of pituitary origin, predominantly a pituitary adenoma and only occasionally pituitary hyperplasia. The symptoms of excessive cortisol include (1) redistribution of body fat so the limbs are thin as compared with the trunk, (2) accumulation of fat pads which provides the buffalo hump and moon facies, (3) increased catabolism results in muscle weakness as well as wasting, (4) loss of elastic

fibers in the skin results in thin skin, purple striae, and a plethoric complexion, (5) friable blood vessels and easy bruisability, (6) mildly abnormal glucose tolerance, and (7) hypertension. Excessive androgen secretion may also be present, which results in acne, oily skin, hirsutism, and oligomenorrhea or amenorrhea and even virilism.

D. *Neoplasms of the adrenal glands*
    1. *Adrenal cortical adenoma.* Hirsute women with cortical adenomas have the characteristics of Cushing's syndrome as already described.
    2. *Adrenal carcinoma.* Adrenal carcinomas are often bilateral and metastasize early. Death is usual.

E. *Miscellaneous causes of hirsutism or virilization*
    1. *Common drugs*
       a) Adrenocorticotropic hormone (ACTH)
       b) Aldomet
       c) Androgenic steroids (testosterone, danazol, etc)
       d) Diazoxide
       e) Dilantin
       f) Glucocorticoids
       g) Oral contraceptives
       h) Phenothiazines
       i) Spironolactone
       j) Streptomycin
    2. *Syndromes and diseases*
       a) Achard-Thiers
       b) Bird-headed dwarf of Seckel
       c) Cornelia de Lange
       d) Gangliosidosis
       e) Hypertrichosis lanuginosa
       f) Leprechaunism
       g) Lipodystrophy

DIAGNOSTIC EVALUATION

Important facts to consider in diagnostic evaluation of the hirsute or virilized female are (1) age of onset, (2) pattern, duration, and progression, (3) presence of familial history, (4) associated findings or diseases, and (5) use of drugs.

A. *Neonates and infants*

A problem of the female infant is ambiguous genitalia which may occur when the fetus is exposed to excessive androgen prior to the twelfth week of gestation. Deficiencies in 21-hydroxylase or 11β-hydroxylase in CAH, maternal drug ingestion, or tumor (adrenal or ovarian) in the mother or the fetus may be the source of excessive androgen.

B. *Premenarchal girls*

Primary diseases to consider are CAH (21-hydroxylase and rarely 11-β-hydroxylase deficiency) and precocious puberty, which is five to eight times more common in girls than in boys and, fortunately, only rarely associated with tumor. Inappropriate timing by the hypothalamus in initiating puberty is the most common cause of precocious puberty in girls.

C. *Adolescent and premenopausal women*

Primary considerations are PCOD including Stein-Leventhal and adult adrenogenital syndromes, Cushing's disease and syndrome, and tumors of the ovaries or adrenal glands. A protocol for diagnostic evaluation is presented in Figure 27–2. Dynamic testing protocols, for suppression of the adrenal cortex with dexamethasone followed by stimulation of the ovaries with human chorionic gonadotropin (hCG) while the adrenal glands remain suppressed, to localize the source of androgen secretion are ineffective. Unfortunately, the ovaries may respond to ACTH by secreting androgens, and adrenal tumors have responded to stimulation with hCG.

Plasma DHEAS between one and two times the normal concentration with or without elevation of A and T is suggestive of excessive adrenal gland secretion. Elevation of A or T with normal DHEAS may indicate either excessive ovarian or adrenal (or both) androgen. Difficulties arise in interpretation when both the ovaries and the adrenal glands are secreting excessively, a problem encountered about 33 percent of the time. Under this circumstance, whichever treatment is selected only partly inhibits hair growth, and addition of the second suppressive agent is required so that both ovarian and adrenal gland suppression is accomplished. Elevated DHT is likely due to excessive ovarian secretion or conversion of T by the liver.

If the patient appears Cushingoid in addition to having hirsutism or being virilized, the simplest screening test for evaluation is a 24-hour urine collection for free cortisol. Results of urinary 17-hydroxycorticosterone (17OH) determination may be difficult to interpret because normal values are based upon body surface area. Obese women have increased body surface area, and, therefore, 17OH may appear elevated and falsely abnormal. Urinary free cortisol is not influenced by obesity or liver disease and is an excellent screening test for revealing excessive cortisol secretion. Most obese hirsute women with buffalo humps that appear Cushingoid do not have Cushing's disease or syndrome. The short dexamethasone suppression test (8 AM plasma cortisol below 10 μg% following 1 mg of oral dexamethasone the previous night at midnight) is falsely negative in 30 percent of patients with Cushing's syndrome and falsely positive in many obese patients who do not have Cushing's syndrome. The long dexamethasone suppression test is clearly the more useful in separating patients with Cushing's disease and syndrome from normal individuals. The long oral dexamethasone suppression test is performed as follows:

Day	Dexamethasone Every 6 Hours	17-Hydroxycor-ticosteroids (mg/ 24-hour urine)	Re-marks
1	None	12 or less	Normal
2	0.5 mg[*]	No collection	
3	0.5 mg[*]	3 or less	Normal
4	2.0 mg	No collection	

(continued)

Day	Dexamethasone Every 6 Hours	17-Hydroxycor- ticosteroids (mg/ 24-hour urine)	Re- marks
5	2.0 mg	Suppression > 50% of the baseline	Cush- ing's disease
		Suppression < 50% or no suppression com- pared to the baseline	Cush- ing's syn- drome

*Weight-adjusted dose of dexamethasone, 20 μg/kg of actual body weight, may improve discrimination.

Further separation of patients with Cushing's syndrome is gained by obtaining blood ACTH levels. Patients with autonomous adrenal secretion of cortisol, adrenal adenomas, or carcinomas suppress pituitary ACTH levels to less than 100 pg/ml. Ectopic secretion of ACTH from a tumor generally results in blood ACTH levels greater than 200 pg/ml.

D. *Postmenopausal women*
   Primary considerations are tumors of the ovaries or adrenal glands (Fig. 27–2).

E. *Other diseases occasionally associated with hirsutism or virilism*
   1. *Anorexia nervosa and starvation.* These patients are extremely thin, have fine lanugo hair over most of their body (not in a male pattern distribution), have dry, rough, coarse skin, have vital signs that are low (de-creased heart rate, respiratory rate, blood pressure, and body temperature), amenorrhea, hyperactivity, and de-nial of any medical problem including thin body image. Appropriate laboratory studies are as follows:
      a) Thyroxine (T_4) is low normal.
      b) T_3 resin uptake (T_3RU) is normal.

    c) Triiodothyronine (T_3) is below normal.

    d) Thyroid-stimulating hormone (TSH) is normal, and the thyrotropin-releasing hormone (TRH) test is characteristically exaggerated and prolonged.

    e) FSH and LH are low.

    f) Estradiol and progesterone are low.

    g) Cortisol and growth hormone are normal or elevated.

2. *Hypothyroidism.* Women with hypothyroidism frequently complain of fatigue, cold intolerance, weight gain, dry skin, constipation, and menorrhagia. Physical findings may include hypothyroid facies, heavy, thick, dry, myxedematous skin, hoarse voice, and slow reflexes and mentation. Laboratory studies are as follows:

    a) T_4 is low.

    b) T_3 is low.

    c) T_3RU is low.

    d) TSH is elevated. Occasionally in mild hypothyroidism the TSH may be normal. However a TRH test is abnormal with elevated TSH.

3. *Intersexuality.* In intersex patients, the genotype (karyotype) does not harmonize with the phenotype (sexual characteristics).

    a) *Female pseudohermaphroditism* (FP) occurs when a fetus with ovaries and a female karyotype (XX) is exposed to excessive androgen in utero prior to gestational week 12 or 13 due to CAH or maternal production of androgens (tumor) or ingestion of drugs (progesterone) with loss of the classic female phenotype.

    b) *Male pseudohermaphroditism* (MP) occurs when the genotype includes a Y chromosome, the gonads contain testicular tissue, and the phenotype reveals varying degrees of femaleness.

       (1) *Enzyme deficiencies* found in CAH may result in deficient cortisol and/or sex steroid production (Fig. 27–1). Some enzyme deficiencies, if severe, result in death because cholesterol is never converted to the basic adrenal and gonadal steroid,

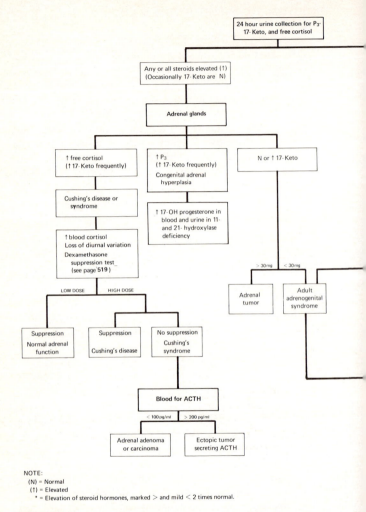

Figure 27–2. A protocol for diagnostic evaluation of the hirsute or virilized female. Additional studies must be employed for localization when a tumor is suspected.

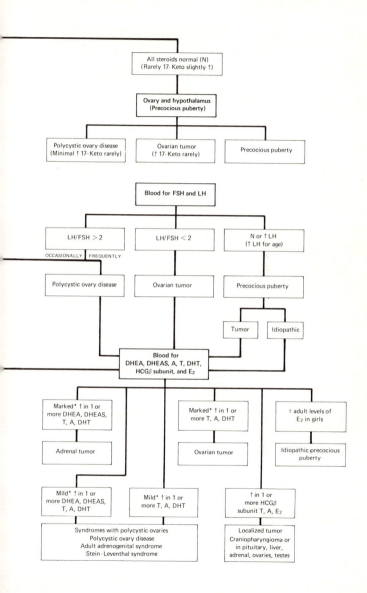

All steroids normal (N)
(Rarely 17-Keto slightly ↑)

Ovary and hypothalamus
(Precocious puberty)

Polycystic ovary disease
(Minimal ↑ 17-Keto rarely)

Ovarian tumor
(↑ 17-Keto rarely)

Precocious puberty

Blood for FSH and LH

LH/FSH > 2

OCCASIONALLY FREQUENTLY

LH/FSH < 2

N or ↑ LH
(↑ LH for age)

Polycystic ovary disease

Ovarian tumor

Precocious puberty

Tumor

Idiopathic

Blood for
DHEA, DHEAS, A, T, DHT,
HCGβ subunit, and E₂

Marked* ↑ in 1 or
more DHEA, DHEAS,
T, A, DHT

Marked* ↑ in 1 or
more T, A, DHT

± adult levels of
E₂ in girls

Adrenal tumor

Ovarian tumor

Idiopathic precocious
puberty

Mild* ↑ in 1 or
more DHEA, DHEAS,
T, A, DHT

Mild* ↑ in 1 or
more T, A, DHT

↑ in 1 or
more HCGβ
subunit T, A, E₂

Syndromes with polycystic ovaries
Polycystic ovary disease
Adult adrenogenital syndrome
Stein-Leventhal syndrome

Localized tumor
Craniopharyngioma or
in pituitary, liver,
adrenal, ovaries, testes

pregnenolone, while some enzyme deficiencies result only in impaired testosterone production with development of MP.

(2) *Testosterone receptor abnormalities* cause resistance at the cellular level to testosterone with lack of male phenotypic differentiation. Testicular feminization is characterized by a normal female phenotype with full breast development and absence of pubic and axillary hair. On examination, the vagina is shortened, the uterus is absent, and normal testes are located anywhere along the normal pathway of descent (intraabdominal to labia majora). An incomplete form may exist in which some receptors are normal, which results in varying amounts of hirsutism and cliteromegaly at puberty.

(3) *5-α-Reductase deficiency* results in inadequate conversion of T to DHT, the androgen required by the urogenital sinus for differentiation into the male phenotype. It should be recalled that the female phenotype is basic and will develop unless domineered by testicular release of testosterone at critical times in embryonic development. Failure to reduce T to DHT in utero results in severe hypospadias and a vagina of varying depth called "pseudovaginal perineoscrotal hypospadias." This deficiency is important to diagnose correctly because at puberty the high levels of testosterone produced by the adult testes causes generalized masculinization and in most patients male psychosexual orientation, if socially possible.

(4) *Gonadal dysgenesis* in genotypic 46,XY phenotypic females, called Swyer's syndrome, is characterized by a normal female phenotype, a normal male karyotype, and streak nonfunctioning gonads. These patients present at puberty with amenorrhea and sometimes hirsutism and/or

cliteromegaly. Gonadoblastomas occur in 30 to 70 percent of these patients and, when present, may produce androgens which cause masculinization.

(5) *Transsexuals* are hormonally normal male or female patients who reject their gonadal and phenotypic sex but cannot reject their karyotypic sex. These adult patients may be in different stages of converting their phenotypic sex from male to female (male to female transsexual) or female to male (female to male transsexual). When fully treated, they are castrated, have the appearance and psychologic adjustment of the opposite sex of their karyotype, and are maintained on sex hormone replacement of the phenotypic sex. Male to female transsexuals have female breasts and a vagina and appropriately seek gynecologic care as women.

c) *Laboratory evaluation* of patients in whom intersex is suspected is directed by the clinical constellation of findings and guided by experience:

(1) Chromosome studies are required to determine if mosaicism is present and for complete genotype.

(2) Barr bodies provide a rapid indication of genotype.

(3) FSH and LH, if elevated, suggest receptor abnormalities or absence of functioning gonadal tissue.

(4) Selection of appropriate steroid tests will depend upon the clinical presentation (Fig. 27–1). Enzyme deficiency, blockade, is located by finding elevation of steroid intermediates with an abrupt stepdown at the blockade.

F. *Special diagnostic procedures*

Special procedures helpful in diagnosis and/or localization of the source of excessive androgen secretion.

1. *Radiological*

a) *X-ray, skull for sella for pituitary evaluation.* Tomograms may be used for initial screening as well as for comparison if continued monitoring is required. Calcium noted in the vicinity of the pituitary is suggestive of craniopharyngioma.

b) *X-ray, wrist for bone age.* Bone age is advanced in precocious puberty, CAH, and sometimes in the presence of tumors in children.

c) *Intravenous pyelogram with tomography* is particularly helpful in identifying adrenal hyperplasia and tumors.

d) *Ultrasonography* is useful in evaluation of pelvic structures, providing information on size and density of one or both ovaries. Solid tumors when detected can be distinguished from cysts.

e) *Computerized tomography* is used for examination of both the head and body for seeking and delineating a tumor. Suprasellar extension of a tumor or an empty sella can also usually be determined, thus avoiding pneumoencephalography in most cases with enlarged sellas.

f) *Selective catheterization* for obtaining blood for hormone analysis from both adrenal glands and ovaries via the femoral vein is most helpful for localization of excessive androgen secretion, especially when noninvasive techniques have failed and tumor is suspected.

2. *Surgical. Laparoscopy* is employed alone or in combination with laparotomy when visualization (and biopsy) of the ovaries or other tissues is desired. This is particularly helpful in women with severe hirsutism and PCOD when the ovaries are extremely different in size. Rarely, ovarian tumor has been missed in laparoscopic-directed ovarian biopsy.

TREATMENT

A. *Medical*
   Medical management is employed predominantly in nonneoplastic diseases. The primary role of the therapy is to provide an exogenous supply of the regulating hormone from the

gland that is to be suppressed so that by negative feedback the hypothalamic-pituitary axis is inhibited. Thus, the target gland is not physiologically stimulated. This form of treatment is not effective when the gland is functioning autonomously or there is tumor.

1. *Corticosteroids*
    a) *Congenital adrenal hyperplasia.* Prednisone is one of several glucocorticoids that may be used. The dose is based upon the body surface area and suppression of blood or urinary levels of 17-hydroxyprogesterone to normal. The dose of prednisone is approximately 6.5 mg/sq cm every eight hours.
    b) *Polycystic ovary disease.* PCOD associated with elevated DHEA or DHEAS (with normal cortisol) is treated with oral prednisone for adrenal suppression with a dose of 2.5 mg every eight hours or 5 mg at bedtime (HS) and 2.5 mg on arising (AM). Whenever the adrenal cortex is suppressed with exogenous glucocorticoids for longer than five days, recovery of cortisol synthesis may be significantly delayed upon discontinuing the glucocorticoid, i.e., prednisone. In addition, while the cortex is in a suppressed state the patient must be given additional glucocorticoid during any stress state, e.g., surgery, common cold with fever. Significant toxicity except for gastric irritation should not be encountered at the above physiologic dose. At higher doses, symptoms of Cushing's syndrome are dependent upon the dose and duration of treatment.

2. *Oral contraceptives (OCs)* are used for treatment of excessive androgen of ovarian origin (DHEA, DHEAS, and cortisol are normal) when neoplasm has been ruled out as far as clinically possible or reasonable. These drugs cause ovarian suppression by decreasing gonadotropin secretion and also increase steroid hormone-binding globulin (SHBG), which causes a decrease in free (biologically active) testosterone. As a general rule, an OC containing the least amount of estrogen compatible

with regular uterine withdrawal bleeding (absence of breakthrough bleeding) is appropriate. There is dispute over potency between ethinyl estradiol and mestranol, the synthetic estrogens employed in OCs. However, ethinyl estradiol appears to exert more biologic activity than mestranol based on weight in most protocols studied. The biologic activity of 0.05 mg of ethinyl estradiol approximates 0.08 mg of mestranol. See Table 23–1 for the specific estrogen and its weight (mg) in commonly prescribed OCs.

3. *Combining OCs with prednisone* even when the adrenal gland is the primary source of androgen secretion may prove helpful because estrogens increase SHBG, which in turn binds more T and DHT leaving less free, biologically active T or DHT. Use of estrogens (OC) is either inappropriate or must be considered specifically in women with (1) history of thrombophlebitis or thromboembolic disease, (2) cerebral vascular or coronary arterial disease, or (3) estrogen-dependent vascular disease, headaches, neoplasms, hypertension, or diabetes when controlled with oral hypoglycemic agents or diet. Breakthrough bleeding or amenorrhea may not be an indication to stop OCs, but the patient should be reevaluated and probably have her OC changed. Two factors that are associated with increased hazard of OCs are age and smoking.

4. *Additional drugs* recently employed for treatment of hirsutism are listed in Table 27–2.

5. *Clomiphene citrate (Clomid),* an antiestrogen, stimulates the ovary by increasing pituitary gonadotropins and is useful for induction of ovulation and should be used in hirsute women primarily for this purpose. Ovarian stimulation with Clomid frequently results in excessive androgen secretion with potentiation of hirsutism often accompanied by regular ovulatory menses.

6. *Mechanical alterations* or removal of excessive hair is effective in women with minimal hirsutism. Most women

Table 27-2. ADDITIONAL DRUGS FOR TREATMENT OF HIRSUITISM

Drug	Dose	Action	Side Effects
Medroxyprogesterone* (Provera)	100 mg IM q 15 days	Suppression of ovulation	Breakthrough bleeding, amenorrhea
Spironolactone (Aldactone)	100 mg PO 2x/day	Blocks DHT binding to androgen receptors	Polyuria, polydipsia, fatigue, weakness, lassitude
Cimetidine (Tagamet)	300 mg PO 5x/day	Blocks DHT binding to androgen receptors	Breakthrough bleeding, nausea

*Used for treatment of idiopathic precocious puberty. Effective in preventing further development of sexual maturation but bone maturation continues with development of a tall child and a short adult.

successful in the use of peroxide for bleaching or plucking or wax removal methods are not identified by the physician. Women in whom hair growth is too rapid for the above methods resort to shaving and electrolysis. Dermatologists claim shaving does not stimulate hair growth, but electrologists claim hair removal is more difficult in areas in which it has previously been removed by wax or shaving. Certainly, electrolysis kills the hair follicle. However, if excessive androgen production continues, new terminal hair will replace previously removed hair. Thus, for effective electrolysis, continued suppression of excessive androgen secretion is mandatory.

7. *Diseases requiring estrogen replacement.* Perimenopausal women and patients with gonadal dysgenesis or intersex disease desiring feminization may require estrogen treatment.

   a) *Perimenopausal women*

   b) *Patients with gonadal dysgenesis or intersex disease* require high levels of estrogen for 12 to 18 months for breast development. Castration should precede hormone therapy if a Y chromosome is present. Estrogen in a dose two to three times the usual replacement dose is prescribed in a cyclic manner, with a progestin also prescribed to insure withdrawal bleeding if a uterus is present. An example is Premarin 5 mg given from day 7 to the end of each month plus Provera 10 mg on the last five days of each month. Withdrawal bleeding occurs during the first six days of each month. After maximal breast development is achieved, a maintenance dose of estrogen, Premarin 1.25 mg and Provera 10 mg taken cyclically, is supplied.

   c) *Transsexuals (male to female),* prior to castration, require estrogen in a dose that prevents spontaneous morning erections. Breast development is maximal when a progestin is also supplied to stimulate alveolar development. (Estrogen stimulates ductal development in breast tissue.) The usual dose of Premarin is 5 to 7.5 mg and Provera 10 mg prescribed as indicated for intersex patients. After castration, the Premarin can be reduced to 1.25 mg plus Provera 10 mg taken in the same cyclic manner.

B. *Surgical*

1. *Polycystic ovary disease.* Ovarian wedge resection is usually reserved for women who desire pregnancy and have failed to ovulate while taking clomiphene citrate. Hirsute women not desiring immediate pregnancy, refractory to adrenal suppression, and unable to take oral contraceptives may also be considered for ovarian wedge resection. Removal of ovarian stromal tissue results in decreased T or A in the ovarian veins, decreased peripheral conversion of T to estradiol, normalization of the plasma LH:FSH ratio, decreased urinary 17-ketosteroids, subsequent ovulation, and a decrease in hirsutism, in that order, in most women.

2. *Neoplasms.* Treatment of hirsutism and/or virilism associated with neoplasms is surgical removal, followed by, when required, chemotherapy and/or radiation.

3. *Transsexuals.* Male to female transsexuals when psychologically ready require sex change surgery, penectomy, orchiectomy, and formation of a vagina. Other plastic surgical procedures may be beneficial, such as breast augmentation and rhinoplasty.

BIBLIOGRAPHY

Books

Gold JJ, Josimovich JB (eds): Gynecologic Endocrinology, 3rd ed. San Francisco, Harper, 1980

Speroff L, Glass, RH, Kase, NG: Clinical Gynecologic Endocrinology and Infertility, 2nd ed. Baltimore, Williams & Wilkins, 1978

Articles

Goldzieher JW: Polycystic ovarian disease. Fertil Steril 35:371, 1980

Maroulis G: Evaluation of hirsutism and hyperandrogenemia. Fertil Steril 36:273, 1981

Yen SSC: The polycystic ovary syndrome. Clin Endocrinol (Oxf) 12:177, 1980

28

Menopause and Climacteric

Frank W. Ling, M.D.

TERMINOLOGY

A. *Climacteric*
   Stage of the aging process during which ovarian function wanes, and the woman moves from the reproductive to nonreproductive phase of life.

B. *Menopause*
   A specific event during the climacteric. The cessation of menses.

C. *Premature menopause*
   Spontaneous cessation of menses before the age of 35.
   1. Exact etiology unknown
   2. Immune mechanism suggested[1]
   3. Possible familial relationship

D. *Postmenopausal*
   Events occurring after 12 months amenorrhea.

MENOPAUSE

A. *Normal range* — 48 to 55 years old.
B. *Average* — 51 years old.
C. Occurs prior to 40 years old in 8 percent.
D. *Expected life expectancy beyond menopause* — 28 years (one third of patient's life predicted to occur after menopause).
E. *Abrupt menstrual cessation* — unusual
    1. Usually preceded by variable cycles with lighter flow
       a) Fewer remaining follicles in ovary.
       b) Relative unresponsiveness to gonadatropin stimulation.
       c) Less estrogen production
         (1) Less estrogen stimulation of endometrium.
         (2) Heavy bleeding around time of menopause is abnormal and cause for concern.
    2. Abrupt cessation of menses may be brought on by surgical castration or radiation.
F. *Not* related to menarche, pregnancy timing or number, environment, education, contraception.

CLIMACTERIC SYMPTOMS

A. *Related to loss of ovarian function (estrogen production)*
    1. Oligoamenorrhea.
    2. Vasomotor symptoms (hot flashes):
       a) Most *common* complaint — approximately 75 percent of women.
       b) May precede menopause by months or years.
       c) Sudden sensation of heat on the face
         (1) Spreads to neck and chest.
         (2) Concurrent flushing of skin.
       d) Actual skin temperature elevation.[2]
       e) Heavy perspiration and shivering.

f) If at night, called "night sweats:"
    (1) Possible source of restlessness and insomnia.
    (2) Leads to fatigue.
g) Other possible associated symptoms: dizziness, headache, nausea, palpitations.
h) Pathophysiology — unknown
    (1) Hot flashes follow pulsatile LH or gonadotropin-releasing hormone surge.[3]
    (2) Possible link with catecholamines.[4]
i) Unlike other symptoms of climacteric, *decreases* in frequency and intensity with time.

3. Dyspareunia, vaginal itching, and irritation, "bulging of vagina" (atrophic vaginal epithelium).
4. Dysuria, urinary frequency (atrophic urethritis/trigonitis.)

B. Unrelated to loss of estrogen production — possible relation to psychosocial ramifications:
  a) Depression
  b) Insomnia
  c) Headache
  d) Fatigue
  e) Palpitations
  f) Irritability
  g) Muscle cramps
  h) Poor concentration
  i) Dizziness
  j) Poor memory
  k) Poor libido
  l) Nervousness

C. Fears:
1. Fear of menopause as a definitive milestone.
2. Fear of pregnancy (as a function of amenorrhea).
3. Fear of aging process.

D. Complaints of appearance (physical changes)
1. Fat redistribution
  a) More on abdomen, buttocks, hips

      b) Less in breasts
2. Loss of hair on scalp and pubis.
3. Hair on upper lip and chin.
4. Poor muscle tone.
5. Change of skin
      a) Hyperkeratosis
      b) Loss of elasticity
      c) Wrinkling

THE CLIMACTERIC OVARY

A. *Perimenopausal alterations*
   1. Decrease in number of remaining follicles
      a) Ovary less responsive to gonadotropin stimulation.[5]
      b) Decreased estrogen production
         (1) Remove feedback inhibition on hypotha-lamus/pituitary.
         (2) Increase gonadotropins FSH, LH.
         (3) Shortened follicular phase.
   2. Irregular follicular maturation
      a) Menstrual irregularity.
      b) Twenty-three percent of women over 50 years old have corpus luteum formation.[6]
B. *Postmenopausal hormone production*
   1. *Estrogens*
      a) Estradiol
         (1) Low levels similar to premenopausal female after oophorectomy.[7]
         (2) Levels same before and after postmenopausal oophorectomy.
         (3) Primary postmenopausal source is adrenal gland.
      b) Estrone
         (1) Serum concentration higher than estradiol.
         (2) Minimal ovarian contribution.

(3) Adrenal gland is major source
    (a) Most circulating estrone from aromatization of androstenedione.[8]
    (b) Occurs in fat, liver, muscle, brain, kidney, and other tissues.
    (c) Conversion rate related to body fat[9] and possibly age.[10]

2. *Androgens*
   a) *Testosterone*
      (1) Significant portion of circulating testosterone derived from ovary.
      (2) Significant decrease of levels after oophorectomy both pre- and postmenopausal.[9]
      (3) From hilus and stromal cells of ovary.[7]
   b) *Androstenedione*
      (1) Primary source is adrenal gland.
      (2) Ovarian contribution is 20 percent of circulating levels.
      (3) Minimal reduction after postmenopausal oophorectomy.[9]
      (4) From hilus and stromal cells.[7]
   c) *Dehydroepiandrosterone*
      (1) Primarily adrenal in origin.
      (2) Twenty-five percent from ovary.
   d) *Dehydroepiandrosterone sulfate* — primarily adrenal.

3. *Hormonal status of the menopause*
   a) Possibly sufficient endogeneous estrogen supply where:
      (1) Enough to prevent hot flashes.
      (2) Enough to prevent genital atrophy.
      (3) Enough to prevent osteoporosis.
      (4) Enough to stimulate endometrium.
   b) Possibly *relative* androgen excess where:
      (1) Defeminization
      (2) Hirsutism
      (3) Virilism

PSYCHOSOCIAL CHANGES

A. Psychologic *and* physical milestone
   1. Physical changes as discussed.
   2. Psychologic changes
      a) More difficult to evaluate than physical changes.
      b) *Any* period of transition is psychologically stressful.
      c) Problems peculiar for this age group:
         (1) Sense of loss
            (a) Loss of femininity (manifest by loss of cycles).
            (b) Loss of youth.
            (c) Loss of reproductive function.
            (d) Loss of dependent children ("empty nest syndrome").
            (e) Loss of sexuality.
            (f) Loss of potential career goals.
         (2) Marital security possibly absent.
         (3) Financial security possibly absent.
B. Role of hormones
   1. Change of hormonal status — an additional stress
      a) Aggravates other difficult situations.
      b) Decreases ability to cope with other life situations.
   2. Estrogen deficiency role confounded by other variables
      a) By effect of the aging process.
      b) By other environmental factors.
   3. *Estrogen is not indicated in treatment of primary psychologic problems*
      a) Possible reduction of emotional reactions to climacteric.[11]
      b) Possible improved memory and mood when compared to placebo.[12]
      c) Any improvement in a and b possibly due to alleviation of physical discomfort associated with menopause.
C. Climacteric not a characteristic time of new and distinctive mental illness.

MANAGEMENT OF MENOPAUSE

A. *Principles*
   1. Regular health maintenance examinations
      a) General history
         (1) Menopause-related symptoms
         (2) Environmental overview (familial, marital, job-related factors)
         (3) Screening for malignancy
            (a) Colon
            (b) Breast
            (c) Lung
            (d) Genital
      b) Physical examination
         (1) Blood pressure
         (2) Urinalysis
         (3) Breast examination
         (4) Pelvic examination
            (a) Note state of vaginal cornification
            (b) Note small uterus
            (c) Note *nonpalpable* ovaries
         (5) Rectal examination
   2. Need for emotional and psychologic support.
   3. Therapy individualized.
   4. Full explanations including risks and benefits of hormonal therapy.
B. *Diagnosis of menopause*
   1. History of amenorrhea and estrogen deficiency symptoms.
   2. FSH
      a) Best single test for ovarian function
      b) No premenopausal/postmenopausal overlap
         (1) > 40 mIU/ml is castrate level.
         (2) Reproductive age rarely > 25 mIU/ml.
   3. Urine estrogens decreased
   4. Serum estrogens decreased

5. Vaginal smear
   a) *Maturation index.* Scraping from upper lateral vaginal sidewall:
      (1) Estrogens → superficial maturation
      (2) Progestogens → intermediate
      (3) Lack of maturing factors → no cellular maturation beyond parabasal
   b) Menopause: 100/0/0
   c) Most helpful in monitoring trend of indices
      (1) Not predictive of problems.[13]
      (2) Can monitor total estrogen effect (endogenous and exogenous).
C. *Advantages of exogenous estrogen*
   1. Vasomotor symptoms
      a) Estrogen more effective than placebo in relief of hot flashes [14]
         (1) Decreases frequency and severity.
         (2) Placebo does help some, however.
      b) Occurrence of hot flashes decreases with time even without treatment.
   2. *Genitourinary atrophy*
      a) Vagina
         (1) Promote epithelial proliferation.
         (2) Treatment of vaginal narrowing, shortening, and loss of elasticity.
         (3) Not helpful for treatment of vaginal relaxation.[15]
      b) Urethra and bladder trigone [16]
         (1) Proliferation of epithelium.
         (2) Treatment of persistent urethral symptoms.
      c) Vulva. No role for estrogen in vulvar dystrophy.
   3. *Osteoporosis*
      a) Reduction in quantity of bony material resulting in structural fragility.
      b) Various locations
         (1) Spine
            (a) Twenty-five percent of females over 60 years develop spinal compression fractures.[17]

   (b) Symptomatic spinal osteoporosis five times more common in females than in males.
  (2) Hip
   (a) Eighty percent of fractures are associated with osteoporosis.
   (b) Seventeen percent die within three months of fracture.
  (3) Wrist
   (a) At age 45, female forearm fractures equal male forearm fracture frequency.
   (b) At age 60, female forearm fractures are 10 times more common than in males.
 c) Incidence:
  (1) Osteoporosis rare in black population.
  (2) Increased incidence in postmenopausal years.
  (3) Oophorectomized females develop osteoporosis sooner and with greater severity.
 d) Other possible etiologic factors:
  (1) Lack of exercise
  (2) Poor diet (calcium, fluoride, and vitamin D)
  (3) Overweight
  (4) Smoking
 e) Estrogen may:
  (1) Decrease incidence of fracture.[18,20]
  (2) Decrease and possibly reverse some of bone loss.[21]

4. *Atherosclerosis*
 a) The role of estrogen in myocardial infarction and atherosclerosis is unclear
  (1) Data only suggestive of protection.[22]
  (2) Premature cessation of ovarian function possibly increases risk of nonfatal myocardial infarction.[23,24]
 b) Alteration of serum lipoproteins to a low-risk profile.[25]
 c) No convincing data to show that customary estrogen doses for postmenopausal replacement increases risk

of thromboembolic phenomenon, stroke, or heart disease in women undergoing a spontaneous menopause.[26]

D. *Disadvantages of exogenous estrogen*
  1. *Endometrial neoplasia*
     a) More common in "high estrogen" conditions.[27,29]
     b) Retrospective data suggest increased risk
        (1) Those associated with exogenous estrogens are lower grade and less advanced.
        (2) Risk decreased with cyclic progestin.[30,31]
     c) Risk possibily increases with duration of use.
     d) Uncertain risk relation to dosage.
     e) Relationship still debatable
  2. *Breast neoplasia*
     a) No significant association.
     b) Data suggest risks possibly confined to postmenopausal women with intact ovaries.[32]
  3. *Gallbladder disease* — 2.5-fold relative risk.[26]
  4. *Side effects*
     a) Breakthrough bleeding
     b) Breast tenderness
     c) Nausea
     d) Edema
     e) Weight gain
     f) Vaginal discharge
     g) Stimulation of leiomyomata
  5. *Contraindications to exogenous estrogen therapy*
     a) Estrogen-dependent neoplasia
     b) Undiagnosed genital bleeding
     c) Thromboembolic phenomenon — past or present
     d) Active or severe liver disease
     e) Patient fear, unresponsive to patient education

E. *Administration of exogenous estrogens*
  1. Patient shown to be estrogen deficient
     a) Lack of withdrawal to progesterone challenge
     b) Poor maturation index
     c) Poor ferning of cervical mucus

2. Use lowest dose to relieve symptoms.
3. When to start therapy?
   a) At time of castration.
   b) At time of diagnosis of menopause.
   c) At onset of symptoms.
4. How to start therapy?
   a) With uterus present
      (1) Conjugated estrogens 0.625 mg (ethinyl estradiol 0.02 mg) daily days 1 to 24 of calendar month.
      (2) Medroxyprogesterone acetate 10 mg per day during the last 7 to 10 days of estrogen therapy.
   b) Uterus absent — three possible regimens
      (1) As in section E4a.
      (2) Conjugated estrogens 0.625 mg daily first three weeks of calendar month.
      (3) Conjugated estrogens 0.625 mg daily.
   c) *Dosage adjusted up or down as symptoms warrant.*
5. When to stop therapy?
   a) Taper to minimum dose needed to treat symptoms.
   b) Variable duration — possibly indefinite for prevention of genital atrophy or osteoporosis.
   c) Until "risks exceed benefits."
6. *Vaginal estrogens*
   a) Local symptoms usually require less estrogen than vasomotor symptoms
      (1) Dyspareunia
      (2) Urethral symptoms
   b) Topical estrogen creams two to three times per week.
   c) Readily absorbed [33]
      (1) Estrogen enters bloodstream without liver metabolism.
      (2) Can have endometrial and systemic effects.
7. *Postmenopausal bleeding*
   a) Must investigate under *any* circumstances regardless of hormone status.
   b) Basic principle: *rule out malignancy.*
      (1) Cervicovaginal cytologic sampling inadequate.

      (2) Endometrial biopsy is *initial* diagnostic tool
         (a) Overall 91 percent accuracy.[34]
         (b) Several acceptable techniques
            (i) Novak suction curette
            (ii) Vakutage
            (iii) Vabra aspiration
            (iv) Endometrial cytologic sampling
      (3) Fractional dilatation and curettage
         (a) As initial procedure in the following circum-
            stances:
            (i) Excessive bleeding
            (ii) Significant pelvic pathology
            (iii) Inability to perform endometrial bi-
              opsy
            (iv) If patient requires hospital procedure
         (b) As secondary procedure for any significant
            pathology found on endometrial biopsy.
  8. *Alternatives to estrogen therapy*
    a) Vaginal atrophy—use of water soluble lubricants (K-
       Y, Lubifax) to prevent mechanical dyspareunia.
    b) Osteoporosis
      (1) Calcium carbonate 2.6 gm daily[35]
         (a) Possibly can cause hypercalcemia.
      (2) Increased physical activity
    c) Vasomotor symptoms
      (1) Medroxyprogesterone acetate (Provera) oral 20
         mg PO daily.[12,36,37]
      (2) Depo-Provera 150 mg IM q three months.[38]
      (3) Clonidine 25 to 75 μg bid.[39]
      (4) Bellergal S one tablet bid
         (a) Contains phenobarbitol, ergotamine, bel-
            ladonna.
         (b) Inhibits sympathetic and parasympathetic hy-
            peractivity.
      (5) Consider mild tranquilizers or sedatives
         (a) When hormonal therapy fails.
         (b) When functional and/or emotional etiology
            suspected.

REFERENCES

1. Coulam CB, Ryan RJ: Premature menopause. Am J Obstet Gynecol 133:639, 1979
2. Meldrum DR, et al.: Elevations in skin temperatures of the finger as an objective index of postmenopausal hot flashes: Standardization of the technique. Am J Obstet Gynecol 135:713, 1979
3. Tataryn IV, et al.: LH, FSH, and skin temperature during the menopausal hot flash. J Clin Endocrinol Metab 49:152, 1979
4. Sturdee DW, et al.: Physiological aspects of menopausal hot flush. Br Med J 2:79, 1978
5. Sherman BM, Korenman SG: Hormonal characteristics of the human menstrual cycle throughout reproductive life. J Clin Invest 55:699, 1975
6. Novak ER: Ovulation after fifty. Obstet Gynecol 36:903, 1970
7. Judd HL, et al.: Endocrine function of the postmenopausal ovary; concentrations of androgens and estrogens in ovarian and peripheral vein blood. J Clin Endocrinol Metab 39:1020, 1974
8. Grodin JM, et al.: Source of estrogen production in postmenopausal women. J Clin Endocrinol Metab 36:207, 1973
9. Judd HL, et al.: Effect of oophorectomy on circulating testosterone and androstenedione levels in patients with endometrial cancer. Am J Obstet Gynecol 118:793, 1974
10. Hemsell DL, et al.: Plasma precursors of estrogens. II. Correlations of the extent of conversion of plasma androstenedione to estrone with age. J Clin Endocrinol Metab 38:476, 1974
11. Kantor HI, et al.: Estrogen for older women. Am J Obstet Gynecol 116:115, 1973
12. Campbell S: Double blind psychometric studies on effects of natural estrogens on postmenopausal women. In Campbell S (ed): The Management of the Menopause and Postmenopausal Years. Baltimore, University Park Press, 1976, pp 149–158
13. Kaufman SA: Limited relationship of maturation index to estrogen therapy for menopausal symptoms. Obstet Gynecol 30:399, 1967
14. Coope J: Double blind cross-over study of estrogen replacement therapy. In Campbell S (ed): The Management of the Menopause and Postmenopausal Years. Baltimore, University Park Press, 1976, pp 159–168
15. Stark M, et al.: Can estrogens be useful for treatment of vaginal relaxation in elderly women? Am J Obstet Gynecol 131:585, 1978
16. Brown ADG: Postmenopausal urinary problems. Clin Obstet Gynecol 4:181, 1977

17. Heaney RP: Estrogens and postmenopausal osteoporosis. Clin Obstet Gynecol 19:791, 1976

18. Weiss NS, et al.: Decreased risk of fractures of the hip and lower forearm with postmenopausal use of estrogen. N Engl J Med 303:1195, 1980

19. Nachtigall LE, et al.: Estrogen replacement therapy. I. A 10 year prospective study in the relationship to osteoporosis. Obstet Gynecol 53:277, 1979

20. Hutchinson TA, et al.: Postmenopausal oestrogens protect against fractures of hip and distal radius. A case-control study. Lancet 2:705, 1979

21. Lindsay R, et al.: Long-term prevention of postmenopausal osteoporosis by estrogen. Lancet 1:1038, 1976

22. Ross RK, et al.: Menopausal oestrogen therapy and protection from death from ischaemic heart disease. Lancet 1:858, 1981

23. Higano N, et al.: Increased incidence of cardiovascular disease in castrated women. N Engl J Med 268:1123, 1963

24. Rosenberg L, et al.: Early menopause and the risk of myocardial infarction. Am J Obstet Gynecol 139:47, 1981

25. Bradley DD, et al.: Serum high-density liproprotein cholesterol in women using oral contraceptives, estrogens and progestins. N Engl J Med 299:17, 1978

26. Boston Collaborative Drug Surveillance Program, Boston University Medical Center: Surgically confirmed gallbladder disease, venous thromboembolism, and breast tumors in relation to postmenopausal estrogen therapy. N Engl J Med 290:15, 1974

27. Smith DC, et al.: Association of exogenous estrogen and endometrial carcinoma. N Engl J Med 293:1164, 1975

28. Ziel HK, Finkle WD: Increased risk of endometrial carcinoma among users of conjugated estrogens. N Engl J Med 293:1167, 1975

29. Mack TM, et al.: Estrogens and endometrial cancer in a retirement community. N Engl J Med 294:1262, 1976

30. Thom MH, Studd JWW: Estrogens and endometrial hyperplasia. Br J Hosp Med 23:506, 1980

31. Paterson MEL, et al.: Endometrial disease after treatment with estrogens and progestogens in the climacteric. Br Med J 280:822, 1980

32. Ross RK, et al.: A case-control study of menopausal estrogen therapy and breast cancer. JAMA 243:1635, 1980

33. Schiff I: Vaginal absorption of estrone and 17β-estradiol. Fertil Steril 28:1063, 1977

34. Merrill JA: Management of postmenopausal bleeding. Clin Obstet Gynecol 24:285, 1981
35. Recker RR, Saville PD, Heaney RP: Effect of estrogens and calcium carbonate on bone loss in postmenopausal women. Am Intern Med 87:649, 1977
36. Bullock HL, et al.: Use of medroxyprogesterone acetate to prevent menopausal symptoms. Obstet Gynecol 46:165, 1975
37. Schiff I, et al.: Oral medroxyprogesterone in the treatment of postmenopausal symptoms. JAMA 244:1443, 1980
38. Morrison JC, et al.: The use of medroxyprogesterone acetate (Depo-Provera) for relief of climacteric symptoms. Am J Obstet Gynecol 138:99, 1980
39. Clayden JR, Bell JW, Pollard P: Menopausal flushing: double blind trial of a non-hormonal medication. Br Med J 1:409, 1974

INDEX

References to figures are indicated by an italic *f*.